# CIVIL RIGHTS
# AND EQUALITY

# CIVIL RIGHTS AND EQUALITY

With an Introduction by Kenneth L. Karst

*Selections from the*
Encyclopedia of the American Constitution
Edited by
Leonard W. Levy, Kenneth L. Karst, and
Dennis J. Mahoney

MACMILLAN PUBLISHING COMPANY

NEW YORK

Collier Macmillan Publishers

LONDON

Macmillan Publishing Company
866 Third Avenue, New York, NY 10022

Collier Macmillan Canada, Inc.


Library of Congress Catalog Card Number: 89-7948


Printed in the United States of America

Printing number

1 2 3 4 5 6 7 8 9 10

Library of Congress Cataloging-in-Publication Data

Encyclopedia of the American Constitution. Selections.
    Civil rights and equality : selections from the Encyclopedia of
the American Constitution / edited by Leonard W. Levy, Kenneth L.
Karst, and Dennis J. Mahoney ; introduction by Kenneth L. Karst.
        p.   cm.
    Bibliography: p.
    ISBN 0-02-897241-4
    1. Discrimination—United States.    2. Race discrimination—Law and
legislation—United States.    3. Afro-Americans—Legal status, laws,
etc.    I. Levy, Leonard Williams, 1923–        .    II. Karst, Kenneth L.
III. Mahoney, Dennis J.    IV. Title.
KF4755.A75E53 1989
342.73′023′03—dc20
[347.3022303]                                               89-7948
                                                              CIP

# CONTENTS

# INTRODUCTION

Although the American ideal of equal citizenship is at least as old as the nation, another persistent American reality has been the subordination of groups. Race, sex, religion, national origin—these and other characteristics have served to mark groups of people for exclusion from full participation in our public life. The term "civil rights" found early expression in the nation's efforts to give tangible meaning to the ideal of equality in the lives of black people following the abolition of slavery. Even today most writers use "civil rights" to refer to matters of civil equality, reserving "civil liberties" for the freedoms guaranteed in the Bill of Rights, including the freedoms of speech, press, assembly, and religion, and a number of protections against abuse of the criminal justice process.

The idea of civil rights was initially narrow, focused on a limited number of substantive rights and a single claimant group. One of the most striking features of American civil rights law has been its capacity for expansion. Today civil rights include a broad range of rights to equal citizenship, and are claimed by many new groups: women, religious and ethnic minorities, the aged, the handicapped. These newer claims find their models, both in politics and in legal doctrine, in the civil rights movement and in the nation's continuing commitment to eradicate racial discrimination and its effects.

America has seen two major civil rights eras. In the aftermath of the Civil War, three amendments to the Constitution and a number of acts of Congress gave promise that the ideal of equal citizenship would be converted into a set of enforceable legal rights. The Thirteenth Amendment (1865) abolished slavery, constitutionalizing the wartime Emancipation Proclamation (1863) and extending its reach throughout the nation. Emancipation itself would seem to imply a considerable measure of civil equality.[1] But a number of southern states had adopted Black Codes, laws aimed at keeping the freed slaves in a subordinate legal status just short of slavery. Congress, unwilling to leave the invalidation of these laws to future judicial interpretations of the meaning of emancipation, adopted the Civil Rights Act of 1866.

---

1. See Arthur Kinoy, The Constitutional Right of Negro Freedom, *Rutgers Law Review* 21:387 (1987).

The senators and representatives understood "civil rights" to include legal rights that were basic: to move freely from place to place, to be protected against private violence, to own and deal with property, to make contracts, to marry and be governed by ordinary family law, to be parties and witnesses in lawsuits. In assuring the freed slaves access to such forms of participation in civil society, the 1866 act guaranteed the very rights the Black Codes had denied. Congress passed the act over the veto of President Andrew Johnson, who challenged its constitutionality. The Fourteenth Amendment (1868) followed, intended immediately as a constitutional foundation for the 1866 act. The Fifteenth Amendment (1870) forbade both the states and the United States to deny or abridge the right to vote on account of race. Several other acts of the Reconstruction Congress authorized both civil remedies (damages and injunctions) and criminal penalties for invasions of civil rights. The Civil Rights Act of 1875 even addressed the question of "social" equality, providing for equal access to hotels, restaurants, and other public accommodations.

Even as the 1875 act was being adopted, the tide was going out for the cause of civil rights. After the Compromise of 1877 ended Reconstruction, both politics and constitutional doctrine took a sharp turn. For American blacks the promise of civil equality was soon betrayed, not just by unconcerned politicians but by judges whose interpretations squeezed most of the substance out of the Civil War Amendments and the Reconstruction civil rights laws. Two Supreme Court decisions were particularly harmful to the cause of civil equality. In the *Civil Rights Cases* (1883) the Court invented the "state action" limitation on the Fourteenth Amendment and held that the amendment had not empowered Congress to forbid private racial discrimination—as it had done in the 1875 act. Then in *Plessy v. Ferguson* (1896), upholding Louisiana's law requiring racial segregation of railroad passengers, the Court put its stamp of approval on the "separate but equal" doctrine that served as a constitutional underpinning for the system called Jim Crow.

Jim Crow was, indeed, a system. Segregation was not just the separation of the races but a symbolically charged instrument of the subordination of one racial group to another.[2] Law and government policy provided a framework for the system, which was

---

2. See Joel Williamson, *The Crucible of Race: Black-White Relations in the American South Since Emancipation* (1984); Kenneth L. Karst, *Belonging to America: Equal Citizenship and the Constitution* ch. 5 (1989).

fleshed out by custom and private behavior. The stigma of subordination was heightened by the very triviality of some forms of segregation: separate Bibles for swearing black and white witnesses in court; separate pay windows for black and white employees at a factory; separate storage for textbooks used by black and white pupils.[3] Even where laws were formally equalized—in defining voting rights, for example—they were administered to exclude most black people from equal citizenship. (In the early 1960s an Alabama voting registrar, concluding that a black citizen had failed the state's literacy test, noted this reason for refusing to register the citizen as a voter: "Error in spilling.")

Not until the years following World War II did a second civil rights era begin. Then, after decades of evasion, the nation once again roused itself to try to make good on the promise of equal citizenship. The Warren Court took the lead in the school segregation case of *Brown v. Board of Education* (1954), surely the Court's most important decision of the twentieth century. Within a few years the Court had not only overruled *Plessy v. Ferguson* but invalidated all forms of racial discrimination commanded or authorized by state law. A newly invigorated civil rights movement captured the nation's political imagination with sit-ins and freedom rides and voting marches. By the mid-1960s Congress weighed in with two major enactments. The Civil Rights Act of 1964 broadly prohibited racial discrimination by employers, operators of public accommodations, and persons who were receiving federal subsidies. The Voting Rights Act of 1965 effectively enfranchised the South's black citizens. The Supreme Court responded with newly generous readings of the Reconstruction civil rights laws. And in 1968 the Court concluded that Congress could, after all, forbid private racial discrimination by way of enforcing the Thirteenth Amendment, which had never been subjected to any "state action" limitation.[4]

By the mid-1970s the second civil rights movement had largely run its course. The wounds of Vietnam and Watergate combined with a slumping economy to confront the nation with an "era of

---

3. See C. Vann Woodward, *The Strange Career of Jim Crow* ch. 3 (second revised edition 1966).

4. Jones v. Alfred H. Mayer Co., 392 U.S. 409 (1968). Surely, too, the Warren Court's expansive interpretation of constitutional guarantees in the criminal justice area reflected the Justices' awareness that members of racial and ethnic minorities compose a disproportionate number of those who are caught up in the criminal process.

limits." The Burger Court's majority took a cautious approach to a new generation of issues focused on race, issues such as the place of intention in defining racial discrimination, or the validity of affirmative action. During the same decade, however, the women's movement was moving to the fore with explosive speed. The same Justices who were applying a "go slow" policy to claims of racial equality moved quickly to recognize a number of protections against sex discrimination. Judicial activism had not started with the Warren Court, and had not ended there.

In these decisions, as in the modern decisions promoting racial equality, the Supreme Court's interpretations of civil rights statutes and of the constitutional guarantee of equal protection were mutually reinforcing. In one set of cases the Court faltered, concluding that discrimination based on pregnancy was not sex discrimination,[5] and Congress responded with the Pregnancy Discrimination Act (1978). In two decades the courts and Congress have added to the subject of civil rights a sophisticated body of sex discrimination law. These new forms of civil equality are crucially bolstered by the recognition of women's constitutional rights to control their own destiny as begetters and bearers of children. If the abortion question is an issue about privacy or the right to life, it is also an issue about women's equality.

For lawyers today, "civil rights" names a branch of law still centered on the problem of racial discrimination but now amplified to include guarantees against many other forms of group subordination. This body of law is increasingly specialized; law school courses devoted to it can be quite technical. Today civil rights law ranges from school segregation to sexual harassment of women employees, from synagogue bombings to discrimination against persons with AIDS, from housing discrimination to mandatory retirement schemes.

A major component of current civil rights law is what lawyers call the law of remedies. Much of that law is derived from the civil rights statues of the Reconstruction era, which today provide remedies for violations of all manner of constitutional rights. If a police officer searches your home illegally, you can sue for damages. If a park administrator unconstitutionally denies you a permit to hold your meeting, you can go to court for injunctive relief. In extreme cases, such as the murder of three civil rights workers in Mississippi in 1964, the violators will be prosecuted for federal crimes. None

---

5. Geduldig v. Aiello, 417 U.S. 484 (1974); General Electric Co. v. Gilbert, 429 U.S. 128 (1976).

of the substantive rights violated in these cases fall within the body of civil rights law, but all of them find their remedies in federal civil rights statutes.

The law and the politics of civil rights have always gone hand in hand. The end of Reconstruction marked not only a retreat from the civil equality that had been written into law but also a waning of political strength for the civil rights cause in both North and South. Similarly, modern efforts to promote civil rights have required strategies combining resort to the courts and political activity within the legislative halls and elsewhere. In law and in politics *Brown v. Board of Education* represented a climax and also a beginning. The decision culminated both a litigation program and a political campaign; in turn it was a catalyst for further efforts in the courts, in the Congress, and in the streets.

If in the recent past civil rights law has been dynamic, it seems likely to go on expanding in the future. Even within the traditional purview of civil rights law, concerns about racial discrimination are deepening into concerns about the marginalizing effects of poverty in the ghetto. Old issues, too, are being redefined: the current legislative attack on pornography takes the forms of ordinances cast as civil rights laws. And more and more groups are resorting to law as a way to achieve their inclusion in the fullness of equal citizenship: lesbians and gay men are one especially deserving example.

The articles in this collection are grouped in four categories: (1) overviews of constitutional developments in some basic areas; (2) racial equality from slavery to the mid-twentieth century (arranged chronologically); (3) racial equality in the modern era (arranged topically, but also with an eye to chronology); and (4) the expansion of civil equality beyond the concerns of racial minorities to other groups defined by other characteristics (sex, "legitimacy" of birth, sexual orientation, alienage, indigency). These articles primarily reflect the perspectives of historians, political scientists, and lawyers on the shaping of American law concerning civil rights and equality. But the term "civil rights" today carries a meaning beyond the enforcement (or nonenforcement) of constitutional guarantees and civil rights laws. In our political life, from the halls of Congress to living-room conversations, "civil rights" calls to mind a broadly shared national aspiration centered on the ideal of civil equality.

Even as the second civil rights movement was fading in the 1970s it became possible to see the emergence in the national government of a broad bipartisan consensus in support of the movement's basic goals. When Lyndon Johnson left the presidency and

Richard Nixon took office, the consensus held, despite President Nixon's "southern strategy" during his campaign. The consensus has endured despite the hostility that radiated from the Executive Branch during the 1980s. A few days before his inauguration as President, George Bush went out of his way to reassert what had been standard presidential doctrine until 1981:

What becomes of Martin Luther King's dreams is up to us.
We must not fail him. We must not fail ourselves. And
we must not fail the nation he loved so much and gave his life for.

President Bush's remarks reflect not only personal commitment but political reality—the same reality that derailed the nomination of Judge Robert Bork to the Supreme Court in 1987. The political constituency for civil rights is not limited to racial and ethnic minorities, or women, or the other groups that supply most of the plaintiffs in civil rights lawsuits. The civil rights constituency today includes large numbers of white and male members of the middle class who want to put yesterday's divisions behind us and to get on with the fulfillment of the promise of equal citizenship. In 1988 the Supreme Court asked the parties in a pending case to argue the question whether the Court should overrule a 1976 Burger Court decision that had generously interpreted the Civil Rights Act of 1866. Almost two-thirds of all United States senators joined in a friend-of-the-Court brief urging the Justices not to overrule that precedent—and surely the Court heard that message.[6] A great many Americans know intuitively that the ideal of civil equality lies at the heart of the culture of American public life. With President Bush, they understand that the protection of civil rights is a measure of our ability to live up to the spiritual meanings that define a nation.

KENNETH L. KARST

---

6. Patterson v. McLean Credit Union, ——— S. Ct. ——— (1989).

# PUBLISHER'S NOTE

The essays in this volume survey the development of civil rights and equality under the law in the United States and explore the constitutional doctrine governing those subjects. They are chosen from the four-volume set of the *Encyclopedia of the American Constitution,* which Macmillan published in 1986.

In these articles the reader will find certain words, names, and court cases set in small capital letters. This cross-referencing system was used in the *Encyclopedia* to refer to separate entries on those subjects. Readers of this volume who want to find out more about these topics will want to consult the *Encyclopedia of the American Constitution* for further information. In addition, each essay has a bibliography that will aid the reader in pursuing his or her own study of the subject.

This volume is the second of a planned series on topics of constitutional interest. We are publishing the series to make the contents of the *Encyclopedia of the American Constitution* more readily accessible to students. The first volume dealt with American constitutional history in general. Future volumes will treat the subjects of criminal justice and the Bill of Rights, among others.

## ABOUT THE EDITOR

Kenneth L. Karst has been professor of law at the University of California, Los Angeles, since 1965. Mr. Karst is Associate Editor of the *Encyclopedia of the American Constitution* (Macmillan, 1986). Among his many books and articles is the recently published *Belonging to America: Equal Citizenship and the Constitution* (1989).

# Overviews

# CIVIL RIGHTS

## Jack Greenberg

The core of the concept "civil rights" is freedom from RACIAL DISCRIMINA-TION. Although the term, not improperly, often refers to freedom from discrimination based on nationality, alienage, gender, age, sexual prefer-ence, or physical or mental handicap—or even RELIGIOUS LIBERTY, immu-nity from official brutality, FREEDOM OF ASSEMBLY AND ASSOCIATION, FREE-DOM OF THE PRESS, FREEDOM OF SPEECH, the RIGHT OF PRIVACY, and additional rights found in the Constitution or elsewhere—other terms can characterize these rights. Sometimes they are referred to as CIVIL LIBERTIES or by particular names (for example, gender or handicap dis-crimination). Although the racial discrimination cases have influenced doctrinal development in many of these other areas, standards governing them often differ at the levels of both judicial scrutiny and appropriate remedies. Racial discrimination deserves separate treatment.

The constitutional law of civil rights begins in the THIRTEENTH, FOURTEENTH, and FIFTEENTH AMENDMENTS. These "Civil War Amend-ments" were adopted during Reconstruction to effect a radical revision of the status of blacks and a sharp change in relations between national and state governments. Until the end of the Civil War, the situation of black people had been dominated by SLAVERY in the South and a regime under which, in the words of the Supreme Court in DRED SCOTT v. SANDFORD (1857), they had no rights that a white man was bound to respect. Their legal rights or disabilities derived from state law, subject to no meaningful control by the national government. The Civil War amendments changed that. The Thirteenth Amendment abolished slav-ery; the Fourteenth, among other things, prohibited states from denying to any person DUE PROCESS OF LAW or EQUAL PROTECTION OF THE LAWS. (Other provisions of the Fourteenth Amendment had little practical effect). The Fifteenth Amendment protected VOTING RIGHTS against gov-ernmentally imposed racial discrimination.

Each amendment empowered Congress to adopt enforcing legisla-tion. Such laws were enacted—most notably the CIVIL RIGHTS ACT OF 1866—but they were not implemented, were interpreted restrictively, or fell into disuse following the COMPROMISE OF 1877 which assured the Presidential election of RUTHERFORD B. HAYES in exchange for his pledge to withdraw Union troops from the South and end Reconstruction. During the same period southern states, effectively free from national

*blacks never hew of gout additional piece*

3

control, implemented BLACK CODES, and later Jim Crow laws, which returned black people to a status that was only nominally free. No significant national civil rights law was adopted again until the mid-1960s.

Between Reconstruction and the mid-twentieth century, the judiciary sporadically found significant content in the Civil War Amendments; yet racial SEGREGATION and discrimination remained pervasive in the South and widespread elsewhere. During the same period, the Fourteenth Amendment was interpreted expansively to protect burgeoning business enterprise. Between BROWN v. BOARD OF EDUCATION (1954) and the CIVIL RIGHTS ACT OF 1964, the main period of the modern civil rights revolution, the doctrinal potential of the amendments to advance the cause of black people became largely realized. Implementation became the main task, taking the form of comprehensive civil rights statutes, lawsuits brought by the United States and private parties, and administrative enforcement. As a result of this process, some whites have charged that remedies for blacks violate *their* constitutional rights: for example, that AFFIRMATIVE ACTION constitutes "reverse discrimination," or that SCHOOL BUSING for integration injures them. Justice OLIVER WENDELL HOLMES's aphorism, "the life of the law has not been logic: it has been experience," is as least as true of civil rights law as of any other branch of law.

The concept of "equal protection of the laws" underwent its greatest evolution between 1896, when PLESSY v. FERGUSON upheld a state law requiring SEPARATE BUT EQUAL segregation of whites and blacks in intrastate rail travel, and 1954, when *Brown v. Board of Education* held that segregated public EDUCATION denied equal protection. Although *Plessy* dealt only with intrastate transportation and *Brown* only with education, each was quickly generalized to other aspects of life.

The very factors which the Supreme Court invoked to uphold segregation in 1896 were reassessed in *Brown* and used to justify a contrary result. The *Plessy* majority held that the framers of the Civil War Amendments did not intend to eliminate segregation in rail travel which the Court characterized as a social, not a political activity. It thereby distinguished STRAUDER v. WEST VIRGINIA (1880), in which the Supreme Court had held that excluding blacks from juries violated the Fourteenth Amendment because it stigmatized them. *Plessy* dismissed the argument that segregating blacks from whites could justify segregating Protestants from Catholics, because that would be unreasonable; racial segregation was reasonable, for state court decisions and statutes had authorized segregation in schools. Finally, the Court addressed what today is called social psychology, writing that although *Plessy* claimed segregation connoted black inferiority, whites would not consider themselves stigmatized if they were segregated by a legislature controlled by blacks. Any harmful psychological effects of segregation were self-inflicted.

*Plessy* became so deeply ingrained in jurisprudence that as late as 1927, in GONG LUM V. RICE, a Court in which Holmes, LOUIS D. BRANDEIS, and HARLAN F. STONE sat unanimously agreed that racial segregation in education "has been many times decided to be within the constitutional power of the state legislature to settle, without the intervention of the federal courts under the Federal Constitution."

Other Supreme Court decisions, however, offered hope that some day the Court might come to a contrary conclusion. In YICK WO V. HOPKINS (1886) the Court invalidated as a denial of equal protection a city ordinance which, under the guise of prohibiting laundries from operating in wooden buildings, where virtually all Chinese laundries were located, excluded Chinese from that business. In BUCHANAN V. WARLEY (1917) it invalidated racial zoning of urban land under the due process clause. Later it struck down state laws prohibiting blacks from participating in primary elections. By 1950, in SWEATT V. PAINTER and MCLAURIN V. OKLAHOMA STATE REGENTS, the Court invalidated segregation in law school and graduate education, without holding segregation unconstitutional per se and without abandoning the separate-but-equal formula. These and other decisions foreshadowed *Brown* and undermined precedents approving segregation.

*Brown* contradicted or distinguished *Plessy* on every score. It read the legislative history of the Civil War Amendments as inconclusive on the question of school segregation, pointing out that although after the Civil War public education had been undeveloped and almost nonexistent for blacks, it had become perhaps the most important function of state government. In effect the amendment was treated as embodying a general evolutionary principle of equality which developed as education became more important. The Court treated early precedents as not controlling school segregation and drew from the 1950 graduate school cases support for a contrary result.

In contrast to *Plessy* 's dismissal of the psychological effects of segregation, *Brown* held that "to segregate them [black children] from others of similar age and qualifications solely because of their race generates a feeling of inferiority as to their status in the community that may affect their hearts and minds in a way unlikely ever to be undone." The Court cited social science literature in support of this response to *Plessy.* This portion of the opinion provoked much adverse commentary, some condemning the decision as based on social science, not law. But of course, *Plessy* had come to its sociological conclusions without any evidence at all.

In BOLLING V. SHARPE, a companion case to *Brown,* the Court decided that the Fifth Amendment's due process clause prohibited school segregation in the District of Columbia. Any other result, the Court said, would be "unthinkable."

The contending arguments in *Plessy* and *Brown* not only exemplify the possibilities of legal advocacy but also raise the question how "equal protection" could be interpreted so differently at different times. After all, the arguments remained the same, but first one side prevailed, then the other. The reason for the change lies in the development of American history. Indeed, *Brown* suggests as much in describing how much public education had changed between Reconstruction and 1954, how essential education had become for personal development, and how much blacks had achieved. By 1954 black citizens had fought for their country in two major World Wars, the more recent of which was won against Nazi racism; had moved from concentration in the South to a more even distribution throughout the country; and had achieved much socially, politically, economically, and educationally, even though their status remained below that of whites.

The courtroom struggle leading to *Brown* showed that blacks were ready to participate effectively in securing their full liberation. It culminated a planned litigation campaign, building precedent upon precedent, directed by a group of mostly black lawyers headed by THURGOOD MARSHALL, then head of the NAACP LEGAL DEFENSE AND EDUCATIONAL FUND and later a Justice of the United States Supreme Court. This campaign had many ramifications, not the least of which was to become a model for development of public interest law, which grew rapidly in the 1970s.

The nation owed black people a debt which it acknowledged officially in several ways. In the late 1940s and in *Brown* itself the solicitor general of the United States joined counsel for black litigants in calling upon the Supreme Court to declare segregation unconstitutional. That the country was generally prepared to accept this argument was further evidenced in the 1947 Report of President HARRY S. TRUMAN's Committee on Civil Rights. The committee called for the end of racial segregation and discrimination in education, PUBLIC ACCOMMODATIONS, housing, employment, voting, and all other aspects of American life.

Despite the storm of controversy stirred by the 1954 decisions, they are firmly rooted in constitutional law and nowadays there is no longer significant criticism of their results. *Brown* was quickly followed by decisions applying its principles to all other forms of state imposed racial segregation. Courts soon ordered desegregation of parks, beaches, sporting events, hospitals, publically owned or managed accommodations, and other public facilities.

But *Brown* could not affect the rights of blacks against privately imposed discrimination, for the equal protection clause is a directive to the states. The admonition that "no state" shall deny equal protection was not addressed to private employers, property owners, or those who managed privately owned public accommodations. In the CIVIL RIGHTS CASES (1883) the Supreme Court made clear not only that the equal protection clause did not apply to private action but that Congress in enforcing the Fourteenth Amendment might not prohibit private persons from discriminating. As a consequence, national civil rights laws could not apply to private restaurants, hotels, transportation, employment, and housing—places where people spend most of their lives.

In 1960 the SIT-INS, freedom rides, and DEMONSTRATIONS burst upon the national scene, aimed first at racial exclusion from privately owned public accommodations and then at other forms of discrimination. This phase of the civil rights struggle sought to move antidiscrimination precepts beyond the limitation of state power to prohibitions against private discrimination. The cases arising out of these efforts necessarily examined the distinction between what is private and what is STATE ACTION, an issue long debated in political theory and constitutional law. On the one hand, it has been argued that privately asserted rights derive from power conferred and enforced by the state and that at bottom there is no such thing as a "private" right. According to this reasoning, applying the TRESPASS laws to enforce an owner's privately held preference against black patronage of his lunch counter would be prohibited by the Fourteenth Amendment: the owner's property interest is a function of state law; the law of trespass is a state creation; prosecution and its consequences are state conduct. Pursuing such reasoning, lawyers for sit-in demonstrators identified the governmental components of otherwise private action, arguing that the Fourteenth Amendment, therefore, protected blacks who were denied service on racial grounds and later prosecuted for refusing to leave the premises. They had some legal support for this argument. Even before 1954 the Supreme Court had held in MARSH v. ALABAMA (1946) that religious proselytizing on company town property was protected by the FIRST AMENDMENT against prosecution for trespass because the town was a governmental entity, notwithstanding private ownership. Similarly, the equal protection clause had been interpreted to forbid enforcement by state courts or racially RESTRICTIVE COVENANTS against purchase or occupancy of real estate by blacks or other minorities. These cases, and their rationales, followed to the end of their logic, would mean that governmental enforcement of private discrimination violates the equal protection clause.

But the courts were not prepared to follow the reasoning to its logical conclusion. In cases in which blacks were arrested and prosecuted for entering or remaining on privately owned public accommodations where they were not wanted because of race, the Supreme Court first avoided deciding whether there was state action by ruling for the defendants on various other grounds, for example, lack of evidence or VAGUENESS of the law. In other cases the Court found state action in special circumstances: a private owner segregated because required by law; an ordinance required segregated toilets, which tended to encourage exclusion of blacks; a private restaurant leased premises from a state agency; private security guards who enforced segregation were also deputy sheriffs. But the Court balked at finding state action in prosecution for trespass to enforce a proprietor's personal decision to discriminate. The resistance grew out of a fear that to extend the state action doctrine would make most private decisions subject to government control. Moreover, if one could not call upon the state to enforce private preferences, personal force might be employed.

Other legal theorists would have differentiated between conduct prohibited by the amendment and that which is not by factoring into the decision-making process the concept of privacy. They would find, for example, that impermissible state action existed in racial exclusion from a restaurant but not from a private home. The policy against racial discrimination would prevail in the restaurant case, where there was no countervailing interest of privacy, but in the private home case the privacy interest would outweigh strictures against racial discrimination.

In 1964 the Court held that the Civil Rights Act of that year invalidated convictions of sit-in demonstrators, even those convicted before its passage. The fundamental question of precisely what level of state involvement in private conduct constitutes state action was left undecided.

The uncertain scope of the state action doctrine was underscored by the constitutional basis advanced for congressional power to pass the 1964 Civil Rights Act. Congress relied on the COMMERCE CLAUSE in addition to the Fourteenth Amendment because the commerce clause does not require state action to justify congressional regulation. The initial Supreme Court decisions upholding the 1964 Civil Rights Act, HEART OF ATLANTA MOTEL V. UNITED STATES (1964) and KATZENBACH V. MCCLUNG (1964), relied on the commerce clause, and upheld applications of the law in cases of minimal effect upon commerce.

The impulse to define fully the meaning of state action was further damped by developments in Thirteenth Amendment law. The Thirteenth Amendment has no state action limitation and, therefore, covers private as well as state action. But early efforts to apply it to discrimination as a BADGE OF SERVITUDE were rejected by the Court, which held that the amendment forbade only slavery itself. The Civil Rights Act of 1866 had made illegal private racially discriminatory refusals to contract or engage in real estate transactions. But not until 1968 did the Supreme Court interpret these laws to forbid private discrimination. By the mid-1960s, through the civil rights acts of that period and the new judicial interpretation of Reconstruction legislation, it was no longer necessary to discover state action in ostensibly private conduct in order to prevent discrimination. With the passing of this need, concerted efforts to expand the courts' views of the state action concept came to a halt.

The contrast between the promise of the Constitution and its performance was nowhere better highlighted than in *Brown* itself. The Supreme Court treated constitutional right and remedy in two separate opinions, *Brown I* and *Brown II,* decided in 1955. *Brown I* decided only that racial segregation was unconstitutional, postponing decisions on the means and the pace of school desegregation. *Brown II* proclaimed that school segregation need not end immediately; it had to be accomplished with ALL DELIBERATE SPEED. The Court required a "prompt and reasonable" start, and permitted delay only for the time necessary for administrative changes. Opposition to desegregation, the Court said, would not justify delay. Nevertheless, southern schools actually integrated at an extremely slow pace. Not until 1969, when the Court announced that the time for "deliberate speed" had passed, did school integration proceed rapidly.

While the "deliberate speed" decision contributed to a sense that desegregation was not urgent and procrastination was tolerable, it is difficult to believe that a different formula would have materially affected the pace of integration. Armed physical opposition in Little Rock and elsewhere in the South was aimed at integration at any time, with or without deliberate speed. One hundred members of Congress signed the SOUTHERN MANIFESTO denouncing the Supreme Court, and Congress came within a single vote of severely restricting the Court's JURISDICTION. Congressional legislation implementing *Brown* would not be adopted until after the civil rights movement of the 1960s.

The refusal of school districts to desegregate was not susceptible to remedy because there was almost no one who would bring integration suits. No southern white lawyers would bring school suits until the 1970s; in many a southern state, there was only a handful of black lawyers with minimal resources; civil rights organizations were few, small, and overburdened; the United States Justice Department and the Department of Health, Education, and Welfare had no authority to bring suit. As a consequence, where school boards resisted or claimed to be in compliance with *Brown,* there was hardly any way to compel change. These conditions, not "deliberate speed," kept school segregation in place. Real opportunities for the judiciary to speed the pace of integration had to await political change. That change came in the 1960s, with the pro-civil rights policies of Presidents JOHN F. KENNEDY and LYNDON B. JOHNSON, culminating in the Civil Rights Act of 1964.

Supreme Court opinions stating in OBITER DICTUM that integration must be achieved rapidly began to be issued at the end of the 1960s. In the 1970s courts began to hand down detailed orders requiring the end of segregation "root and branch." Because black and white families were segregated residentially, the only way to integrate schools in many communities was to combine in single attendance zones areas separated by some distance, thus employing SCHOOL BUSING. Numerical standards also were employed to measure whether acceptable levels of integration had been reached. These techniques—particularly busing and RACIAL QUOTAS—have stimulated controversy and political opposition.

The integration of the 1970s in most instances was carried out as quickly as possible when courts ordered it. Although the deliberate speed doctrine had by then been overruled, such rapid desegregation met its literal requirements. In a typical case, the revision of boundaries and regulations and the reassignment of students and teachers took a few months. Conditions in the nation, not "deliberate speed," caused the long delay.

*Brown,* of course, concerned states where segregation had been required or permitted by statute. By the 1970s the Supreme Court faced the issue of northern segregation which was not caused by state statute. It differentiated between "de facto" segregation (resulting from racially segregated housing patterns) and "de jure" segregation (resulting from deliberate official decisions). Some commentators argued that there is no such thing as de facto segregation, for children always are assigned to schools by governmental action. But only where some intent to discriminate was demonstrated did the courts require desegregation. However, where an intent to discriminate has been shown in part of a district, a presumption has been held to arise that single-race schools elsewhere in the district have been the product of such intent. Under this doctrine many northern districts have been desegregated.

Often a city school district is nearly all black and surrounded by white suburban districts. The Court held in MILLIKEN v. BRADLEY (1974) that integration across district lines may not be ordered without proof of an interdistrict violation. A number of lower courts have found such violations and have ordered integration across district lines.

All of these standards were implemented, particularly in the 1970s, by the Departments of Justice and Health, Education, and Welfare (later the Department of Education). The private bar brought a considerable number of cases facilitated by congressional legislation authorizing the award of counsel to prevailing parties in school segregation, to be paid by defendants. But the intimate relation between politics and implementation of constitutional civil rights became apparent once more in the 1980s when a new administration opposed to busing and numerical standards for gauging integration virtually ceased bringing school cases to court, undertook to modify or revoke INJUNCTIONS in already decided cases, and opposed private plaintiffs in others.

Following *Brown* and in response to the demonstrations of the 1960s, the Civil Rights Acts of 1964, 1965, and 1968 were enacted with the goal of implementing the ideals of the Civil War amendments. But results of these laws varied according to their political, social, and legal settings. Public accommodations, for example, integrated easily; housing has been intractable. Affirmative action policies have been devised to assure certain levels of minority participation, but they have stimulated opposition by whites who claim they are being disfavored and illegally so. Controversy has also developed over the question of whether antidiscrimination orders might be entered only upon a showing of official discriminatory intent, or whether such orders are also justified to remedy the racially discriminatory effects of official policies. Affirmative action and discriminatory intent, the twin central legal issues of civil rights in the 1980s, have in common a concern with distributive fairness. Both issues have been contested in political, statutory, and constitutional arenas.

In general, the courts have sustained the constitutionality of affirmative action as a congressional remedy for past discriminations and as an appropriate judicial remedy for past statutory or constitutional violations. In medical school admissions, for example, four Justices of the Supreme Court thought a fixed racial quota favoring minorities violated the Civil Rights Act of 1964, and a fifth Justice found an equal protection violation; a different majority, however, concluded that an admissions policy favoring racial and other diversity, which assured the admission of a substantial but not fixed number of minorities, would be valid as an aspect of a university's First Amendment exercise of academic freedom. The Court, with three dissents, has sustained a congressionally mandated quota assuring ten percent of certain government contracts to minority contractors. And in school integration numerical measures of integration have been commonplace. In employment and voting as well, affirmative action has been incorporated into efforts to undo discrimination and has been upheld by the courts. [See REGENTS OF University of California v. Bakke (1978), and FULLILOVE v. KLUTZNICK 1980).]

The courts usually have required a showing of discriminatory intent in order to establish an equal protection violation, but intent may be inferred from conduct. In any event, the intent requirement may be dispensed with where Congress has legislated to make discriminatory results adequate to trigger corrective action.

The public accommodations portions of the 1964 Act prohibited discrimination in specific types of establishments (typified by those providing food or amusement) that affect INTERSTATE COMMERCE. An exception for private clubs reflected uncertainty about the lack of power (perhaps arising out of countervailing constitutional rights of association) and the desirability of controlling discrimination in such places. But the meaning of "private" in this context has not been explicated. Clubs where a substantial amount of business is conducted may not be exempt and an amendment has been proposed to make this clear.

Immediately following passage of the law the Department of Justice and private plaintiffs brought successful suits against recalcitrant enterprises. Most public accommodations complied rapidly. Large national enterprises that segregated in the South integrated because they could not afford the obloquy of resistance, threat of boycott, and consequent loss of business in the North. Many small southern businesses opened to all without problems. Even proprietors who wished to continue discriminating soon bowed to the law's commands. Today one rarely hears of public accommodations discrimination.

Before adoption of the civil rights legislation of the 1960s, the only significant federal regulations of employment discrimination were the Fifth Amendment and Fourteenth Amendment, which prohibited federal and state employment discrimination, and executive order prohibition of discrimination by certain government contractors. The Railway Labor Act and the NATIONAL LABOR RELATIONS ACT were construed to forbid discrimination by covered unions. But all such limitations were difficult to enforce. The Civil Rights Act of 1964 and the 1968 Equal Employment Opportunity (EEO) Act were the first effective prohibitions against discrimination in employment. Private suits (with counsel fees payable to prevailing plaintiffs), suits by the Equal Employment Opportunity Commission against private defendants, and suits by the Justice Department against state and local government are the primary mechanisms of enforcement. As elsewhere in modern civil rights law, the two most important issues with constitutional overtones under this law have been whether a plaintiff must prove that discrimination was intentional and whether courts may award affirmative relief, including racial quotas. As to intent, the EEO statute has been interpreted to forbid hiring and promotion criteria that have an adverse impact on a protected group but bear no adequate relationship to ability to perform the job. Thus, an intelligence test for coal handlers, or a height requirement for prison guards, which screen out blacks or women and do not indicate ability to do the job, violate the statute even absent a showing of intent to discriminate. On the other hand, when the statute is not applicable, a plaintiff can secure relief under the Constitution only by showing intentional discrimination.

Affirmative action in the form of hiring and promotion goals and timetables have been prescribed by courts and all branches of the federal government with enforcement responsibility. Moreover, some private employers have adopted these techniques as a matter of social policy or to head off anticipated charges of discrimination. The legality of such programs has been upheld in the vast majority of cases. Affirmative action has substantially increased minority and female participation in jobs it covers but continues to be attacked by nonprotected groups as unconstitutional, illegal, or unwise. In 1984 the Supreme Court held that the EEO Act prohibits enjoining layoffs of black beneficiaries of a consent decree requiring certain levels of black employment where that would result in discharging whites with greater seniority.

Although the Fifteenth Amendment expressly protects the right to vote against racial discrimination and the Fourteenth Amendment's equal protection clause also has been interpreted to do so, voting discrimination was widespread and blatant well into the 1960s, and to some extent it still persists. Apart from physical violence and intimidation, which lasted until the mid-1960s, a long line of discriminatory devices has been held to be in violation of the Constitution and statutes, only to be succeeded by new ones. Very early, southern states adopted GRAND-FATHER CLAUSES, requiring voters to pass literacy tests but exempting those who were entitled to vote in 1866, along with their lineal descendants—which meant whites only. When the courts struck down the grandfather clause, it was succeeded by laws permitting registration only during a very brief period of time without passing a literacy test. Thereafter even those who could pass the test were not permitted to register. Very few blacks could take advantage of this narrow window, but the stratagem was not outlawed until 1939. Most southern states through the 1920s had laws prohibiting blacks from voting in party PRIMARY ELECTIONS. In the South, the Democratic party excluded blacks, and the winner of the Democratic primary always was elected. These laws were held unconstitutional in the 1940s and 1950s on the grounds that the party primary was an integral part of the state's electoral system, despite its nominal autonomy. As the white primary fell, laws and practices were widely adopted requiring registrants to read and understand texts like the Alabama State Constitution or to answer registrars' questions such as "how many bubbles are there in a bar of soap." These tests were held unconstitutional. Racial GERRYMANDERING, a not uncommon practice where blacks in fact voted, also was enjoined as unconstitutional. Other impediments to voting were not motivated solely by racial considerations but affected blacks disproportionately, such as the POLL TAX, later prohibited by constitutional amendment. LITERACY TESTS also lent themselves to discriminatory administration.

The VOTING RIGHTS ACT OF 1965 invalidated any and all racially discriminatory tests and devices. But, more important, states in which there was a history of voting discrimination (identified by low registration or voter turnout) could not adopt new voting standards unless those standards were certified as nondiscriminatory by the Department of Justice. This prohibition ended the tactic of substituting one discriminatory device for another. Where they were needed, federal officials could be sent to monitor registration and voting or, indeed, to register voters.

Although the 1965 law significantly reduced racial discrimination in the electoral process, abuses persisted in the forms of inconvenient registration procedures, gerrymandering, occasional intimidation, and creation of MULTIMEMBER DISTRICTS. This last device has its roots in post-Reconstruction efforts to dilute black voting strength. The use of single-member districts to elect a city council would result in the election of blacks from those districts where blacks constitute a majority. By declaring the entire city a multimember district, entitled to elect a number of at-large candidates, the majority white population can, if votes are racially polarized, elect an all-white council—a result that has occurred frequently. The Supreme Court required a showing of discriminatory intent if such a voting system were to be held unconstitutional. But the interplay between Court and Congress produced an amendment of the Voting Rights Act in 1982, permitting proof of a violation of the act by a showing of discriminatory effect.

Affirmative action has been an issue in voting as in other areas. The Supreme Court has held that, upon a showing of past voting discrimination, the attorney general may condition approval of legislative redistricting upon a race-conscious drawing of district lines to facilitate election of minority candidates.

Until 1968, the most important federal prohibition of housing discrimination was the equal protection clause, which was held in SHELLEY V. KRAEMER (1948) to prohibit judicial enforcement of restrictive covenants among property owners forbidding occupancy of property by members of racial minorities. The Fifth and Fourteenth Amendments prohibit racial segregation in public housing, but the construction of public housing has virtually ceased.

The Fair Housing Act of 1968 marked the completion of the main statutory efforts to satisfy the prescriptions of President HARRY S. TRUMAN's 1947 Committee on Civil Rights. On the eve of the law's passage, the Supreme Court interpreted the Civil Rights Act of 1866 to forbid refusals to engage in real property transactions on racial grounds. Nonetheless, the 1866 and 1968 acts have been the least effective of the civil rights acts. Their failure owes to deep, persistent opposition to housing integration, to a lack of means of enforcement commensurate with the extent of the problem, and to a shortage in the housing market of houses in the price range which most minority buyers can afford. Because the housing market is atomized, a single court order cannot have widespread effect. (Housing is thus unlike education, where an entire district may be desegregated, or employment, where government agencies and other large employers can be required to take steps affecting thousands of employees.)

An effort to address the relationship between race and economics in housing foundered at the constitutional level when the Court held that large-lot zoning—which precluded construction of inexpensive housing, thereby excluding minorities—was not invalid under the Constitution absent a demonstration of racially discriminatory intent. The 1968 Fair Housing Act authorizes judicial relief when such laws produce discriminatory effects, without demonstration of intent. Nevertheless, economic factors and political opposition have prevented the statutory standard from having a significant practical impact. In several states where state law has invalidated such zoning, the actual change in racial housing patterns has been slight.

Some legislative efforts to desegregate housing have run into constitutional obstacles. A municipality's prohibition of "For Sale" signs to discourage panic selling by whites in integrated neighborhoods has been held to violate the First Amendment. A judge's award of damages for violation of the Fair Housing Act has been held to violate the Sixth Amendment right of TRIAL BY JURY (subsequently, contrary to civil rights lawyers' expectations, jury verdicts often have been favorable to plaintiffs). A large governmentally assisted housing development's racial quota, set up with the aim of preventing "tipping" (whites moving out when the percentage of blacks exceeds a certain point), was still being contested in the mid-1980s.

From constitutional adoption, through interpretation, and judicial and statutory implementation, the law of civil rights has interacted with the world that called it into being. No great departures from settled doctrine are to be anticipated in the near future. But similar assertions might have been made confidently at various points in the history of civil rights, only to be proved wrong in years to come.

Bibliography

BLACK, CHARLES L., JR.   1967   Foreword: State Action, Equal Protection, and California's Proposition 14. *Harvard Law Review* 81:69–109.

EASTLAND, TERRY and BENNETT, WILLIAM J.   1979 *Counting by Race.* New York: Basic Books.

GREENBERG, JACK   1968   The Supreme Court, Civil Rights and Civil Dissonance. *Yale Law Journal* 77:1520–1544.

JOINT CENTER FOR POLITICAL STUDIES   1984   *Minority Vote Dilution,* Chandler Davidson, ed. Washington, D.C.: Howard University Press.

KIRP, DAVID L.   1983   *Just Schools: The Idea of Racial Equality in American Education.* Berkeley: University of California Press.

KLUGER, RICHARD   1975   *Simple Justice: The History of Brown v. Board of Education and Black America's Struggle for Equality.* New York: Knopf.

KONVITZ, MILTON R.   1961   *Century of Civil Rights.* New York: Columbia University Press.

KUSHNER, JAMES A.   1983   *Fair Housing: Discrimination in Real Estate, Community Development, and Revitalization.*  New York: Shepard's/McGraw-Hill.

SCHLEI, BARBARA and GROSSMAN, PAUL   1983   *Employment Discrimination Law,* 2nd ed. Washington, D.C.: Bureau of National Affairs.

U.S. COMMISSION ON CIVIL RIGHTS   1981   *Affirmative Action in the 1980's: Dismantling the Process of Discrimination.*  Washington, D.C.: U.S. Commission on Civil Rights.

# RACIAL DISCRIMINATION

Owen M. Fiss

The nation was founded with the enslavement of blacks as an established and ongoing institution, and though we were not particularly proud of the institution, we were prepared to live with it. The Constitution did not mention the word "slave," and contemplated the eventual closing of the slave trade (referred to simply as the "importation of persons"), but, through similar circumlocutions, also created obligations to return fugitive slaves, and included a proportion of the slaves within the population base to be used for the apportionment of representatives and taxes. In DRED SCOTT V. SANDFORD (1857) the Supreme Court viewed slaves as property and declared that the right of slaveholders to take their slaves to the territories was protected by the DUE PROCESS CLAUSE of the Fifth Amendment.

The Civil War brought slavery to an end and reversed the basic commitment of the Constitution toward blacks. The law sought equality rather than enslavement, and it was through the elaboration of this egalitarian commitment that the concept of racial discrimination emerged. Prohibiting racial discrimination became the principal strategy of the American legal system for achieving equality for blacks. The laws against racial discrimination typically protect all racial minorities, not just blacks, and yet, for purely historical reasons, the development of those laws would be unimaginable apart from the struggle of blacks for equality in America. That struggle has been the source both of the achievements of antidiscrimination law and of its recurrent dilemmas.

The three amendments adopted following the Civil War constitute the groundwork of this branch of the law, although only one—the FIFTEENTH AMENDMENT—actually speaks of racial discrimination. It provides that "the right . . . to vote shall not be denied or abridged . . . on account of race, color, or previous condition of servitude." The other Civil War amendments are not cast in terms of racial discrimination. The THIRTEENTH AMENDMENT prohibits slavery and involuntary servitude, and the FOURTEENTH AMENDMENT, in relevant aspect, prohibits states from denying "the EQUAL PROTECTION OF THE LAWS." But the Supreme Court has interpreted both these amendments to prohibit racial discrimination. With respect to the Thirteenth Amendment, the Court reasoned in JONES V. ALFRED H. MAYER CO. (1968) that racial discrimination is a badge or incident of slavery. (See BADGES OF SERVITUDE.) Similarly, in interpreting the Fourteenth Amendment, the Court, as early as STRAUDER V. WEST VIRGINIA (1880), declared racial discrimination to be the kind of unequal treatment that constitutes a denial of equal protection of the laws. Indeed, over the years, racial discrimination came to be seen as the paradigmatic denial of equal protection, and supplied the standard against which all other equal protection claims came to be measured, even when pressed by nonracial groups such as the poor or women. They too had to show that they were discriminated against on the basis of some impermissible criterion such as their wealth or sex. The promise of equal protection was thus transformed into a promise not to discriminate.

It was, moreover, through the enforcement of the Fourteenth Amendment that the prohibition against racial discrimination achieved its greatest prominence. Antidiscrimination was the instrument that finally put to an end the system of white supremacy that emerged in the late nineteenth and early twentieth centuries and that worked by separating whites and blacks—Jim Crow. The discrimination appeared on the very face of Jim Crow laws and a principle that condemned racial discrimination easily brought those laws within the sweep of the Fourteenth Amendment. All that was needed was an understanding of how the separatism of Jim Crow worked to the disadvantage of blacks; that was the burden of BROWN V. BOARD OF EDUCATION (1954) and the cases that followed. As the principle controlling the interpretation of the Fourteenth Amendment, antidiscrimination was a limitation only upon the actions of states, but once the step entailed in *Brown* was taken, the federal government was, in BOLLING V. SHARPE (1954), made subject to an identical prohibition by a construction of the due process clause of the Fifth Amendment. Racial discrimination was deemed as inconsistent with the constitutional guarantee of liberty as it was with equal protection.

Statutes, too, have been concerned with racial equality. In the years immediately following the Civil War, Congress passed a comprehensive program to protect the newly freed slaves, and defined the conduct it sought to prohibit in a variety of ways. In the CIVIL RIGHTS ACT OF 1866 Congress promised that blacks would enjoy the same rights as whites; in the FORCE ACTS (1870, 1871) it guaranteed all citizens the rights and privileges arising from the Constitution or laws of the United States. In the decades following *Brown v. Board of Education,* however, when the antidiscrimination principle of the Fourteenth Amendment received its most strenuous affirmation and the nation embarked on its Second Reconstruction, Congress cast the substantive standard in terms of a single idiom—do not discriminate. (See CIVIL RIGHTS ACT OF 1964; VOTING RIGHTS ACT OF 1965; CIVIL RIGHTS ACT OF 1968.)

During this period, Congress introduced new mechanisms to enforce the equal protection clause; for example, it authorized the attorney general to bring injunctive school desegregation suits, required federal administrative agencies to terminate financial assistance to segregated school systems, and provided for criminal prosecutions against those who forcibly interfered with desegregation. Congress also broadened the reach of federal antidiscrimination law beyond the scope of the Fourteenth Amendment by regulating, in the name of racial equality, activities of private agencies (for example, restaurants, employers, or landlords), which otherwise would not have been covered by that amendment because of its "state action" requirement. In each of these measures, Congress used the language of antidiscrimination. So did the President in promulgating EXECUTIVE ORDER 11246 (1965), which regulates government contractors. Many state legislatures also intervened on behalf of racial equality during the Second Reconstruction, and these enactments were also couched in terms of prohibiting discrimination.

Sometimes Congress and the state legislatures exempted certain discriminatory practices from the laws they enacted. One instance is the federal open housing law, which exempts discrimination by small residences ("Mrs. Murphy's roominghouse"); another is the federal fair employment statute, which exempts from its coverage small businesses (at first businesses with fewer than twenty-five employees, later reduced to fifteen). Apparently Congress viewed the interest in associational liberty present in these settings as sufficiently strong to justify limited exemptions to the ban on racial discrimination. Yet, putting these exemptions and a handful of others to one side, it is fair to say that today, primarily as a result of the Second Reconstruction, the prohibition against racial discrimination is all-encompassing. It has both constitutional and statutory bases and is the subject of an executive order. It is a pervasive feature of both federal and state law and calls forth a broad array of civil and criminal remedies. It almost has the status of a moral imperative, like the norm against theft or killing. The issue that divides Americans today is thus not whether the law should prohibit racial discrimination but what, precisely, doing so entails.

The antidiscrimination norm, as already noted, was largely fashioned at a time when the nation was swept by the SEPARATE-BUT-EQUAL DOCTRINE of Jim Crow and when blacks were disadvantaged in a rather open and crude manner. In such a context, the principle of antidiscrimination invites a color blindness: When allocating a scarce opportunity, such as a job or a place in a professional school, the decision maker should not prefer a white candidate over a black one on the basis of the individual's color or race. Here antidiscrimination requires that individuals be judged independently of race. This much is settled. Interpretive problems arise, however, when the social context changes—when we have moved beyond Jim Crow and blacks have come to be disadvantaged primarily in ways that are hidden and systematically entrenched. Then we confront two issues. One arises from the exclusion of blacks on the basis of a seemingly innocent criterion such as performance on a standardized test; the other from the preference given to blacks to correct for long-standing unequal distributional patterns.

To clarify the first issue, it should be understood that the appearance of innocence might be misleading. Although a black scores higher than a white on a test, the employer might manipulate or falsify the scores so that the white is given the job. In this case, the apparent use of an innocent criterion is simply a mask for racial discrimination. The decision is still directly based on race and would be deemed unlawful. The most straightforward remedy would be to set aside the decision and allow an honest application of the test.

There are, moreover, situations when a test is honestly administered and yet the very decision to use the test in the first place is based on an illegitimate concern, namely, a desire to exclude blacks. A highly sophisticated verbal aptitude test might be used, for example, to select employees for manual work because the employer, wanting to maintain a predominantly white work force, assumes that fewer whites than blacks will be screened out by the test. Here again, the "real" criterion of selection is race; a court would disallow the use of the irrelevant test, and require the employer to choose a criterion that serves a legitimate end. In both of these cases—the dishonest application of legitimate criteria and the honest application of illegitimate criteria—the appearance of color blindness is a sham and a court could use the simple, colorblind form of the antidiscrimination norm to void the results.

The more troublesome variant of the first issue arises when (1) the facially innocent criterion is adopted in order to serve a legitimate interest; (2) the criterion in fact furthers that interest; and (3) the application of the criterion disadvantages the racial minority in much the same way as would the use of race as the criterion of selection. The job may in fact require sophisticated verbal skills and the test that measures these skills may screen out more blacks than whites. The test is job-related but has a disparate adverse impact on blacks. The question then is whether an employment decision based on the test violates the anti-discrimination prohibition. This is a question of considerable difficulty because while the law, strictly speaking, prohibits distinctions based on race, this particular decision is based on a criterion other than race.

One school of thought answers this question in the negative. This view stresses process, and interprets antidiscrimination in terms of the integrity of the selection process: A selection process based on race is corrupt and cannot be allowed. A selection process free of racial influence might redound to the benefit of the racial minority, since it would allow them to compete on equal footing with other groups and thus give them a chance to alter the distributional inequalities that occurred under a regime such as Jim Crow, where they were penalized because of their race. Any actual effect on their material status as a group, however, would represent just an agreeable by-product, or a background assumption, not the purpose of antidiscrimination law. According to this school, the aims of antidiscrimination law are fulfilled when the process of selection is purified of all racial criteria or motivations.

Another viewpoint stresses results or effects, not process; it would find the use of the innocent criterion unlawful even if it serves legitimate ends. What is decisive, according to this school of thought, is the actual disadvantaging of blacks, not the way the disadvantage comes about. If the application of a criterion has a disproportionately adverse impact on the racial minority, in the sense that it excludes substantially more blacks than whites, the criterion should be treated as the functional equivalent of race.

At the heart of this interpretation of antidiscrimination is a concern for the social status of blacks. It is motivated by a desire to end all practices that would tend to perpetuate or aggravate their subordinate position. Admittedly, the costs of this program are real, for it is stipulated that the contested criterion serves some legitimate end; the test is job-related. But these costs are seen as a necessary price of justice. Only when the costs become extraordinarily large or achieve a special level of urgency, as when the criterion serves some "compelling" (and not just a "legitimate") interest, will the use of the criterion be allowed.

The theorist who so emphasizes effects rests his argument principally on the Fourteenth Amendment and ascribes to it the grandest and noblest of purposes—the elimination of caste structure. He insists that antidiscrimination, as the principle that controls the application of that amendment, be construed with this broad purpose in mind and if need be, that a new principle—the group-disadvantaging principle—be articulated in order to make this purpose even more explicit. He also insists that the various statutes that prohibit discrimination—the principal argumentative props of the process school—should be construed derivatively. These statutes, unlike the Fourteenth Amendment, may contain in so many words a specific ban on "discrimination based on race," but, so the effects theorist argues, these statutes should be seen as a legislative adoption of the prevailing constitutional principle. When that principle is interpreted to forbid the use of criteria that effectively disadvantage blacks, the statutes should be interpreted in a similar fashion.

The process school emphasizes not only the precise language in which the statutory norm is cast but also the traditional rule that conditions judicial intervention on a finding that the defendant is at fault. This fault exists when a white is given a job over a black even though the black scored higher on a test; the employer is said to be acting wrongfully because race is unrelated to any legitimate purpose and is a factor over which individuals have no control. But the requisite fault is said to be lacking when the selection is made on the basis of the individual's performance under some nonracial standard, such as a job-related test. On the other hand, those who subscribe to an effects test emphasize the prospective nature of the remedy typically sought in these cases (an injunction to forbid the use of the criterion in the future) and deny the need for a finding of fault. Such a finding may be necessary to justify damages or the criminal sanction, because these remedies require the defendant to pay for what he did in the past, and presumably such a burden can be placed only on someone who acted wrongfully. But an injunction simply directs that the defendant do what is just and does not presuppose that the defendant has acted wrongfully. Alternatively, the effects theorist might contend that if fault is necessary, it can be found in the defendant's willingness to persist in the use of the contested criterion with full knowledge of its consequences for the racial minority. Such persistence connotes a certain moral indifference.

The disadvantaging that the effects test seeks to avoid is usually defined in terms of the status of a group (for example, the criterion has a greater adverse impact on blacks than on whites and thus tends to perpetuate their subordinate position). Some see this group orientation as alien to our jurisprudence, and thus find a further reason for turning away from an effects test. Borrowing the Court's language in SHELLEY v. KRAEMER (1948), they insist that "[t]he rights created by the first section of the Fourteenth Amendment are, by its terms, guaranteed to the individual" and that "[t]he rights established are personal rights." But those who subscribe to the effects test see the well-being of individuals and of groups as inextricably linked: They believe that the status of an individual is determined in large part by the status of the group with which he is identified. Slavery itself was a group phenomenon, and any corrective strategy must be structured in group terms. Effects theorists also point to practices outside the racial context that display a concern for the welfare of groups such as religious minorities, women, the handicapped, labor, and consumers, and for that reason insist that a group orientation is thoroughly compatible with American legal principles.

In the late 1960s and early 1970s, the Supreme Court responded to these arguments and moved toward adopting an effects test in cases such as *Gaston County v. United States* (1969), GRIGGS v. DUKE POWER CO. (1971), and SWANN v. CHARLOTTE-MECKLENBURG BOARD OF EDUCATION (1971). There was, however, an element of ambiguity or hesitation in the Court's response. The Court prohibited the use of seemingly innocent criteria that disadvantaged blacks, even when their use served some legitimate interests, but the Court did not justify its decisions solely in terms of the adverse effects of the criteria. In addition, the Court characterized the adverse effect as a vestige of an earlier use of race. For example, a literacy test was disallowed as a qualification for voting not simply because it disqualified more blacks than whites but also because it perpetuated the disadvantages previously imposed on blacks in segregated schools. This insistence on analyzing the disadvantage as a vestige of past discrimination may have reflected a commitment to the process test insofar as the Court treated the earlier procedural imperfection (the assignment to schools on the basis of race) as the legally cognizable wrong and the present practice (the literacy test) as merely a device that perpetuates that wrong. But at the same time, the concern with past discrimination surely reflected some commitment to the effects test, for it resulted in the invalidation of facially innocent criteria that in fact served legitimate ends. Disallowing today's literacy test would avoid perpetuating yesterday's discrimination in the educational system, but only by compromising an interest the Court had previously deemed legitimate, namely, that of having a literate electorate. In fact, an interpretation of antidiscrimination law to forbid practices that perpetuate past discrimination could become functionally coextensive with an interpretation that makes effects decisive if some global practice such as slavery is taken as the relevant past discrimination, if the victims of past discrimination are identified in group terms, and if the remedial burden is placed on parties who had no direct role in the earlier discrimination. All disparate effects can be seen as a vestige of the special and unfortunate history of blacks in America.

By the mid-1970s, however, it became clear that the Court was not inclined to broaden its concern with past discrimination so as to make it the functional equivalent of the effects test. In fact, the Court turned in the opposite direction—away from effects and toward process. As Justice POTTER STEWART announced, "Reconstruction is over." The Court did not flatly repudiate its earlier decisions, but instead tried to limit them by confining the effects test to those antidiscrimination norms that were embodied in statutes. For constitutional claims of discrimination, the Court in cases such as WASHINGTON v. DAVIS (1976) and MOBILE v. BOLDEN (1980) required a showing that the process was flawed, or more precisely, that the defendant "intended to discriminate." The plaintiff had to show that the defendant's decision was based on race, or that he chose the seemingly innocent criterion not to further legitimate ends but to exclude or disadvantage blacks. The Court continued to honor claims of past discrimination, but by and large insisted that those claims be advanced by individually identifiable victims of the earlier discrimination, that past acts of discrimination be defined with a great deal of specificity, and that the causal links of those acts to the present racially disparate effects be manifest. No global claims of past discrimination have been allowed.

There is a certain irony in this distinction between statutory and constitutional claims, and in the Supreme Court's decision to confine the effects test to the statutory domain, for the statutes are couched in terms less congenial to such a test. The statutes speak specifically in terms of decisions based on race, while the Fourteenth Amendment speaks of equal protection. (Antidiscrimination is but the judicially constructed principle that is to guide the application of that provision.) Arguably, the distinction between statute and Constitution might reflect the Court's desire to find some way of limiting the practical impact of the effects test, for under the Fourteenth Amendment an effects test would have the widest scope and present the greatest possibilities of judicial intervention. The Fourteenth Amendment extends to all state practices and, because of its universality (it protects every "person"), could be used to protect even those groups that are not defined in racial terms. Indeed, in *Washington v. Davis* the Court expressed the fear that under the effects test the Fourteenth Amendment might even invalidate a sales tax because of its disproportionately adverse impact on the poor (never for a moment pausing to consider whether suitable limiting principles could be developed for avoiding such a result). The Court's distinction between statutory and constitutional claims might also stem from a desire to devise a means for sharing with other political institutions responsibility for the sacrifice of legitimate interests entailed in the application of an effects test. When attached to the statute, the effects test and its disruptive impact become the responsibility of both Court and Congress, since Congress remains free to repeal the statute or otherwise disavow the test.

In the mid-1970s, at the very moment the Court was struggling to identify the circumstances in which the use of a seemingly innocent criterion could be deemed a form of racial discrimination and was moving away from an effects test, it also had to confront the other major interpretive issue posed by antidiscrimination law, the issue of AFFIRMATIVE ACTION. The Court had to decide whether the norm against racial discrimination prohibits giving preference to blacks.

For much of our history, it was assumed that race-based action would be hostile to blacks and that therefore colorblindness would work to the advantage of blacks or at least shield them from hostile action. During the Second Reconstruction, however, as the drive for racial equality grew stronger, an assertedly "benign" use of race became more common. Many believed that even the honest application of legitimate criteria would not significantly alter the unequal distributional patterns that were produced among the races first under slavery and then under

Jim Crow, and that it would be necessary, at least for the immediate or foreseeable future, to give blacks a preference in order to improve their status relative to other groups.

These affirmative action programs typically included other minorities, such as Hispanics, as beneficiaries, but were primarily seen as addressed to blacks and did not extend to all disadvantaged groups, such as the poor or white ethnic minorities. They had a distinctive racial cast and were sometimes described as a form of "reverse discrimination." These programs were also typically structured so as to require the decision maker to achieve a certain number of blacks or other minorities within the institution, say, as employees or students. Often that number equaled the percentage of blacks or other minorities in the general population, and was variously described as a goal or quota, depending on which side of the issue one was on. A "goal" was said to establish the minimum rather than the maximum and to be more flexible than a "quota." But more significantly, the term "goal" did not have the odious connotations of the term "quota," which had been used in the past to describe numerical limits on the admission of minorities, limits that were designed to preserve rather than eradicate the caste structure.

For the most part, these affirmative action programs were not treated as a constitutional or statutory requirement. Some of those who subscribed to an effects test argued that the failure to institute preferential programs would constitute a practice that perpetuated the subordinate position of blacks and thus would be itself a form of racial discrimination. But this argument equated inaction with action, and either for that reason or because the effects test was having difficulties of its own, this argument never established a toehold in the law. Equally unsuccessful were the arguments that emphasized those antidiscrimination laws, such as the federal fair employment statute or the executive order governing government contractors, that not only prohibited discrimination but also commanded in so many terms "affirmative action"; the inclusion of these two words were deemed insufficient to alter or add to the basic obligations of the law. The issue posed by affirmative action programs was therefore one of permissibility, rather than obligation: Were these programs consistent with the prohibition against racial discrimination?

Sometimes the purported beneficiaries of the programs (or people speaking on their behalf) objected to them on the theory that the use of race was not wholly benign. Affirmative action was premised on the view that the racial minorities would not fare well under a colorblind policy, thus implying that these minorities are not as well equipped as whites to compete under traditional meritocratic criteria. They are being told, as they were under Jim Crow, that they are inferior—nothing "reverse" about this distinction. This complaint forced those who ran affirmative action programs to be secretive or discreet about what they were doing, but it did not bring those programs to an end or even present an especially formidable obstacle. The proponents of affirmative action explained that the race-based preference was premised on an assessment of the group's history in America, on the wrongs it suffered, not on a belief about innate ability, and as such could not justifiably be seen as giving rise to a slight. The use of race is benign, they insisted, because it improves the status of blacks and other racial minorities by giving them positions, jobs, or other concrete material advantages that they otherwise would not enjoy, at least not in the foreseeable future.

Affirmative action programs have also been attacked by whites, especially when there are discernible differences in the applicants under standard nonracial criteria and when scarce goods, such as highly desired jobs or places in professional schools, are being allocated. In such circumstances favoring a black because of his race necessarily means disfavoring a white because of his race; a job given to one is necessarily denied another. The rejected white applicant cannot truly claim that he is stigmatized even in these circumstances; no one is suggesting he is inferior. His exclusion comes as the by-product or consequence of a program founded on other principles—not to hurt him or the members of his group, but to help the disadvantaged. On the other hand, the rejected white applicant does not rest his complaint solely on the fortuity of the general, racially unspecific language of the antidiscrimination norm, the fact that discrimination based on *any* race is prohibited. The white applicant can also claim that he is being treated unfairly, since he is being judged on the basis of a criterion over which he has no control and which is unrelated to any conception of merit. The rejected white applicant might not be stigmatized, but he can insist that he is being treated unfairly.

This claim of individual unfairness finds support in the process theory of antidiscrimination: If the purpose of antidiscrimination law is to preserve the integrity of a process, to insure that individuals are treated fairly and to prevent them from being judged on the basis of irrelevant criteria, then it would not seem to matter whether the color used in the process were white or black. In either instance, the selection process would be unfair. The program may be well-intentioned, but the intention is of little solace to the rejected white applicants who, as Justice LEWIS F. POWELL put it, are being forced "to bear the burdens of redressing grievances not of their making."

Some of the proponents of affirmative action deny that there is any unfairness to the rejected white applicant. They argue that the claim of unfairness presupposes a special moral status for certain nonracial or meritocratic standards of evaluation, such as grades or performance on a standardized test, and that the requisite moral status is in fact lacking. The white has no "right" to be judged on the meritocratic standard. The more widely shared view among the proponents of affirmative action, however, acknowledges the unfairness caused to individual whites by the preference for blacks but treats it as a necessary, yet regrettable cost of eliminating caste structure. As Justice HARRY A. BLACKMUN put it, "In order to get beyond race, we must first take account of race. There is no other way." Those who take this position, like those who support an effects test, argue that the purpose of antidiscrimination law is to guard against those practices that would perpetuate or aggravate the subordinate position of blacks and other racial minorities and that it would be a perversion of history now to use that law to stop programs designed to improve the status of these groups.

The Supreme Court confronted the issue of affirmative action and weighed these arguments in two different settings. In one, affirmative action was undertaken at the behest of a court order. The theory underlying such orders is not that affirmative action is directly required by an antidiscrimination statute or by the Constitution but rather that it is needed to remedy a pattern or practice of discrimination. Affirmative action is part of the court's corrective plan. A court might, for example, require a company to grant a preference in the seniority system to blacks who were previously excluded from the company and thus unable to earn seniority rights equal to those of whites. The Supreme Court has accepted such remedial uses of race, although it has insisted that this kind of preference be limited to identifiable victims of past discrimination and that some regard be given to the interests of the innocent whites who might be adversely affected by the preferences. For example, blacks might be preferred for vacancies, but will not necessarily be allowed to force the layoff of whites.

The second setting consists of the so-called voluntary affirmative action programs, which are adopted not under orders from a court but out of a sense of moral duty or a belief that the eradication of caste structure is a desirable social policy. These voluntary affirmative action programs have proved more troublesome than the remedial ones, in part because they are not limited to individually identifiable victims of past discriminations (they are truly group oriented), but also because they are not preceded by a judicial finding that the institution has previously discriminated and they are not carried out under the close supervision of a court. The Supreme Court approved these affirmative action programs, but its approval has not been a blanket one. By the mid-1980s, it was established that under certain circumstances color consciousness is permissible, but the Court has been divided in its effort to define or limit these circumstances.

These divisions have been especially pronounced when the voluntary programs were used in higher education. In the first case, DeFunis v. Odegaard (1974), involving admissions to a state law school, the Court heard arguments and then dismissed the case on grounds of MOOTNESS because the rejected white applicant had graduated by the time the Court came to decide the case—a disposition that underscored the difficulty of the issue and the internal divisions on the Court. A few years later, the Court took up the issue again, in REGENTS OF UNIVERSITY OF CALIFORNIA V. BAKKE (1978), this time at the insistence of a rejected white applicant to a state medical school. In this case the Court reached the merits, but the divisions were even more apparent. No single opinion commanded a majority.

Four Justices thought the preferential program in *Bakke* unlawful. They stressed an antidiscrimination statute, which prohibited, in so many terms, discrimination based on race. These Justices reasoned that a preference for blacks is as much a discrimination based on race as one for whites. No discrimination means no discrimination. Another Justice thought preferential programs could be justified as a means of diversifying the student body, but he objected to the manner in which the particular program before the Court had been implemented. He would allow race to be considered in the admissions process, but would not permit separate tracks for applicants according to race. The remaining four Justices joined in an opinion that would sustain the program as it was in fact implemented, but two of these Justices also wrote separate opinions.

These deep-seated divisions did not resolve themselves substantially in the years following *Bakke*. One voluntary program received a slightly more resolute acceptance by the Court, however, in FULLILOVE V. KLUTZNICK (1980). This program was established by Congress and required a preference for minority-owned businesses in awarding contracts for federally funded public works projects. Although, once again, no single opinion commanded a majority of the Court, the vote of the Justices shifted from 1–4–4 to 6–3, and Chief Justice WARREN E. BURGER, who had objected (without qualification) to the preferential program in *Bakke,* voted to uphold this one. He also wrote one of three opinions that supported the constitutionality of the program. The Chief Justice studiously avoided choosing among "the formulas of analysis" articulated in *Bakke;* that is, he refused to say whether the affirmative action program had to meet the "compelling" interest standard or whether it was sufficient if the corrective ends of the program were deemed "important" or just "legitimate" and the means substantially related to those ends. He simply said, whatever the standard, this program meets it. He did, however, specifically and repeatedly mention one factor that might be the key to the change in his position and the Court's attitude in general: "Here we pass, not on a choice made by a single judge or a school board, but on a considered decision of the Congress and the President."

With this emphasis on the role played by the coordinate branches of government in the affirmative action program, the Chief Justice returned to an idea that emerged in the analysis of the Court's treatment of facially innocent criteria, and that might well explain the Court's determination to confine the effects test to statutes: The Court is more prepared to accept the costs and dislocations that are entailed in the eradication of caste structure when it can share the responsibility for this project with the other branches of government. The Court does not want to go it alone. This suggests that the fate of equality will depend not only on the substantive commitments of the Justices, on their determination to bring the subordination of blacks and other racial minorities to an end, but also on their views about the role of the Court. The content of antidiscrimination law will in good measure depend on the willingness of the Justices to use their power to lead the nation, or if that impulse is lacking, on the willingness of the other branches of government to participate aggressively in the reconstruction of a society disfigured by one century of slavery and another of Jim Crow.

## Bibliography

BELL, DERRICK 1980 *Race, Racism and American Law.* Boston: Little, Brown.

BREST, PAUL 1976 In Defense of the Antidiscrimination Principle. *Harvard Law Review* 90:1–54.

COHEN, MARSHALL; NAGEL, THOMAS; and SCANLON, THOMAS 1977 *Equality and Preferential Treatment.* Princeton, N.J.: Princeton University Press.

EISENBERG, THEODORE 1981 *Civil Rights Legislation.* Charlottesville, Va.: Michie Co.

FISHKIN, JAMES 1983 *Justice, Equal Opportunity and the Family.* New Haven, Conn.: Yale University Press.

FISS, OWEN 1971 A Theory of Fair Employment Laws. *University of Chicago Law Review* 38:235–314.

—————— 1976 Groups and the Equal Protection Clause. *Philosophy and Public Affairs* 5:107–177.

FREEMAN, ALAN 1978 Legitimizing Racial Discrimination through Antidiscrimination Law: A Critical Review of Supreme Court Doctrine. *Minnesota Law Review* 62:1049–1119.

GARET, RONALD 1983 Communality and Existence: The Rights of Groups. *Southern California Law Review* 56:1001–1075.

GUNTHER, GERALD 1972 In Search of Evolving Doctrine on a Changing Court: A Model for Newer Equal Protection. *Harvard Law Review* 86:1–48.

KARST, KENNETH and HOROWITZ, HAROLD 1974 Affirmative Action and Equal Protection. *Virginia Law Review* 60:955–974.

RAE, DOUGLAS 1981 *Equalities.* Cambridge, Mass.: Harvard University Press.

TUSSMAN, JOSEPH and TEN BROEK, JACOBUS 1949 The Equal Protection of the Laws. *California Law Review* 37:341–381.

# EQUAL PROTECTION
# OF THE LAWS

Kenneth L. Karst

The ancient political ideal of equality did not find explicit recognition in the text of the Constitution until the FOURTEENTH AMENDMENT was ratified in 1868. Yet equality was an American ideal from the earliest colonial times. There was irony in the expression of the ideal in the DECLARATION OF INDEPENDENCE; the newly independent states generally limited voting to white male property owners, and THOMAS JEFFERSON, the Declaration's author, was the troubled owner of slaves. Even so, one feature of white American society that set it apart from Europe was an egalitarian climate for social relations. The Constitution's ban on TITLES OF NOBILITY symbolized the nation's determination to leave behind the old world's privileges of monarchy and aristocracy.

Jefferson, who believed in an aristocracy of "virtue and talents," understood that equality of opportunity was consistent with wide disparities among individuals' wealth and power. The equality he envisioned was, above all, equality before the law. The principle of universal laws, equally applicable to all citizens, itself provided a foundation for a market economy whose competitive struggles would lead to further inequalities. An equality that was formal, or legal, thus would undermine the "equality of condition" that attracted some of Jefferson's contemporaries. Yet formal equality was something that mattered greatly in the nation's first decades, and it matters greatly today. When Europeans remark, as they still do, on America's relatively high degree of equality, they are referring not to equality of wealth or political power but to equality of social status. With pardonable literary exaggeration, Simone de Beauvoir said it this way: "the rich American has no grandeur; the poor man no servility; human relations in daily life are on a footing of equality. . . ."

The Fourteenth Amendment's wording emphasizes legal equality. A state is forbidden to "deny to any person within its jurisdiction the equal protection of the laws." On its face this language seems to demand no more than even-handed enforcement of laws as they are written. Such a reading, however, would drain all life from the guarantee of equal protection. On this view even a law barring blue-eyed persons from state employment would pass constitutional muster if the state applied it equally, without discrimination, to all applicants, refusing jobs only to those who were blue-eyed. No one has ever seriously argued for so restricted a scope for the equal protection clause. The Supreme Court casually dismissed the idea with a passing comment in YICK WO v. HOPKINS (1886): "the equal protection of the laws is a pledge of the protection of equal laws."

At the other extreme of silliness, the *Yick Wo* statement might be taken literally, interpreting the equal protection clause to forbid the enforcement of any law that imposed any inequality. As Joseph Tussman and JACOBUS TEN BROEK showed nearly forty years ago, so sweeping a reading would convert the clause into a constitutional prohibition on legislation itself. All laws draw lines of classification, applying their rules only to some people (or some transactions or phenomena) and not to others. Furthermore, the very existence of law—that is, of governmental regulation of human behavior—implies inequality, for some individuals must evaluate the behavior of others and enforce the state's norms by imposing sanctions on the recalcitrant. In Ralf Dahrendorf's biting formulation, "all men are equal *before* the law but they are no longer equal *after* it." Given the diverse characteristics of humans, the achievement of equality as to one aspect of life necessarily implies inequalities as to other aspects. And if it were possible to construct a society characterized by total, uncompromising equality, no one would want to live in that society.

Then what kinds of inequality are prohibited by the equal protection clause? The abstraction, equality, cannot resolve cases; the question always remains, equality as to what? To give meaning to the equal protection clause requires identification of the substantive values that are its central concern. The inquiry begins in the history leading to the adoption of the Fourteenth Amendment, but it does not end there. To understand the substantive content of the equal protection clause, we must consider not only what it meant to its framers, but also what it has come to mean to succeeding generations of judges and other citizens.

Just what role the framers had in mind for the equal protection clause remains unclear; the amendment's sketchy "legislative history" has been given widely divergent interpretations. All the interpreters agree, however, that the framers' immediate objective was to provide an unshakable constitutional foundation for the CIVIL RIGHTS ACT OF 1866. That act had been passed over the veto of President ANDREW JOHNSON, who had asserted that it exceeded the powers of Congress.

The 1866 act had declared the CITIZENSHIP of all persons born in the United States and subject to its JURISDICTION. This declaration, later echoed in the text of the Fourteenth Amendment, had been designed to "overrule" the assertion by Chief Justice ROGER B. TANEY in his opinion for the Supreme Court in DRED SCOTT V. SANDFORD (1857) that black persons were incapable of being citizens. Taney had said that blacks—

not just slaves but any blacks—were incapable of citizenship, because blacks had not been members of "the People of the United States" identi-fied in the Constitution's PREAMBLE as the body who adopted that docu-ment. Blacks has been excluded from membership in the national com-munity, according to Taney, because they were "considered as a subordinate and inferior class of beings, who had been subjugated by the dominant race, and, whether emancipated or not, yet remained subject to their authority. . . ." Discriminatory state legislation in force when the Constitution was adopted, Taney said, negated the conclusion that the states "regarded at that time, as fellow-citizens and members of the sovereignty, a class of beings whom they had thus stigmatized; . . . and upon whom they had impressed such deep and enduring marks of inferiority and degradation. . . ."

This dubious reading of history is beside the point; *Dred Scott*'s relevance to our inquiry is that Taney's assumptions about racial inferior-ity and restricted citizenship were just what the drafters of the 1866 act sought to destroy. There was to be no "dominant race" and no "subordinate and inferior class of beings," but only citizens. Indeed the act's conferral of various CIVIL RIGHTS was aimed at abolishing a new system of serfdom designed to replace SLAVERY in the southern states. That system rested on the BLACK CODES, laws methodically imposing legal disabilities on blacks for the purpose of maintaining them in a state of dependency and inferiority.

The 1866 act, after its declaration of citizenship, provided that "such citizens, of every race and color [including former slaves], shall have the same right [to contract and sue in court and deal with property, etc.] as is enjoyed by white citizens. . . ." The "civil rights" thus guaran-teed were seen as the equal rights of citizens. When President Johnson vetoed the bill, he similarly linked the ideas of citizenship and equality, and argued that the THIRTEENTH AMENDMENT was an insufficient basis for congressional power. Congress overrode Johnson's veto, but from the time of the veto forward, a major purpose of the promoters of the Fourteenth Amendment, then under consideration in Congress, was to secure the constitutional foundations of the 1866 act.

The amendment, like the act, begins with a declaration of citizenship. In the same first section, the amendment goes on to forbid a state to "abridge the PRIVILEGES OR IMMUNITIES of citizens of the United States," to "deprive any person of life, liberty, or property, without DUE PROCESS OF LAW," or to deny a person "the equal protection of the laws." No serious effort was made during the debates on the amendment to identify separate functions for the three clauses that followed the declaration of citizenship. The section as a whole was taken to guarantee the equal enjoyment of the rights of citizens.

Beyond those specific goals, nothing in the consensus of the Fourteenth Amendment's framers would have caused anyone to anticipate what the Supreme Court made of the amendment in the latter half of the twentieth century. Yet the Fourteenth Amendment was not written in the language of specific rights, such as the right to contract or buy or sell property, but was deliberately cast in the most general terms. The broad language of the amendment strongly suggests that its framers were proposing to write into the Constitution not a "laundry list" of specific civil rights but a principle of equal citizenship.

To be a citizen is to enjoy the dignity of membership in the society, to be respected as a person who "belongs." The principle of equal citizenship presumptively forbids the organized society to treat an individual either as a member of an inferior or dependent caste or as a nonparticipant. As Taney recognized in his *Dred Scott* opinion, the stigma of caste is inconsistent with equal citizenship, which demands respect for each individual's humanity. Further, a citizen is a participant in society, a member of a moral community who must be taken into account when community decisions are made. Citizenship also implies obligations to one's fellow citizens. The values of participation and responsibility contribute to the primary citizenship value of respect, but they are also independently significant as aspects of citizenship.

For the first eight decades of the Fourteenth Amendment's existence, its interpretation by the Supreme Court was largely a betrayal of the constitutional ideal of equal citizenship. First by inventing the STATE ACTION limitation on the Fourteenth Amendment in the CIVIL RIGHTS CASES (1883), and then by giving racial SEGREGATION the stamp of constitutional validity in the SEPARATE BUT EQUAL decision of PLESSY V. FERGUSON (1896), the Supreme Court delivered virtually the entire subject of race relations back into the hands of the white South. The equal citizenship principle was left to be articulated in dissenting opinions. Notable among those dissents were the opinions of Justice JOSEPH P. BRADLEY in the SLAUGHTERHOUSE CASES (1873) and of Justice JOHN MARSHALL HARLAN in the *Civil Rights Cases* and *Plessy v. Ferguson.* The latter dissent included a passage that is now famous: "In view of the Constitution, in the eye of the law, there is in this country no superior, dominant, ruling class of citizens. There is no caste here. Our Constitution is color-blind, and neither knows nor tolerates classes among citizens." For half a century, those words expressed not a reality but a hope.

Outside the field of RACIAL DISCRIMINATION, the equal protection clause had little force even during the period when the due process clause of the Fourteenth Amendment was in active use as a defense against various forms of ECONOMIC REGULATION. By the 1920s, Justice OLIVER WENDELL HOLMES could say in BUCK V. BELL (1927), with accuracy if not with compassion, that the equal protection clause was the "usual last resort of constitutional arguments."

Even during the years when Holmes's "last resort" epithet summarized equal protection jurisprudence, the NAACP was pinning its hopes for racial justice on the federal judiciary, and was winning some victories. The Supreme Court had struck down LITERACY TESTS for voting that contained GRANDFATHER CLAUSES exempting most white voters, in GUINN v. UNITED STATES (1915) and *Lane v. Wilson* (1939); the Court had begun the process of holding "white primaries" unconstitutional; and it had invalidated racial zoning in BUCHANAN v. WARLEY (1917). And after the nation had emerged from the Great Depression and World War II, the judicial climate was distinctly more hospitable to equal protection claims.

The Depression had brought to dominance a new political majority, committed to active governmental intervention in economic affairs for the purpose of achieving full employment and major improvements in wages and the conditions of labor. The judiciary's main contribution to those egalitarian goals was to free the legislative process from the close judicial supervision of economic regulation that had attended the flowering of SUBSTANTIVE DUE PROCESS doctrines in the recent past. The war not only ended the Depression; it was a watershed in race relations. The migration of blacks from the rural South to northern and western cities, which had slowed during the Depression, dramatically accelerated, as wartime industry offered jobs that black workers had previously filled only rarely. Urban blacks were soon seen as a potent national political force. By the end of the war, the Army had begun the process of racial integration. Wartime ideology, with its scorn for Nazi racism, had lasting effects on the public mind. Even as the Supreme Court was upholding severe—and racist—wartime restrictions in the JAPANESE AMERICAN CASES (1943–1944), it reflected a new national state of mind in its celebrated OBITER DICTUM in KOREMATSU v. UNITED STATES (1944): "All legal restrictions which curtail the civil rights of a single racial group are immediately suspect. . . . [C]ourts must subject them to the most rigid scrutiny."

In the immediate postwar years the Supreme Court held unconstitutional the judicial enforcement of RESTRICTIVE COVENANTS in SHELLEY v. KRAEMER (1948), and it even ruled that the equal protection clause forbade some forms of segregation in state universities. (See SWEATT v. PAINTER, 1950.) The expected return to economic depression did not materialize. Instead, the country entered a period of unprecedented economic expansion. Good times are the most propitious for egalitarian public policies; it is relatively easy for "haves" to share with "have-nots" when they see their own conditions as steadily improving. The time was ripe, in the 1950s, for important successes in the movement for racial equality.

On the national scene, however, the political branches of government remained disinclined to act. One-party politics in the South had given

disproportionate influence in the Congress to Southerners whose seniority gave them chairs of major committees. With President DWIGHT D.
EISENHOWER reluctant to intervene, the prospects for effective civil rights
legislation seemed dim. Thus was the stage furnished when Eisenhower
appointed EARL WARREN to the Chief Justiceship in 1953.

In Warren's first term the Court decided BROWN V. BOARD OF EDUCA-
TION (1954)—still the leading authoritative affirmation that the Constitution forbids a system of caste—and in so doing began what Philip Kurland
has called an "egalitarian revolution" in constitutional law. *Brown* was
a major event in modern American history. Race relations in America
would never again be what they were on the eve of the decision. The
political movement for racial equality took on new vitality, and other
egalitarian movements drew encouragement from that example. The
constitutional law of equal protection gained powerful momentum, and
the doctrinal effects went well beyond the subject of racial equality. If
*Brown* itself represented JUDICIAL ACTIVISM, it was no more than a shadow
of what was to come. The equal protection clause became the cutting
edge of the WARREN COURT's active intervention into realms that previously had been left to legislative choice.

Two doctrinal techniques served these egalitarian ends. First, the
Court heightened the STANDARD OF REVIEW used to test the constitutionality of certain laws, insisting on STRICT SCRUTINY by the courts of legislation
that employed a SUSPECT CLASSIFICATION or discriminated against the
exercise of a FUNDAMENTAL INTEREST. Second, the Court relaxed the
"state action" limitation on the Fourteenth Amendment, bringing new
forms of private conduct under the amendment's reach. Although the
BURGER COURT later revitalized the "state action" limitation and slowed
the advance of equal protection into new doctrinal territory, it made
its own contributions to the development of the principle of equal citizenship.

Once the Court had firmly fastened the "suspect classification" label
to racial discrimination, other forms of discrimination were attacked in
the same terms. Some Justices have refused to find any legislative classification other than race to be constitutionally disfavored, but most of
them have been receptive to arguments that at least some nonracial
discriminations deserve heightened scrutiny. Thus, while only discrimination against ALIENS has been assimilated to the "suspect classifications"
category—and even that assimilation is a sometime thing—the Court
has announced clearly that judicial scrutiny should be heightened in
some significant degree for SEX DISCRIMINATION or legislative classifications based on ILLEGITIMACY. Not only in these opinions but also in
opinions refusing to apply similar reasoning to other forms of discrimination, the Court has developed a consensus on two sets of factors that
are relevant in determining a classification's degree of "suspectness" or

disfavor, and thus the level of justification which courts should demand for it.

The first set of factors emphasizes the equal citizenship value of respect; these factors reflect the judiciary's solicitude for the victims of stigma. A classification on the basis of a trait that is immutable and highly visible—such as race or sex—promotes stereotyping, the automatic assignment of an individual to a general category, often implying inferiority. The second set of factors, emphasizing the equal citizenship value of participation, focuses on the historic disadvantages (especially political disadvantages) of DISCRETE AND INSULAR MINORITIES. Both the phrase and the idea antedate Warren Court activism; they come from Justice HARLAN FISKE STONE's opinion for the Court in UNITED STATES v. CAROLENE PRODUCTS CO. (1938). Legislation that burdens a group likely to be neglected by the legislature is a natural candidate for special judicial scrutiny.

The equal citizenship themes of respect, participation, and responsibility also informed the Warren Court's decisions demanding close examination of the justifications for legislative discrimination against the exercise of "fundamental interests." Those decisions, in theory, might have been rested on grounds of substantive due process rather than equal protection. In fact, the Burger Court, which refused to recognize any new "fundamental" interests in equal protection doctrine, employed similar reasoning under the heading of due process, with corresponding attention to the values of equal citizenship. (See ABORTION AND THE CONSTITUTION; FAMILY AND THE CONSTITUTION; RIGHT OF PRIVACY.) The equal protection cases, however, identify only three clusters of interests as "fundamental": VOTING RIGHTS and related interests in equal access to the electoral process; certain rights of ACCESS TO THE COURTS (which have come to be explained more recently on due process grounds); and rights concerning marriage, procreation, and family relations. (See FREEDOM OF INTIMATE ASSOCIATION.)

Voting, of course, is one of the core responsibilities of citizenship. Perhaps more important, it is the citizen's preeminent symbol of participation as a valued member of the community. Access to the courts, like voting, is instrumentally valuable as a way to protect other interests. But—also like voting—the chance to be heard is an important citizenship symbol. To be listened to, to be treated as a person and not an object of administration, is to be afforded the dignity owed to a citizen. Finally, the marriage and family cases similarly implicate the citizenship values of respect, responsibility, and participation. Marriage and parenthood do not merely define one's legal obligations; they define one's status and social role and self-concept. For the state to deny a person the right and responsibility of choice about such matters is to take away the presumptive right to be treated as a person, one of equal worth among citizens. None of these "fundamental" interests is entirely immune from state interference; what the principle of equal citizenship requires is that government offer weighty justification before denying their equal enjoyment.

In retrospect the whole apparatus of differential standards of review can be seen as judicial interest-balancing, thinly disguised: the more important the interest in equality, the more justification was required for its invasion by the government. Perhaps the Warren Court's majority chose to clothe its decisions in a "judicial"-sounding system of categories because the Justices were sensitive to the charge that they were writing their own policy preferences into the equal protection clause, and not just "interpreting" it. As a consequence, the Court extended the reach of equal protection without ever explicitly articulating the substantive content of the equal protection clause.

The Warren Court, in its final years, was well on the way to effective abandonment of the "state action" limitation on the Fourteenth Amendment, finding "significant state involvement" in all manner of private racial discriminations that denied their victims full participation in the public life of the community. Once Congress passed the CIVIL RIGHTS ACT OF 1964, however, it became unnecessary for the Court to complete its dismantling job; now there was a federal statutory right of access to PUBLIC ACCOMMODATIONS such as hotels, restaurants, and theaters. When the Court in JONES v. ALFRED H. MAYER CO. (1968) discovered the Thirteenth Amendment as a source of congressional power to forbid most other private racial discrimination, the chief practical motivation for doing away with the "state action" doctrine was removed. In later years, a different majority of Justices has gone far to restore the "state action" limitation to its former status but at the same time it has both reaffirmed the power of Congress to stamp out private racial discrimination and promoted that purpose with an expansive interpretation of existing civil rights acts.

The right to participate in the community's public life—even those portions of public life that are owned and managed by private persons—is an essential ingredient of effective citizenship, part of what it means to be a respected member of society. The "state action" limitation, when the Supreme Court invented it, insulated the "private" choices of the owners of public accommodations and other commercial businesses not only from the direct reach of the Fourteenth Amendment's guarantee of equal protection but also from congressional vindication of the rights of equal citizenship. Although "state action" remains an impediment to the application of the equal protection clause to some private conduct, Congress can protect, and has protected, the most important claims to participation by all citizens in society's public life.

To say that the principle of equal citizenship is the substantive core of the equal protection clause, and that the Supreme Court's recent equal protection jurisprudence has centered on the values of equal citizenship, is not to decide particular cases. Equal citizenship is not a decisional machine but a principle that informs judgment by reference to certain substantive values. Like other constitutional principles, it is inescapably open-ended. The Warren Court's expansion of the content of equal protection doctrine was regularly greeted with the criticism that the Court had not specified exactly how far its egalitarian principles would reach. The critics did no more than echo what Jeremy Bentham had said more than a century earlier: the abstraction, equality, is insatiable; where would it all end?

This "stopping-place" problem is implicit in any constitutional guarantee of equality. Most obviously, it lies at the center of the question of affirmative governmental obligations to reduce inequality. In a few decisions over the past three decades the Supreme Court has imposed on government the duty to compensate for the inability of INDIGENTS to pay various costs or fees required for effective access to the courts. The Burger Court's consciousness of the stopping-place problem produced two types of response. Some claims of access, although accepted, were explained as resting on rights to procedural fairness, and thus on due process rather than equal protection grounds. (See BODDIE V. CONNECTICUT, 1971.) Other access claims were rejected, halting further extension of the demands of equal protection. (See ROSS V. MOFFITT, 1974.) Yet the Court has not been willing to put an end to the notion that some inequalities, although not caused directly by the state, are constitutionally intolerable, requiring governmental action to relieve their victims from some of their consequences.

Similarly, consciousness of the stopping-place problem has influenced the Court's definition of what constitutes a legislative discrimination based on race, or gender, or, presumably, any other disfavored classification. After flirting in some school segregation cases with a view that would equate de facto with de jure segregation, the Court declared in the employment discrimination case of WASHINGTON V. DAVIS (1976) that it was not enough, in making a claim of racial discrimination, to show that legislation had a racially discriminatory impact. To succeed, such a claim must be based on a showing of official discriminatory purpose. (See LEGISLATION.) The "impact" principle, said the Court, "would be far reaching and would raise serious questions about, and perhaps invalidate, a whole range of tax, welfare, public service, regulatory, and licensing statutes that may be more burdensome to the poor and to the average black than to the more affluent white." In other words, where would it all end?

What is needed, in dealing with the stopping-place problem as with any other aspect of equal protection interest-balancing, is the guidance that can be found in the Fourteenth Amendment's substantive values. Some inequalities will invade the core values of equal citizenship, and others will touch them hardly at all. The level of justification required for governmental action—or failure to act—will vary according to the magnitude of that invasion. Some economic inequalities may be so severe as to impose a stigma of caste, but most do not. Part of our tradition of responsible citizenship, after all, is to provide for oneself and one's family. The principle of equal citizenship is not a charter for economic leveling but a presumptive guarantee against those inequalities that dehumanize or seriously impair one's ability to participate as a member of society. To say that such determinations turn on questions of degree is merely to acknowledge that no constitutional principle is a substitute for judicial judgment.

Since the late 1960s a number of governmental and private bodies have voluntarily taken steps to compensate for inequalities that are the legacy of past societal discrimination, and generally to integrate various institutions by race and by gender. These AFFIRMATIVE ACTION programs, sometimes in the form of racial or gender-based quotas for employment or housing or admission to higher education, do not merely equalize. Every equality begets another inequality. Even absent a quota, when a person's race becomes a relevant qualification for a job, all other relevant factors are diminished in weight. To put the matter more concretely, an individual can lose the competition for the job on the basis of his or her race. If affirmative action is constitutionally justified—and the Supreme Court has largely validated it—the reasons lie not in any lack of sympathy for such arguments, but in the weight of countervailing considerations supporting the programs. The Justices' various opinions upholding affirmative action have mainly sounded the theme of remedying past discrimination, but other arguments emphasize the urgency of integrating American institutions in the present generation.

The debate over affirmative action has touched a more general issue: the appropriate role of groups in equal protection analysis. In one view, group membership is simply irrelevant. The text of the equal protection clause provides its guarantees to "any person," and much of our constitutional tradition is individualistic. Yet, inescapably, a claim to equality is a claim made on behalf of a group. If every law draws some line of classification, then it is also true that every individual is potentially classifiable according to an enormous variety of characteristics. Legislative classification implies a selection of certain attributes as the relevant ones—the "merits" that justify conferring a benefit (or "demerits" that justify a burden). Once such a classification is written into law, any individual is classified either with the group of persons who possess the "merits" (or "demerits") or with the group of those who do not. To complain against a classification scheme is not merely to say "I am wronged," but to say "We—the whole group of individuals disadvantaged—are wronged." Indeed, any claim based on a rule of law is intelligible only as a demand to be treated the same as other members of a group, that is, all others who share the relevant "individual" attributes specified by the rule.

The origins of the Fourteenth Amendment strongly suggest that a group, defined by race just as the *Dred Scott* opinion had defined it, was intended to be the amendment's chief beneficiary. If today the equal protection clause prohibits other forms of inequality, there is nothing incongruous about viewing that development in one perspective as the recognition of the claims of groups of people: women, aliens, illegitimate children, homosexuals, the handicapped. When equal citizenship is denied, the denial typically takes a form that affects not merely isolated individuals but classes of people.

The equal protection clause limits only the states; nothing in the constitutional text expressly imposes an analogous limit on the federal government. Yet since BOLLING v. SHARPE (1954) the Supreme Court has consistently interpreted the Fifth Amendment's due process clause to guarantee equal protection against federal denial. This interpretation has roots in the original Constitution's assumption that the new national government would have a direct relationship with individuals. The idea of national citizenship was current long before the Civil Rights Act of 1866. And that citizenship, as Justice Bradley argued in his dissent in the *Slaughterhouse Cases,* implies some measure of equality before the law. *Bolling,* a companion case to *Brown v. Board of Education,* presented a challenge to school segregation in the District of Columbia. *Brown* held the segregation of state schools unconstitutional, and Chief Justice Warren said it would be "unthinkable" if a similar principle were not applied to the national government. After the Fourteenth Amendment's reaffirmation of national citizenship, such a result would, indeed, have been unthinkable.

The Warren Court's expansion of constitutional guarantees of equality necessarily implied an expansion of the powers of the national government. The Civil War amendments were reinterpreted to give Congress sweeping powers to reach virtually all racial discriminations, public and private. The Fourteenth Amendment's equal protection clause became the basis for intensified intervention by the federal courts into areas previously governed by local law and custom, as a new body of uniform national law replaced local autonomy. As the "state action" limitation was relaxed, the Constitution brought the commands of law to areas previously regulated by private institutional decision. In ALEXANDER BICKEL's phrase, the Warren Court's main themes were "egalitarian, legalitarian, and centralizing."

The desegregation of places of public accommodations in the South is an instructive example. The Supreme Court first held unconstitutional all forms of state-sponsored segregation, including segregation of public beaches, parks, golf courses, and restaurants. Then, cautiously, it began to apply the same reasoning to some privately owned public accommodations, finding "state action" in the most tenuous connections between public policy and the private decision to segregate. Finally, in HEART OF ATLANTA MOTEL CO. v. UNITED STATES (1964) the Court moved swiftly to validate the Civil Rights Act of 1964, which forbade segregation in most public accommodations that mattered. In all these actions the Court promoted the extension of a body of uniform national law to replace the local laws and customs that had long governed southern communities, with an earlier Supreme Court's blessing.

These changes in the law governing racial discrimination in public accommodations were, in one perspective, a repetition of a course of events that had been common in the Western world since the seventeenth century. An older system, basing a person's legal rights on his or her status in a hierarchical structure, came to be replaced by a newer law that applied impersonally to everyone. The abolition of slavery, the 1866 Civil Rights Act, the Civil War amendments—all had been earlier episodes in this same historical line. And the law that liberated individuals from domination based on race, like the law that previously had broken feudal hierarchies and the power of the guilds, was the law of the centralized state. If one were asked to compress three centuries of Western political history into three words, the words might be: "egalitarian, legalitarian, and centralizing."

Justice ROBERT H. JACKSON, concurring in EDWARDS v. CALIFORNIA (1941), remarked that the Fourteenth Amendment's privileges and immunities clause was aimed at making United States citizenship "the dominant and paramount allegiance among us." Whatever the historical warrant for that assertion, it reflects today's social fact. We think of ourselves primarily as citizens of the nation, and only secondarily as citizens of the several states. The Constitution itself has become our pre-eminent symbol of national community, and the judiciary's modern contributions to our sense of community have centered on the principle of equal citizenship.

It is hard to overstate the importance of the ideal of equality as a legitimizing force in American history. For the SOCIAL COMPACT theorists of the eighteenth century whose thinking was well-known to the Framers of the original Constitution, some measure of equality before the law was implicit in the idea of citizenship. DANIEL WEBSTER, speaking of "the LAW OF THE LAND," agreed: "The meaning is, that every citizen shall hold his life, liberty, property, and immunities, under the protection of the general rules which govern society." By Webster's time, support for the principle of equality of opportunity could be found even among the most comfortable Americans, who saw in that principle a way to justify their advantages. More generally, the egalitarian spirit that has promoted a national consciousness has also lent legitimacy to government. There has been just enough truth in the belief that "anyone can grow up to be President" to provide a critical measure of the diffuse loyalty that is an essential ingredient of nationhood.

Never in our history has it been true that *anyone* might aspire to the presidency. Slavery and racial discrimination are only the most obvious and uglier counterexamples; not until our own time have women's aspirations to such high position become realistic. Yet the guarantee of equal protection of the laws, even during the long decades when lawyers deemed it a constitutional trifle, stood as a statement of an important American ideal. Much of the growth in our constitutional law has resulted when the downtrodden have called the rest of us to account, asking whether we intend to live up to the principles we profess. Vindication of the constitutional promise of equal citizenship did not take its rightful place on our judicial agenda for an unconscionably long time, and it remains far from complete. What is most remarkable, however, is the nourishment that the promise—the promise alone—has provided for a national community.

Bibliography

BELL, DERRICK A., JR.    1980    *Race, Racism, and American Law,* 2nd ed. Boston: Little, Brown.

BICKEL, ALEXANDER M.    1970    *The Supreme Court and the Idea of Progress.* New York: Harper & Row.

BLACK, CHARLES L., JR.    1969    *Structure and Relationship in Constitutional Law.* Pages 51–66. Baton Rouge: Louisiana State University Press.

ELY, JOHN HART    1980    *Democracy and Distrust: A Theory of Judicial Review.* Cambridge, Mass.: Harvard University Press.

FISS, OWEN M.    1976    Groups and the Equal Protection Clause. *Philosophy and Public Affairs* 5:107–177.

KARST, KENNETH L.    1977    The Supreme Court, 1976 Term—Foreword: Equal Citizenship under the Fourteenth Amendment. *Harvard Law Review* 91:1–68.

KINOY, ARTHUR    1967    The Constitutional Right of Negro Freedom. *Rutgers Law Review* 21:387–441.

MICHELMAN, FRANK I.    1969    The Supreme Court, 1968 Term—Foreword: On Protecting the Poor Through the Fourteenth Amendment. *Harvard Law Review* 83:7–59.

POLE, J. R.    1978    *The Pursuit of Equality in American History.* Berkeley: University of California Press.

RAE, DOUGLAS    1981    *Equalities.* Cambridge, Mass.: Harvard University Press.

TOCQUEVILLE, ALEXIS DE   1945   *Democracy in America,* P. Bradley, ed., 2 vols. New York: Vintage Books.

TUSSMAN, JOSEPH and TEN BROEK, JACOBUS   1949   The Equal Protection of the Laws. *California Law Review* 37:341–381.

WESTEN, PETER   1982   The Empty Idea of Equality. *Harvard Law Review* 95:537–596.

# STATE ACTION

## Charles L. Black, Jr.

The phrase "state action," a term of art in our constitutional law, symbolizes the rule—or supposed rule—that constitutional guarantees of human rights are effective only against *governmental* action impairing those rights. (The word "state," in the phrase, denotes any unit or element of government, and not simply one of the American states, though the "state action" concept has been at its most active, and most problematic, with respect to these.) The problems have been many and complex; the "state action" doctrine has not reached anything near a satisfactory condition of rationality.

A best first step toward exploring the problems hidden in the "state action" phrase may be a look at its development in constitutional history. The development has revolved around the first section of the FOURTEENTH AMENDMENT, wherein the problem is in effect put forward by the words here italicized:

All persons born or naturalized in the United States, and subject to the jurisdiction thereof, are citizens of the United States and of the State wherein they reside. *No State* shall make or enforce any law which shall abridge the privileges or immunities of citizens of the United States; *nor shall any State* deprive any person of life, liberty, or property, without due process of law; nor deny to any person within its jurisdiction the equal protection of the laws.

An early "state action" case under this section, *Ex parte Virginia* (1880), raised an audacious claim as to the limiting effect of the words emphasized above. A Virginia judge had been charged under a federal statute forbidding racial exclusion from juries. He was not directed by a state statute to perform this racial exclusion. The judge argued that the action was not that of the state of Virginia, but rather the act of an official, proceeding wrongfully on his own. On this theory, a "state" had not denied EQUAL PROTECTION. The Fourteenth Amendment, the judge contended, did not therefore forbid the conduct charged, or authorize Congress to make it criminal. The Supreme Court, however, declined to take such high ground.

"The constitutional provision," it said, ". . . must mean that no agency of the state, or of the officers or agents by whom its powers are exerted, shall deny . . . equal protection of the laws." But probably the only fully principled and maximally clear rule as to "state action" would have been that the "state," as a state, does not "act" except by its official enactments—and so does not "act" when one of its officers merely abuses his power. "Fully principled and maximally clear"—but, like so many such "rules," aridly formalistic, making practical nonsense of any constitutional rule it limits. There were gropings, around the year of this case, toward a "state action" requirement with bite, but the modern history of the concept starts with the CIVIL RIGHTS CASES of 1883, wherein many modern problems were foreshadowed. In the CIVIL RIGHTS ACT OF 1875, Congress had enacted "[t]hat all persons . . . shall be entitled to the full and equal enjoyment of the accommodations, advantages, facilities, and privileges of inns, public conveyances on land or water, theatres, and other places of public amusement . . . [regardless of race]."

Persons were indicted for excluding blacks from hotels, theaters, and railroads. The Court considered that the only possible source of congressional power to make such a law was section 5 of the Fourteenth Amendment: "The Congress shall have power to enforce, by appropriate legislation, the provisions of this article." This section the Court saw as authorizing only those laws which *directly* enforced the guarantees of the amendment's section 1 (quoted above), which in turn referred only to a *state.* The amendment therefore did not warrant, the Court held, any congressional dealing with racially discriminatory actions of individuals or CORPORATIONS.

Few judicial opinions seem to rest on such solid ground; at the end of Justice JOSEPH BRADLEY's performance, the reader is likely to feel, "Q.E.D." But this feeling of apparent demonstration is attained, as often it is, by the passing over in silence of disturbing facts and thoughts. Many of these were brought out in the powerful dissent of Justice JOHN MARSHALL HARLAN.

One of the cases involved racial discrimination by a railroad. The American railroads, while they were building, were generally given the power of EMINENT DOMAIN. Eminent domain is a sovereign power, enjoyed par excellence by the state, and given by the state to "private" persons for public purposes looked on as important to the state; the Fifth Amendment's language illustrates the firmness of the background assumption that "private property" shall be taken, even with JUST COMPENSATION, only for PUBLIC USE. The American railroads were, moreover, very heavily assisted by public subsidy from governmental units at all levels. Both these steps—the clothing of railroad corporations with eminent-domain power, and their subsidization out of public funds—were justified, both rhetorically and as a matter of law, on the grounds that the railroads were *public instrumentalities,* fulfilling the classic state function of furnishing a transportation system. Regulation of railroads was undertaken under the same theory.

Railroads and hotel-keepers, moreover, followed the so-called common callings, traditionally entailing an obligation to take and carry, or to accommodate, all well-behaved persons able to pay. The *withdrawal* of protection of such a right to equal treatment might be looked on as "state action," and Congress might well decide, as a practical matter, either that the right had been wholly withdrawn as to blacks (which was in many places the fact of the matter) or that the state action supporting these rights of access was insufficient and required supplementation; only the most purposefully narrow construction could deny to such supplementation the name of "enforcement."

Indeed, this line of thought, whether as to the *Civil Rights Cases* or as to all other "equal protection" cases, is fraught with trouble for the whole "state action" doctrine, in nature as in name. "Action" is an exceedingly inapt word for the "denial" of "protection." Protection against lynching was, for example, usually "denied" by "inaction." Inaction by the state is indeed the classic form of "denial of protection." The Civil Rights Cases majority did not read far enough, even for the relentless literalist; it read as far as "nor shall any State . . ." but then hastily closed the book before reading what follows: ". . . *deny* to any person . . . the equal *protection* of the laws." Contrary to the majority's reading, the state's affirmative obligation of protection should have extended to the protection of the traditional rights of resort to public transport and common inns; it was notorious that the very people (blacks) whose "equal protection" was central to the Fourteenth Amendment were commonly the only victims of nominally "private" denial of these rights.

Justice Harlan pointed out that in its first sentence, conferring CITI-ZENSHIP on the newly emancipated slaves, the first section of the Fourteenth Amendment did not use any language in any way suggesting a "state action" requirement, so that there was not even the verbal support for the "state action" requirement that the Court had found in the other phrases of that section. The question then became, in Harlan's view, what the legal consequences of "citizenship" were; for purposes of the particular case at hand, he said:

But what was secured to colored citizens of the United States—as between them and their respective States—by the national grant to them of State citizenship? With what rights, privileges, or immunities did this grant invest them? There is one, if there be no other—exemption from race discrimination in respect of any civil right belonging to citizens of the white race in the same State. . . . Citizenship in this country necessarily imports at least equality of civil rights among citizens of every race in the same State. It is fundamental in American citizenship that, in respect of such rights, there shall be no discrimination by the State, or its officers, or by individuals or corporations exercising public functions or authority, against any citizen because of his race or previous condition of servitude. . . .

There is a third, most interesting aspect to Harlan's dissent. The majority had summarily rejected the argument that under the THIR-TEENTH AMENDMENT—forbidding SLAVERY and involuntary servitude and giving Congress enforcement power—racial exclusion from public places was one of the "badges and incidents" of slavery. Harlan argued that forced segregation in public accommodations was a BADGE OF SERVI-TUDE, and he pointed out that no "state action" requirement could be found in the words of the Thirteenth Amendment. This argument was plowed under and was heard from no more for many decades, but it is of great interest because it was revived and made the basis of decision in a leading case in the 1960s, JONES v. ALFRED H. MAYER CO. (1968).

The *Civil Rights Cases,* in the majority opinion, brushed past contentions that were in no way frivolous. Very many discriminatory actions of public scope are taken by persons or corporations enjoying special favor from government and heavily regulated by government; one cannot easily see their actions as isolated from public power. "Denial of equal protection," the central constitutional wrong in racial cases, seems to refer at least as naturally to inaction as it does to action. If any positive rights at all inhere in citizenship—and if there are no such rights, the citizenship clause is a mere matter of nomenclature—these rights are set up by the Fourteenth Amendment without limitation as to the source of their impairment. Nevertheless, the holdings and doctrine of the *Civil Rights Cases* fell on a thirstily receptive society. The "state action" doctrine became one of the principal reliances of a racist nation, North as well as South.

In a society where so much of access to goods and values is managed by nominally "private" persons and corporations—railroads, restaurants, streetcars, cinemas, even food and clothing—a protection that runs only against the government, strictly defined, can work out to very little effective protection. If the official justice system is hampered by inconvenient constitutional safeguards, the sheriff can play cards while the lynch mob forms, and there is "no state action." A nightclub may refuse to serve a black celebrity, and there is "no state action." The "state action" doctrine protected from constitutional scrutiny an enormous network of racial exclusion and humiliation, characterizing both North and South.

Paradoxically, the "state action" requirement may for a long time have been more important to the maintenance of northern racism than to that of the cruder racism of the South. The South developed SEGREGA-TION by law, in all phases of public life, and this regime was broadly validated by the notorious 1896 decision in PLESSY v. FERGUSON. For complex political reasons—and perhaps because of a faintly lingering adherence to scraps of Civil War idealism—segregation by official law was not widely imposed in the North. But the practices of real-estate agents, mortgage lenders, restaurant keepers, and a myriad of other "private" people and corporations added up to a pervasive custom of racial segregation in many phases of life, a custom less perfectly kept than the official legal dictates of the southern regime, but effectively barring most blacks from much of the common life of the communities they lived in.

A striking case in point was *Dorsey v. Stuyvesant Town Corporation* (1949–1950). The Metropolitan Life Insurance Company, having much money to invest, struck a complicated deal with the State and the City of New York. The contemplated end-result was the conversion of a large section of New York City—from 14th to 23rd Streets, and from Avenue A to the East River—into a vast complex of apartments, to be owned and run by a Metropolitan subsidiary. By formal statute and ordinance, the State and City acquiesced in this scheme, agreeing to use (and later using) the sovereign "eminent domain" power to acquire title to all the needed land, which was, as prearranged, later transferred to Metropolitan. Again by formal arrangement, a quarter-century tax exemption was granted on "improvements"—that is to say, on the immensely valuable apartment buildings. The public easement on certain streets was extinguished, and control over them turned over to Stuyvesant Town Corporation, a Metropolitan subsidiary; various water, sewage, and fire-protection arrangements were altered to suit the needs of the project. And all this was done, visibly and pridefully, as a joint effort of public and "private" enterprise; politicians as well as insurance men took bows. Then, when the whole thing was built, with "title" safely vested in "private" hands, Stuyvesant Town Corporation announced that no blacks need apply for apartments. The suit of a black applicant reached the highest court of New York, and that court held, 4–3, that there was not enough "state action" in all this to make applicable the Fourteenth Amendment prohibition of racial discrimination. The Supreme Court of the United States denied CERTIORARI.

The *Stuyvesant Town* case illustrates very well what could be done with the "state action" formula. With the fullest cooperation from government at all levels, as much of any city as might be desired (strictly public buildings alone excepted) could be turned into a "whites only" preserve. With the necessary cooperation, the process could be extended to a whole county, or a whole state. If they were prudent, the political partners in such deals would not put anything in writing about the racial exclusion contemplated.

But the essentiality of the "state action" formula to the success of northern racism must not obscure its considerable strategic importance even in the South. Segregation by law had in the main been validated, and this was the South's main reliance, but there were gaps, and the "state action" formula filled them in.

First, there was the role of nominally "private" violence against blacks, as the ultimate weapon of the racist regime—with lynching at the top of the arsenal's inventory. At this point the disregard of the Fourteenth Amendment's words, "nor shall any State *deny* . . . equal *protection* of the laws," is most surprising. But for a long time a whole lot of seemingly serious people saw no "denial of protection" in the de facto denial of protection to blacks against a great deal of "private" violence.

Second, outright racial residential zoning by law—just one form of segregation—had been struck down by the Supreme Court, in the 1917 case of BUCHANAN V. WARLEY. The opinion in that case does not adequately distinguish *Plessy v. Ferguson,* but it was the law, and nominally "private" methods of racial zoning had often to be resorted to in the South—just as they were, pervasively, in the North. Real-estate agents and mortgage banks played their accustomed part; until astonishingly recent times, the actually published codes of "ethics" of "realtors" forbade (under some transparent euphemism) actions tending toward spoiling the racial homogeneity of any neighborhood. But more was needed, and that more was found—South and North—in the "racially RESTRICTIVE COVENANT." These "covenants" were neither necessarily nor commonly mere casual contractual arrangements between parties dickering at random. Very commonly, when an "addition" was "subdivided," all the first deeds restricted ownership or occupancy, or both, to whites only— or to white Gentiles only, or to white Gentiles of northern European extraction. These covenants, recorded at the courthouse in a registry furnished by the State for this purpose, were ordained by many states' laws to "run with the land"—that is, they had to be put in all subsequent deeds forever, and usually were binding whether so inserted or not, since any buyer, examining title, could find them in the title-chain. These "covenants"—often functionally equivalent to racial zoning by law, enforced by court orders, and kept on file at the courthouse—were for a long time looked on as "merely private" action, in no way traceable to the state, and so not amenable to constitutional command.

A third and even more important use of the "state action" doctrine (or a doctrine closely akin) was peculiar to the South, and was the rotting-out base of southern politics for generations. The FIFTEENTH AMENDMENT forbade racial exclusions from voting—but, like the Fourteenth, it directed its prohibition at governments: "The right of citizens of the United States to vote shall not be denied or abridged by the United States or by any State on account of race, color, or previous condition of servitude."

The general response in the South to this politically inconvenient constitutional mandate was the all-white Democratic PRIMARY ELECTION. This primary was colloquially known as "the election"; its nominees virtually always won in the November balloting, when all the whites who had voted in the Democratic primary were expected to vote for its nominee, and enough did so to wipe out any scattered Republican votes, including the votes of those blacks who could surmount the other barriers to their voting—LITERACY TESTS, difficult registration procedures, and even more violent discouragements. This plain fraud on the Constitution did not rest wholly on the concept that the action of the Democratic party was not "state action," but the even bolder idea behind it—the idea, namely, that the practical substitution of a "party" election for the regular election could altogether escape the Fifteenth Amendment mandate, even when the State commanded the all-whiteness of the Party—was related in more than spirit to the "state action" doctrine as illustrated in the Stuyvesant Town case. Its basis was the thought that racial voting requirements were not "official" if a nominally "private" organization was put in as a buffer between the wrong done and state power. And the all-white primary in the end had to rely (vainly, as at last it turned out) on the "state action" requirement.

The "state action" doctrine is not a mere interesting footnote in constitutional law. It has served as an absolutely essential and broadly employed component in the means by which black equality, theoretically guaranteed by the post-Civil War amendments, was made to mean next to nothing. It could do this because of the fact that, in our society, vast powers over all of life are given to formally private organizations—the Democratic party, the realtors' association, the mortgage bank, the telephone company, and so on—and because, further and indispensably, the courts were (as is illustrated by a line of decisions from the *Civil Rights Cases* to the Stuyvesant Town case) willing in case after case to gloss over the fact that large organized enterprises can rarely if ever be successfully conducted without very considerable help from the government. Intermixed in these racial cases was, moreover, the disregard of the Fourteenth Amendment's textual condemnation of governmental *inaction,* where that inaction amounted to *denial of equal protection,* as inaction obviously may. And constitutional guarantees that were implicit rather than explicit as limits on government were mostly ignored. A doctrine that went to the length of seeming to make of lynching a thing untouched by the Constitution and (as in UNITED STATES v. CRUIKSHANK, 1875) untouchable by Congress was and could be again a powerful tool indeed for bringing national human rights, nationally enjoyed, to nothing, on the plane of life as lived.

The "state action" requirement thus served the major strategic goal of a nation to which racism, in practice, was utterly essential. But even outside the field of race, its incidence, though spotty, was wide-ranging. As late as 1951, in *Collins v. Hardyman,* the Supreme Court, obviously under the influence of the doctrine though not directly relying on it, forcibly construed a federal statute, in plain contradiction to the law's clear terms, as not to reach the "private" and violent breaking up of a political meeting of citizens.

But a strong countercurrent developed in the 1940s. Without entire consistency, the Supreme Court uttered a striking series of decisions that promised to clip the claws of the "state action" requirement. The Court declared the all-white Democratic primary unlawful in SMITH v. ALLWRIGHT (1944) and extended this ruling in TERRY v. ADAMS (1953) to a local primary serving the same function under another name and form. MARSH v. ALABAMA (1946) held that the FIRST AMENDMENT, as incorporated into the Fourteenth, forbade the barring of Jehovah's Witnesses from distributing leaflets in a company-owned town. And SHELLEY v. KRAEMER (1948) held that judicial enforcement of restrictive covenants was unlawful.

In the "white primary" cases the Court was doing no more than refusing to persevere in self-induced blindness to an obvious fraud on the Fifteenth Amendment. But *Marsh v. Alabama* suggested that the formality of "ownership" could not immunize from constitutional scrutiny the performance of a governmental function—an idea big with possibility. And the *Shelley* case even more profoundly stirred the foundations. Of course it was difficult to say that judicial enforcement of a racial-restrictive covenant, recorded at the courthouse, with the attendant implication that such covenants are not (as some others are) "against public policy," did not amount to "state action of some kind"—the requirement as worded in the fountainhead *Civil Rights Cases* of 1883. The difficulty in assimilation of *Shelley* arose from the fact that "state action of some kind" underpins and in one way or another enforces every nominally "private" action; the states had facilitated and lent their aid, indeed, to the very acts of discrimination considered in the 1883 cases. *Shelley,* therefore, forced a more searching analysis of the theory of "state action"; academic commentators became exceedingly eager and thorough, and in later decisions the Court became more willing to find "state action" and to move toward a fundamental doctrinal revision.

This process was accelerated by the civil rights movement that gained strength in the late 1950s, and grew to major force in the 1960s. In 1954, the famous case of BROWN v. BOARD OF EDUCATION had outlawed racial segregation in the public schools; a number of other decisions had extended this rule to all forms of segregation imposed by law or by uncontestable official action. Though enforcement of these decisions was to be difficult, the first of two principal jural supports of American racism—legal prohibition of participation by blacks in the common society—had crumbled. Naturally attention turned—whether with the aim of continuing racism or of completing its demolition—to the second of the pillars of American racism, the "state action" requirement.

Segregation and state action were now clearly seen to have a close functional similarity. Before the decisions following *Brown,* the blacks in a typical southern town could not eat in the good restaurants because state law commanded their exclusion. After these decisions, the proprietors of the restaurants, by and large, went on excluding blacks. (In this they were simply following a practice widely followed in the North already). There was a difference in legal theory, but no difference to the black people. The city-owned bus system could not make black people sit in the back—but most bus companies were "private" in form; seating in the back was "privately" commanded.

The resistance to this widespread public segregation under "private" form was led (actively in part and symbolically throughout) by Dr. Martin Luther King, Jr. Thousands of black people—most, but not all, young—defied the system by "sitting-in"—insisting upon service at "private" establishments open to the general public. They were in great numbers convicted of "crimes" selected with careful attention to the appearance of neutrality, such as "trespass after warning" or BREACH OF THE PEACE, and their cases reached the Supreme Court in some number.

The net result up to about 1965 was a considerable practical loosening up of the "state action" requirement, but no satisfactory theoretical reworking of that doctrine. A very few examples must be selected from the abundant case law.

The 1961 case of BURTON v. WILMINGTON PARKING AUTHORITY is an interesting example. The parking authority, a state agency, leased space in its parking building to a restaurateur, who forthwith refused to serve blacks. One might have thought it all but frivolous to contend that "state action of some kind" was absent here. The state had gone with open eyes into a transaction that empowered the restaurateur to insult and inconvenience citizens, in a public building owned by itself, and its police stood ready to make his rule stick. The state had done this—in effect certainly, if not in intent—for rent money. It had had the easy recourse of inserting in the lease a provision against racial discrimination; one has to wonder how the omission of that provision, obviously available under "the laws," can be anything but a "denial" of "equal protection of the laws," on the part of government. Yet the Court majority, though striking down the discrimination in the very case, roamed back and forth amongst the minutiae of facts—gas, service for the boiler-room, responsibility for structural repairs—and carefully confined its ruling to a lease of public property "in the manner and for the purpose shown to have been the case here. . . ." Still, the Wilmington case might have contributed toward some generality of constitutional theory.

As the "sit-in" issue heated up, however, the Court became even more evasive of the central issues. As cases reached the Court in great numbers, no "sit-in" conviction was ever affirmed. But neither the whole Court nor any majority ever reached and decided the central issue— whether *Shelley v. Kraemer* fairly implied that the knowing state use of state power to enforce discrimination, in publicly open facilities, consti- tuted such action of the state as "denied equal protection of the laws." Instead the cases were decided on collateral grounds peculiar to each of them.

The culminating case was BELL V. MARYLAND (1964). Trespass convic- tions of Maryland civil-rights "sitters-in" were reversed, on the grounds (available by chance) that a newly enacted Maryland antidiscrimination statute might be held, in the state courts, to "abate" prosecution for prior attempts to get the service now guaranteed; nothing was actually decided on the more fundamental issues. Six Justices reached the "state action" issue, but of those six, three would have found it and three would not.

At this dramatic moment, with indefinite postponement of a major doctrinal decision seemingly impossible, Congress stepped in and solved the immediate problem, by passing the CIVIL RIGHTS ACT OF 1964, Title 2 of which made unlawful nearly all the discriminatory exclusions that had generated the sit-in prosecutions, making future prosecutions of sit-ins impossible. Then, in 1964, in *Hamm v. City of Rock Hill,* the Court held that the act compelled dismissal of all such prosecutions begun before its passage. Thus vanished the immediate problem of the sit- ins, and of many other claims to nondiscrimination previously based purely on the Constitution. It is noteworthy that Congress chose to base this Title 2, dealing with PUBLIC ACCOMMODATIONS, mainly on the COMMERCE CLAUSE rather than on the Fourteenth Amendment. This legislative decision reflected uncertainty as to whether the Court could be persuaded to overrule the 1883 *Civil Rights Cases,* which had severely limited congressional power to enforce the Fourteenth Amendment. In HEART OF ATLANTA MOTEL V. UNITED STATES (1964) and KATZENBACH V. McCLUNG (1964) the Court construed the 1964 provisions broadly, and upheld them under the commerce clause theory that Congress had emphasized. The public accommodations crisis was over, and with it the really agonizing social crisis as to "state action."

Nevertheless, important problems continued to present themselves after 1964. It seemed for a time that, though no longer under the intense pressure of the public accommodations issue, the Court might be moving along the road toward relaxation of the state action requirement—a road along which travel had begun at least as early as the cases of *Smith v. Allwright* (1944—knocking out the all-white Democratic primary), *Marsh v. Alabama* (1946—the "company-town" case), and *Shelley v. Kraemer* (1948—the case of the racial-restriction covenants). (Indeed, no case actually denying relief on the "no-state-action" ground was decided by the Supreme Court from 1906 to 1970, except the 1935 case upholding the white primary, overruled nine years later).

In 1966 the Court held, in *Evans v. Newton,* that a huge public park in the center of Macon, Georgia, could no longer be operated as a park "for whites only," pursuant to the directions in the 1911 will of the man who had given it to the city, even though the city, for the purpose of seeing this all-white status maintained, had resigned as trustee, and had acquiesced in the appointment of a set of "private" trustees. In *Amalgamated Food Employees v. Logan Valley Plaza* (1968) the Court applied *Marsh v. Alabama* to hold a large SHOPPING CENTER subject to the First Amendment, and REITMAN V. MULKEY (1967) struck down under the Fourteenth Amendment a California constitutional amendment that would have forbidden state or local "fair" (i.e., antiracist) housing ordinances until such time as the state constitution might be amended again— a process substantially more difficult than the enactment of ordinary legislation. This opinion, by Justice BYRON R. WHITE, encouraged much hope, because it explicitly undertook to judge this state constitutional amendment "in terms of its 'immediate objective,' its 'ultimate effect,' and its 'historical context and the conditions existing prior to its enactment.' " This attitude, if adhered to, would in every case bring the "state action" question down to the earth of reality. The Court would recognize the impact of formal state "neutrality" on the actual patterns of American racism, and would ask in each case whether such seeming "neutrality" operated as a *denial of equal protection* to the group principally marked for protection. This hope was further encouraged in 1969 in *Hunter v. Erickson* wherein the Court struck down an Akron, Ohio, requirement that fair-housing ordinances run an especially difficult gauntlet before they became effective; it was especially striking that Justices JOHN MARSHALL HARLAN and POTTER STEWART, who had dissented in *Reitman,* found the Akron provision too much, because on its face it discriminated against antiracist laws.

But the current of doctrine changed after President RICHARD M. NIXON made the most of his chance to put his stamp on the Court. The change was signaled by the 1970 decision in EVANS V. ABNEY, a follow-up to the first Macon park case, *Evans v. Newton,* above. After the Newton decision, the heirs of the donor of the park applied for a reverter to them. The Court held this time that the state court's decision in their favor, in effect imposing a penalty on the citizens of Macon for their being unable under the Fourteenth Amendment to keep the park all-white, did not constitute "such state action" as to implicate the equal protection clause.

In 1971, in PALMER V. THOMPSON, the Court upheld the City of Jackson in its closing the city swimming pools and leasing one of them to the "private" YMCA, rather than having blacks swim in them. Here the Court found no state encouragement of discrimination, although the pools had been closed in response to a desegregation order. This was a total turn-about, in just four years, from the *Reitman v. Mulky* resolution to tie the operation of state-action law to the facts of life, and Justice White, the author of the *Reitman* opinion, dissented, with three other pre-Nixon Justices.

In 1974 the Court decided JACKSON V. METROPOLITAN EDISON COMPANY. A heavily regulated "private" electric company, enjoying a monopoly and a state-issued certificate of public convenience, terminated service to a customer without offering her any chance to be heard. This practice was allowed by a "tariff" on file with and at the least acquiesced in by the Public Utilities Commission. Justice WILLIAM H. REHNQUIST's opinion for the Court found insufficient "state action" in any of this to implicate the DUE PROCESS clause. This opinion and judgment, if adhered to in all their implications, would put us at least as far back as the 1883 Civil Rights Cases. Then, in 1976, HUDGENS V. NATIONAL LABOR RELATION BOARD explicitly overruled the *Logan Valley Shopping Center* case and made authoritative for the time being a very narrow view of *Marsh v. Alabama*.

Meanwhile, however, a new doctrinal thread had become visible. In the 1883 *Civil Rights Cases* the first Justice Harlan had argued that the Thirteenth Amendment, which contains no language to support a state-action requirement, proscribes all "badges and incidents" of slavery—which, historically, would mean a great many if not all racially discriminatory and degrading actions. This argument was a long time in coming into its own, but in 1968, in *Jones v. Alfred H. Mayer Co.*, the Court made it the ground of a decision upholding an old act of Congress which the Court interpreted to command nondiscrimination in the sale of housing. And in 1976, GRIFFIN V. BRECKENRIDGE, overruling *Collins v. Hardyman,* based decision solidly on the Thirteenth Amendment, holding that the amendment authorizes Congress to secure its beneficiaries against "racially discriminatory private action aimed at depriving them of . . . basic rights. . . ." Under the very formula of the 1883 *Civil Rights Cases* themselves—Congress may "enforce" only that which is substantively there—this should imply a large substantive content in the Thirteenth Amendment, far beyond literal "slavery." In RUNYON V. McCRARY (1976) the Court extended much the same rationale to the condemnation of racial exclusion from a "private, commercially operated, nonsectarian" school.

"State action" doctrine has remained intractable to being made rational. What is wanted is attention to these points:

1. In almost any impingement by one person or more on another person or more, there is some contribution by the state: empowerment,

support, or threatened support. Thus the presence or absence of "state action" is not a "test" at all; this has led to the spinning out of enormous series of subtests, hard to express and even harder to comprehend, none of which has much if any warrant in law.

2. Concomitantly, "state action" may not legitimately be confined—as the Supreme Court's recent opinions have confined it—to one or more neatly defined categories such as "command," "encouragement," or "public function." One may identify ten ways in which so infinitely complicated and subtle a being as the "state" may act—and the "state" may then act in an eleventh and then in a twelfth way—all "state action."

3. There is no warrant whatever in law for the assumption that "state action," to be significant, must be at a *high level* of involvement, or that a *very close* "nexus" must be found between "state action" and the wrong complained of.

4. Many constitutional guarantees do not explicitly require "state action" as a component. The modern "state action" requirement purported to draw its life from the words of the Fourteenth Amendment. Many rights and relationships set up by the Constitution and enforceable by Congress do not refer to the state at all, for example, the prohibition of slavery (and, as now held, its badges and incidents), the right to vote for congressmen and senators, the RIGHT TO TRAVEL. It is only custom-thought, which usually means half-thought, that would think it obvious that an impediment to INTERSTATE COMMERCE would be unconstitutional only if it were state-created.

5. A citizen of the United States should be regarded as having *relational* rights—rights of membership in the organized community—which nobody, state or private person, may interfere with. This principle has some life in the cases; in *Bewer v. Hoxie School District* (8th Cir. 1956), for example, an INJUNCTION was upheld that restrained private persons from interfering with state officials' attempts to comply with the national Constitution. But the principle deserves a greater generality. Anybody who tries forcibly to keep another person from getting his mail is interfering with a legitimate relation between citizen and government, even though the wrongdoer's own actions may not be "state action" at all. (See also UNITED STATES v. GUEST, 1966.)

6. There is broad scope in the natural meaning of the Fourteenth Amendment's words: "deny to any person within its jurisdiction the equal protection of the laws." These words, even as a matter of "narrow verbal criticism," do not require "action."

7. Above all, while much of the defense of the "state action" requirement is conducted in the name of the private, personal lives of people whose conduct, it is said, ought not to be constitutionalized, it is very, very rare that any real "state action" case involves these values at all. The conduct of public transportation and restaurants, the operation of

carnivals and parks, dealings with city swimming pools, the way the light company collects its bills, the character of a whole section of town—these are the usual stuff of "state action" problems in real life. If anybody ever files a lawsuit praying a mandatory injunction that he be included on somebody else's dinner list, that will be time enough to begin devising a well-founded "rule of reason" fencing constitutional prohibition out of the genuinely private life. This "genuinely private" life may be hard to define, but surely no harder to define than the "state action requirement" has turned out to be, and continues to be. And at least one would be trying to define the right thing.

Bibliography

BLACK, CHARLES L., JR.   1962   The Constitution and Public Power. *Yale Review* 52:54–66.

BLACK, CHARLES L., JR.   1967   "State Action," Equal Protection, and California's Proposition 14. *Harvard Law Review*  81:69–109.

HALE, ROBERT L.   1952   *Freedom through Law.*  Chap. 11. New York: Columbia University Press.

HOROWITZ, HAROLD W.   1957   The Misleading Search for "State Action" under the Fourteenth Amendment. *Southern California Law Review*  30:208–221.

VAN ALSTYNE, WILLIAM W.   1965   Mr. Justice Black, Constitutional Review, and the Talisman of State Action. *Duke Law Journal*  1965:219–247.

# Racial Equality from Slavery to the Mid-Twentieth Century

# SLAVERY AND THE CONSTITUTION

## John Hope Franklin

Long before the CONSTITUTIONAL CONVENTION OF 1787 the question of slavery had become the prime concern of many Americans. In the first and second Continental Congresses, the matter arose when several groups of slaves petitioned for their manumission. Nothing came of their pleas, of course. In THOMAS JEFFERSON's draft of the DECLARATION OF INDEPENDENCE, he accused the king of waging cruel war against human nature itself, "violating its most sacred rights of life and liberty in the persons of a distant people . . . captivating and carrying them into slavery in another hemisphere. . . ." Although slavery existed throughout the English colonies in 1776, the southern slaveholders in Congress forced rejection of this indictment of the king. If they won their independence on the basis of such an argument, they feared that there would no longer be any justification for slavery.

In some colonies the sentiment against slavery grew during the war for Independence; and the eventual use of slaves as soldiers in the war contributed to the feeling that they should be free. As the states gained their independence some prohibited the slave trade. Some went beyond that enacting legislation looking to the abolition of slavery altogether. Pennsylvania and Massachusetts passed such laws in 1780, followed by Connecticut and Rhode Island in 1784, New York in 1785, and New Jersey in 1786. While no states south of Pennsylvania abolished slavery during this period, several enacted laws facilitating manumission by slaveholders.

Meanwhile, the Continental Congress began to look at the question of slavery as it undertook to develop a national land policy. When Thomas Jefferson framed the ORDINANCE OF 1784 for the organization of government in the western territory, he included a provision that after the year 1800 there should be no slavery or involuntary servitude in any of the states to be organized. That provision was rejected. The idea persisted, however, that slavery should not be extended indefinitely. In the NORTHWEST ORDINANCE of 1787 Jefferson's language of 1784 was adopted with the caveat that fugitive slaves escaping into the Northwest Territory from one of the original states "may be lawfully reclaimed and conveyed to the person claiming his or her labor or service. . . ."

The Ordinance did not apply south of the Ohio River, where slaveholders were more likely to settle than in the Northwest Territory.

It was inevitable that slavery should have been an important consideration at the Constitutional Convention. At a time when slavery was waning in the North, the southern states saw in slavery an increasing source of wealth both in the market value of slaves and in what slaves could produce. An economic interest so important could not be ignored by a convention one of whose major concerns was to protect property and to advance the economic interests of those who were to live within the new frame of government. Although there were numerous points at which the emerging document affected the institution of slavery, four were of prime significance to the future of slavery and, indeed, the fate of the Constitution.

One point had to do with the TAXING POWER of Congress. Southern delegates generally feared that in levying taxes, especially POLL TAXES, the federal government might discriminate against the South in the way it counted slaves. Closely connected with this was the perception that in apportioning representation, the South would suffer from any arrangement that did not recognize and count slaves as people. After considerable debate, some of it acrimonious, a compromise was reached. Direct taxes were to be apportioned among the several states according to population, thus making it impossible to raise a major portion of federal revenue by taxing property that existed only in one section of the country. In determining the basis of taxation *and* representation, five slaves were to be counted as equal to three free persons. The cryptic language in Article I, Section 2, reads: "Representatives and direct Taxes shall be apportioned among the several States which may be included within this Union, according to their respective Numbers, which shall be determined by adding to the whole Number of free Persons, including those bound to Service for a Term of Years, and excluding Indians not taxed, three fifths of all other persons."

The other two points regarding slavery were handled with some dispatch, not because they were unimportant but because they did not come up until late in the session, when the weary delegates were eager to return to their homes. On the slave trade, several southern delegates were uncompromising. While those from Virginia and Maryland appeared to favor a prohibition of the trade, those from South Carolina and Georgia were unalterably opposed to the prohibition. To avoid a rupture between the delegates of the upper South and the North, who favored prohibition, and those of the lower South, the compromise was reached that the slave trade could not be ended before twenty years had elapsed. This language was added in Article II, Section 9: "The Migration or Importation of such Persons as any of the States now shall think proper to admit, shall not be prohibited by the Congress prior to the Year one thousand eight hundred and eight, but a Tax or duty may be imposed on such Importation, not exceeding ten dollars for each Person."

Significantly, there was almost no opposition to the proposal that fugitive slaves be returned to their masters. The public obligation to return slaves, which had already been provided for in several Indian treaties between 1781 and 1786, was established in the Northwest Territory in 1787 along with the prohibition of slavery in that region. When the provision came before the Convention in late August, the delegates were in no mood for a protracted debate. The slaveholders had already won such sweeping constitutional recognition of slavery, moreover, that the question of fugitive slaves was something of an anticlimax. Without serious challenge, the provision was inserted in Article IV, Section 2: "No person, held to Service or Labour in one State, under the Laws thereof, escaping into another, shall, in Consequence of any Law or Regulation therein, be discharged from such Service or Labour, but shall be delivered up on Claim of the party to whom such Service or Labour may be due."

In dealing with slavery the delegates to the Convention made certain, as if out of a sense of guilt or shame, never to use the word "slave" or any of its variations in the Constitution itself. "Three fifths of all other persons," "Persons held to Service or Labour," and "Migration or Importation of Such Persons," were all mere euphemisms. Everyone knew what they meant. They were meant to shield the consciences of the delegates just as the clauses themselves were meant to protect the institution of slavery. In none of the deliberations did the delegates give serious consideration to abolishing slavery, even though slavery made a mockery of freedom, equality, and the rights of man. It did not make a mockery, however, of the rights of property. American independence and the new Constitution had the effect of giving slavery a longer life than it was to have in the British Empire.

It was the business of the Congress to enact legislation to carry out the objectives set forth in the Constitution. As far as slaves were concerned, this meant the enactment of legislation to facilitate the recovery of runaway slaves by their masters. The impetus for legislation came, however, not from concerns about fugitive slaves but in the call for a statute to facilitate the surrender of FUGITIVES FROM JUSTICE. When the governor of Pennsylvania was unable to persuade the governor of Virginia to give up three white men accused of kidnapping a Pennsylvania free Negro, he presented the facts in the case to President GEORGE WASHINGTON. When the President transmitted the matter to Congress, it responded by passing the Fugitive Slave Act of 1793. After dealing with the matter of the surrender of fugitives from justice in the first two sections, the law turned to the rendition of fugitive slaves.

Under the law a slaveholder could apply to a federal district or circuit judge for a certificate authorizing him to return his slave to the state from which he had fled. This certificate was to be granted after the master had captured his slave, and there were few federal judges at the time; therefore, the master was compelled to go to considerable expense and travel before enjoying the protection of the federal courts. The law did not authorize judges to issue warrants for the arrest of slaves and it did not compel federal authorities to aid in the pursuit of fugitive slaves. The lack of such provisions generated criticism by slaveholders for years to come.

Although under the law of 1793 many fugitives were recaptured and returned to the places from which they had fled, masters continued to complain about the difficulties of reclaiming their human property. Meanwhile, as antislavery sentiment gained momentum in the first decade of the century, opponents of slavery placed additional obstacles in the way of slaveholders seeking the return of their runaways. They began actively to aid fugitives, to urge federal judges not to issue certificates for the return of runaways, and to persuade local officers not to cooperate in their rendition. Slavemasters soon called for a more effective law, and in 1818, a stronger bill was introduced in the House of Representatives. As it made its way through Congress, it was burdened with amendments introduced by antislavery legislators requiring proof of ownership before a court of record and making masters criminally liable for false claims. Although a version of the proposed law passed both houses, it was tabled when the conference committee was unable to resolve the problem of amendments.

As the new century began, many Americans turned their thoughts to the provision of the Constitution prohibiting Congress from closing the slave trade before 1808. The slave trade was flourishing, and the slave interests faced a curious dilemma. If the trade continued they risked increasing the chances of violence as unruly blacks from Africa or revolutionary and resourceful blacks from the Caribbean were imported. On the other hand, they required a larger number of slaves to tend their burgeoning plantations. Hoping that the national and state governments would provide safeguards against uprisings and insurrections, they were tempted to favor the continued importation of slaves. At least, they wished to keep their options open.

Ending the slave trade under the provision set forth in the Constitution was not a foregone conclusion, and the antislavery forces knew it. All through the decade they pressed for stringent federal legislation to end the trade. In January 1800, a group of free Negroes in Philadelphia called on Congress to revise its laws on the slave trade and on fugitives. When South Carolina reopened its ports to the trade in 1803, antislavery groups began to press Congress to act. Several resolutions were introduced in Congress condemning the slave trade, but that body took no conclusive steps. The question was brought dramatically before the country in December 1805, when Senator Stephen R. Bradley of Vermont introduced a bill to prohibit the slave trade after January 1, 1808, but the bill was indefinitely tabled. This measure set the stage for President Jefferson to address the issue in his annual message to Congress in December 1806. He called attention to the approaching date when Congress could constitutionally prohibit "all further participation in those violations of human rights which have been so long continued on the unoffending inhabitants of Africa, and which the morality, the reputation, and the best interests of our country have long been eager to proscribe."

Pursuant to the President's eloquent call, which was reminiscent of his draft of the Declaration of Independence, Congress proceeded to consider legislation outlawing the trade. Every provision of the proposed law was debated vigorously. Slaveholders, fearing that Africans smuggled into the United States would not be under the control of the law, wanted them seized and sold into slavery. The antislavery members of Congress strongly objected. The PROHIBITION OF THE SLAVE TRADE ACT (1807) was a compromise. It directed federal officers to be "governed by the provisions of the laws, now existing, of the several states prohibiting the admission or importation . . . of any Negro, mulatto, or other person of color."

In 1818 in the first supplementary act to the law of 1807, Congress sought to make the trade less attractive by increasing the penalty for anyone engaged in it. For example, a fine of $20,000 was replaced by a lowered fine and imprisonment for three to seven years. There were stiffer penalties for persons who knowingly purchased illegally imported Negroes; one-half of all forfeitures and fines were to go to informers. In 1819 Congress directed the President to use armed cruisers on the coasts of the United States and Africa to suppress the trade. Half the proceeds of a condemned ship would go to the captor as bounty, and the captured slaver was to be returned to the port from which it sailed. In the following year Congress provided that direct participation in the slave trade was an act of piracy, punishable by death.

The slave trade was profitable, and it continued despite federal legislation. State laws on the disposition of illegally imported Africans varied. North Carolina directed that such Africans "be sold and disposed of for the state." Georgia directed that the Africans either be sold or given to the Colonization Society for transportation to Africa, with the Society bearing all expenses. Despite these laws, most imported slaves seem to have escaped capture. There were so few captures and the federal officials did so little to enforce the statute of 1807 that it was nearly a dead letter. Slavers introduced their cargo into the United

States from Galveston, then a part of Mexico, from Amelia Island in Florida, until 1819 a part of the Spanish Empire, and at various ports on the eastern and southern coasts of the United States. Secretary of the Treasury William H. Crawford confessed that the United States had failed to enforce the law.

Estimates regarding the numbers involved in the illicit slave trade varied. In the decades following passage of the supplementary acts, slavers easily evaded federal authorities, and enforcement received no more than lip service in Washington. In 1839 President MARTIN VAN BUREN called for revision of the laws covering the slave trade in order that "the integrity and honor of our flag may be carefully preserved." A decade later President Zachary Taylor invited the attention of Congress "to an amendment of our existing laws relating to the African slave trade, with a view to the effectual suppression of that barbarous traffic." Nothing happened, and the trade continued down through the Civil War. Because of its clandestine nature, precise figures are impossible; a recent student of the trade estimates that some 51,000 slaves were illegally imported by 1860.

Shortly after the United States purchased Louisiana in 1803, inhabitants from the older states began to settle in the newly acquired territory. When Louisiana entered the Union in 1812 as a slave state, eastern and northern interests began to appreciate the political and economic consequences of slave states entering the Union. They believed that under the Constitution the federal government could prevent the creation of slave states in the territories. They were determined, therefore, to prevent slave states from entering the Union, or, failing that, to limit the number of new slave states. When Missouri sought admission in 1818, northern members of Congress said that they would agree only on condition that the Missouri constitution forbid slavery. Southerners claimed that the restriction was discriminatory; some threatened disunion. After bitter debate, the impasse was resolved when Maine sought admission. Congress admitted Maine as a free state and Missouri as a slave state and declared that in the Louisiana territory slavery should not exist north of the southern boundary of Missouri.

The MISSOURI COMPROMISE stimulated the rivalry between the slave and free states, with each side searching for ways to enhance its advantage. While southern spokesmen insisted that the problems of slavery were local, they relied on the federal Constitution and laws to protect slavery in defiance of the FIRST AMENDMENT; they demanded that antislavery petitions to Congress be laid on the table without receiving notice. At the same time they demanded that Congress act to facilitate the return of fugitive slaves. As antislavery sentiment in the North increased and abolitionists became more active in obstructing the return of fugitives, the Southerners' demands for protection became more shrill. There were numerous dramatic moments between 1830 and 1860, when abolitionists seized fugitive slaves from their captors or interrupted court proceedings to give accused fugitives the opportunity to flee.

In some northern states residents feared that the Fugitive Slave Law of 1793 would operate to the disadvantage of kidnapped whites and free Negroes accused of being runaway slaves. Consequently, state legislatures empowered state courts to rule in matters arising out of the 1793 law. The Pennsylvania statute of 1826 required the master to present to a magistrate proof of his claim to the alleged fugitive. If the magistrate was convinced the claim was well founded, he was to issue a certificate authorizing the removal of the runaway from the state. If, on the other hand, anyone had seized a person suspected of being a runaway and wrongfully removed him, he would, upon conviction, be deemed guilty of a felony and suffer fine and imprisonment. In due course and by amicable arrangement the Supreme Court ruled on the constitutionality of the Pennsylvania statute in PRIGG v. PENNSYLVANIA (1842), thereby significantly affecting the slavery question for the next two decades.

Edward Prigg, a slave catcher, seized a Negro woman and her children in Pennsylvania with the intention of returning them to their alleged owner in Maryland. When Prigg sought a certificate authorizing their removal, the magistrate, dissatisfied with the proof of ownership, declined to issue the certificate. Prigg took them anyway and was subsequently convicted for violating the 1826 law. The Supreme Court reversed the state court in a decision that had far greater significance than merely exonerating Prigg. Speaking for the Court, Associate Justice JOSEPH STORY declared the Pennsylvania PERSONAL LIBERTY LAW unconstitutional, because it invaded a field placed within the exclusive domain of the federal government by the Fugitive Slave Act of 1793 and by the Constitution itself. "Under the Constitution," said Story, the right to seize a runaway and the duty to deliver him pervaded "the whole Union with an equal and supreme force, uncontrolled and uncontrollable by State SOVEREIGNTY or State legislation." States could enforce the law of 1793, if they wished; but they could not be required to do so, Story added. Further, if an owner recaptured his fugitive slave he did not need a state magistrate's permission to return him to his place of abode.

By placing the fugitive slave question within the exclusive JURISDICTION of the federal government, Justice Story implicitly encouraged northern states that did not wish to cooperate in the enforcement of federal legislation on the subject. The decision promoted the belief, moreover, that antislavery forces could work through sympathetic state and local officials to prevent the recovery of fugitive slaves. Accordingly ten free states enacted personal liberty laws.

When slaveholders felt the impact of *Prigg* in relieving states of responsibility in enforcing the Fugitive Slave Law, they agitated for a more stringent federal law that neither abolitionists nor hostile state laws could nullify. Because the annual pecuniary loss in fugitive slaves was in the hundreds of thousands of dollars, slaveholders increased their pressure on Congress to act. Despite its validation in *Prigg,* the Act of 1793 was inadequate. State courts seemed to vie with abolitionists in their disregard for federal authority. What was needed was a new act of Congress providing effective federal machinery for its successful enforcement. Early in 1850, Senator James Mason of Virginia introduced a bill to that end. Thus began the long and tortuous route by which a new fugitive slave law made its way through Congress.

The debate on the bill was extensive and, at times, acrimonious, connected as it was with other matters that were to constitute the COMPROMISE OF 1850. In the Senate, WILLIAM H. SEWARD of New York wanted to guarantee to every alleged fugitive slave the right to TRIAL BY JURY. HENRY CLAY of Kentucky, on the other hand, wished to emphasize the right of the aggrieved master to recover his property from any place, including a free state, where the slave had fled. DANIEL WEBSTER of Massachusetts, to the surprise of many Northerners and Southerners, agreed with Clay and declared that "in regard to the return of persons bound to service, who have escaped into the free States . . . it is my judgment that the South is right, and the North is wrong." After the bill passed both houses, President Millard Filmore signed it on September 18, 1850.

The new fugitive slave law undertook to establish adequate federal machinery for its enforcement. Circuit courts were to appoint commissioners who, concurrently with circuit and district judges, had authority to grant certificates for the return of fugitive slaves. United States marshals were to execute warrants issued under the act, and a failure of diligent execution was punishable by a $1,000 fine. If a fugitive should escape from a marshal's custody, the marshal was liable for the slave's full value. When the marshal or claimant brought the slave before the court to request a certificate for his return, the alleged fugitive was not permitted to testify in his own behalf. Court disturbances, aiding or abetting fugitives, and harboring or concealing fugitives were punishable by a $1,000 fine and six months imprisonment.

Abolitionists and others attacked the Fugitive Slave Law as unconstitutional. Horace Mann said that it made war on the fundamental principles of human liberty. CHARLES SUMNER called it a "flagrant violation of the Constitution, and of the most cherished rights—shocking to Christian sentiments, insulting to humanity, and impudent in all its pretensions." Others argued that the fugitive slave clause of the Constitution did not confer on Congress any power to enact laws for the recovery of fugitive slaves. They questioned the power of Congress, moreover, to give commissioners authority to render judgments that only United States judges could properly render under the Constitution. The denial to fugitives by the law of 1850 of the right to trial by jury and to CONFRONT and cross-examine witnesses was itself an unconstitutional denial of DUE PROCESS, its opponents argued. The fact that commissioners received fees instead of fixed salaries meant that they were themselves interested parties in fugitive slave cases. If the commissioner turned over the fugitive to his claimant, he received a ten dollar fee. If he freed the fugitive, the commissioner received only five dollars. What commissioner could be trusted to render impartial justice when his income depended on the kind of decision that he rendered?

The flight into Canada from northern cities of numerous free Negroes and fugitive slaves dramatized for many Northerners the new role of the federal government in obstructing the efforts of those who sought freedom. Many Northerners vowed to prevent enforcement of the new fugitive slave law. Fugitive slave cases increased, but so did rescues, accompanied by denunciations of federal officials. Friends of fugitives resorted to desperate measures such as kidnapping slave hunters and poisoning their bloodhounds. They organized vigilance committees not only to engage in action but also to express their moral revulsion to every effort to enforce the new law. In 1852 the Boston committee unsuccessfully attempted to prevent the rendition of Thomas Sims, an alleged fugitive from Georgia. Composed of such men as Theodore Parker, Wendell Phillips, Horace Mann, and Charles Sumner, the committee, on April 13 at 3 A.M., watched as the United States marshal walked Sims down State Street, past the spot where Crispus Attucks fell and to the wharf where the ship was waiting to take him back to Savannah. Six days later Sims was publicly whipped in Savannah, the first slave Massachusetts had returned.

Opponents of the Fugitive Slave Law of 1850 challenged it in the same way that opponents had challenged its predecessor. The Supreme Court ruling in STRADER v. GRAHAM (1851) could well have controlled the problem for years to come. After Jacob Strader, a citizen of Kentucky, helped several Negroes leave Kentucky, their alleged master sued Strader for damages. Strader claimed that the blacks were not slaves and that they made regular visits to Ohio where they worked as entertainers. These visits, Strader claimed, had caused them to become free even if they had previously been slaves because the Ordinance of 1787 forbade slavery in the Northwest Territory of which Ohio had been a part. When the case reached the Supreme Court, Chief Justice ROGER B. TANEY, speaking for the entire bench, declared that whatever the status of the blacks while outside Kentucky, they were subject to Kentucky laws upon their return. Nothing in the Constitution, he insisted, could control the law of Kentucky on this subject.

Meanwhile, opposing forces in Kansas were attempting to settle the issue in their own way. The bill to organize Kansas and Nebraska as territories had repealed the Missouri Compromise and left to the inhabitants of the respective territories the decision whether the states-to-be would be slave or free. Abolitionists, believing there should be no more slave states under any circumstances, were determined to make Kansas as well as Nebraska free states. To that end, they undertook first to settle Kansas with persons who would vote for a free constitution and thus to discourage slaveholders from settling in Nebraska, which they were certain would become a free state. Proslavery forces were determined at least to make Kansas a slave state. Both sides were certain they had the Constitution on their side. After bitter arguments and bloody battles, Kansas voted for a free constitution. The South felt that its ambitions had been frustrated and its rights under the Constitution violated as well.

The antislavery forces would not let the decision in *Strader* stand without challenge. They hoped it might be modified, or even overruled, in another decision offering some protection to slaves who had been in free states. Soon another case, DRED SCOTT V. SANDFORD (1857), presented an ideal opportunity, they thought, to secure an unequivocal statement on the status of slaves in the free states and in the territories. Dred Scott, a Missouri slave, traveled with his master to the free state of Illinois, where they lived for a time, then to Minnesota, a free territory under the provisions of the Missouri Compromise. Upon their return to Missouri, his master sold Scott to a New York resident in a vain attempt to establish federal DIVERSITY JURISDICTION when Scott subsequently sued for his freedom. When the Supreme Court announced its decision on March 6, 1857, Chief Justice Taney was again the spokesman.

Taney declared that because Negroes had been viewed as belonging to an inferior order at the time that the Constitution was ratified, they were not citizens within the meaning of the Constitution's provision defining the permissible JURISDICTION of federal courts in cases between citizens of different states. Moreover Scott had not become free by virtue of the Missouri Compromise, because the Compromise was unconstitutional; Congress had no authority to prohibit slavery in the territories. In any case, Taney concluded, once Scott returned to Missouri his status was determined by Missouri law. In Missouri he was still a slave, and thus not a citizen of any state. The case was dismissed for want of jurisdiction.

The decision gave the proslavery forces more support than they could possibly have expected. Slavery's opponents called the decision wicked, atrocious, and abominable. Others hoped the decision would settle once and for all the grievous sectional issues that were about to destroy the Union. But the decision remained controversial. Its impact on events of the next few years is unclear. Perhaps it did not contribute significantly to the critical disputes and eventual divisions in the Democratic party. Perhaps the decision did not greatly stimulate the growth of the Republican party. Yet, as Don E. Fehrenbacher, the leading historian of the decision, has said, "it was a conspicuous and perhaps an integral part of a configuration of events and conditions that did produce enough changes of allegiance to make a political revolution and enough intensity of feeling to make that revolution violent."

The abolitionists, although embittered by the decision, did not relent in their effort to secure judicial support for their position. In a Wisconsin case, which came to the Supreme Court as ABLEMAN v. BOOTH (1859), they attempted once again to have the Fugitive Slave Law of 1850 declared unconstitutional. Sherman M. Booth, an abolitionist editor in Milwaukee, had been arrested for helping a Negro escape from a United States deputy marshal. The state courts pronounced the law unconstitutional and ordered Booth released. When the case reached the Supreme Court in 1859, Chief Justice Taney reversed the state courts, censured them for presuming to pass judgment on federal laws, and held that the Fugitive Slave Law was fully authorized by the Constitution.

*Booth* was the last opportunity the abolitionists would have to take their cause to the Supreme Court. They would win local victories, such as the denial of the right of transit by slaves through a free state, but the Fugitive Slave Law remained intact until the Civil War. It would take much more than court challenges or even local disturbances to dislodge the institution of slavery. The fact remained that slavery was so deeply imbedded in the Constitution itself and so firmly protected by it that both violent action and a constitutional amendment would be required to effect far-reaching and lasting change.

The violent action was not long in coming, but the outbreak of the Civil War did not put an end to slavery. President ABRAHAM LINCOLN insisted that the Confederate states were still in the Union and continued to enjoy the constitutional protection of slave property. Once the war began in earnest, however, there was no enforcement of the fugitive slave laws, and as slaves escaped to the Union lines, their emancipation became increasingly a part of the war's objectives. Congress early took steps to free certain slaves. The CONFISCATION ACT of August 6, 1861, declared that owners forfeited slaves engaged in hostile military service. In July 1862 Congress took additional steps in the Second Confiscation Act by granting freedom to slaves of traitors. Furthermore, the slaves of all persons supporting the rebellion were "forever free of their servitude. . . ." Although Lincoln had serious doubts about the constitutionality of the act, he signed it.

Meanwhile, Congress was moving speedily to emancipate the slaves whom it constitutionally could. It could not pass a universal emancipation bill, but it could and did abolish slavery in the DISTRICT OF COLUMBIA and the TERRITORIES. The emancipation bill for the District of Columbia precipitated a lengthy debate, during which President Lincoln persuaded the lawmakers to include an appropriation of $1,000,000 for compensation to owners not exceeding $300 for each slave and for the removal and colonization of the freedmen. Even so, Lincoln was reluctant to sign the bill. He signed it after Senator CHARLES SUMNER of Massachusetts and Bishop Daniel A. Payne of the African Methodist Episcopal Church pleaded with him to approve it. On June 19, 1862, Congress passed and sent to the President a bill abolishing slavery in the territories, with no provision for the compensation of owners, and Lincoln signed it.

The President continued to argue that the federal government could not emancipate the slaves unless it also compensated the owners and colonized the freedmen. Unfortunately for him, his arguments convinced neither the representatives of the border slave states nor the Negro delegations that visited him. Consequently, he was compelled to face the mounting pressures to free the slaves without any apparent constitutional means of doing so. Even as he moved toward an emancipation policy, Lincoln kept his own counsel. He listened patiently to the constant stream of delegations, some urging him to free the slaves, others insisting that he do nothing. The only thing he revealed was that the matter was on his mind, day and night, "more than any other."

In the late spring of 1862 Lincoln decided that he would emancipate the slaves by proclamation. The bleak military outlook pressed the decision on Lincoln. In July he read to the Cabinet a recently completed draft and solicited suggestions regarding language and timing. The members confined their remarks to possible political and military consequences. Lincoln agreed that a propitious moment to issue it would be in the wake of a Union victory, lest some view it as an act of desperation.

Although the battle of Antietam, September 17, 1862, was not the clear-cut victory for which Lincoln had been waiting, he decided to act anyway. On September 22, 1862, he issued the Preliminary EMANCIPATION PROCLAMATION, to take effect on January 1, 1863. Abandoning the notion of colonization, the President, in the final Proclamation, declared free those slaves in states or parts of states under Confederate control. He further declared that the freedmen would be received into the armed service of the United States "to garrison forts, positions, stations, and other places, and to man vessels in said service." Even without a comprehensive emancipation policy, Lincoln is reported to have said as he signed the document, "I never, in my life, felt more certain that I was doing right than I do in signing this paper."

Lincoln realized, of course, that his proclamation, primarily a war measure, did not actually free the slaves. Although military action set many of them free, either state or federal action or both were needed to achieve real and permanent freedom in law and practice. By early 1865, Tennessee, West Virginia, Maryland, and Missouri had taken steps to free their slaves. Delaware and Kentucky, like the Confederate states, had taken no such action by the end of the war.

It early became clear that only national action, preferably through a constitutional amendment, could provide a uniform emancipation policy. Yet some doubted the wisdom or even the prudence of using the Constitution to reform a domestic institution such as slavery. Others questioned the legality of amending the Constitution while eleven states remained outside the Union. The latter circumstance was a major reason why the proposed amendment to forbid slavery throughout the nation initially failed to get the necessary two-thirds approval of the House after it had passed the Senate in the spring of 1864. After the election of 1864 and with the war winding down, the House finally approved the amendment on January 31, 1865. The following day, Lincoln was pleased to sign the resolution submitting the amendment to the states for ratification.

By December 18, 1865, twenty-seven states, including eight former Confederate states, had ratified the THIRTEENTH AMENDMENT, and it became part of the Constitution. One of the ironies was that the amendment could not have been ratified without the concurrence of the slave states whose governments Congress did not recognize in 1865. This seemed an appropriate way to end slavery, which was itself the most remarkable anomaly in the history of the country.

Bibliography

BECKER, CARL (1942)1953 *The Declaration of Independence: A Study in the History of Political Ideas.* New York: Knopf.

BOWEN, CATHERINE DRINKER 1966 *Miracle at Philadelphia: The Story of the Constitutional Convention May to September 1787.* Boston: Little, Brown.

CURTIN, PHILIP 1969 *The Atlantic Slave Trade: A Census.* Madison: University of Wisconsin Press.

DUBOIS, W. E. BURGHARDT (1896)1954 *The Suppression of the African Slave Trade to the United States of America.* New York: Social Science Press.

FEHRENBACHER, DON E. 1978 *The Dred Scott Case: Its Significance in American Law and Politics.* New York: Oxford University Press.

FINKELMAN, PAUL   1981   *An Imperfect Union: Slavery, Federalism, and Comity.* Chapel Hill: University of North Carolina Press.

FRANKLIN, JOHN HOPE   1963   *The Emancipation Proclamation.* Garden City, N.Y.: Doubleday.

LEVY, LEONARD W.   1950   Sims' Case: The Fugitive Slave Law in Boston in 1851. *Journal of Negro History* 35:39–74.

ZILBERSMIT, ARTHUR   1967   *The First Emancipation: The Abolition of Slavery in the North.* Chicago: University of Chicago Press.

# ABOLITIONIST CONSTITUTIONAL THEORY

William M. Wiecek

American abolitionists developed comprehensive but conflicting theories about the place of slavery in the American constitution. Though these ideas did not positively influence political and legal debate until the 1850s, they exercised profound influence over subsequent constitutional development, merging with constitutional aspirations of nonabolitionist Republicans after the Civil War to provide the basis for what one writer has called the "Third Constitution": the THIRTEENTH through FIFTEENTH AMENDMENTS. From abolitionist constitutional ideals embedded in section 1 of the FOURTEENTH AMENDMENT, there emerged some principal trends of constitutional development in the century after the Civil War: SUBSTANTIVE DUE PROCESS, equality before the law, protection for the privileges of national and state CITIZENSHIP.

By the time abolitionists began systematically to expound constitutional ideas in the 1830s, the constitutional aspects of the controversy over slavery were well developed. Even before American independence, Quakers in the Middle Colonies and some Puritan ministers in New England had attacked slavery on religio-ethical grounds. In SOMERSET'S CASE (1772) WILLIAM MURRAY (Lord Mansfield), Chief Justice of King's Bench, suggested that slavery could be established only by positive law and that, as a legal institution, it was "odious." The American Revolution witnessed the total abolition, exclusion, or disappearance of slavery in some northern jurisdictions (Vermont, Massachusetts and Maine, New Hampshire, the Northwest Territory) and its gradual abolition in the rest (Pennsylvania, New York, New Jersey, Connecticut, Rhode Island). Early antislavery groups, federated as the American Convention of Abolition Societies, worked in legal and paternalistic ways to protect freed blacks and provide them jobs and education. Yet these Revolutionary-era inhibitions on slavery were offset by gains slavery made in the drafting of the United States Constitution, in which ten clauses promoted slavery's security, most notably in the federal number clause (Article I, section 2, clause 3), the slave trade clause (Article I, section 9, clause 1), and the fugitive slave clause (Article IV, section 2, clause 3).

Constitutional controversy flared over slavery in several early episodes: the federal abolition of the international slave trade and its incidents, the Missouri crisis (1819–1821), the disputes over federal aid to colonization of free blacks, Denmark Vesey's slave revolt (Charleston, 1822), and the Negro Seamen's Acts of the southern coastal states (1822–1830). But not until the ideas of immediate abolition rejuvenated the antislavery movement did abolitionists begin a systematic constitutional assault on slavery. When they organized the American Anti-Slavery Society (AASS) in 1833, abolitionists, in a document drafted by WILLIAM LLOYD GARRISON, pledged themselves to tolerate the continued existence of slavery in the states and rejected the possibility that the federal government could abolish it there. But they insisted that slavery should be abolished immediately, that blacks should not suffer legal discrimination because of race, and that Congress should abolish the interstate slave trade, ban slavery in the DISTRICT OF COLUMBIA and the TERRITORIES, and refuse to admit new slave states.

The newly reorganized movement promptly encountered resistance that directed its thinking into constitutional modes. Federal efforts to suppress abolitionist mailings and to gag abolitionists' FREEDOM OF PETITION, together with mobbings throughout the northern states, diverted abolitionists briefly from the pursuit of freedom for blacks to a defense of CIVIL LIBERTIES of whites. At the same time, they assaulted slavery's incidents piecemeal, attempting to protect fugitive slaves from rendition, and seeking repeal of statutes that permitted sojourning masters to keep their slaves with them for limited periods of time in northern states. They secured enactment of PERSONAL LIBERTY LAWS: statutes that protected the freedom of black people in the northern states by providing them HABEAS CORPUS relief when seized as fugitives and by prohibiting state officials or public facilities from being used in the recapture of fugitives.

In 1839–1840, the unified antislavery movement split apart into three factions. Ironically, this organizational disaster stimulated abolitionists' systematic constitutional theorizing and broadcast their ideas widely outside the movement. Because of theological and tactical disagreements, the movement first broke into Garrisonian and political action wings, the Garrisonians condemning conventional electoral politics and the activists organizing a third party, the Liberty party, which ran its own presidential candidate in 1840 and 1844. The political action group subsequently split into those who believed slavery to be everywhere illegitimate and who therefore sought to have the federal government abolish slavery in the states, and those who continued to maintain the position of the original AASS Constitution, namely, that Congress lacked constitutional power to abolish slavery in the states. The Garrisonians, meanwhile, had concluded that the United States Constitution supported slavery and therefore called on northern states to secede from the Union and on individuals to disavow their allegiance to the Constitution.

Those who always maintained slavery's universal illegitimacy relied first on the DUE PROCESS clause of the Fifth Amendment, arguing that slaves were deprived of life, liberty, and property without legal justification, but they soon broadened their attack, ingeniously interpreting nearly a third of the Constitution's clauses, from the PREAMBLE to the TENTH AMENDMENT, to support their untenable thesis that slavery had usurped its preferred constitutional status. The 1840 publication of JAMES MADISON's notes of proceedings at the CONSTITUTIONAL CONVENTION OF 1787 was an embarrassment to them, disclosing as it did the concessions the Framers willingly made to the political power of slavery. Exponents of the universal-illegitimacy theory included Alvan Stewart, G. W. F. Mellen, Lysander Spooner, Joel Tiffany, and later, Gerrit Smith, JAMES G. BIRNEY, Lewis Tappan, and Frederick Douglass. Their principal contributions to later constitutional development included: their insistence on equality before the law irrespective of race; their vision of national citizenship protecting individuals' rights throughout the Union; their reliance on the PRIVILEGES AND IMMUNITIES clause (Article IV, section 2, clause 1) as a protection for persons of both races; and their uncompromising egalitarianism, which led them to condemn all forms of RACIAL DISCRIMINATION. They were scorned as extremists in their own time, even by fellow abolitionists, and modern scholars such as Robert Cover dismiss their ideas as "utopian."

Political action abolitionists who conceded the legality of slavery in the states remained closest to the mainstream of American politics and established a political alliance with like-minded men outside the abolitionist movement to create the Free Soil party in 1848. Their insistence that, as the federal government could not abolish slavery, neither could it establish it, led them to proclaim the doctrines of "divorce" and "freedom national." "Divorce" called for an immediate and absolute separation of the federal government from the support of slavery (for example, by abolishing the interstate slave trade and repealing the Fugitive Slave Act of 1793), coupled with an aggressive attack on the political bases of slavery's strength (repeal of the federal number clause, refusal to appoint slaveholders to federal posts). "Divorce" provided the doctrinal basis of the three-way Free Soil coalition of 1848, comprised of Conscience Whigs, Barnburner Democrats, and former Libertymen. Liberty leaders in the Free Soil group included SALMON P. CHASE (later Chief Justice of the United States), Gamaliel Bailey, STANLEY MATTHEWS (a future justice of the United States Supreme Court), Representative Owen Lovejoy, and Joshua Leavitt.

Stimulated by the widespread popularity of the WILMOT PROVISO (1846) in the north, which would have excluded slavery from all territories acquired as a result of the Mexican War, the abolitionist Free Soilers demanded "non-extension": the refusal to permit slavery in any American territories, and the nonadmission of new slave states. This became transformed into "freedom national," a constitutional doctrine holding that, under *Somerset*, freedom is the universal condition of humans, and slavery a local aberration created and continued only by local positive law. These ideas were cordially received by Whigs who formed a nucleus of the Republican party after the demise of the Free Soilers and the fragmentation of the regular parties as a result of the KANSAS-NEBRASKA ACT (1854): Joshua Giddings, CHARLES SUMNER, Charles Francis Adams, and Horace Mann. Other Republicans such as ABRAHAM LINCOLN and WILLIAM SEWARD refused to accept "divorce" but made nonextension the cornerstone of Republican policy. "Freedom national" even influenced anti-abolitionists such as Lewis Cass and then STEPHEN A. DOUGLAS, who promoted a modified version of it as the FREEPORT DOCTRINE of 1858.

Garrisonians dismissed the United States Constitution as the "covenant with death and agreement with hell" denounced by Isaiah, but they too influenced later constitutional development, principally through their insistence that the proslavery clauses of the Constitution would have to be repealed or nullified, and the federal government fumigated of its contamination with support of slavery. Though they included competent lawyers (Wendell Phillips, William I. Bowditch), the Garrisonians were distinguished chiefly by literary and polemical talent (Edmund Quincy, Lydia Maria Child) and consequently made little contribution to systematic constitutional exposition.

The crises of the union in the 1850s, beginning with enactment of the Fugitive Slave Act in 1850, leading through the dramatic fugitive recaptures and rescues, the Kansas-Nebraska Act (1854) and "Bleeding Kansas," and culminating, constitutionally, in DRED SCOTT V. SANDFORD (1857), ABLEMAN V. BOOTH (1859), and the pending appeal of *People v. Lemmon* (1860), together with legislative activity (chiefly enactment of ever broader personal liberty laws, including Vermont's Freedom Act of 1858), enabled abolitionists to work together toward common goals, and to overcome or survive their sectarian quarrels of the 1840s. Though fragmented as a distinct movement, abolitionists permeated the press, parties, and the churches, diffusing their ideas widely among persons who had not been theretofore involved in the antislavery movement. Thus egalitarians like Sumner and THADDEUS STEVENS, conservative lawyers like JOHN BINGHAM and William Lawrence, and political leaders like WILLIAM PITT FESSENDEN and ROSCOE CONKLING were influenced by abolitionist constitutional ideas, appropriating them after the war and injecting them into the Constitution and its interpretation, both in cases and in statutes.

Bibliography

DUMOND, DWIGHT L.    1961    *Antislavery*. Ann Arbor: University of Michigan Press.

FEHRENBACHER, DON    1978    *The Dred Scott Case: Its Significance in American Law and Politics*. New York: Oxford University Press.

GRAHAM, HOWARD J.    1968    *Everyman's Constitution*. Madison: State Historical Society of Wisconsin.

TEN BROEK, JACOBUS    1965    *Equal under Law*. New York: Collier Books.

WIECEK, WILLIAM M.    1977    *The Sources of Antislavery Constitutionalism in America, 1760–1848*. Ithaca, N.Y.: Cornell University Press.

# ROBERTS v. CITY OF BOSTON

5 Cush. (Mass.) 198 (1850)

Leonard W. Levy

In Brown v. Board of Education (1954) the Court observed that the separate but equal doctrine "apparently originated in *Roberts* v. *City of Boston*." Chief Justice Lemuel Shaw's opinion in that case had an extraordinary influence. The courts of at least ten states relied on it as a precedent for upholding segregated education. In Hall v. DeCuir (1878) the Supreme Court cited it as an authority for the rule that "equality does not mean identity." In Plessy v. Ferguson (1896) the Court relied on it as the leading precedent for the validity of state legislation requiring racial segregation in places where whites and blacks "are liable to be brought in to contact," and in Gong Lum v. Rice (1927) the Court explained *Roberts* as having sustained "the separation of colored and white schools under a state constitutional injunction of equal protection, the same as the Fourteenth Amendment. . . ."

*Roberts* arose as a test case to determine the validity of Boston's requirement that black children attend segregated schools. Charles Sumner, attacking that requirement, denied that a racially separate school could be equal, because it imposed a stigma of caste and fostered prejudice.

Shaw, for a unanimous Supreme Judicial Court, agreed that the case presented the question whether the separate schools for blacks violated their constitutional right to equality. But he reasoned that all rights must depend on laws adapted to the "respective relations and conditions" of individuals. He believed that the school committee had exercised "a discriminating and honest judgment" in deciding that the good of both races was best promoted by the separate education of their children. The law, Shaw said in reply to Sumner, did not create prejudice, probably could not change it, and might only foster it by "compelling" both races to attend "the same schools." Thus, by a singular absence of considered judgment, the court found no constitutional violation of equal protection in compulsory racial segregation as long as blacks had an equal right to attend public schools.

# SLAVERY IN THE TERRITORIES

William M. Wiecek

Slavery was confirmed by statute or royal decree in all the English, Spanish, and French colonies of North America. After American Independence, slavery therefore enjoyed a legal existence in all the states. In the NORTHWEST ORDINANCE of 1787, the Confederation Congress prohibited slavery in the Northwest Territory, although it also provided for the recapture of slaves escaping there. The First Congress reenacted this ban, but in legislation for the area southwest of the Ohio River it omitted the exclusion of slavery, so that slavery was free to penetrate into the TERRITORIES ceded by Virginia, New York, North Carolina, South Carolina, and Georgia. Slavery also existed in the French settlements that were to become Louisiana, Missouri, Illinois, and Indiana. The treaty of cession with France (1803), by which the United States acquired the LOUISIANA PURCHASE, guaranteed extant property rights, thus assuring slavery's perpetuation in those territories.

Despite the ban of the Northwest Ordinance, settlers in Ohio (particularly in the Virginia Military Reserve in the southwest quadrant of the territory), Indiana, and Illinois tried to introduce slavery, with the connivance of Indiana territorial governor William Henry Harrison in the case of Ohio, and at least the tacit consent of President THOMAS JEFFERSON. They failed in Ohio and Indiana, but in Illinois slavery continued in subterfuge forms in the lead mines of Galena and the salt mines of Shawneetown, and only a vigorous abolitionist effort prevented its legalization throughout the state in 1822.

The Constitution contained no direct allusion to slavery in the territories; the new states and territories clauses did not refer to it, although the fugitive slave clause permitted recapture of fugitives only from the states, not the territories. Consequently, when Missouri sought admission as a slave state in 1819, Congress had no textual guidance, and for the first time it had to extrapolate from what it could determine of the Framers' intent concerning the territories. The result was a long and bitter debate in which restrictionists argued that slavery was hostile to the spirit of republican government and should not be extended to the new lands, while slavery's supporters insisted that Congress lacked power to exclude slavery from any territory. Jefferson at the time joined the antirestrictionists, arguing that as slavery spread it would diffuse to the point where the black population, relative to the white, would dwindle in both the old states and the new territories. The Missouri controversy was settled by admitting Missouri as a slave state and Maine as a free state, while prohibiting slavery in all the Louisiana Purchase territory north of Missouri's southern boundary (36°30′). (See MISSOURI COMPROMISE.) Jefferson likened the Missouri debates to a "firebell in the night," the "knell of the union."

As the confrontation over slavery intensified in the 1830s, abolitionists and defenders of slavery amplified their constitutional and policy arguments about slavery's future in the territories. Abolitionists found two sources of congressional power to exclude slavery. They saw the territories clause (Article IV, section 3) as a plenary grant of power to the national government to regulate all matters of property and personal status in the territories. Further, the new states clause (Article IV, section 3) implicitly permitted restriction because it gave Congress power to prohibit a state's admission if it recognized slavery. Abolitionists also maintained that slavery was contrary to the principles of a republican form of government, which the United States must guarantee to each of the states.

Alarmed by such doctrines, JOHN C. CALHOUN in the period 1837–1847 elaborated doctrines that denied any exclusionary power to Congress. He insisted that the territories were the common property of all the states, and that it would be unjust to the slave states to exclude one form of property and its owners (slaves) when all other forms of property were not similarly restricted. Calhoun regarded Congress as the agent of the states (they being the principals) or as their trustee (they being the beneficiaries). By either legal metaphor, Congress lacked power to exclude slavery because that would discriminate against one group of states. He maintained that slavery was not only a positive good but also an essential element in the domestic and political structure of the slave states. Efforts to impede its spread were therefore not only insulting but threatening to the security of the states themselves.

This debate remained academic until 1845. Arkansas had been admitted as a slave state in 1836, the unorganized Indian Territory (modern Oklahoma) was not then targeted for white settlement, and many still considered the remainder of the Louisiana Purchase uninhabitable. But Texas's independence, followed by its request for admission, thrust the territorial debates to center stage, and for over a decade after the outbreak of the Mexican War the territorial issue eclipsed all other topics of the slavery controversy except the problem of fugitive slaves. Texas, a slaveholding Republic that had struck for Independence partly because the Mexican constitution had abolished slavery, presented the potential for more than one slave state; the JOINT RESOLUTION admitting it to statehood recognized its potential subdivision into five states.

When war with Mexico broke out in 1846, the future of the territories to be acquired from that country became a more urgent issue. A few persons suggested that the United States acquire no new territories, but that idea was lost in the tide of Manifest Destiny flooding the country in the 1840s. In 1846, Representative David Wilmot, a Pennsylvania Democrat, offered a proviso to an appropriations bill that used the language of the Northwest Ordinance to exclude slavery from all territories acquired as a result of the Mexican War. Democrats and other defenders of slavery were alarmed by the WILMOT PROVISO's popularity in the North (nearly all free state legislatures endorsed it), and especially by the Proviso's appeal to Northern Democrats, who resented Southern dictation of party policy on slavery-related subjects and wanted to preserve the new territories for free white settlement.

The Proviso's opponents introduced four alternative proposals. Many Southerners at first found the idea of extending the Missouri Compromise line attractive. The Polk administration, Justice JOHN CATRON of Tennessee, the NASHVILLE CONVENTION of 1850, and Senator JOHN J. CRITTENDEN of Kentucky in 1860 all suggested extrapolating the 36°30′ line as a simple and arbitrary solution to the Gordian knot of slavery in the territories. Despite its simplicity, the idea repeatedly failed. One of the reasons for its failure was that other Southern leaders, more determined to protect the South than to compromise the territorial issue, revised their 1820 position and insisted that any exclusion of slavery from the territories was unconstitutional. Their theories for a time were subsumed under the shorthand term "non-intervention," a name for a cluster of doctrines that adopted Calhoun's premises and went on to demand that the federal government protect slavery in all the territories and even establish it there by a federal territorial slave code if necessary.

Northern Democrats rejected this position, but they did not want to split the party by endorsing the Wilmot Proviso. Under the leadership of Lewis Cass of Michigan and STEPHEN A. DOUGLAS of Illinois, they proposed a third alternative: the doctrine of territorial sovereignty, more often but less accurately referred to as POPULAR SOVEREIGNTY or squatter sovereignty. Cass and Douglas insisted that the future of slavery in the territories be decided by the settlers of the territories themselves, not by Congress. After 1850, they also began to adopt the Southern position that slavery's exclusion was not only unnecessary and gratuitously offensive to the South but also unconstitutional. Territorial sovereignty contained a central ambiguity: when were the settlers to decide? If, as Southern spokesmen demanded, territorial settlers could not exercise this prerogative until the eve of statehood, then slavery would establish a foothold, as it had in Missouri, and be impossible to dislodge. Northern proponents of territorial sovereignty, on the other hand, insisted that the settlers had a right to exclude slavery at any point after the organization of the territory. This view, in turn, forced Southerners to another doctrinal redoubt, when they claimed that just as Congress could not exclude slavery, neither could its creature, the territorial legislature. In this view, slavery could establish itself anywhere in American territories.

The Free Soil coalition of 1848, made up of New York Democrats, antislavery Whigs, and former political abolitionists, adopted the Wilmot Proviso as a principal plank in their program. But the COMPROMISE OF 1850 decisively rejected the Wilmot Proviso. In admitting California as a free state and organizing New Mexico and Utah Territories without restrictions as to slavery, Congress also rejected the Missouri Compromise line. But it also adopted the fourth alternative to the Wilmot Proviso, the "Clayton Compromise." Senator John Clayton of Delaware had proposed that all questions arising in TERRITORIAL COURTS concerning title to slaves or a black's claim to freedom be appealable directly to the United States Supreme Court, in effect inviting the Justices of the high court to try their hand at resolving the seemingly insoluble territorial issue. By adopting the Clayton Compromise, Congress admitted its inability to deal with the most exigent political issue of the day. Its desperate grasp at nonpolitical solutions not only confessed its impotence but also assumed the finality of an unpredictable resolution of a question that was ultimately metajudicial.

The KANSAS-NEBRASKA ACT of 1854 adopted the principle of territorial sovereignty, along with some vague and ambiguous allusions to nonintervention. It declared the Missouri Compromise defunct and implied that it was unconstitutional, thus representing a victory for both northern Democrats and Southerners. But this accommodation did not last long, as Kansas filled with authentic settlers and Missouri sojourners. Because most of the former hoped to see Kansas free and because all the latter were determined to make it a slave state, political controversy erupted into guerrilla warfare in the period known as "Bleeding Kansas." President JAMES BUCHANAN tried to force the proslavery LECOMPTON CONSTITUTION on the territory, over the wishes of a large majority of bona fide settlers, and thereby split the Democratic party into Southern-dominated and Douglas wings.

Meanwhile, Chief Justice ROGER B. TANEY and his colleagues took up the invitation tendered by Congress in DRED SCOTT v. SANDFORD (1857). Taney held, in the latter part of his opinion, that the Missouri Compromise was unconstitutional, and that Congress could not exclude slavery from a territory. He adopted three Calhounite positions in OBITER DICTA: the federal government had to protect slavery in the territories; territorial legislatures could not exclude slavery at any time before statehood; and the federal government was the trustee of the states or the territories. In passing, Taney suggested that congressional exclusion would deprive a slaveowner of rights to property protected by the DUE PROCESS clause of the Fifth Amendment. This adumbration of SUBSTANTIVE DUE PROCESS was merely a passing allusion, however, the emphasis of Taney's opinion lying instead in his interpretation of the new states clause.

In the LINCOLN–DOUGLAS DEBATES of 1858, ABRAHAM LINCOLN challenged Douglas to explain what was left of territorial sovereignty after *Dred Scott.* Douglas suggested the FREEPORT DOCTRINE: that Congress could for all practical purposes exclude slavery from a territory simply by not enacting a territorial slave code or extending any other protection for it there. Under one interpretation of SOMERSET v. STEWART (1772), there being no positive law to keep a person enslaved, slavery effectively could not establish itself. This led Mississippi Senator JEFFERSON DAVIS to demand that the federal courts protect slavery in the territories somehow, and, if this proved unavailing, that Congress enact a territorial slave code.

The Constitution of the Confederate States of America extended full federal protection to slavery in any territories the Confederacy might acquire. The Congress of the United States abolished slavery in all federal territories in 1862 (Act of June 19, 1862).

Bibliography

BESTOR, ARTHUR   1961   State Sovereignty and Slavery: A Reinterpretation of Proslavery Constitutional Doctrine, 1846–1860. *Journal of the Illinois State Historical Society* 54:117–180.

QUAIFE, MILO M.   1910   *The Doctrine of Non-Intervention with Slavery in the Territories.* Chicago: Chamberlin.

RUSSEL, ROBERT R.   1966   Constitutional Doctrines with Regard to Slavery in the Territories. *Journal of Southern History* 32:466–486.

# DRED SCOTT v. SANDFORD

## 19 Howard 393 (1857)

### Don E. Fehrenbacher

Closely associated with the coming of the Civil War, DRED SCOTT V. SANDFORD remains one of the most famous decisions of the United States Supreme Court. It is certainly the prime historical example of judicial power exercised in the interest of racial subordination, and, as such, it stands in sharp contrast with BROWN V. BOARD OF EDUCATION (1954), handed down almost a century later.

Scott was a Missouri slave owned by an army medical officer named John Emerson, who took him to live at military posts in Illinois and in federal territory north of 36°30' where SLAVERY had been prohibited by the MISSOURI COMPROMISE. In 1846, Scott brought suit against Emerson's widow in St. Louis, claiming that he had been emancipated by his residence on free soil. Missouri precedent was on his side, and after two trials he won his freedom. In 1852, however, the state supreme court reversed that judgment. By a 2–1 vote and in bitterly sectional language, it declared that the state would no longer enforce the antislavery law of other jurisdictions against Missouri's own citizens. Scott's residence elsewhere, it held, did not change his status as a slave in Missouri.

Normally, the next step should have been an APPEAL to the United States Supreme Court, but a recent decision in the somewhat similar case of STRADER V. GRAHAM (1851) may have persuaded Scott's legal advisers that the Court would refuse to accept JURISDICTION. They decided instead to initiate a brand new suit for freedom in the federal CIRCUIT COURT for Missouri against Mrs. Emerson's brother, John F. A. Sanford of New York, who had been acting as her agent in the Scott litigation and may even have become the slave's owner. Sanford's New York CITIZENSHIP provided the foundation for DIVERSITY JURISDICTION. So began the case of *Dred Scott v. Sandford* (with Sanford's name misspelled in the official record).

Up to this point, the principal issue in Scott's suit had been how residence on free soil affected the legal status of a slave. It was a familiar issue that dated back to the noted British case of *Somerset v. Stewart* (1772) and had been dealt with in a number of state court decisions. (See SOMERSET'S CASE.) During the early decades of American independence, a tacit sectional accommodation had prevailed. Southerners accompanied by slaves were generally able to travel and sojourn in free states without interference. At the same time, southern courts joined in upholding the rule that a slave domiciled in a free state became forever free. Beginning in the 1830s, however, this arrangement broke down under antislavery pressure. State after state in the North withdrew the privilege of maintaining slaves while sojourning, and there was growing judicial acceptance of the view that any slave other than a fugitive became free the moment he set foot on free soil. (See COMMONWEALTH v. AVES, 1836.) To Southerners the change meant not only inconvenience but also insult, and by the 1850s they were retaliating in various ways.

*Dred Scott v. Sandford* raised an additional issue. In order to maintain a suit in federal court, Scott had to aver that he was a citizen of Missouri. Sanford's counsel challenged this assertion with a plea in abatement arguing that Negroes were not citizens and that the Court therefore lacked jurisdiction. The trial judge ruled that any person residing in a state and legally capable of owning property was qualified to bring suit under the diverse-citizenship clauses of the Constitution and the JUDICIARY ACT. On the merits of the case, however, he instructed the jury in favor of the defendant. Like the Missouri Supreme Court in *Scott v. Emerson,* he declared that Scott's status, after returning to Missouri, depended entirely upon the law of that state, without regard to his residence in Illinois and free federal territory. The jury accordingly brought in a verdict for Sanford.

The case then proceeded on WRIT OF ERROR to the United States Supreme Court, whose membership at the time consisted of five southern Democrats, two northern Democrats, one northern Whig, and one Republican. Argument before the Court in February 1856 introduced another new issue. For the first time, Sanford's lawyers maintained that Scott had not become free in federal territory because the law forbidding slavery there was unconstitutional. This, of course, was the issue that had inflamed national politics for the past decade and would continue to do so in the final years of the sectional crisis. With a presidential contest about to begin, the Justices prudently ordered the case to be reargued at the next session. On March 6, 1857, two days after the inauguration of James Buchanan, Chief Justice ROGER B. TANEY finally read the decision of the Court.

Although Taney spoke officially for the Court, every other member had something to say, and only one concurred with him in every particular. The effect of the decision was therefore unclear, except that Dred Scott had certainly lost. Seven Justices concluded that at law he remained a slave. Taney, in reasoning his way to that judgment, also ruled that free blacks were not citizens and that Congress had no power to prohibit SLAVERY IN THE TERRITORIES. But were these declarations authoritative parts of the decision?

According to some contemporary critics and later historians, Taney did not speak for a majority of the Court in excluding Negroes from citizenship. Their conclusion rests upon the assumption that only those Justices expressly agreeing with him can be counted on his side. Yet, since Taney's opinion was the authorized opinion of the Court, it seems more reasonable to regard only those Justices expressly disagreeing with him as constituting the opposition. By this measure, the opinion never encountered dissent from more than two Justices at any major point. Furthermore, five Justices in their opinions spoke of the citizenship question as having been decided by the Court. In other words, the authoritativeness of that part of Taney's opinion was attested to by a majority of the Court itself.

More familiar is the charge that Taney indulged in OBITER DICTUM when he ruled against the constitutionality of the Missouri Compromise restriction after having decided that Scott was not a citizen and-so had no right to bring suit in a federal court. "Obiter dictum" was the principal battle cry of the Republicans in their attacks on the decision. By dismissing Taney's ruling against territorial power as illegitimate, they were able to salvage the main plank of their party platform without assuming the role of open rebels against judicial authority. What the argument ignored was Taney's not unreasonable contention that throughout his opinion he was canvassing the question of jurisdiction. Having concluded that Scott could not be a citizen because he was a *Negro,* the Chief Justice elected to fortify the conclusion by demonstrating also that Scott could not be a citizen because he was a *slave.* Such reinforcement was especially appropriate because some of the Justices were convinced that the Court could not properly review the citizenship question.

It therefore appears that none of Taney's major rulings can be pushed aside as unauthoritative. In any case, the long-standing argument over what the Court "really decided" has been largely beside the point; for Taney's opinion was accepted as the opinion of the Court by its critics as well as its defenders. As a matter of historical reality, the *Dred Scott* decision is what he declared it to be.

Taney devoted about forty-four percent of his opinion to the question of Negro citizenship, thirty-eight percent to the territorial question, sixteen percent to various technical issues, and only two percent to the original question of whether residence on free soil had the legal effect of emancipating a slave. Throughout the entire document, he made not a single concession to antislavery feeling but instead committed the JUDICIAL POWER OF THE UNITED STATES totally to the defense of slavery. Behind his mask of judicial propriety, the Chief Justice had become privately a fierce southern sectionalist, seething with anger at "Northern insult and Northern aggression." His flat legal prose does not entirely conceal the intensity of emotion that animated his *Dred Scott* opinion.

The citizenship issue concerned the status of free Negroes only;

for everyone agreed that slaves were not citizens. Yet Taney persistently lumped free Negroes and slaves together as one degraded class of beings who "had been subjugated by the dominant race, and, whether emancipated or not, yet remained subject to their authority." Thus all blacks, in his view, stood on the same ground. Emancipation made no difference. Negroes could not have been regarded as citizens by the Framers of the Constitution, he declared, because at the time they "had no rights which the white man was bound to respect." These notorious words were not mere historical commentary as defenders of the Chief Justice have often insisted. Taney also held that the constitutional status of Negroes had not changed at all since 1787, which meant that in 1857 they still had no federal rights that white men were bound to respect. His reasoning excluded blacks not only from citizenship but also from every protection given to *persons* by the Constitution.

Much more forceful in its political impact was Taney's ruling against the constitutionality of the antislavery provision in the Missouri Compromise. He began by dismissing as irrelevant the one clause of the Constitution in which the word "territory" appears, preferring instead to derive the territorial power of Congress by implication from the power to admit new states. No less remarkable is the fact that he never said precisely why the antislavery provision was unconstitutional. Historians have inferred from one brief passage that he based his holding on the DUE PROCESS clause of the Fifth Amendment. Yet there is no explicit statement to that effect, and in the end he did not declare that congressional prohibition of slavery in the territories *violated* any part of the Constitution; he said only that it was "not warranted" by the Constitution, a phrasing that suggests reliance on the principle of strict construction.

Not satisfied with ruling in effect that the Republican party was organized for an illegal purpose, the Chief Justice also struck a hard blow at northern Democrats and the doctrine of POPULAR SOVEREIGNTY. If Congress could not prohibit slavery in a territory, he said, neither could it authorize a territorial legislature to do so. This statement, being on a subject that did not arise in the case, was *dictum*. It exemplified Taney's determination to cover all ground in providing judicial protection for slavery. The dissenting Justices, JOHN MCLEAN and BENJAMIN R. CURTIS, rejected Taney's blanket exclusion of Negroes from citizenship. Having thus affirmed Scott's capacity to bring suit in a federal court, they proceeded to the merits of the case while denying the right of the Court majority to do so. Both men upheld the constitutionality of the Missouri Compromise restriction by interpreting the territory clause, in Republican style, as an express and plenary delegation of power to Congress. They went on to maintain that antislavery law, state or federal, dissolved the legal relationship between any master and slave coming within its purview, thereby working irrevocable emancipation.

Antislavery critics made good use of the dissenting opinions in launching an angry, abusive attack upon the Court majority and its judgment. The influence of the decision on the sectional conflict is difficult to assess. No doubt it contributed significantly to the general accumulation of sectional animosity that made some kind of national crisis increasingly unavoidable. It also aggravated the split in the Democratic party by eliciting STEPHEN A. DOUGLAS's FREEPORT DOCTRINE and inspiring southern demands for a territorial slave code. At the same time, there is reason to doubt that the decision enhanced Republican recruiting or had a critical effect on the election of ABRAHAM LINCOLN.

For the two principals in the case, the verdict of the Court made little difference. John Sanford died in an insane asylum two months after the reading of the decision. Dred Scott was soon manumitted, but he lived only sixteen months as a free man before succumbing to tuberculosis. The constitutional effect of the decision likewise proved to be slight, especially after the outbreak of the Civil War. The wartime Union government treated *Dred Scott v. Sandford* as though it had never been rendered. In June 1862, Congress abolished slavery in all the federal territories. Later the same year, Lincoln's ATTORNEY GENERAL issued an official opinion holding that free men of color born in the United States were citizens of the United States. The THIRTEENTH AMENDMENT (1865) and the FOURTEENTH AMENDMENT (1868) completed the work of overthrowing Taney's decision.

The *Dred Scott* case damaged Taney's reputation but did not seriously weaken the Supreme Court as an institution. Aside from its immediate political effects, the case is significant as the first instance in which a major federal law was ruled unconstitutional. It is accordingly a landmark in the growth of JUDICIAL REVIEW and an early asserton of the policymaking authority that the Court would come to exercise more and more.

Bibliography

EHRLICH, WALTER   1979   *They Have No Rights: Dred Scott's Struggle for Freedom.* Westport, Conn.: Greenwood Press.

FEHRENBACHER, DON E.   1978   *The Dred Scott Case: Its Significance in American Law and Politics.* New York: Oxford University Press.

SWISHER, CARL B.   1974   *The Taney Period, 1836–1864,* Volume V of the Oliver Wendell Holmes Devise *History of the Supreme Court of the United States.* New York: Macmillan.

# ABRAHAM LINCOLN

## (1809–1865)

### Harry V. Jaffa

Abraham Lincoln of Illinois served as President of the United States during the nation's greatest crisis, the Civil War. He had previously represented Illinois in the House of Representatives for a single term (1847–1849), during which he introduced the SPOT RESOLUTIONS, implicitly critical of President JAMES K. POLK's administration of the Mexican War, and supported the WILMOT PROVISO, which would have banned slavery from the territory acquired in that war. Lincoln rose to national prominence opposing the policies of Senator STEPHEN A. DOUGLAS, especially Douglas's KANSAS-NEBRASKA ACT, which extended SLAVERY IN THE TERRITORIES on a local-option basis. In 1856 he joined the fledgling Republican party. Lincoln opposed Douglas's reelection to the Senate in 1858, and the two candidates toured the state together, publicly debating the issues of slavery, POPULAR SOVEREIGNTY, and CONSTITUTIONALISM. During the LINCOLN-DOUGLAS DEBATES, Lincoln severely criticized Chief Justice ROGER B. TANEY's decision in DRED SCOTT V. SANDFORD (1857) as a betrayal of the principles embodied in the DECLARATION OF INDEPENDENCE.

Lincoln's election to the presidency in 1860 triggered the long-impending SECESSION of several slaveholding southern states. Lincoln's presidency was devoted to saving the Union, which meant, in his mind, the rededication of the nation to the principles of the Declaration of Independence, and especially to the proposition that all men are created equal. This work of saving the Union, tragically cut short by an assassin's bullet, was Lincoln's great contribution to American constitutionalism.

In the Lincoln Memorial, directly behind the statue of the Great Emancipator, these words are inscribed:

> In this temple
> as in the hearts of the people
> for whom he saved the Union
> the memory of Abraham Lincoln
> is enshrined forever.

Lincoln did indeed save the Union. But the Union Lincoln saved was older than the Constitution; the Constitution was intended to form a "more perfect Union." When Lincoln began the Gettysburg Address with the magisterial "Fourscore and seven years ago . . ." he intended his listeners to understand that the birth date of the nation was 1776, not 1787, and that the principles of "government of the people, by the people, for the people" were those of the Declaration of Independence. The Constitution was intended to implement those principles more perfectly than had been done by the ARTICLES OF CONFEDERATION. Lincoln at Gettysburg also intended his listeners—and the world—to know that there would be "a new birth of freedom" that would be accomplished by the EMANCIPATION PROCLAMATION, followed, as he intended that it would be, by the THIRTEENTH AMENDMENT. (We may be confident that, had he lived, Lincoln would also have given his support to the FOURTEENTH and FIFTEENTH AMENDMENTS, as part of that same "new birth.")

To understand the Constitution as Abraham Lincoln did must mean, primarily and essentially, to understand the Constitution as an expression of the principles of the Declaration. To do this is to separate the interpretation of the Constitution from all forms of legal positivism, historicism, and moral relativism, that is to say, from all those forms of interpretation that are dominant today in the law schools, universities, and courts of the nation. For, contrary to Lincoln's expectations, his words at Gettysburg have been greatly noted and long remembered: it is their meaning that has been forgotten.

Lincoln did indeed save the Union. At the time of his inauguration, March 4, 1861, seven states had already seceded and joined together to form an independent government called the Confederate States of America. JAMES BUCHANAN, the outgoing President, had been confronted with the SOUTH CAROLINA ORDINANCE OF SECESSION on December 20, 1860, six weeks after Lincoln's election, and more than ten weeks before his inauguration. Buchanan declared secession to be unconstitutional, but coupled his denunciation of secession with a much harsher denunciation of abolitionism. He denied, moreover, that he as President could take any lawful action against secession. Whatever action the federal government ought to take, he lamely concluded, must originate in laws enacted by Congress. But Buchanan had nothing to suggest to Congress, and Congress, at this juncture—the representatives of eight slave states remaining on March 4, 1861—was as divided as the nation itself. No congressional majority could have been formed then for decisive action against the rebellion. Lincoln waited until Congress had gone home, and cannily maneuvered the South Carolinians into firing those shots against Fort Sumter that electrified the North and consolidated public opinion behind his leadership. He then issued his call for 75,000 troops, and set on foot those measures that eventually resulted in the forcible subjugation of the rebellion.

Lincoln insisted that the Constitution ought not to be construed in such a way as to deny to the government any power necessary for carrying out the Constitution's commands. The Constitution required the President to take an oath "to preserve, protect, and defend the Constitution," and made it the duty of the President to "take care that the laws be faithfully executed." Lincoln held it to be absurd to suppose that it was unlawful for him to do those things that were indispensably necessary to preserve the Constitution by enforcing the execution of the laws. Even an action that might otherwise be unlawful, he said, might become lawful, by becoming thus indispensable. Lincoln never conceded that any of his wartime actions were unconstitutional. But supposing that one of them had been so, he asked, ". . . are all the laws but one to go unexecuted, and the Government itself go to pieces, lest that one be violated?"

Lincoln saved the Union. He prevented the United States from being divided into two or more separate confederacies. It was entirely likely that the North American continent would have been "Balkanized" had the initial secession succeeded. Like the Balkan states, the petty American powers would have formed alliances with greater powers, and North America would have become a cockpit of world conflict. All the evils that the more perfect Union was designed to prevent, those particularly described in the first ten numbers of THE FEDERALIST—large standing armies, heavy taxation, the restriction of individual liberties characteristic of an armed camp—would have come to pass. Civil and religious liberty, the supreme ends of republican government, would, with the failure of the American experiment, "perish from the earth." The "central idea of secession," Lincoln held, "is the essence of anarchy." A constitutional majority, checked and limited, and able to change easily with deliberate changes in public opinion and sentiment, "is the only true sovereign of a free people." To reject majority rule is to turn necessarily either to anarchy or to despotism.

The Lincoln Memorial says that Lincoln saved the Union for "the people." At the outset of the war Lincoln said, "This is essentially a people's contest." Today, when the foulest despotisms call themselves "people's republics," it requires a conscious effort to restore to our minds the intrinsic connection in Lincoln's mind between the cause of the people and fidelity to individual liberty under the rule of law in a constitutional regime. "Our adversaries," Lincoln said, at the outset of the war, "have adopted some declarations of independence, in which, unlike the good old one, penned by THOMAS JEFFERSON, they omit the words 'all men are created equal.' Why? They have adopted a temporary national constitution, in the preamble of which they omit, 'We the People,' and substitute 'We, the deputies of the sovereign and independent States.' Why? Why this deliberate pressing out of view the rights of men and the authority of the people?" Here is the core constitutional question of the Civil War. Lincoln was elected on a platform that called for the recognition of STATES' RIGHTS, "and especially the right of each State to order and control its own domestic institutions according to its own judgment exclusively." Such rights, the Republican platform asserted, and Lincoln repeated in his inaugural, were "essential to that balance of power on which the perfection and endurance of our political fabric depend." For Lincoln, however, the rights of the states were themselves the political expression of the rights of the people, which in turn were the political expression of the rights of men. The proposition that embodied the rights of men was that to which—as he said at Gettysburg—the nation was dedicated at its conception. The Civil War was a result of the fact that the idea of states' rights, and of popular sovereignty, had become divorced, in the public mind of the Confederacy, from the original doctrine of equality in the Declaration of Independence.

The question posed by the Civil War, Lincoln said, was addressed to "the whole family of man." That Lincoln conceived of mankind as in some sense a "family" was of course but another expression of his belief in human equality. Lincoln's question was essentially the same as that addressed by ALEXANDER HAMILTON in *The Federalist* #1: "whether societies of men are really capable or not of establishing good government from reflection and choice, or whether they are forever destined to depend for their political constitutions upon accident and force." The election of Abraham Lincoln was a deliberate decision of the American people, in accordance with the canons of reflection and choice embodied in the Constitution. It remained to be seen therefore whether, in Lincoln's words, "discontented individuals, too few in numbers to control administration according to organic law [can arbitrarily] break up their government, and thus practically put an end to free government upon the earth." But because the leaders of the rebellion "knew their people possessed as much of moral sense, as much devotion to law and order . . . as any other civilized and patriotic people," it was necessary for them to invent "an ingenious sophism which, if conceded, was followed by perfectly logical steps . . . to the complete destruction of the Union. The sophism itself is, that any State of the Union may, consistently with the national Constitution . . . withdraw from the Union without the consent of the Union or of any other State."

The secessionists claimed that membership in the Union resulted from the acts by which the states had ratified the Constitution and that they might therefore withdraw by the same procedure. The Constitution itself, according to this theory, had no higher authority than the will of the people of the several states, acting in their constituent capacity.

In contradiction of this position, Lincoln presented a historical argument, that the Union was older than the states, that the rights of the states were only rights within the Union, and never rights outside of it or independent of it. Although the Declaration of Independence speaks, in its next to last sentence, of all those "Acts and Things which Independent States may of right do," none of them were ever done by any of the United States independently of each other. This argument, however, is not as conclusive as that other argument, independent of history, which follows from that "abstract truth applicable to all men and all times," to which, at Gettysburg, Lincoln said the nation had been dedicated. This argument Lincoln had been developing throughout his mature life, and is the ground of his constitutionalism, as indeed it is of all his moral and political thought. According to Lincoln, the Civil War was a "people's contest" because the rights of the states, and of the United States, were the rights of the people, either severally or generally. But what are the rights of the people? They are the rights with which the Creator has equally endowed all men—all human beings. These are the unalienable rights, among which are the rights to life, to liberty, and to the pursuit of happiness. Since all men have these rights equally, no man can rule another rightfully except with that other man's consent. Nothing better illuminates the division within the American mind that brought about the Civil War than this passage from a speech in reply to Douglas in 1854: "Judge Douglas," said Lincoln, "frequently, with bitter irony and sarcasm, paraphrases our argument by saying: 'The white people of Nebraska are good enough to govern themselves, *but they are not good enough to govern a few miserable negroes!* !' Well, I doubt not that the people of Nebraska are, and will continue to be as good as the average of people elsewhere. I do not say the contrary. What I do say is, that no man is good enough to govern another man, *without that other's consent.* I say this is the leading principle—the sheet anchor of American republicanism." Slavery, Lincoln observed, is a violation of this principle, not only because "the Master . . . governs the slave without his consent; but he governs him by a set of rules altogether different from those which he prescribes for himself." Republicanism, for Lincoln, meant that those who live under the law share equally in the making of the law they live under, and that those who make the law live equally under the law that they make. Here in essence is the necessary relationship between equality, consent, majority rule, and the rule of law in Lincoln's thought. Here in essence is what unites the principles of the Declaration with the forms of the Constitution. Here is what enables us to distinguish the principles of the Constitution from the compromises of the Constitution (in particular, the compromises with slavery). Here is the essence of Lincoln's understanding of why the argument against slavery and the argument for free government are distinguishable but inseparable aspects of one and the same argument.

The people are collectively sovereign because the people individually, by their consent, have transferred the exercise of certain of their unalienable rights—but not the rights themselves—to civil society. They have done so, the better "to secure these rights." A just government will act by the majority, under a constitution devised to assure with a reasonable likelihood that the action of the majority will fulfill its purpose, which is the equal protection of the indefeasible and equal rights of all. The majority is the surrogate of the community, which is to say, of each individual. Majority rule is not merely obliged to respect minority rights; in the final analysis it has no higher purpose than to secure the rights of that indefeasible minority, the individual. The sovereignty of the people—or of the states—cannot be exerted morally or lawfully for any purpose inconsistent with the security of those original and unalienable rights. Although Lincoln denied any constitutional right to secede, he did not deny a revolutionary right, which might be exercised justly if "by the mere force of numbers, a majority should deprive a minority of any clearly written constitutional right."

In his inaugural address Lincoln repeated his oft-repeated declaration that he had no purpose, "directly or indirectly, to interfere with slavery where it exists." He had, he said, "no lawful right to do so" and he had "no inclination to do so." This, he held, was implied constitutional law, but he was willing to make it express, by an amendment to the Constitution. Lincoln would not, however, agree to any measures that might have as their consequence the extension of slavery to new lands where it did not already exist. As he wrote to his old friend ALEXANDER H. STEPHENS in 1861, "You think slavery is *right,* and ought to be extended; while we think it is *wrong* and ought to be restricted. That I suppose is the rub. It certainly is the only substantial difference between us." Many complex and elaborate explanations have been made of the causes of the Civil War. Lincoln's is at once the shortest and the most profound.

The South claimed the right to extend slavery on the ground that it was a violation of the fundamental equality of the states to allow the citizens of one state or section to emigrate into a federal TERRITORY with their property, while prohibiting the citizens of any other state or section from emigrating into that same federal territory with their property. Lincoln dealt with this argument in 1854—in his first great antislavery speech—as follows: "Equal justice to the South, it is said, requires us to consent to the extending of slavery to new countries. That is to say, inasmuch as you do not object to my taking my hog to Nebraska, therefore I must not object to you taking your slave. Now, I admit this is perfectly logical, if there is no difference between hogs and negroes."

Southerners had come to deny the essential difference between hogs and Negroes, in part because of the enormous economic stake that they had come to have in slave labor, because of the enormous burgeoning of the cotton economy. This was one cause of the change in their opinion of slavery, from a necessary evil to a positive good. Another may be seen in the following from one of Lincoln's 1859 speeches. Douglas, Lincoln said, had "declared that while in all contests between the negro and the white man, he was for the white man . . . that in all questions between the negro and the crocodile he was for the negro." Lincoln interpreted Douglas's statements as "a sort of proposition in proportion, which may be stated thus: As the negro is to the white man, so is the crocodile to the negro; and as the negro may rightfully treat the crocodile as a beast or reptile, so the white man may rightfully treat the negro as a beast or reptile." Douglas's references to "contests" between negroes and crocodiles, and between negroes and whites, reflected popular ideas of "the survival of the fittest" in the evolutionary process. Lincoln, in commenting on these remarks of Douglas, also went out of his way to deny the necessity of any such "contests." Alexander Stephens, who was inaugurated vice-president of the Confederacy in February 1861, conceded that the United States had been founded upon the proposition "that all men are created equal," and that that proposition had indeed (contrary to what Chief Justice Roger B. Taney had said in *Dred Scott v. Sandford*) included black men as well as white. But, Stephens went on, the Confederacy was "founded [and] its corner stone rests upon . . . the great truth that the negro is not the equal to the white man. That slavery—the subordination to the superior race, is his natural and normal condition." "This our new Government," Stephens added, "is the first in the history of the world, based upon this great physical and moral truth." The doctrine of racial superiority became a vital element in the conviction that slavery was a positive good. Without the conviction and the doctrine there could not have been a belief in the South of a constitutional right to extend slavery. That science, in one or another version of evolution, had established the inequality of the races, became the ground for the rejection of the doctrine that all men are created equal.

In fact, the doctrine of racial inequality involves the denial that there is any natural right, or that there are any "laws of nature and of nature's God." And this is to deny that constitutionalism and the RULE OF LAW rest upon anything besides blind preference. Justice would then be nothing but the interest of the stronger. Abraham Lincoln's speeches, before and during the Civil War, are the supreme repository for that wisdom that teaches us that we as moral beings ought to live under the rule of law. According to this wisdom, it is also in our interest to do so, because upon our recognition of the humanity of other men depends the recognition of our own humanity. And upon the recognition of our own humanity—by ourselves and by others—depends the possibility of our own happiness as human beings. Surely Lincoln was right in saying that the source of all moral principle—no less than of all political and constitutional right—was the proposition "that all men are created equal."

It is doubtful that the history of the world records another life displaying an integrity of speech and deed equal to that of Abraham Lincoln. With an almost perfect understanding of the theoretical ground of free, constitutional government was united an unflinching courage, and a practical wisdom, in doing what had to be done, lest popular government "perish from the earth." Whether, in the third century of the Constitution, Lincoln's legacy will survive in deed depends upon whether we can recover anything of his character and intelligence. But whether or not this republic lasts, as long as the world lasts Lincoln's speeches and deeds will remain as an emblem and a beacon of humanity to all men everywhere who may be struggling out of the dark valley of despotism and aspiring to the broad, sunlit uplands of freedom.

Bibliography

BELZ, HERMAN   1969   *Reconstructing the Union.*  Ithaca, N.Y.: Cornell University Press.

FEHRENBACHER, DON E.   1978   *The Dred Scott Case: Its Significance in American Law and Politics.*  New York: Oxford University Press.

———   1979   Lincoln and the Constitution. Pages 121–166 in Cullom Davis, ed., *The Public and Private Lincoln: Contemporary Perspectives.*  Carbondale: Southern Illinois University Press.

JAFFA, HARRY V.   (1952)1983   *Crisis of the House Divided: An Interpretation of the Lincoln–Douglas Debates.*  Chicago: University of Chicago Press.

NEVINS, ALAN   1950   *The Emergence of Lincoln.*  2 Vols. New York: Scribner's.

RANDALL, JAMES G.   1951   *Constitutional Problems under Lincoln,*  rev. ed. Urbana: University of Illinois Press.

# EMANCIPATION PROCLAMATION

## 12 Stat. 68 (1863)

### Harold M. Hyman

ABRAHAM LINCOLN, employing the Constitution's WAR POWERS, announced the Emancipation Proclamation on September 22, 1862. It had its roots in ABOLITIONIST CONSTITUTIONAL THEORY. Although Lincoln's swift rise in the Republican party was due in part to his outspoken opposition to the extension of slavery, on the outset of the war he was bound by the Constitution (Article IV, section 2) and federal laws on fugitive slaves that required federal officials to return runaways, even to disloyal owners. Politically ambitious Union general George B. McClellan, a conservative would-be Democratic presidential candidate, sternly enforced the 1850 law; generals BENJAMIN F. BUTLER and John Charles Frémont, by contrast, refused to return runaways in their commands and armed some against rebel guerrillas. Lincoln countermanded the latter's orders to dim the issue of arming Negroes and to keep policy in civilians' hands.

Negroes continued to flee to Union lines no matter what orders civilians or generals issued. Awareness grew in the Union army and among bluecoats' families and other correspondents that almost the only trustworthy southerners were blacks. Gradually, sentiment increased that to return runaways was indecent and illogical, for slaves were the South's labor force. In Congress, with few exceptions, Democrats remained uneducable on the runaway issue and damned as unconstitutional any mass emancipation whether by EXECUTIVE ORDER or statute and whether or not involving colonization of freedmen abroad or compensation to loyal owners. Republicans, from Lincoln down, altered their opinions on race matters. Some northern states softened racist BLACK CODE clauses in constitutions and civil and criminal laws; some made laws color-blind. Congress, in addition to the CONFISCATION ACTS and with Lincoln's assent, enacted laws in March, April, and June 1862, respectively, that prohibited military returns of disloyal owners' runaways without requiring a judicial verdict of disloyalty, ended slavery in the DISTRICT OF COLUMBIA with compensation to owners, and forbade slavery in the federal TERRITORIES, thus challenging part of DRED SCOTT V. SANDFORD (1857). In effect,

Republicans, retaining their basic view of the Constitution as an adaptable instrument, were adopting aspirations that abolitionist constitutionalists had long advanced.

Fearing conservative gains in the 1862 congressional and state elections, congressional Republicans then marked time. Lincoln did not have this option. He determined to reverse two centuries of race history *if* continued Confederate intransigence forced further changes and *if* the Union won the war.

Therefore, following the Antietam "victory," Lincoln proclaimed that unless slaveowners in still-unoccupied states of the Confederacy (he excluded unseceded slaveholding states) publicly renounced the rebellion by January 1, 1863, their slaves "shall be then, thenceforward, and forever free." All Union military personnel must positively assist, not merely not impede, runaways from slavery. With respect to unseceded slaveholding states, Lincoln encouraged "immediate or gradual" emancipation by state initiative, with compensation to loyal owners and colonization of freedmen abroad.

The Proclamation was not an immediate success. It diminished opinion abroad favoring recognition of the Confederacy. Few southern whites abjured the rebellion before the deadline. Lincoln, on New Year's Day 1863, announced the Proclamation to be in effect. But he had enlarged his horizons, adding an announcement that he would recruit blacks for the Union's armies. Relatively few blacks lived in northern states. Lincoln's new policy, if successful—which meant if Union voters persevered, if enough slaves kept coming into Union lines, and if Union forces occupied enough Confederate areas—could drain the South of its basic labor force and augment the Union's military power.

The policy eventually succeeded. Almost 200,000 black bluecoats, overwhelmingly southern in origin, helped to crush the rebellion. *Dred Scott* was made irrelevant. Though black Union soldiers and sailors suffered inequities in rank, pay, and dignity compared to whites, their military record made it impossible for the nation to consider them again as submen in law, though racists advocated the retrograde view. Compared to their prewar status even in the free states, blacks' legal and constitutional conditions improved as a result of the Proclamation. It initiated also an irreversible revolution in race relationships leading to the WADE-DAVIS BILL, the THIRTEENTH AMENDMENT, and the CIVIL RIGHTS ACT OF 1866. But the eventual consequence of the Emancipation Proclamation was Appomattox; thereby, alternatives forbidden by *Dred Scott,* by the 1861 Crittenden Compromise, and by the aborted Thirteenth Amendment of 1861, became options. This society could be slaveless, biracial, and more decently equal in the constitutions, laws, and customs of the nation and the states.

Bibliography

BELZ, HERMAN 1978 *Emancipation and Equal Rights: Politics and Constitutionalism in the Civil War Era.* New York: Norton.

HYMAN, HAROLD M. and WIECEK, WILLIAM M. 1982 *Equal Justice under Law: Constitutional Development 1835–1875.* Pages 252–255. New York: Harper & Row.

OATES, STEPHEN B. 1977 *With Malice Toward None: The Life of Abraham Lincoln.* New York: Harper & Row.

VOEGELI, V. JACQUES 1967 *Free But Not Equal: The Midwest and the Negro During the Civil War.* Chicago: University of Chicago Press.

# THIRTEENTH AMENDMENT

## (Framing)

### Harold M. Hyman

Scholars and jurists have virtually ignored the Thirteenth Amendment, the Constitution's first formal addition in sixty-one years. Reasons for this indifference seem, initially, to be both obvious and adequate. The Thirteenth Amendment, ratified in December 1865, appears to be a simple, brief statement of the noble, limited effect of the Civil War.

Its succinct text, written by Illinois Senator LYMAN TRUMBULL, echoed clauses of the NORTHWEST ORDINANCE. In the Civil War's last weeks, during the closing session of the 38th Congress, Senator CHARLES SUMNER tried to substitute for the proposed Amendment's second section one specifying that every person was equal before both national and state laws. Trumbull, a constitutional specialist, favored section 2 in its present form. Sumner and many other congressmen assumed that all parts of the Constitution, including amendments, implicitly authorized enforcement; Trumbull wished to have the amendment empower enforcement explicitly. There was almost no other discussion on the amendment. In a sense, abolition had been before the congressmen and the nation since 1861.

Persons who celebrated abolition's arrival in 1865 did not foresee that race problems and derivative strains in federal relations were to require a FOURTEENTH and a FIFTEENTH AMENDMENT plus enforcement legislation, and would lead to the first IMPEACHMENT of a President. Celebrants of 1865 stressed the "war-gulf" that separated the ratified Thirteenth Amendment from one in early 1861 that Congress had proposed and three states had ratified in a desperate effort to seduce the South from seceding. The aborted Thirteenth Amendment would have forbidden the nation perpetually from curtailing slavery in states where it existed. Thereafter the nation steadily raised both its sense of self-interest and its moral sights. Union troops in the South reported that the only trustworthy residents were black. Though few Negroes lived outside the South, most Northern states had long been racist in laws and customs, if never so fiercely as in the slave states. During the war Northern racism softened, partially as a result of pro-Negro reports from Union soldiers and partly from the diffusion of ABOLITIONIST CON-

STITUTIONAL THEORY. Before the war, abolitionists, long hard-pressed even in the North, had come to scorn the Constitution, for it did not protect them against unpunished harassments. But once the war started, Union and abolition became identified. Gradually, Congress and ABRAHAM LINCOLN caught up to Union soldiers' needs, constituents' altering race sentiments, and abolitionists' aspirations and perceptions.

In 1861 and 1862, CONFISCATION ACTS threatened disloyal individuals with the loss of their title to property, including slaves, after individual prosecutions in federal courts. In September 1862, Lincoln's EMANCIPATION PROCLAMATION, an executive, war-power order, offered slaveowners ninety days in which to give up the rebellion or lose their slaves. That grace period having expired, Lincoln in January 1863 ordered also the recruitment of Negroes, most of whom lived in the South, into the Union's armies. In December 1863 and July 1864 respectively, Reconstruction policies issued by the President and the Congress provided for emancipation as a prerequisite for state restorations. The fall 1864 election proved the growth of a Northern consensus in favor of irreversible emancipation as a war result, though, save for abolitionists, it had not been an original war aim. Therefore the 38th Congress, with Lincoln's warm support, prepared the present Thirteenth Amendment, and when the war ended it sent it to the states for ratification.

Despite its simplicity, the Thirteenth Amendment was a momentous, perhaps revolutionary change in constitutional relationships. It prohibited not only the national or state governments or officials but every American institution and person from allowing slavery or involuntary servitude to exist, and it specifically authorized Congress to enforce the prohibition. If states, the traditional parents of slavery, did not comply with the prohibition and allowed individuals to hold other people in a slave status, the nation now had authority to punish directly either the oppressing persons or the states.

Democrats strongly opposed ratification. Even before the Civil War, most Democrats rejected a view of the Constitution as an adaptable, organic instrument. The amendment's enforcement clause allowed Congress to initiate changes in race relationships beyond abolition. Some Democrats insisted that abolition was illicit even by means of an amendment; that slave property remained totally a state's right to define; and that the unrepresented Southern states could not properly be asked to ratify the amendment.

Republicans argued for the amendment's ratification, in part because Lincoln's Emancipation Proclamation might have left slavery alive in the unseceded border states and in some Confederate areas earlier reconquered. It was clear also that individual confiscation trials could never reach the millions of slaveholders and slaves. Republicans also worried because the amendment voided the Constitution's THREE-FIFTHS CLAUSE.

The South's Negroes were now to count as whole persons in determining the size of a state's congressional representation. Ironically, the South, after initiating and carrying on a civil war for four years, would substantially increase its strength in the House of Representatives. "Radical" Republicans looked at the Thirteenth Amendment as the culmination of abolitionist constitutional theory. Radicals asserted that the amendment, freeing slaves, also equalized all Americans in the protections due to them in their states for the exercise of both public and private rights. The DECLARATION OF INDEPENDENCE and the BILL OF RIGHTS defined the duties all states owed to every resident; the nation's duty was to see to state performance. State justice, down to the remotest hamlet, must protect every resident equally against hurtful positive acts or discriminatory nonacts by public officers and private persons, in both civil and criminal relationships.

No Republicans advocated centralization; all Republicans were STATES' RIGHTS nationalists. State sovereignty was dead but state rights flourished. State wrongs that diminished individuals' rights as defined by state laws, were, however, unacceptable; they again threatened the nation's stability. Republicans assumed that the ex-rebel states would emulate, in their formal law at least, the lessened racism of the rest of the nation, and afford Negroes the same protections that whites enjoyed. But it became apparent from evidence such as the BLACK CODES that the South would not behave as expected.

All through 1865, Democrats criticized the fact that President ANDREW JOHNSON required the reconstructing states to ratify the Thirteenth Amendment, and they insisted that those states were entitled to be represented in Congress. The Johnson provisional states, excepting Florida and Texas where reconstruction proceeded slowly, did ratify the Thirteenth Amendment, though reluctantly, with spokesmen expressing special distaste for the enforcement clause. Johnson pressured recalcitrant states with threats of indefinite military rule if ratification failed; Secretary of State WILLIAM SEWARD calmed Southerners by asserting that the amendment restricted Congress to enforcing only a prohibition of formal slavery, a dubious interpretation. On December 15, 1865, Seward proclaimed the amendment to be in effect. Were the southern states truly states for the purposes of ratification? The question asked in 1865 and again in 1868 and 1870 when the Fourteenth and Fifteenth Amendments were ratified, and repeated endlessly since, has a metaphysical quality. Ratification was a mandate to the nation by a clear majority of the American people, not an act of the national government. Lincoln's insight that the South's states were still states, although out of their proper relationship to the Union of states, neither supported immediate restorations of those states nor diminished their capacities to perform certain state functions including ratification of amendments. In 1865 the southern states ratified in number beyond the Constitution's requirement (Article V) that three-fourths of the states approve an amendment. Additional states ratified subsequently to end all doubts as to the amendment's validity. But in 1865, those doubts existed and enhanced the doubts that Democrats spread, and Republicans also felt, about President Johnson's unlimited authority over the South.

The 39th Congress assembled in December 1865 for its first postwar session. Its Republican members, upon examination of the Black Codes and other evidence from the South of lingering vestiges of servitude, resorted immediately to the just-ratified Thirteenth Amendment's enforcement clause. Sharing a mobile, organic view of the Constitution, Republicans were ready to confirm that the nation had an interest in and a duty to personal equality in states, as defined by state law and customs; their readiness is evident in the quick formulation of the CIVIL RIGHTS BILL (the world's first), the second FREEDMAN'S BUREAU BILL, and the Fourteenth Amendment. Republicans created these measures in light of the Thirteenth Amendment, a far more complex and inclusive statement than most accounts suggest.

Bibliography

BUCHANAN, SIDNEY G.   1976   *The Quest for Freedom: A Legal History of the Thirteenth Amendment.*   Houston: Reprint from *Houston Law Review.*

HOWE, MARK A. DEWOLFE   1965   Federalism and Civil Rights. [Massachusetts Historical Society] *Proceedings* 77:15–67.

HYMAN, HAROLD M. and WIECEK, WILLIAM M.   1982   *Equal Justice under Law: Constitutional Development 1835–1875.*   Chaps. 10–11. New York. Harper & Row.

TEN BROEK, JACOBUS   1951   *The Antislavery Origins of the Fourteenth Amendment.*   Chap. 13. Berkeley: University of California Press.

# THIRTEENTH AMENDMENT

## (Judicial Interpretation)

### Kenneth L. Karst

Ratification of the Thirteenth Amendment in 1865 not only diminished the urgency of the debate over the constitutionality of the EMANCIPATION PROCLAMATION but also wrote a new substantive value into the Constitution. The amendent's first section abolished slavery and involuntary servitude throughout the nation, and its second section empowered Congress to enforce abolition. If any of the amendment's framers expected it to end the system of racial dominance and dependence, they were soon divested of that illusion. The persistence of a plantation economy and the adoption in southern states of the BLACK CODES kept blacks in a position of subordination that was not only economic but political and social as well.

The question thus arose whether section 2 of the Thirteenth Amendment gave Congress the power to do more than provide sanctions against slavery or involuntary servitude, narrowly defined. Over a presidential veto, Congress adopted the CIVIL RIGHTS ACT OF 1866, which not only declared the CITIZENSHIP of the freed slaves but also protected them against the sort of RACIAL DISCRIMINATION that had been embodied in the Black Codes, such as disqualification to own property, to make contracts, or to serve on juries. President ANDREW JOHNSON had explained his veto of the bill partly on the ground that the Thirteenth Amendment had not empowered Congress to adopt legislation aimed at such purposes. Reacting to this argument, Congress proposed the FOURTEENTH AMENDMENT as a means of assuring the validity of the 1866 Act and placing beyond doubt the power of Congress to enforce the CIVIL RIGHTS of the freed slaves.

From the beginning it was arguable that the abolition of slavery implied that the persons so freed would take on the status of free citizens—that the amendment should be read broadly as a response to the whole social system of racial subordination associated with slavery. But in the early years, this view did not prosper in the Supreme Court; it was found mainly in OBITER DICTA and in dissenting opinions. All agreed that section 1 of the amendment was self-executing: slavery and involuntary servitude were abolished, whether or not Congress enacted civil or criminal sanctions to enforce the abolition. Because the amendment contained no STATE ACTION limitation, it operated directly, of its own force, against either public or private conduct that imposed slavery. But the Court limited the notion of "involuntary servitude" to personal servitude, refusing to extend it (by analogy to feudal servitudes) to cover the granting of monopolies or other similar privileges. (See SLAUGHTER-HOUSE CASES, 1873). By the end of the nineteenth century, the Court was saying that slavery implied no more than "a state of bondage," and the lack of "a legal right to the disposal of [one's] own person, property, and services"; thus the Thirteenth Amendent standing alone did not even forbid a state to impose racial segregation on seating in railroad cars. (See PLESSY V. FERGUSON, 1896.)

This narrow view of the Thirteenth Amendment's self-executing reach was reflected in the Supreme Court's treatment of the power granted to Congress by section 2. In the CIVIL RIGHTS CASES (1883) the Court, in the face of a powerful dissenting opinion by Justice JOHN MARSHALL HARLAN, held invalid the CIVIL RIGHTS ACT OF 1875, a congressional statute forbidding racial discrimination in such PUBLIC ACCOMMODATIONS as hotels, theaters, and railroads. Both the majority and the dissent agreed that the Thirteenth Amendment was designed to put an end to the "incidents" of slavery as well as slavery itself. The question was whether racially based refusals of access to public accommodations amounted to "badges of slavery and servitude," and the majority held that they did not. This severely restrictive interpretation of the power of Congress to enforce the Thirteenth Amendment culminated in 1906, when the Court decided HODGES V. UNITED STATES. Congress could prohibit no more than the "entire subjection" of one person to another, as in laws forbidding PEONAGE; Congress was not empowered by section 2 to go further in erasing "badges" or "incidents" of slavery.

So matters stood for six decades. The Thirteenth Amendment, like the Fourteenth Amendment's guarantee of the EQUAL PROTECTION OF THE LAWS, lay dormant, offering no effective protection against racial discrimination. The judicial interpretation of the Thirteenth Amendment mirrored the nation's political history; Congress adopted no civil rights legislation from the time of Reconstruction to the late 1950s. The first modern civil rights law of major importance was the CIVIL RIGHTS ACT OF 1964; its public accommodations provisions were upheld by the Supreme Court, but on the basis of the COMMERCE CLAUSE, not the Thirteenth or Fourteenth Amendments. (See HEART OF ATLANTA MOTEL V. UNITED STATES, 1964; *Katzenbach v. McClung,* 1964.) The Court seemed determined to uphold congressional legislation aimed at establishing racial equality, and in UNITED STATES V. GUEST (1966) six Justices agreed in two separate opinions that Congress could reach even private conduct that interfered with the exercise of Fourteenth Amendment rights. The state action limitation, in other words, would not bar congressional enforcement of the equal protection clause of the Fourteenth Amendment's prohibition on private discrimination.

The reach of the equal protection clause, of course, is not limited to racial inequalities. Perhaps some of the Justices were reluctant to pursue the line of doctrinal development suggested by the separate opinions in *Guest,* for fear of giving Congress an invitation without apparent limitation. The solution to this puzzle—if it was a puzzle—came only two years after the *Guest* decision, in the form of a complete turnabout in the interpretation of the power of Congress to enforce the Thirteenth Amendment.

The turnabout came in JONES v. ALFRED H. MAYER CO. (1968), when the Court interpreted the 1866 Civil Rights Act to prohibit all racial discrimination in the sale of property and upheld the act as so construed. The Court overruled the *Hodges* decision and essentially adopted the dissenting views of Justice Harlan in the *Civil Rights Cases.* The Thirteenth Amendment was held to empower Congress not only to eliminate slavery but also to eliminate slavery's "badges and incidents." Furthermore, said the Court, it is for Congress itself "rationally to determine what are the badges and incidents of slavery," and to enact laws to eradicate any such "relic of slavery" it might find.

This broad language is not limited to racial discrimination. Commentators have asked whether the Court, in seeking to avoid an open-ended interpretation of congressional power under the Fourteenth Amendment, has offered Congress a different set of constitutional bootstraps. In the quoted passage from the *Jones* opinion, the Court appears to authorize Congress to define a given right—any right—as one that is essential to freedom, to define its impairment as an incident of slavery, and to enact a law protecting the right against both public and private interference.

When the right in question is a right to be free from racial discrimination, this line of reasoning accords not only with the language of the *Jones* opinion but also with the decision's place in the historical process of constitutional validation of modern civil rights legislation. Outside the racial context, however, the reasoning is unlikely to be adopted by the Supreme Court. Of course the Thirteenth Amendment prohibits the enslavement of anyone, of any race. And the Court has upheld an application of the 1866 act to a case of racial discrimination against whites, evidently (but without discussion) on the basis of Congress's power to enforce the Thirteenth Amendment, in *McDonald v. Santa Fe Trail Transportation Co.* (1976). The decision is defensible, despite the lack of historic links between slavery and discrimination against whites. There is a basis in experience for a congressional conclusion that discrimination against one racial group affects attitudes toward race generally and promotes discrimination against other races. It would be much harder to justify a similar conclusion about the effects of discrimination on the basis of gender, or sexual preference, or physical handicap. Even if the analogy were stronger, the doctrinal context of the *Jones* decision cautions against a prediction that its "badges and incidents" reasoning will be extended beyond cases of racial discrimination. The Thirteenth Amendment seems to have had its main appeal as a basis for congressional power precisely because that power could be contained within the confines of remedies for racial discrimination. The "badges and incidents of slavery" which justify congressional intervention are to be found in racial discrimination if they are to be found at all.

The power of Congress to enforce the Thirteenth Amendment, like any other congressional power, is subject to the limitations of the BILL OF RIGHTS. Without question, the amendment empowers Congress to prohibit racial discrimination in all the public areas of life, including commercial dealings. In RUNYON v. McCRARY (1976), for example, the Supreme Court relied on the Thirteenth Amendment to uphold application of the 1866 act to a private school that accepted applicants from children in the public at large but excluded blacks. The potential limitations of the Bill of Rights found expression in that case. Justice LEWIS F. POWELL, concurring, cautioned that some hypothetical congressional enforcements of the Thirteenth Amendment might violate constitutional rights of PRIVACY or associational freedom, as when a litigant might seek application of the 1866 act to a case of racial discrimination in the selection of a home tutor or babysitter.

The expansion of the power of Congress to enforce the Thirteenth Amendment has not been accompanied by a corresponding expansion of the amendment's reach as a self-executing provision. The *Jones* opinion left open the question whether the amendment "by its own terms did anything more than abolish slavery," and although MEMPHIS v. GREENE (1981) raised the issue, the Court did not reach it. Thus, even though a great many forms of private racial discrimination may constitute "badges and incidents of slavery" justifying congressional action to secure their elimination, if Congress has not acted, these same "badges and incidents" are insufficient to trigger the operation of the amendment's section 1. The practical significance of this difference, however, is slight. The Supreme Court has construed existing civil rights legislation broadly enough to prohibit a wide range of private acts of racial discrimination.

Even assuming that the Thirteenth Amendment's self-executing force is limited to cases of bondage to personal service, there is room for debate about the kinds of compulsion that constitute involuntary servitude. Debt bondage—the requirement that a person work in discharge of a debt—is a classic case of peonage and is plainly forbidden by the amendment. However, compulsory military service (or alternative service for CONSCIENTIOUS OBJECTORS), hard labor for persons imprisoned for crime, and restrictions on the right to strike all have been sustained against Thirteenth Amendment attacks.

Bibliography

CASPER, GERHARD    1968    Jones v. Mayer: Clio, Bemused and Confused Muse. *Supreme Court Review* 1968:89–132.

FAIRMAN, CHARLES    1971    *Reconstruction and Reunion: 1864–1888, Part One.* Chapter XIX. New York: Macmillan Company.

NOTE 1969 The "New" Thirteenth Amendment: A Preliminary Analysis. *Harvard Law Review* 82:1294–1321.

# BLACK CODES

## William M. Wiecek

In 1865–1866, the former slave states enacted statutes, collectively known as the "Black Codes," regulating the legal and constitutional status of black people. The Black Codes attempted to accomplish two objectives: (1) to enumerate the legal rights essential to the status of freedom of blacks; and (2) to provide a special criminal code for blacks. The latter objective reflected the two purposes of the antebellum law of slavery: race control and labor discipline.

In the view of white Southerners, emancipation did not of its own force create a civil status or capacity for freedmen. The southern state legislatures accordingly specified the incidents of this free status: the right to buy, sell, own, and bequeath property; the right to make contracts; the right to contract valid marriages, including so-called common-law marriages, and to enjoy a legally recognized parent–child relationship; the right to locomotion and personal liberty; the right to sue and be sued, and to testify in court, but only in cases involving black parties.

But the Codes also reenacted elements of the law of slavery. They provided detailed lists of civil disabilities by recreating the race-control features of the slave codes. They defined racial status; forbade blacks from pursuing certain occupations or professions; prohibited blacks from owning firearms or other weapons; controlled the movement of blacks by systems of passes; required proof of residence; prohibited the congregation of groups of blacks; restricted blacks from residing in certain areas; and specified an etiquette of deference to whites, such as by prohibiting blacks from directing insulting words at whites. The Codes forbade racial intermarriage and provided the death penalty for blacks raping white women, while omitting special provisions for whites raping black women. (See MISCEGENATION.) They excluded blacks from jury duty, public office, and voting. Some Black Codes required racial SEGREGATION in public transportation or created Jim Crow schools. Most Codes authorized whipping and the pillory as punishment for freedmen's offenses.

The Codes salvaged the labor-discipline elements of slave law in master-and-servant statutes, VAGRANCY and pauper provisions, apprenticeship regulations, and elaborate labor contract statutes, especially those pertaining to farm labor. Other provisions permitted magistrates to hire out offenders unable to pay fines. These statutes provided a basis for subsequent efforts, extending well into the twentieth century, to provide a legal and paralegal structure forcing blacks to work, restricting their occupational mobility, and providing harsh systems of forced black labor, sometimes verging on PEONAGE.

The Black Codes profoundly offended the northern ideal of equality before the law. Northerners lost whatever sympathies they might have entertained for the plight of southern whites trying to make the revolutionary transition from a slave society, based on a legal regime of status, to a free, capitalist society based on will and contract. Northerners determined to force the former slave states to create new structures of racial equality. Consequently, the Black Codes were repealed or left unenforced during the congressional phase of Reconstruction. Later Redeemer and Conservative state legislatures reenacted the Jim Crow provisions and labor contract statutes to provide the statutory component of the twilight zone of semifreedom that characterized the legal status of southern blacks through World War I.

Bibliography

WILSON, THEODORE B.    1965    *The Black Codes of the South*.  University: University of Alabama Press.

# CIVIL RIGHTS ACT OF 1866

(Framing)
14 Stat. 27

Harold M. Hyman

Responding to the Black Codes, Congress in 1866 passed its first CIVIL RIGHTS bill to enforce the THIRTEENTH AMENDMENT. The bill's definition of national CITIZENSHIP superseded the decision in DRED SCOTT V. SANDFORD (1857), which had excluded blacks. A citizen was any person not an Indian or of foreign allegiance born in any state or territory, regardless of color. All citizens were to enjoy full and EQUAL PROTECTION of all laws and procedures for the protection of persons and property, and be subject to like punishments without regard to former slave status. In all jurisdictions citizens were to have equal rights to sue, contract, witness, purchase, lease, sell, inherit, or otherwise convey personal or real property. Anyone who, "under color of any law . . . or custom," prevented any person from enjoying those rights, or who subjected any person to discriminatory criminal punishments because of race or previous involuntary servitude, was subject to MISDEMEANOR prosecutions in federal courts. Congress further authorized the REMOVAL OF CASES from state to federal courts of persons denied civil rights and of federal officer defendants, prosecuted by states, protecting civil rights; that provision connected the civil rights bill to the FREEDMEN'S BUREAU and the HABEAS CORPUS statutes. All federal officials could initiate proceedings under the bill. Federal judges were to appoint special commissioners to enforce judgments under the bill (a use of fugitive slave law processes for opposite purposes). Alternatively, judges could employ the army or state militias, under the President's command, as posses. Last, Congress expanded the Supreme Court's APPELLATE JURISDICTION to include questions of law arising from the statute.

President ANDREW JOHNSON's powerful veto of the Civil Rights Bill, though overridden by Congress, touched both honorable traditions of the states' monopoly of rights and ignoble concepts of race hierarchy. He insisted that the bill would create a centralized military despotism and invoked the recent EX PARTE MILLIGAN (1866) decision. Congress, he argued, was creating black citizens of the same states it was excluding from representation.

Though trenchant, the veto never touched on the question of the remedies available to injured citizens or the nation, when states failed to carry out their duty to treat their own citizens equally. If no statutory remedies existed, then both nation and states were returned to the conditions of 1860. Anxious to make clear the fact of the nation's advance from that pitiable condition, the Congress pushed ahead with a FOURTEENTH AMENDMENT proposal and, in 1867, resorted to military reconstruction as a desperate stop-gap.

But the Fourteenth Amendment, unlike the Thirteenth (which the Civil Rights Act enforced) constrained only STATE ACTION, at least according to Supreme Court judgments commencing with the *Slaughterhouse* case (1873). In May 1870, the Congress "re-enacted" the 1866 Civil Rights law, this time under the Fourteenth and FIFTEENTH AMENDMENTS (though section 16 of the 1870 law still punished discriminatory felonious private acts). In 1874, a revision of the federal statutes appeared, breaking up the text of the 1866 statute into scattered sections.

Bibliography

HOWE, M. A. DEWOLFE  1965  Federalism and Civil Rights. [Massachusetts Historical Society] *Proceedings* 77:15–27.

HYMAN, HAROLD M. and WIECEK, WILLIAM M. 1982  *Equal Justice under Law: Constitutional Development 1835–1875.* Chaps. 9–11. New York: Harper & Row.

KACZOROWSKI, ROBERT J.  1971  Nationalization of Civil Rights: Theory and Practice in a Racist Society, 1866–1883. Ph.D. diss., University of Minnesota.

# CIVIL RIGHTS ACT OF 1866

## (Judicial Interpretation)

### Theodore Eisenberg

Judicial interpretation has transformed the Civil Rights Act of 1866 from a simple effort to dismantle the BLACK CODES into one of the most important existing CIVIL RIGHTS laws. In assessing judicial treatment of the act, it is helpful to consider section one of the act separately from section three. Other sections have not led to noteworthy judicial development. Section one of the act, which granted all persons the same rights as white persons to make and enforce contracts, sue, be parties, give EVIDENCE, inherit, purchase, lease, sell, hold, and convey real and personal property, and to the full and equal benefit of all laws and proceedings for the security of person and property, was reenacted in modified form by the Civil Rights Act of 1870, was divided into two sections by the REVISED STATUTES OF 1874, and survives as sections 1981 and 1982 of Title 42, United States Code. Section three of the act, which set forth the procedures for vindicating rights protected by section one, was scattered throughout the United States Code. Portions of it survive as CIVIL RIGHTS REMOVAL statutes and as part of section 1988 of Title 42. Judicial interpretation of the 1866 act is not unrelated to these statutory reshufflings. Cut adrift from their moorings in the entire 1866 act, the act's remnants are amenable to many more interpretations than the original provision.

Cases decided in the years immediately following the 1866 act's passage are particularly important in ascertaining its original meaning. The REVISED STATUTES of 1874 would strip the act's descendants of any close resemblance to the original measure. And once the courts became accustomed to applying the FOURTEENTH AMENDMENT, much of the 1866 act would become superfluous. In addition, ratification of the Fourteenth Amendment eliminated most doubts about the act's constitutionality.

Prior to ratification of the Fourteenth Amendment, most courts were willing to sustain the act under Congress's THIRTEENTH AMENDMENT power to proscribe SLAVERY. But at least Kentucky's highest court in *Bowlin v. Commonwealth* (1867) declared the act unconstitutional. Other courts avoided such a declaration only by interpreting the act not to prohibit some forms of RACIAL DISCRIMINATION that the act's words arguably covered.

In the reported interpretations of the act, for example, courts divided over whether states could continue to outlaw marriages between whites and blacks. State courts in Tennessee (1871), Indiana (1871), and Alabama (1878) found marriage not to be a contract within the meaning of section 1, and therefore rejected attacks on antimiscegenation laws that relied on the 1866 act. State courts in Louisiana (1874) and Alabama (1872) relied at least in part on the 1866 act to find intermarriage legal, but the Alabama case was soon overruled. Not until LOVING v. VIRGINIA (1967) did the Supreme Court hold the Fourteenth Amendment to ban antimiscegenation laws.

State courts also divided over whether the 1866 act abrogated state laws prohibiting blacks from testifying against whites. The Kentucky court found Congress's effort to do so unconstitutional, but an 1869 Arkansas decision found the act to authorize such testimony. In 1869, the California Supreme Court relied on the 1866 act's evidentiary provision to dismiss an INDICTMENT against a mulatto, because Chinese witnesses had testified at his trial and state law prohibited them from testifying against white men. But a year later, despite the 1866 act, the California court sustained the state's evidentiary ban on testimony by Chinese against whites.

After the 1870s, section 1 diminished in importance. The state laws against which it most successfully operated, laws mandating racial discrimination in areas covered by section 1, could also be attacked directly under the Fourteenth Amendment. And with section 1 and the Fourteenth Amendment undermining the most egregious provisions of the Black Codes, there remained only one important area to which section 1 might be applied—private discrimination. When the CIVIL RIGHTS CASES (1883), UNITED STATES v. HARRIS (1883), and UNITED STATES v. CRUIKSHANK (1876) limited Congress's Thirteenth and Fourteenth Amendment power to legislate against private racial discrimination, there was doubt about whether section 1 constitutionally could be applied to private discrimination. One early lower federal court opinion, *United States v. Morris* (1903), suggested the 1866 act's applicability to private discrimination, but Supreme Court statements in *Virginia v. Rives* (1880) and CORRIGAN v. BUCKLEY (1926) suggested that the act did not apply to private conduct. (See STRAUDER v. WEST VIRGINIA, 1880.)

*Hurd v. Hodge* (1948), a companion case to SHELLEY v. KRAEMER (1948), gave section 1 some new life. The court applied section 1 to prohibit courts in the DISTRICT OF COLUMBIA from enforcing a racially RESTRICTIVE COVENANT. The breakthrough came in JONES v. ALFRED H. MAYER CO. (1968), where the Court held both that Congress meant the 1866 act to proscribe private discrimination and that Congress constitutionally could outlaw private discrimination under the Thirteenth Amendment. As the result of *Jones, Johnson v. Railway Express Co.* (1974), and RUNYON V. MCCRARY (1976), the remnants of the 1866 act were transformed from historical relics into federal laws broadly prohibiting private racial discrimination in the sale or lease of all housing, in schools, in employment and in virtually all other contracts. In many respects the 1866 act's newly discovered coverage exceeds that of comprehensive modern civil rights laws. *General Building Constructors Association, Inc. v. Pennsylvania* (1982) limited the 1866 act's reach by holding that liability may not be imposed under the act without proof of intentional discrimination.

Section 3 of the 1866 act traveled a less visible path through the courts. Its primary significance has been to determine when a violation of former section 1 authorizes an original or removal action in federal court. (See REMOVAL OF CASES.) In *Blyew v. United States* (1872), over the dissents of Justices JOSEPH P. BRADLEY and NOAH SWAYNE, the Court held that Kentucky's testimonial disqualification of black witnesses did not confer ORIGINAL JURISDICTION on a lower federal court to hear a state murder case at which the black witnesses were to testify. In a series of civil rights removal cases, the Court held that what had been section 3 authorized removal to federal court where state laws expressly mandated a racial distinction that prevented blacks from receiving equal justice, as when blacks were excluded from juries. But the Court found removal not to be authorized where the same result was achieved through other than formal state statutory command.

Under section 3's remnants, actions that arise under state law but are removed to federal court are tried in federal court by applying state law. In *Robertson v. Wegmann* (1978), however, the Court misconstrued the shred of the 1866 act commanding this result to require application of state law to cases arising under *federal* law. The same remnant, section 1988, also has been relied on in *Sullivan v. Little Hunting Park, Inc.* (1969) to authorize damages for violations of section 1 rights and in *Tomanio v. Board of Regents* (1980) to require the use of state statutes of limitations in federal civil rights cases.

Bibliography

BARDOLPH, RICHARD 1970 *The Civil Rights Record.* Pages 84–87, 94–96, 200–201, 532–533. New York: Thomas Y. Crowell.

CARR, ROBERT K. 1947 *Federal Protection of Civil Rights.* Ithaca, N.Y.: Cornell University Press.

EISENBERG, THEODORE 1981 *Civil Rights Legislation.* Charlottesville, Va.: Michie Co.

# FOURTEENTH AMENDMENT

## (Framing)

### William E. Nelson

The Fourteenth Amendment to the United States Constitution consists of a variety of provisions addressed to several problems that arose when the Civil War and the abolition of slavery transformed the American political order. One sentence—"No State shall make or enforce any law which shall abridge the PRIVILEGES OR IMMUNITIES of citizens of the United States; nor shall any State deprive any person of life, liberty, or property without DUE PROCESS OF LAW; nor deny to any person within its jurisdiction the EQUAL PROTECTION OF THE LAWS"—has become the text upon which most twentieth-century constitutional law is a gloss. But this sentence may not have been the most important part of the amendment as it was conceived by its framers, adopted by Congress, and ratified by the states between 1865 and 1868.

The sentence was addressed most pointedly to one of the lesser problems that Congress faced in the winter of 1865–1866. During that winter congressional legislation protecting the CIVIL RIGHTS of former slaves had been vetoed by President ANDREW JOHNSON in part, he contended, because the Constitution entrusted the protection of civil rights to the states. The Republican proponents of the CIVIL RIGHTS ACT OF 1866 mustered the necessary two-thirds vote to override the veto, but doubt remained about the power of the federal government to protect civil rights. The quoted sentence in section 1 of the Fourteenth Amendment was written, at least in part, to resolve that doubt.

Another concern of some Northerners in the winter of 1865–1866 was that some future Congress might repudiate the debt that the federal government had amassed during the Civil War or might undertake to pay the Confederate debt or compensate former slaveholders for the loss of their slaves. Section 4 of the amendment guaranteed the national debt, prohibited the payment of the Confederate debt, and barred compensation to slaveholders.

However, the most urgent task that the Thirty-ninth Congress confronted when it began its first session in December 1865 was to establish governments in the South that would be loyal to the Union and send loyal representatives to Congress. The problem was compounded by the ratification of the THIRTEENTH AMENDMENT, which not only abolished slavery but also put an end to the original Constitution's THREE-FIFTHS CLAUSE. With the abolition of slavery, the former slaves would be fully counted as part of the population of the former Confederate states; as a result those states would have more power in Congress and the ELEC-TORAL COLLEGE than they had had before the Civil War. Something had to be done to insure that the war did not increase the political power of the disloyal groups that had brought the war about.

Three solutions were advanced to prevent those who had lost the Civil War from enhancing their power as a result of it. One was to confer the franchise on Southern blacks, whose votes were expected to bring about the election of loyal candidates. A second solution was to deny political rights—both the right to vote and the right to hold office—to some or all who had participated in the rebellion against national authority. This scheme would increase the number of districts in which Union loyalists had a majority or at least some power to tip the electoral balance in favor of loyal candidates.

A third solution was to alter the basis of representation: to base a state's number of representatives in the House and hence its votes in the Electoral College not on total population but on the number of people eligible to vote. Thus, if a state excluded blacks from the right to vote, they would not be counted in determining its representation in Congress and its vote in the Electoral College. Thus the abolition of slavery and the end of the three-fifths compromise would reduce South-ern political power in Congress unless Southern states gave blacks the right to vote and hence a share in that power.

The JOINT COMMITTEE ON RECONSTRUCTION, established by CONCUR-RENT RESOLUTIONS of the House and Senate in the opening days of the Congress, sought to put the possible solutions into some sort of order. Four members of this fifteen-man committee were most prominent in its activities: JOHN A. BINGHAM and THADDEUS STEVENS from the House and WILLIAM PITT FESSENDEN and JACOB M. HOWARD from the Senate.

At the third meeting of the Joint Committee on January 12, 1866, Bingham proposed a constitutional amendment that would give Congress "power to make all laws necessary and proper to secure to all persons in every State within this Union equal protection in their rights of life, liberty and property." The proposal was referred to a subcommittee which eight days later returned it to the Joint Committee in the following form: "Congress shall have power to make all laws necessary and proper to secure to all citizens of the United States, in every State, the same political rights and privileges; and to all persons in every State equal protection in the enjoyment of life, liberty, and property." In this form the proposal addressed two of the problems then pending, because it gave Congress power to protect civil rights and to legislate VOTING RIGHTS for blacks. This proposal, however, was never presented to Congress. The committee spent two weeks debating its language, finally agreeing on February 3 to the following: "The Congress shall have power to make all laws which shall be necessary and proper to secure to citizens of each State all privileges and immunities of citizens in the several States [Art. IV, Sec. 2]; and to all persons in the several States equal protection in the rights of life, liberty and property [5th Amendment]." A key issue that subsequent judges and scholars have long debated is whether this change in language was meant to deprive Congress of power to legislate black suffrage or merely to put that power into more acceptable language.

On the same day that the subcommittee submitted the early version of the amendment to the Joint Committee, it also submitted a proposal basing representation on population, but further providing "[t]hat whenever the elective franchise shall be denied or abridged in any State on account of race or color, all persons of such race or color shall be excluded from the basis of representation." Thus, the total package as of January 20 not only gave Congress power to legislate civil rights and black suffrage—power which Congress might or might not exercise—but also deprived a state of representation based on its black population if blacks were not given suffrage either by Congress or by the state. The package, as altered by the language change of February 3, was submitted to the full House as two separate constitutional amendments.

On February 28, the House postponed consideration of the Bingham amendment conferring legislative power on Congress, and never again considered that amendment as a separate entity. Earlier it had passed and sent to the Senate the amendment depriving states of representation if blacks were denied the right to vote. The Senate, however, never acted on the proposal. Thus, by the end of February 1866, the two forerunners of the Fourteenth Amendment had come to nought.

Both reappeared in slightly different language, however, in the omnibus measure which the Joint Committee presented to both houses of Congress on April 30, 1866. Section 1 of the measure was the sentence containing today's privilege and immunities, due process, and equal clauses, while section 2 reduced the representation of states who denied the right to vote to males over the age of twenty-one. Section 3 deprived all persons who had voluntarily supported the Confederate cause of the right to vote in federal elections prior to 1870, while section 4 dealt with the war debt. Section 5 gave Congress power to enforce the other four sections.

The omnibus amendment passed the House as proposed, but it faced difficulties in the Senate. When it emerged from the Senate on

June 8, it had been changed in two significant respects. One of the changes added to section 1 a definition of CITIZENSHIP. The Senate also weakened section 3; instead of disfranchising those who had supported the Confederacy, it merely barred from federal office those Confederate supporters who prior to the Civil War had taken an oath to support the Constitution.

After the House had concurred on June 13 in the Senate's changes, the amendment was sent to the states. Twelve days later, on June 25, Connecticut became the first state to ratify. Five additional states ratified the amendment in 1866, and eleven added their RATIFICATIONS in January 1867. By June of 1867, one year after the amendment had been sent to the states, a total of twenty-two had ratified it.

Ratification by six more states was needed, however, and that did not occur until July 1868. By that time two of the states that had previously ratified the amendment, New Jersey and Ohio, had voted to withdraw their assent. Nonetheless Congress ruled that their ratifications survived the subsequent efforts at withdrawal and remained valid. On July 28, 1868, Secretary of State WILLIAM SEWARD accordingly proclaimed the Fourteenth Amendment part of the Constitution of the United States.

In recent decades, historians and judges have extensively debated three questions about the meaning which the Thirty-Ninth Congress and the ratifying states attached to the Fourteenth Amendment, especially to section 1. First, does section 1 give Congress power to protect voting rights? Second, does section 1 overrule BARRON v. BALTIMORE (1833) and require the states to abide by the provisions of the BILL OF RIGHTS? Third, does section 1 prohibit compulsory racial SEGREGATION?

Did section 1 of the Fourteenth Amendment give Congress power to protect voting rights? The Justices of the Supreme Court have been divided in their answer to this question, although the weight of historical scholarship leans toward the view that section 1 was not concerned with voting rights. As the above summary of the progress of the amendment in Congress suggests, resolution of the issue depends on whether the privileges and immunities language in section 1 was meant to alter the substance or only the form of an earlier version of the section, which explicitly gave Congress power to secure to all citizens in every state "equal political rights and privileges." The question can never be answered definitively, for the substitution was made in committee and the committee left no record of its reasoning. The record of congressional debates is equally ambiguous. When the present language of section 1 was on the floor, some congressmen suggested that the section gave Congress power to protect voting rights, but others disagreed. Similarly, some congressmen claimed after the amendment had been adopted that it gave them power to legislate protection of voting rights—and again others disagreed.

Was section 1 meant to overrule *Barron v. Baltimore* and compel the states to abide by the provisions of the Bill of Rights? Justice HUGO L. BLACK, relying on explicit statements during congressional debates that the section would accomplish that end, declared in a dissenting opinion in ADAMSON v. CALIFORNIA (1947) that the Fourteenth Amendment did incorporate the Bill of Rights and apply it to the states. Some scholars have supported Black's position. However, two years after *Adamson* Charles Fairman wrote an article challenging Black. Fairman noted that many states in the 1860s did not follow procedures mandated by the Bill of Rights, but that no one during state ratification proceedings seemed concerned that adoption of the Fourteenth Amendment would require changes in state practice. He thought it probable that, if the states were concerned that the amendment, through INCORPORATION of the Bill of Rights, would require changes in their practices, they would at least have discussed the issue. He concluded from the lack of discussion that the amendment had no such purpose. The view of several recent scholars has been that, in light of the conflicting and insubstantial evidence, the question raised by Justice Black can never be conclusively answered.

Finally, there is the question whether section 1 was intended to prohibit racial segregation. After asking the litigants in BROWN v. BOARD OF EDUCATION (1954) to address this question, the Court concluded that the historical evidence was too ambiguous to permit an answer. Some scholars, however, have been more confident. Raoul Berger concluded that the framers of the amendment did not intend to prohibit racial segregation. On the other hand, ALEXANDER BICKEL had argued some years earlier that the framers had consciously framed section 1 in broad, open-ended language that would permit people in the future to interpret it as prohibiting the practice of segregation. The historical record itself is sparse. During the debates in Congress on the amendment, little was said about segregation. Earlier, however, Congress had engaged in lengthy debates about the legality of segregation on DISTRICT OF COLUMBIA streetcars. Moreover, school segregation was opposed by some members of Congress, notably CHARLES SUMNER who had been counsel in ROBERTS v. CITY OF BOSTON, an 1849 school desegregation case. In the 1860s, however, Congress was permitting racially segregated schools to exist in the District of Columbia.

Questions about whether the Thirty-Ninth Congress and the states that ratified the Fourteenth Amendment intended it to protect voting rights, make the Bill of Rights binding on the states, or outlaw segregation can never be answered confidently. All that the person who inquires into the historical record in search of an answer can do is make a guess—a guess more likely to reflect his political beliefs than to reflect the state of the historical record. The questions that judges and historians have asked about the original meaning of the Fourteenth Amendment are simply the wrong ones, because they do not address the issues that Congress and the ratifying states in fact debated and decided during the era of Reconstruction.

On one point of political philosophy, nearly all Americans of the 1860s agreed. President Andrew Johnson stated the point in his 1865 State of the Union address: "Monopolies, perpetuities, and class legislation are contrary to the genius of free government, and ought not to be allowed. Here there is no room for favored classes or monopolies; the principle of our Government is that of equal laws. . . . We shall but fulfill our duties as legislators by according 'equal and exact justice to all men,' special privileges to none." Innumerable Republicans argued that the purpose of section 1 of the Fourteenth Amendment was to enact this political principle into law. John A. Bingham, the draftsman of section 1, said what others repeated: that he proposed "by amending the Constitution, to provide for the efficient enforcement, by law, of these 'equal rights of every man' "—of "the absolute equality of all men before the law." Even Democrats from former slave states accepted the principle that the law should treat all persons equally. There was neither division nor sustained debate in the Thirty-Ninth Congress over the contrary principle that people who are in fact the same should receive equal treatment before the law and that people who are different may be treated differently. The issue on which Republicans and Democrats divided was whether black people, in essence, were equal to white people or inherently inferior.

Garrett Davis, a Democratic senator from Kentucky, used typical racist rhetoric. During an 1866 debate on the question whether blacks should be permitted to vote in the District of Columbia, Davis said:

[T]he proposition that a nation of a superior race should allow an inferior race resident in large numbers among them to take part in their Government, in shaping, and controlling their destinies, is refuted by its mere statement. And the further proposition that a nation composed of the Caucasian race, the highest type of man, having resident in it more than four million negroes, the lowest type, of which race no nation or tribe, from the first dawning of history to the present day, has ever established a polity that could be denominated a Government, or has elaborated for itself any science or literature or arts or even an alphabet, or characters to represent numbers, or been capable of preserving those achievements of intellect when it has received them from the superior race; such a proposition is, on examination, revolting to reason, and in its practical operation would be productive of incalculable mischief.

Republicans responded to this "prejudice," which "belong[ed] to an age of darkness and violence, and is a poisonous, dangerous exotic when suffered to grow in the midst of republican institutions." Jacob M. Howard, a key member of the Joint Committee, told the Senate:

For weal or for woe, the destiny of the colored race in this country is wrapped up with our own; they are to remain in our midst, and here spend their years and here bury their fathers and finally repose themselves. We may regret it. It may not be entirely compatible with our taste that they should live in our midst. We cannot help it. Our forefathers introduced them, and their destiny is to continue among us; and the practical question which now presents itself to us is as to the best mode of getting along with them.

Justin Morrill of Vermont added: "We have put aside the creed of the despot, the monarchist, the aristocrat, and have affirmed the right and capacity of the people to govern themselves, and have staked the national life on the issue to make it good in practice. . . . To deny any portion of the American people civil or political rights common to the citizen upon pretense of race or color, is to ignore the fundamental principles of republicanism." The only proper policy for the Government, according to Lyman Trumbull, chairman of the Senate Judiciary Committee, was "to legislate in the interest of freedom. Now, our laws are to be enacted with a view to educate, improve, enlighten, and Christianize the negro; to make him an independent man; to teach him to think and to reason; to improve that principle which the great Author of all has implanted in every human breast, which is susceptible of the highest cultivation, and destined to go on enlarging and expanding through the endless ages of eternity."

Trumbull and his fellow Republicans understood that God had created blacks as the equals of whites and that, if the law gave blacks an opportunity, they would demonstrate their equality. The Republicans made this equalitarian faith the basis of the Fourteenth Amendment. Although the faith was forgotten within a decade of the Fourteenth Amendment's ratification, it still offers a perspective from which to begin analysis of the issues of Fourteenth Amendment jurisprudence that confront us today.

Bibliography

BERGER, RAOUL  1977  Government by Judiciary: The Transformation of the Fourteenth Amendment. Cambridge, Mass.: Harvard University Press.
BICKEL, ALEXANDER M.  1955  The Original Understanding and the Segregation Decision. Harvard Law Review  69:1–65.
FAIRMAN, CHARLES  1949  Does the Fourteenth Amendment Incorporate the Bill of Rights? The Original Understanding. Stanford Law Review  2:5–173.
HYMAN, HAROLD M. and WIECEK, WILLIAM M.  1982 Equal Justice under Law: Constitutional Development 1835–1875.  New York: Harper & Row.
JAMES, JOSEPH B.  1956  The Framing of the Fourteenth Amendment.  Urbana: University of Illinois Press.
TEN BROEK, JACOBUS  1951  The Antislavery Origins of the Fourteenth Amendment. Berkeley: University of California Press.

# FIFTEENTH AMENDMENT

## (Framing and Ratification)

### William Gillette

In January 1869 adult black males could vote in only twenty states. Blacks had received the franchise in ten states of the South under the Reconstruction Act of March 1867 as part of the price of readmission to the Union set by the Republicans in Congress. Because Republicans also controlled the state government of Tennessee, blacks were enfranchised there. But many lived in the ex-slave border states that had been loyal to the Union, and they were not enfranchised. In the North, most blacks did not have the right to vote; however, there were minor exceptions in those states where the black population was small. The New England states except Connecticut allowed black suffrage, as did four midwestern states, Wisconsin, Nebraska, Minnesota, and Iowa. But especially in the lower North, where most northern blacks lived, white voters in REFERENDUM after referendum had rejected their unrestricted enfranchisement. Indeed in 1868 the issue of black suffrage was thought to be so dangerous and debilitating to the Republican party that at the party's national convention the framers of the platform devised a double standard by endorsing black voting in the South while trying not to antagonize white voters in the North: thus each northern state could decide black suffrage without federal interference, but southern states must accept black voting as a matter of national policy.

In the presidential election of 1868 Republican candidate ULYSSES S. GRANT captured most of the electoral vote and the Republicans retained control of Congress. But beneath the surface the situation was not reassuring. Grant's electoral victory was much greater than his popular vote (only 52 percent). Without the southern black voter Grant would have lost the popular, though not the electoral, vote. In state after state Grant squeaked by with narrow margins. Indeed, a switch of a mere 29,862 votes out of the 5,717,246 cast for the two major party candidates (.52 percent) would have made the Democratic candidate president. Moreover, the Democrats gained seats in the House of Representatives in Washington. And Republican majorities in state after state were slim indeed. Finally, Republican politicians throughout the South reported that little reliance could be placed on the southern black voter in the long run because of strong white influence and intimidation and because of black poverty, illiteracy, and inexperience. Danger signals in the South, defeats in state referenda in the North, and a narrow escape from defeat in the presidential election of 1868 taught the Republicans that their platform pledge to the North had to be ignored. Something must be done by the final session of the Fortieth Congress before the Democrats arrived in force.

The Republicans decided it was necessary to augment their strength by enfranchising more blacks, who could be expected to vote Republican en masse. Although egalitarians had begun the advocacy of black enfranchisement, politicians had made its achievement possible. Two years before, Congress had enfranchised blacks in the South because the Republicans then needed southern black votes to counter southern white votes. Now the Republicans also needed the support of northern and border blacks, especially in closely balanced states, and were willing to run limited risks and promote political reform in order to maintain power.

Therefore, during early 1869 the Republicans in the lame-duck Congress pressed for a constitutional amendment to secure impartial manhood suffrage in every state, thereby avoiding further popular rejection in state referenda. They opted for the usual but more indirect method of having Republican state legislatures that were still in session ratify the amendment. Thus they avoided the risk of possible rejection by special conventions.

The amendment finally passed Congress in late February 1869 after a number of compromises. To secure enough moderate votes, the sponsors had to omit a clause that would have outlawed property qualifications and LITERACY TESTS. Such a clause was dispensable because the tests would affect more Negroes in the South than in the North, and because the proponents of the amendment were intent primarily upon securing the northern Negro voter for the Republican party. For the same reasons, they omitted any provision banning RACIAL DISCRIMINATION in qualifications for officeholding. A provision for federal authority over voter qualifications was defeated, and so the potential for evasion in the southern and border states was left wide open.

The legislative history of the Fifteenth Amendment indicated no triumph of radical idealism but rather served to demonstrate its failure—a fact underscored by the fury and frustration of that band of radicals who had favored idealistic and uncompromising reforms. A moderate measure, the amendment had the support of those who understood the limits of party power and who had practical goals in mind; they took into account the possible difficulties of ratification. Time was short, the pressures were great, and the options were limited.

The primary objective—the enfranchisement of blacks in the northern and border states—was clearly understood, stated, and believed by the politicians, the press, and the people during the time when the amendment was framed and then considered by the state legislatures. As the abolitionist organ, the *National Anti-Slavery Standard,* declared, "evenly as parties are now divided in the North, it needs but the final ratification of the pending Fifteenth Amendment, to assure . . . the balance of power in national affairs." A black newspaper, the Washington *New National Era,* predicted the same for the border states. Indeed, most newspapers both in the North and in the South during 1869 and 1870 unequivocally, incontrovertibly, and repeatedly spoke of the Republican objective of ensuring party hegemony by means of the Fifteenth Amendment. Moreover, congressmen and state legislators, in arguing for passage and ratification, referred again and again to the partisan need for those votes. The southern black, already a voter, was not irrelevant; an important secondary purpose of the amendment was to assure the continuance of black suffrage in the South by forbidding racial discrimination as to the franchise in a virtually unrepealable amendment to the federal Constitution. Still, the anticipated importance of the black electorate in the North and in the borderland was clearly the overriding concern.

To be sure, the political motives of many Republican politicians were not incompatible with a sincere moral concern. The idealistic motive reinforced the pragmatic one: there was no conflict at the outset between the ideal and the practical or between the interests of the black electorate and those of the Republican party. A radical Republican congressman declared, "party expediency and exact justice coincide for once." A black clergyman from Pittsburgh observed that "the Republican Party had done the negro good but they were doing themselves good at the same time." Indeed, the amendment as framed was both bold and prudent: bold in enfranchising blacks despite concerted opposition and in ordering change by establishing constitutional guidelines; prudent in adapting methods to circumstances so that the amendment would not only pass Congress but also be ratified by the states.

Although the struggle over ratification lasted only thirteen months, it was hard going and the outcome was uncertain until the very end. To be sure, ratification was easy in safe Republican territory (New England and most of the Middle West) and in the South where Republican legislators did their duty. But the fight was especially close in the Middle Atlantic states and in Indiana and Ohio, where the parties were competitive and a black electorate had the potential for deciding victory or defeat. In the Democratic border states and on the Pacific Coast, where racial feeling ran high, Republicans feared that pushing the amendment would lose them votes; so they refrained from pressing for ratification in these regions. Nevertheless, in clear-cut conflicts of interest between state and national Republican party organizations, the national party was everywhere victorious. Mutinies in Rhode Island and Georgia were suppressed. The amendment had the backing of the Grant administration, with its rich patronage. By endorsing the amendment in his inaugural address, Grant placed the indispensable prestige of the presidency behind it; he then went beyond pronouncements by swinging Nebraska to ratify it. Those Republican politicians who held or aspired to hold national office added the weight of their influence. As one Ohioan advised, "By hook or by crook you must get the 15th amendment through or we are gone up."

The Fifteenth Amendment became law on March 30, 1870. Republican euphoria followed the hard battle for ratification. Grant, in his message to Congress, wrote that the amendment "completes the greatest civil change and constitutes the most important event that has occurred since the nation came to life." Blacks everywhere celebrated; they regarded the Fifteenth Amendment as political salvation, as a solemn written guarantee that would never be abridged. They now felt secure, protected by both the vote and the "long strong arm of the Government." Whites believed that since the Negro was now a citizen and a voter, he could take care of himself. Antislavery societies throughout the country disbanded, now confident that equality before the law was sufficient and that in any event, "no power ever permanently wronged a voting class without its own consent." But subsequent events made a mockery of such predictions in the South where Democrats denied blacks the franchise for almost a century.

Bibliography

GILLETTE, WILLIAM   (1979)1981   *Retreat from Reconstruction, 1869–1879.* Baton Rouge: Louisiana State University Press.

———   (1965)1969   *The Right to Vote: Politics and the Passage of the Fifteenth Amendment.* Baltimore: Johns Hopkins University Press.

MITTRICK, ROBERT   1985   *A History of Negro Voting in Pennsylvania during the Nineteenth Century.* Unpublished Ph.D. dissertation, Rutgers University, chap. 5.

# FIFTEENTH AMENDMENT

## (Judicial Interpretation)

### Ward E. Y. Elliott

The judicial interpretation of the Fifteenth Amendment has been closely intertwined with that of the FOURTEENTH AMENDMENT, largely in a Southern context. Within a year of ratification (1870) Congress passed three FORCE ACTS forbidding both public and private interference with voting on the basis of race or color. Federal officials tried hard at first to enforce these laws, but they were daunted by hostility in the South and growing indifference in Congress and the Supreme Court. Prosecutions dropped sharply in 1874; Reconstruction ended in 1877; the Jim Crow era of systematic SEGREGATION began around 1890; and the conspiracy provisions of the Force Acts were dropped in 1894.

From Reconstruction to World War I the Supreme Court showed more ingenuity in voiding VOTING RIGHTS actions than in upholding them. Although it was willing, under Article I, section 4, to uphold convictions and damage awards for ballot box fraud in federal elections, as in EX PARTE YARBROUGH (1884), it would not allow INDICTMENTS for conspiracy to bribe, even in federal elections as in JAMES V. BOWMAN (1903). It steadfastly refused to uphold convictions for private interference with voting rights in state or local elections in UNITED STATES V. REESE (1875) and UNITED STATES V. CRUIKSHANK (1876), or to uphold civil actions for a state official's refusal to register blacks, in *Giles v. Teasley* (1904).

The Court did shrug off arguments in *Myers v. Anderson* (1915) that the Fifteenth Amendment was itself void for diluting the votes of enfranchised whites and thereby depriving their states of equal suffrage in the Senate without their consent. But it did almost nothing to thwart the new franchise restrictions of the Jim Crow era—literacy, property, POLL TAX, residence, character, and understanding tests—designed to cull black and upcountry white voters. (See WILLIAMS V. MISSISSIPPI, 1898.) Only in GUINN V. UNITED STATES (1915) did it strike down a GRANDFATHER CLAUSE exempting descendants of 1867 voters from Oklahoma's LITERACY TEST—without, however, striking down the test itself. *Guinn* had no practical impact on voting registration, but it was important for serving notice that the Fifteenth Amendment bars subtle as well as blatant discrimination.

The Court moved against white PRIMARY ELECTIONS with more deliberation than speed. Party primary elections emerged in response to the regional party monopolies, Republican in the North, Democratic in the South, which followed the "realigning" election of 1896. By World War I, primaries were universal. The dominant party's nomination became the choice that counted, and general elections merely rubber-stamped the dominant party's nominee. This trend was earliest and most pronounced in the South. It weakened party discipline, lowered turnout drastically in general elections, strengthened the dominance of plantation whites, and froze out blacks almost completely.

Blacks challenged this exclusion in a famous series of Texas cases. In NIXON v. HERNDON (1927) and NIXON v. CONDON (1932) NAACP attorneys successfully attacked statutes barring blacks, and letting the parties bar blacks, from voting in primary elections. Counsel for both sides in *Herndon* argued the Fifteenth Amendment, but Justice OLIVER WENDELL HOLMES, speaking for a unanimous Court, found the statute instead a "direct and obvious infringement of the Fourteenth." The Court followed this precedent in *Condon*.

In attacking the discriminatory law under the Fourteenth, rather than the denial of a voting right under the Fifteenth, the Court ignored its earlier view that the pertinent section of the Fourteenth was not intended to protect voting rights. (See MINOR v. HAPPERSETT, 1875.) It also left Texas free to repeal the *Condon* statute, while permitting the Democrats to exclude blacks legally through their own "private" action. (See GROVEY v. TOWNSEND, 1935.)

The Court returned to the Fifteenth Amendment to overrule *Grovey* in SMITH v. ALLWRIGHT (1944), finding STATE ACTION in laws governing the timing and conduct of primary elections and by the "fusing [in UNITED STATES v. CLASSIC (1941)] of primary and general elections into a single instrumentality for the choice of officers." Later, in TERRY v. ADAMS (1953), the Court extended this concept of "fusion into a single instrumentality" to invalidate a whites-only "preprimary" election used by the Jaybird party since 1889 to capture Democratic nominations in a Texas county.

Without the white primary, segregationist whites had only franchise restrictions to block black votes. These restrictions had reduced black registrations by a third in the nineteenth century, but they had only limited and temporary effect by the 1950s. Black literacy was up, and only three of the eleven Southern states—Alabama, Mississippi, and Louisiana—retained blatantly discriminatory literacy tests. These the Court struck down, along with nondiscriminatory tests where blacks had been segregated in inferior schools.

Congress greatly aided in expanding the black vote with judicial protection in the CIVIL RIGHTS ACTS OF 1957, 1960, and 1964, and especially with the VOTING RIGHTS ACT OF 1965, which authorized suspension of state literacy and character tests and provision of federal examiners to register blacks where discrimination was found. In 1970, Congress wholly forbade literacy tests as a condition on voting in state elections.

Though the Court took almost seventy-five years to give the Fifteenth Amendment much practical effect, its interventions since World War II have greatly changed both the constitutional and political landscapes. *Smith v. Allwright,* with its broad reading of the Fifteenth Amendment looking through form to substance foreshadowed such great Fourteenth Amendment cases as SHELLEY v. KRAEMER (1948) and BROWN v. BOARD OF EDUCATION (1954). GOMILLION v. LIGHTFOOT (1960), which struck down a racial GERRYMANDER under the Fifteenth Amendment, was a bridge to BAKER v. CARR (1962).

Opening the primaries and the franchise to blacks brought them out of political exile. Black registration in the South, only five percent in 1940, grew to twenty-eight percent in 1960 and sixty-three percent in 1976, narrowing the gap between black and white registrations from forty-four percent to five percent. Black elected officials in the South increased from fewer than 100 to more than 1,000. White politicians stopped waving ax handles, standing in the doorways of segregated schools, and using terms like "burrhead" in public debate. The Court's enforcement of the Fifteenth Amendment may properly be described as late, but not little.

Bibliography

ELLIOTT, WARD E. Y.    1975    *The Rise of Guardian Democracy: The Supreme Court's Role in Voting Rights Disputes, 1845–1969.* Cambridge, Mass.: Harvard University Press.

KEY, V. O., JR.    1949    *Southern Politics.* New York: Knopf.

KOUSSER, J. MORGAN    1974    *The Shaping of Southern Politics: Suffrage Restriction and the Establishment of the One-Party South, 1880–1910.* New Haven, Conn.: Yale University Press.

LAWSON, STEVEN F.    1976    *Black Ballots: Voting Rights in the South, 1944–1969.* New York: Columbia University Press.

# VOTING RIGHTS

Louis H. Pollak

"The right to vote freely for the candidate of one's choice is of the essence of a democratic society, and any restrictions on that right strike at the heart of representative government." So spoke Chief Justice EARL WARREN, on behalf of the Supreme Court, in REYNOLDS v. SIMS (1964).

The Chief Justice's words were in direct philosophic succession to principles of the primacy of representative political institutions announced by the FIRST CONTINENTAL CONGRESS 190 years before, in the Declaration and Resolves of October 14, 1774:

[T]he foundation of English liberty, and of all free government, is a right in the people to participate in their legislative council: and as the English colonists are not represented, and from their local and other circumstances, cannot properly be represented in the British parliament, they are entitled to a free and exclusive power of legislation in their several provincial legislatures, where their right of representation can alone be preserved, in all cases of taxation and internal policy, subject only to the negative of their sovereign, in such manner as has been heretofore used and accustomed.

The failure of King George III, through his ministers, to recognize the urgency of the colonists' demand for true representative institutions was one of the chief causes of revolution set forth in the DECLARATION OF INDEPENDENCE: "He has dissolved Representative Houses repeatedly, for opposing with manly firmness his invasions in the rights of the people. He has refused for a long time, after such dissolutions, to cause others to be elected; whereby the Legislative Powers, incapable of Annihilation, have returned to the People at large for their exercise."

The severing of the ties with Britain required the establishment, at the state level and at the national level, of new and more representative institutions of government. American constitutional history is characterized in part by the continuing enlargement of the right to vote, the mechanism which, in the American political tradition, has become the *sine qua non* of a valid system of REPRESENTATION. An anomaly presents itself: The Constitution, as amended, addresses aspects of the right to vote with far greater frequency than any other topic. Nonetheless, it has never been the function of the Constitution affirmatively to define the universe of voters. The Constitution's function has been narrower—progressively to limit the permissible grounds of disenfranchisement.

Prior to the American Revolution, eligibility to vote was not uniform among the colonies, but the variations were relatively minor. Broadly speaking, voting for colonial (as distinct from township or borough) officials was reserved to adult (generally meaning twenty-one or older) "freeholders." In equating property ownership and suffrage, the colonies were following a familiar English model. But landowning was far more widely dispersed in the colonies than in the mother country, so the proportion of colonists eligible to vote was larger.

There were not more than a few black or women freeholders in any of the colonies, and pursuant either to convention or to formal legal specification those few did not vote. Religious restrictions were also commonplace but varied somewhat among the colonies and at different times. In general, the franchise was the prerogative of the propertied, Protestant, white male.

With the coming of independence, all of the newly sovereign states except Connecticut and Rhode Island adopted new charters of government—"constitutions." Impelled by the rhetoric of revolution and the eagerness of thousands of militiamen to participate in the processes of governance, the drafters of the new state constitutions relaxed but did not abandon the property and religious qualifications for voting for state officials (and the correlative, and generally more stringent, qualifications for holding state office). As Max Farrand observed, Americans

might declare that "all men are created equal," and bills of rights might assert that government rested upon the consent of the governed; but these constitutions carefully provided that such consent should come from property owners, and, in many of the States, from religious believers and even followers of the Christian faith. "The man of small means might vote, but none save well-to-do Christians could legislate, and in many states none but a rich Christian could be a governor." In South Carolina, for example, a freehold of 10,000 currency was required of the Governor, Lieutenant Governor, and members of the council; 2,000 of the members of the Senate; and, while every elector was eligible to the House of Representatives, he had to acknowledge the being of a God and to believe in a future state of rewards and punishments, as well as to hold "a freehold at least of fifty acres of land, or a town lot."

Under the ARTICLES OF CONFEDERATION, the state delegates in Congress constituted the nation's government. The Articles limited the numbers of delegates (no fewer than two and no more than seven per state) but left each state legislature free to determine the qualifications of those selected and the mode of their annual selection. The Articles did not preclude popular election of delegates, but the word "appointed," in the phrase "appointed in such manner as the legislature of each State shall direct," suggests that it was not anticipated that legislatures would remit to their constituents the power to choose those who would speak and vote for the states in Congress.

At the CONSTITUTIONAL CONVENTION OF 1787, the Framers divided on how the lower house was to be selected. JAMES MADISON told his fellow delegates that he "considered an election of one branch at least of the legislature by the people immediately, as a clear principle of true government." Madison's view carried the day. But then the Convention faced the question whether the Constitution should set the qualifications of those who were to elect representatives. GOUVERNEUR MORRIS of Pennsylvania proposed that only freeholders should vote. Colonel GEORGE MASON of Virginia found this proposal regressive: "Eight of nine States have extended the right of suffrage beyond the freeholders. What will the people there say, if they should be disfranchised." OLIVER ELLSWORTH of Connecticut also challenged Morris's proposal: "How shall the freehold be defined? Ought not every man who pays a tax to vote for the representative who is to levy and dispose of his money?" Morris was unpersuaded: "He had long learned not to be the dupe of words. . . . Give the votes to people who have no property, and they will sell them to the rich who will be able to buy them." But BENJAMIN FRANKLIN took decisive issue with his fellow Pennsylvanian: "It is of great consequence that we should not depress the virtue and public spirit of our common people; of which they displayed a great deal during the war, and which contributed principally to the favorable issue of it." Morris's proposal was decisively defeated. The Convention instead approved the provision that has endured ever since, under which eligibility to vote for representatives is keyed, in each state, to that state's rules of eligibility to vote for members of the most numerous house of the state legislature.

When it came to designing the method of selecting the President and vice-president, the Convention devised the indirect election system of the ELECTORAL COLLEGE. The expectation was that the electors—themselves chosen from among the leading citizens of their respective states—would, through disinterested deliberation, select as the nation's chief executive officials the two persons of highest civic virtue, wholly without regard for the vulgar demands of "politics." According to ALEXANDER HAMILTON in THE FEDERALIST #68, "[t]he mode of appointment of the Chief Magistrate of the United States is almost the only part of the system, of any consequence, which has escaped without severe censure, or which has received the slightest mark of approbation from its opponents." But, measured against its intended purpose, no other structural aspect of the Constitution has wound up wider of the mark. The Framers of the Constitution wholly failed to anticipate the development of national political parties whose chief political goal would be the election of the party leader as President. That development has meant that since the fourth presidential election—that of 1800, in which THOMAS JEFFERSON defeated JOHN ADAMS—the electors in each state have themselves been selected as adherents of the political party prevailing in that state and thus have, with the rarest of exceptions, cast their electoral votes for the party's presidential and vice-presidential candidates. The system of electors remains to this day, but it has been entirely drained of its intended function.

Those who drafted the Constitution in 1787, and who saw it through ratification to the launching of the new ship of state in 1789, were America's aristocracy. The transformation of American politics from 1789 to the Civil War can be measured in the marked shift in class status of those who occupied the Presidency. The Presidents from GEORGE WASHINGTON to JOHN QUINCY ADAMS were all patricians. Most of the Presidents from ANDREW JACKSON to ABRAHAM LINCOLN were not. The growth of national parties, beginning with Jefferson and accelerating with Jackson, democratized politics by putting politicians in the business of seeking to enlarge their voting constituencies. Property qualifications gave way, for the most part, to taxpayer qualifications. And, in many states, these in turn were soon largely abandoned.

The erosion of property tests for voting did not mean that anything approximating universal suffrage was at hand. As one political scientist has summarized the situation:

Apart from a few midwestern states, hungry for settlers, no one was very warm to the prospect of aliens and immigrants at the polls; all the states but Maine, Massachusetts, Vermont, New Hampshire, Rhode Island, and New York explicitly barred free blacks from voting, and New York imposed special property requirements on blacks which, while repeatedly challenged, were repeatedly upheld in popular referenda. Even in the tiny handful of northern states that did not exclude blacks by law, social pressures tended to accomplish the same end. New Hampshire and Vermont in 1857 and 1858 had to pass special laws against excluding blacks from voting. Chancellor James Kent concluded that only in Maine could the black man participate equally with the white man in civil and political rights. Women were universally denied the vote [Elliott 1974, p. 40].

In 1848, a year of revolution in Europe, 300 people gathered in a church in the little upstate New York town of Seneca Falls to consider the status of women. The most revolutionary item on the agenda was voting. Half a century before there had been a small outcropping of female voting in New Jersey, whose 1776 constitution had, perhaps inadvertently, used the word "inhabitants" to describe those who, if they met the property qualifications, could vote. It appears that by 1807, respectable New Jersey opinion had reached the consensus that laxity was slipping into license (at a local election in Trenton even slaves and Philadelphians were said to have cast ballots). At this point, "reform" was clearly called for: the legislature promptly altered the electoral code to bring New Jersey's voting qualifications back into conformity with the white maleness that characterized the electorate in the rest of the country and remained the accepted order of things until Seneca Falls.

The chief driving energies behind the Seneca Falls Convention were

Elizabeth Cady Stanton and Lucretia Mott. Stanton drafted the "Declaration of Principles" and the several resolutions which the convention was asked to adopt. The only resolution to receive less-than-unanimous endorsement was the ninth: "Resolved, that it is the duty of the women of this country to secure to themselves their sacred right to the elective franchise." That the franchise was a far more chimerical goal than other concerns (for example, property rights for married women) was recognized by Mott. She had asked Stanton not to submit the ninth resolution for the reason that "Thou will make us ridiculous." The factor that may have tipped the balance in Stanton's decision not to subordinate her principle to Mott's pragmatism was the strong encouragement of Frederick Douglass. The great black leader supported the ninth resolution. He joined the cause of equal rights for women to the cause of abolition.

The women's movement maintained its close association with abolitionism through the Civil War. After the freeing of the slaves, the country's attention focused on the terms on which American blacks were to be brought into the mainstream of American life. The leaders of the women's movement hoped that the drive for women's suffrage would complement and be reinforced by the drive for black suffrage. But that was not to be. As the war neared its end, a number of Republican leaders began to recognize a strong partisan interest in creating black voters to counter the feared resurgence of the Democratic party; there were no comparable reasons for creating women voters. Many of the women leaders, recognizing the political realities, accepted—albeit with no enthusiasm—the priority given to the rights of blacks. But not Elizabeth Cady Stanton and Susan B. Anthony. Said Anthony: "I will cut off this right arm before I will ever work for or demand the ballot for the Negro and not the woman." (Anthony and Stanton then formed the National Woman Suffrage Association, while the other leaders worked through the American Woman Suffrage Association; the split was not to be healed for twenty-five years.)

In 1864 Abraham Lincoln appointed SALMON P. CHASE—Lincoln's former secretary of the treasure and one of his chief rivals for the Republican presidential nomination in 1860—to succeed ROGER B. TANEY as CHIEF JUSTICE of the United States. Chase's elevation to the Court did not abate his presidential ambitions and his attendant interest in promoting a favorable political environment. The new Chief Justice wrote to Lincoln, as he subsequently wrote to President ANDREW JOHNSON, urging that black suffrage be made a condition of the reconstruction of the rebel states. And by 1867 Chase had taken the position that Congress had constitutional authority to enfranchise blacks as a mode of enforcing the THIRTEENTH AMENDMENT: "Can anything be clearer than that the National Legislature charged with the duty of 'enforcing by appropriate legislation' the condition of universal freedom, is authorized and bound to provide for universal suffrage? Is not *suffrage* the best security against *slavery* and *involuntary servitude* ? Is not the legislation which provides the *best* security the most *appropriate* ?" Chase lost interest in active promotion of black voting when it became apparent that his modest chances of being nominated for the presidency were more likely to be realized in the Democratic party than in the Republican party. In any event, the question whether the Thirteenth Amendment could have been a platform for enlarging the franchise became moot upon the adoption of the two other post-Civil War Amendments, both of which expressly addressed the franchise—for blacks, not for women.

The FOURTEENTH AMENDMENT, ratified in 1868, dealt with black voting by indirection. By declaring that "[a]ll persons born or naturalized in the United States, and subject to the jurisdiction thereof, are citizens of the United States and of the State wherein they reside," the first sentence of the first section of the amendment overruled Roger B. Taney's pronouncement in DRED SCOTT v. SANDFORD (1857), that blacks, whether slave or free, could not be citizens within the contemplation of the Constitution. The second sentence of the first section sought to protect the CIVIL RIGHTS of blacks: First, it guaranteed "the privileges and immunities of citizens of the United States" against state abridgment and, second, it prohibited state denial to any person, whether citizen or not, of "life, liberty or property without DUE PROCESS OF LAW," or deprivation of the "EQUAL PROTECTION OF THE LAWS." The second section of the amendment spoke to the political rights of blacks. It provided that any state that denied participation in federal or state elections to "any of the male inhabitants of such State, being twenty-one years of age, and citizens of the United States . . . except for participation in rebellion, or other crime," should have its allocation of representatives and of presidential electors proportionately reduced. The framers of the amendment thus preserved the states' entitlement to discriminate but proposed a substantial penalty as the price of discrimination.

By 1869, after General ULYSSES S. GRANT's narrow victory in the 1868 presidential election, the Republican party recognized that black votes were essential to its survival. So the Republican leadership in Congress fashioned the FIFTEENTH AMENDMENT. That amendment, ratified in 1870, addressed the question of black voting directly. A citizen's entitlement to vote could not be "abridged by the United States or by any State on account of race, color, or previous condition of servitude."

Notwithstanding that the express language of the Fourteenth Amendment addressed male voting, and that the express language of the Fifteenth Amendment addressed discriminations rooted in "race, color or previous condition of servitude," some leaders of the women's movement contended that women were constitutionally entitled to vote. Arguing that the right to vote in a federal election was a privilege of national citizenship protected by section 1 of the Fourteenth Amendment, Susan B. Anthony actually persuaded election officials in Rochester, New York, to let her vote in 1872 notwithstanding that the New York constitution limited the franchise to men. Anthony was promptly charged with the crime of casting a ballot in a federal election in which she was not an eligible voter. The presiding judge was Justice WARD HUNT of the Supreme Court. Justice Hunt rejected Anthony's constitutional claim in the following words:

The right of voting, or the privilege of voting, is a right or privilege arising under the constitution of the state, and not under the Constitution of the United States. The qualifications are different in the different states. Citizenship, age, sex, residence, are variously required in the different states, or may be so. If the right belongs to any particular person, it is because such person is entitled to it by the laws of the state where he offers to exercise it, and not because of citizenship of the United States. If the state of New York should provide that no person should vote until he had reached the age of thirty years, or after he had reached the age of thirty years, or after he had reached the age of fifty, or that no person having grey hair, or who had not the use of all his limbs, should be entitled to vote, I do not see how it could be held to be a violation of any right derived or held under the Constitution of the United States. We might say that such regulations were unjust, tyrannical, unfit for the regulation of an intelligent state; but, if rights of a citizen are thereby violated they are of that fundamental class, derived from his position as a citizen of the state, and not those limited rights belonging to him as a citizen of the United States.

Read through the prism of a century of doctrinal hindsight, Justice Hunt's words seem—at least at first blush—somewhat surprising. The surprise is not occasioned by the fact that the Justice gave such short shrift to arguments based on the Fourteenth Amendment's PRIVILEGES AND IMMUNITIES CLAUSE, for we are accustomed to the fact that, ever since the SLAUGHTERHOUSE CASES (1873), the Supreme Court has read the grant of privileges and immunities flowing from national citizenship very restrictively. The surprise stems from Hunt's failure—which may also have been counsel's failure—to approach sex-based denial of the franchise (not to mention the assertedly analogous hypothetical denials based on age, physical handicap, or color of hair) in equal protection terms. The likely explanation is that in *Slaughterhouse* the Court doubted that "any action of a State not directed by way of discrimination against the negroes as a class, or on account of their race, will ever be held to come within the" equal protection clause.

Justice Hunt directed the jury to return a verdict of guilty and imposed a fine of $100.

Justice Hunt's rejection of Anthony's privileges and immunities claim was vindicated two years later by Chief Justice MORRISON R. WAITE's opinion for the unanimous Court in MINOR v. HAPPERSETT (1875). This was a civil suit brought in a Missouri state court by Virginia L. Minor, and her lawyer husband Francis Minor, to challenge the refusal of a Missouri election official to register her as a voter. The Minors contended that the provision of the Missouri constitution limiting the electorate to male citizens transgressed the privileges and immunities clause. In rejecting the Minors' contention, Chief Justice Waite demonstrated that limitation of the franchise to males had been the norm, despite the fact that women were citizens. Voting had not been a privilege of national citizenship prior to the Fourteenth Amendment. As the amendment "did not add to the privileges and immunities of a citizen," but merely "furnished an additional guaranty for the protection of such as he already had," Missouri's refusal to let Minor vote was not unconstitutional. *Minor v. Happersett* ended attempts to win the campaign for woman's suffrage by litigation. The road to the ballot box was to be political—persuading male legislators to pass laws giving women the vote.

It was to be a long road. In 1870 Wyoming's territorial legislature enacted a law entitling women to vote. Utah followed suit, but the victory there was temporary. An 1887 congressional statute forbidding Utah's Mormons from practicing polygamy also overrode the territorial legislature's grant of the franchise to women. Three years later Wyoming's first state constitution called for women's suffrage. Thereafter progress was slow. Many state campaigns were fought and most were lost. In the South, votes for women were seen as a harbinger of votes for blacks, and the states resisted accordingly; in the East, many industrialists mistrusted the links between some women's suffragists and trade union and other reform groups; in the Midwest, the women's suffrage movement was seen by the brewing interests as the advance guard of prohibition. By 1913 women could vote in only nine states; in that year Illinois admitted women to participation in presidential elections.

In 1912, THEODORE ROOSEVELT's Progressive party endorsed women's suffrage. This endorsement served as a reminder that Susan B. Anthony and her associates had sought to achieve women's suffrage not state-by-state but by amending the Constitution. Pressure for a women's suffrage amendment mounted during World War I when women entered the work force in record numbers. In 1918 WOODROW WILSON announced support for the proposed amendment, notwithstanding that women's suffrage was anathema to the white Democratic South. In 1919, with Democrats divided and Republicans strongly in favor, Congress submitted to the states a proposed amendment barring denial or abridgment of the right to vote in any election on grounds of sex. In 1920, the NINETEENTH AMENDMENT was ratified. In the 1920 elections one of the voters was Charlotte Woodward Pierce who, as a nineteen-year-old farm girl, had attended the Seneca Falls Convention in 1848.

Following the Civil War, the military occupation of the South ushered in a period in which blacks not only voted but were elected to office.

With the adoption of the Fifteenth Amendment, there appeared to be some ground for supposing that black voting had achieved a legal infrastructure which might suffice even after the army departed. However, although the amendment bars race, color, and previous condition of servitude as criteria of eligibility to vote, it does not proscribe other criteria—such as literacy or taxpayer status—susceptible of adaptation as surrogates for racism. The lesson was that most blacks might be prevented from voting by educational or property qualifications.

Following the COMPROMISE OF 1877, which led to the withdrawal from the South of the last military units, the twilight of black participation in the southern political process began. Through the 1880s, some black voting continued—frequently in Populist alliance with poor whites. But in the 1890s, as a corollary of the spreading gospel of Jim Crow, the southern white political leadership forged a consensus to exclude blacks from the ballot box. Some of this was achieved by force, and some by skulduggery, but in large measure the forms of law were utilized. LITERACY TESTS and POLL TAXES were common exclusionary devices, as was closing Democratic primaries—the only real elections in most of the South—to blacks. The underlying rationale was that offered by Senator James Vardaman of Mississippi: "I am just as much opposed to Booker Washington as a voter, with all his Anglo-Saxon reinforcements, as I am to the cocoanut-headed, chocolate-covered, typical little coon, Andy Dottson, who blacks my shoes every morning. Neither is fit to perform the supreme function of citizenship."

By and large, the legal stratagems employed by the southern states to disenfranchise blacks succeeded. Poll taxes and literacy tests which did not on their face show a discriminatory purpose easily passed constitutional muster from BREEDLOVE V. SUTTLES (1937) to *Lassiter v. Northampton Election Board* (1959). To be sure, the Supreme Court did intervene in those rare instances in which the purpose to discriminate was evident on the face of the challenged restraint. A flagrant example was the so-called GRANDFATHER CLAUSE in Oklahoma's 1910 constitution, which exempted from the literacy requirement any would-be voter "who was, on January 1, 1866, or at any time prior thereto, entitled to vote under any form of government, or who at that time resided in some foreign nation, and [any] lineal descendant thereof." In GUINN V. UNITED STATES (1915) the Supreme Court held this literacy test invalid.

Because during the first half of the twentieth century the decisive voting in the South took place in Democratic primaries, not in the general elections, the cases of greatest practical as well as doctrinal consequence were those that challenged devices to maintain the whiteness of the "white primary."

In NIXON V. HERNDON (1927) a unanimous Court, speaking through Justice OLIVER WENDELL HOLMES, sustained the complaint of L. A. Nixon, who contended that he had been unconstitutionally barred from voting in a Texas Democratic primary through enforcement of a Texas statute that recited that "in no event shall a negro be eligible to participate in a Democratic party primary election held in the state of Texas." The Court held that this statutory racial exclusion contravened the Fourteenth Amendment.

The consequence of this ruling was described by Justice BENJAMIN N. CARDOZO in his opinion in NIXON V. CONDON (1932): "Promptly after the announcement of [the Herndon] decision, the legislature of Texas enacted a new statute . . . repealing the article condemned by this court; declaring that the effect of the decision was to create an emergency with a need for immediate action; and substituting for the article so repealed another bearing the same number. By the article thus substituted, 'every political party in this State through its State Executive Committee shall have the power to prescribe the qualifications of its own members and shall in its own way determine who shall be qualified to vote or otherwise participate in such political party. . . .' " Thereupon the executive committee of the Texas Democratic party voted to limit party membership and participation to whites, and L. A. Nixon was once again barred from voting in the Democratic primary. Once again Nixon brought a lawsuit, and once again he prevailed in the Supreme Court. Justice Cardozo, speaking for a majority of five, concluded that the new Texas statute delegated exercise of the state's power over primaries to party executive committees, with the result that the racial exclusion decided on by the executive committee was in effect the racially discriminatory act of the State of Texas and hence prohibited by the Fourteenth Amendment. Justice JAMES C. McREYNOLDS, joined by three other Justices, dissented.

Three years later, in GROVEY V. TOWNSEND (1935), the Court considered the next refinement in the Texas Democratic primary—exclusion of blacks by vote of the party convention. Speaking through Justice OWEN J. ROBERTS, the Court this time unanimously concluded that the action taken by the Texas Democratic party was an entirely private decision for which the State of Texas was not accountable; accordingly, neither the Fourteenth nor the Fifteenth Amendment was transgressed.

Nine years later, toward the end of World War II, the Court, in SMITH V. ALLWRIGHT (1944), again considered the *Grovey v. Townsend* question. In the interval, seven of the Justices who had participated in *Grovey v. Townsend* had died or retired. Approaching the matter in a common sense way, the Court, with Justice Roberts dissenting, concluded that the role of the primary as a formal and vital predicate of the election made it an integral part of the state's voting processes and hence subject to the requirement of the Fifteenth Amendment. Accordingly, the Court in *Smith v. Allwright* overruled *Grovey v. Townsend*.

The resumption, after three-quarters of a century, of significant black participation in the southern political process dates from the decision in *Smith v. Allwright*. But the elimination of the most egregious legal barriers did not mean that all blacks were automatically free to vote. Hundreds of thousands of would-be black voters were still kept from the polls by fraud or force or both. In 1957, three years after the Court, in BROWN V. BOARD OF EDUCATION (1954), held that legally mandated racial SEGREGATION contravened the Fourteenth Amendment, Congress passed the first federal civil rights law enacted since the 1870s: a voting rights law which authorized modest federal supervision of the southern voting process. And the year 1964 witnessed ratification of the TWENTY-FOURTH AMENDMENT, barring exclusion of American citizens from voting in any federal election on grounds of failure to pay any poll tax or other tax. But as black demands for equal treatment multiplied, responsive abuses escalated.

In the spring of 1965, a Boston minister, one of scores of clergymen who had gone to Selma, Alabama, to help MARTIN LUTHER KING, JR., launch a voter registration drive, was murdered. A few days later, on March 15, 1965, President LYNDON B. JOHNSON addressed Congress:

Many of the issues of civil rights are very complex and most difficult. But about this there can and should be no argument. Every American citizen must have an equal right to vote. There is no reason which can excuse the denial of that right. There is no duty which weighs more heavily on us than the duty we have to ensure that right.

Yet the harsh fact is that in many places in this country men and women are kept from voting simply because they are Negroes.

Every device of which human ingenuity is capable has been used to deny this right. The Negro citizen may go to register only to be told that the day is wrong, or the hour is late, or the official in charge is absent. And if he persists and if he manages to present himself to the registrar, he may be disqualified because he did not spell out his middle name or because he abbreviated a word on the application. And if he manages to fill out an application, he is given a test. The registrar is the sole judge of whether he passes this test. He may be asked to recite the entire constitution, or explain the most complex provisions of state laws. And even a college degree cannot be used to prove that he can read and write.

For the fact is that the only way to pass these barriers is to show a white skin.

Experience has clearly shown that the existing process of law cannot overcome systematic and ingenious discrimination. No law that we now have on the books—and I have helped to put three of them there—can ensure the right to vote when local officials are determined to deny it. . . .

This time, on this issue, there must be no delay, or no hesitation or no compromise with our purpose.

We cannot, we must not refuse to protect the right of every American to vote in every election that he may desire to participate in. And we ought not, we must not wait another eight months before we get a bill. We have already waited a hundred years and more and the time for waiting is gone. . . .

But even if we pass this bill, the battle will not be over. What happened in Selma is part of a far larger movement which reaches into every section and state of America. It is the effort of American Negroes to secure for themselves the full blessings of American life.

Their cause must be our cause too. Because it is not just Negroes, but really it is all of us, who must overcome the crippling legacy of bigotry and injustice. And we shall overcome.

As a man whose roots go deeply into Southern soil I know how agonizing racial feelings are. I know how difficult it is to reshape the attitudes and the structure of our society.

But a century has passed, more than a hundred years, since the Negro was freed. And he is not fully free tonight.

It was more than a hundred years ago that Abraham Lincoln, the great President of the Northern party, signed the Emancipation Proclamation, but emancipation is a proclamation and not a fact.

A century has passed, more than a hundred years since equality was promised. And yet the Negro is not equal.

A century has passed since the day of promise. And the promise is unkept.

The time of justice has now come. I tell you that I believe sincerely that no force can hold it back. It is right in the eyes of man and God that it should come. And when it does, I think that day will brighten the lives of every American.

Congress enacted the VOTING RIGHTS ACT OF 1965. The act provided, among other things, for the suspension of literacy tests for five years in states or political subdivisions thereof in which fewer than "50 per cent of its voting-age residents were registered on November 1, 1964, or voted in the presidential election of November, 1964." This and other major provisions of the 1965 act were thereafter sustained in SOUTH CAROLINA V. KATZENBACH (1966), *Rome v. United States* (1980), and KATZENBACH V. MORGAN (1966), as appropriate ways of enforcing the Fifteenth and Fourteenth Amendments. Subsequent amendments to the 1965 act have broadened its coverage.

The 1944 decision in *Smith v. Allwright* was more than a new and hospitable judicial approach to the right of blacks to participate in the American political process. It was a major advance (as, four years later, was SHELLEY V. KRAEMER, 1948) toward the day—May 17, 1954—when a unanimous Court, speaking through Chief Justice Warren, was to hold, in *Brown v. Board of Education,* that the equal protection clause barred the legally mandated racial segregation of school children. Subsequent decisions, building on *Brown v. Board of Education,* soon made it plain that the equal protection clause barred all the legal trappings of Jim Crow. *Brown v. Board of Education* worked a fundamental change in the Court's and the nation's perception of the scope of judicial responsibility to vindicate those values.

In 1962, eight years after *Brown v. Board of Education,* the Court, in *Baker v. Carr,* held that allegations that a state legislature suffered from systematic malapportionment, under which districts of widely different populations were each represented by one legislator, stated a claim cognizable under the equal protection clause. The importance of *Baker v. Carr* cannot be overestimated. Chief Justice Warren thought it the most significant decision handed down by the Court during his sixteen years in the center chair. Even those who rank *Brown v. Board of Education* ahead of *Baker v. Carr* must nonetheless acknowledge that the latter decision set in motion a process that resulted in the redesign of numerous state legislatures and a myriad of local governing bodies, and, indeed, of the House of Representatives. That redesign has been required to meet the Court's pronouncement, in GRAY v. SANDERS (1963), that "[t]he conception of political equality from the Declaration of Independence, to Lincoln's Gettysburg Address, to the Fifteenth, Seventeenth, and Nineteenth Amendments can mean only one thing—one person, one vote." Long-standing patterns of malapportionment in which rural districts with relatively few inhabitants were represented on equal terms with heavily populated urban districts have become a thing of the past. (See REAPPORTIONMENT.)

Guaranteeing the voting rights of women and blacks and overcoming rampant malapportionment have cured the major inexcusable deficiencies of the American political process. In recent decades, certain lesser inequalities have also begun to be addressed.

From the beginning of the republic, Americans residing in the continental United States but not within any state—for example, those who lived in federal territories—had no way of voting in national elections. In the most egregious of anomalies, residents of the nation's capital were voiceless in the selection of the President who dwelt and governed in their own home town. So matters stood until 1964, when the TWENTY-THIRD AMENDMENT was added to the Constitution, giving the DISTRICT OF COLUMBIA a minimum of three electoral votes in presidential elections.

In the late 1960s, profound divisions in American opinion about America's military involvement in the VIETNAM WAR forced recognition of another anomaly—that tens of thousands of young men were being drafted to fight in an unpopular foreign war although they were not old enough to vote in national elections choosing the officials responsible for making decisions for war or for peace. In 1970, Congress, in amending the Voting Rights Act, included a provision forbidding abridgment of the right of any citizen to vote "on account of age if such citizen is eighteen years or older." The statute was promptly challenged in OREGON v. MITCHELL (1970). Four Justices concluded that Congress had the power to lower the voting age to eighteen. Four Justices concluded that Congress had no such power. The casting vote was that of Justice Hugo L. Black, who held that Congress could regulate the voting age in national elections but not in state elections. Because Americans vote every two years for state and national officials at the same time, *Oregon v. Mitchell* was an invitation to chaos. Within six months, Congress proposed and the requisite three-fourths of the states ratified, the TWENTY-SIXTH AMENDMENT which accomplished by constitutional mandate what Congress had been unable to achieve by statute.

In the course of two centuries law and conscience have combined to make the American suffrage almost truly universal. One massive obstacle remains: apathy. In recent national elections in the European democracies, seventy-two percent of the eligible electorate voted in Great Britain, seventy-nine percent in Spain, eighty-five percent in France, and eighty-nine percent in Italy and West Germany. By contrast, in the American presidential election of 1980, only fifty-three percent of those eligible voted. In America's 1984 presidential election, after both major parties had made massive efforts to register new voters, not more than fifty-five percent of those who could have voted made their way to the ballot box. A fateful question confronting American democracy is whether tens of millions of self-disenfranchised Americans will in the years to come find the energy and good sense to exercise the precious right won at such great labor at the Constitutional Convention, in Congress and state legislatures and the Supreme Court, and at Selma and Seneca Falls.

Bibliography

CHUTE, MARCHETTE G.   1969   *First Liberty: A History of the Right to Vote in America, 1619–1850.*  New York: Dutton.

DUBOIS, ELLEN CAROL, ed.   1981   *Elizabeth Cady Stanton, Susan B. Anthony: Correspondence, Writings, Speeches.*  New York: Shocken.

ELLIOTT, WARD E. Y.   1974   *The Rise of Guardian Democracy: The Supreme Court's Role in Voting Rights Disputes, 1845–1969.*  Cambridge, Mass.: Harvard University Press.

FAIRMAN, CHARLES   1971   *Reconstruction and Reunion, 1864–1888.*  New York: Macmillan.

FARRAND, MAX, ed   1921   *The Fathers of the Constitution.*  New Haven, Conn.: Yale University Press.

———, ed.   1911   *The Records of the Federal Convention of 1787.*  New Haven, Conn.: Yale University Press.

FLEXNER, ELEANOR   1975   *Century of Struggle: The Woman's Right to Vote Movement in the United States.*  Rev. ed. Cambridge, Mass.: Harvard University Press.

HIGGINBOTHAM, A. L., JR.   1984   "States' 'Rights' and States' 'Wrongs' ": Apartheid, Virginia and South African Style." Dubois Lecture, Harvard University.

MCKAY, ROBERT B.   1965   *Reapportionment: The Law and Politics of Equal Representation.*  New York: Twentieth Century Fund.

WILLIAMSON, CHILTON   1960   *American Suffrage from Property to Democracy, 1760–1860.*  Princeton, N.J.: Princeton University Press.

WOODWARD, C. VANN   1951   *Origins of the New South, 1877–1913.*  Baton Rouge: Louisiana State University Press.

———   1957   *The Strange Career of Jim Crow.*  New York: Oxford University Press.

# POLL TAX

Kenneth L. Karst

A poll tax (CAPITATION TAX, head tax) is typically levied on every adult (or adult male) within the taxing JURISDICTION. An old technique for raising revenue, the tax in its compulsory form raises no important constitutional questions. (Under Article I, section 9, Congress can levy a poll tax only by apportionment to the national census. Congress has not in fact raised revenue this way.)

Serious constitutional issues have been raised in this century by poll taxes whose payment is "voluntary," enforced only by conditioning voter registration on their payment. Early in the nation's history, payment of such taxes came to replace property ownership as a qualification for voting. By the Civil War, however, widespread acceptance of universal suffrage had virtually eliminated the poll tax as a condition on voting.

In a number of southern states, the poll tax returned in the 1890s along with SEGREGATION as a means of maintaining white supremacy. In theory and in early practice, poor whites as well as blacks were kept from voting by this means. Later, however, some registrars learned to use the device mainly for purposes of RACIAL DISCRIMINATION, requiring only black would-be voters to produce their receipts for poll tax payments—in some states for payments going back to the voter's twenty-first year. The poll tax gradually fell from favor as a means of keeping blacks from voting; "good character" requirements and LITERACY TESTS, for example, were more readily adapted to this purpose. By 1940 only seven states retained the poll tax as a voting condition.

In BREEDLOVE V. SUTTLES (1937), a case involving a white applicant for registration, the Supreme Court upheld Georgia's use of the poll tax as a condition on voting. The poll tax remained a CIVIL RIGHTS issue, kept alive in Congress by the regular introduction of bills to abolish its use. Southern committee chairmanships and senatorial filibusters succeeded in sidetracking this legislation. When the TWENTY-FOURTH Amendment was finally submitted to the states in 1962, it forbade the use of poll taxes as a condition on voting only in federal, not state, elections. The Amendment was ratified in 1964.

Two years later, the Supreme Court held, in HARPER V. VIRGINIA BOARD OF ELECTIONS (1966), that conditioning voting in state elections on poll tax payments denied the EQUAL PROTECTION OF THE LAWS. Only four states still retained the device, but its elimination eloquently symbolized the relation between VOTING RIGHTS and the equal CITIZENSHIP of all Americans.

Bibliography

MYRDAL, GUNNAR   1944   *An American Dilemma: The Negro Problem and Modern Democracy.*  Chaps. 22–23. New York: Harper & Brothers.

# LITERACY TEST

Kenneth L. Karst

Many states used to require voters to be literate in English. The main constitutional problems raised by this practice arose from the use of literacy tests in southern and border states as a form of RACIAL DISCRIMINATION aimed at denying black citizens their VOTING RIGHTS in violation of the FIFTEENTH AMENDMENT. A typical law conditioned voter registration on the ability to read and write a provision of the state constitution selected by the registrar, to the registrar's "satisfaction." (An Alabama registrar once wrote this explanation for rejecting a black applicant: "Error in spilling.") Some laws also required the applicant to "interpret" or "explain" the constitutional provision, offering even greater opportunities for discriminatory application.

In *Davis v. Schnell* (1949) the Supreme Court summarily affirmed a lower court decision invalidating a requirement that a voter "understand and explain" an article of the United States Constitution; the registrar's discretion was so great that the test was an obvious "device to make racial discrimination easy." However, in LASSITER V. NORTHAMPTON COUNTY BOARD OF ELECTIONS (1959) the Court unanimously upheld a bare literacy requirement, in the absence of any showing of discriminatory application. This distinction had been suggested by the Court as early as WILLIAMS V. MISSISSIPPI (1898).

Meanwhile, the Court had fought two minor voting rights skirmishes with Oklahoma. That state had required voters to pass a literacy test, but excepted any voter whose ancestors had been registered to vote in 1866. Because of this GRANDFATHER CLAUSE, only black registrants were required to take literacy tests; the Court readily invalidated this law in GUINN V. UNITED STATES (1915). After the decision, Oklahoma adopted a law requiring all new voters to register within a twelve-day period; because virtually all the new voters were black, this onerous procedure fell before the Fifteenth Amendment, which "nullifies sophisticated as well as simple-minded modes of discrimination," in *Lane v. Wilson* (1939).

The death blow to voter literacy tests was delivered not by the Court but by Congress, which approached the question gingerly. The VOTING RIGHTS ACT OF 1965 required certain states and counties to suspend their use of literacy tests for five years. This feature of the law was upheld in SOUTH CAROLINA V. KATZENBACH (1966). In the same year, KATZENBACH V. MORGAN (1966) upheld another feature of the 1965 act requiring states to confer the vote on some citizens who, having been educated in Puerto Rico, were literate in Spanish. In 1970, Congress suspended literacy tests for voting throughout the nation, a provision which the Court upheld in OREGON v. MITCHELL (1970) as a valid exercise of the power to enforce the Fifteenth Amendment. Finally, in 1975, Congress made the ban on literacy tests permanent. In practical terms, literacy tests for voters are a thing of the past, and the Supreme Court is unlikely to confront the *Lassiter* issue again.

Bibliography

LEIBOWITZ, ARNOLD H.    1969    English Literacy: Legal Sanction for Discrimination. *Notre Dame Lawyer* 45:7–67.

# BADGES OF SERVITUDE

Kenneth L. Karst

There was truth in the claim of slavery's defenders that many a northern "wage slave" worked under conditions less favorable than those of his enslaved counterpart down South. The evil of slavery was not primarily its imposition of hard work but its treatment of a person as if he or she were a thing. The laws governing slaves carried out this basic theme by systematically imposing a wide range of legal disabilities on slaves, preventing them not only from entering into the public life of the community (by voting, being members of juries, or speaking in public meetings) but also from owning property, making contracts, or even learning to read and write. All these disabilities were designed not merely to preserve a system of bondage to service, but to serve as badges of servitude, symbolizing the slaves' degraded status. In a moment of racist candor, Chief Justice ROGER B. TANEY extended this view of the stigmatized status of slaves to all black persons, slave or free. His opinion for the Supreme Court in DRED SCOTT V. SANDFORD (1857) spoke of blacks as "a subordinate and inferior class of beings," upon whom had been impressed "deep and enduring marks of inferiority and degradation."

Although slaves were often physically branded, the "marks" of which Taney spoke were metaphorical; they were the aggregate of legal restrictions imposed on slaves. When slavery was abolished by the THIRTEENTH AMENDMENT (1865), those marks did not disappear. The amendment, however, did not stop with the abolition of slavery and involuntary servitude; it also empowered Congress to enforce the abolition. From an early time it was argued that the amendment authorized Congress to enact laws to eradicate not only slavery itself but the "badges of servitude" as well. This view was at first accepted in principle by the Supreme Court, and then rejected in the early twentieth century. However, in JONES V. ALFRED H. MAYER CO. (1968), the Court reverted to the earlier interpretation, concluding that RACIAL DISCRIMINATION was the sort of "badge of servitude" that Congress could prohibit.

In the meanwhile, a parallel doctrinal development has become apparent. The CIVIL RIGHTS ACT OF 1866 and the FOURTEENTH AMENDMENT both recognized the CITIZENSHIP of the freed slaves. Both were designed to end the notion of superior and inferior classes of persons and to replace a system of sociopolitical subordination with the status of equal citizenship. (See EQUAL PROTECTION OF THE LAWS.) Because the principle of equal citizenship protects against the imposition of stigma, it often operates in the same symbolic universe that produced badges of servitude. To give full effect to the symbol and substance of equal citizenship is one of the major challenges of the nation's third century.

Bibliography

KINOY, ARTHUR 1967 The Constitutional Right of Negro Freedom. *Rutgers Law Review* 21:387–441.

# MISCEGENATION

Kenneth L. Karst

The fear of racial mixture migrated to the New World with the earliest colonists. In 1609, planters headed for Virginia were reminded by a preacher of the injunction that "Abrams posteritie keepe to themselves." Of course, they did no such thing. From the beginning, there was a shortage of women; white men freely interbred with both Indian and black women, even before the great waves of slave importation. During the era of slavery, interracial sex cut across all strata of the white male population, from the poorest indentured servants to the wealthiest planters. THOMAS JEFFERSON was merely the most celebrated of the latter. Mulattoes were, in fact, deliberately bred for the slave market. Miscegenation laws, forbidding an interracial couple to marry or live together, were not designed to prevent interracial sex but to prevent the transmission of wealth and status from white fathers to their interracial offspring. Laws governing ILLEGITIMACY served a similar purpose, particularly in southern states. To this day, a majority of "blacks" in the United States are of interracial descent.

The adoption of the FOURTEENTH AMENDMENT offered an obvious opportunity for the Supreme Court to hold miscegenation laws unconstitutional on EQUAL PROTECTION grounds. When the occasion arose in PACE V. ALABAMA (1883), however, the Court unanimously upheld such a law, saying that it applied equally to punish both white and black partners to an intimate relationship. The constitutional validity of miscegenation laws went largely unquestioned until the great mid-twentieth-century rediscovery of racial equality as the Fourteenth Amendment's central meaning. Following BROWN V. BOARD OF EDUCATION (1954), it was only a matter of time before the miscegenation issue would reach the Supreme Court. As it happened, the period of time was short. In *Naim v. Naim* (1955–1956) the Court fudged, dismissing an appeal in a jurisdictional evasion that Herbert Wechsler properly scored as "wholly without basis in the law." Unquestionably, the Court adopted this avoidance technique because of the political storm that had greeted the *Brown* decision. Playing on the white South's fear of race mixture was a standard scare tactic of politicians favoring SEGREGATION. Recognizing this fear, the NAACP, in planning its assault on segregated higher education, had deliberately chosen as its plaintiff in McLAURIN V. OKLAHOMA STATE REGENTS (1950) a sixty-eight-year-old graduate student. The *Brown* opinion itself had been carefully limited to the context of education, and the *Naim* evasion was cut from the same political cloth.

For a decade, the Court was spared the inevitable confrontation. In *Mclaughlin v. Florida* (1964), it invalidated a law forbidding unmarried cohabitation by an interracial couple. Assuming for argument the validity of the state's law forbidding interracial marriage, the Court nonetheless held that the cohabitation law denied equal protection. The reasoning of *Pace v. Alabama*, the Court said, had not withstood analysis in more recent decisions. Finally, in LOVING v. VIRGINIA (1967), the Court put an end to the whole ugly pretense about "racial purity," holding invalid a law forbidding interracial marriage. Equal protection and SUBSTANTIVE DUE PROCESS grounds served as alternative basis for the decision. *Loving* thus stands not only for a principle of racial equality but also for a broad "freedom to marry." (See FREEDOM OF INTIMATE ASSOCIATION.) The principle of equality is often liberty's cutting edge.

Bibliography

FRAZIER, E. FRANKLIN   1939   (rev. ed. 1966). *The Negro Family in the United States.* Chap. IV. Chicago: University of Chicago Press.

MYRDAL, GUNNAR   1944   *An American Dilemma: The Negro Problem and Modern Democracy.* Chap. 5. New York: Harper & Brothers.

# PEONAGE

William M. Wiecek

Peonage is a system of debt bondage, in which a laborer is bound to personal service in order to work off an obligation to pay money. The system originated in the newly independent countries of Spanish America early in the nineteenth century, and in Hawaii and the Philippines later, as a substitute for various institutions used in the colonial era to marshal a labor force. In some of these countries the system continues to exist. In its classic form, peonage involves a trivial advance of money to a worker, in exchange for a contractual obligation to work for a term, or until the debt is repaid. From then on, the laborer is bound by law to serve the employer, and efforts to quit are met with the force of the state: arrest, imprisonment, return to the employer's service.

Peonage was also part of a larger system of involuntary servitude that emerged in the American South after the Civil War. As such, though whites have sometimes been its victims, peonage has served as a substitute for black slavery. After the slave states were forced by emancipation to shift from a labor regime based on status and force to one of free labor based on contract and choice, peonage emerged as a system that hid the wolf of involuntary servitude in the sheep's clothing of contract.

Peonage as a customary system for coerced black labor had its origin in the contract-enforcement sections of the BLACK CODES (1865–1875) and other labor-related statutes of the era. These provided both civil and criminal penalties for breach of labor contracts, punished VAGRANCY, prohibited enticement of laborers from their jobs, and hampered or penalized agents inducing the emigration of laborers. Southern states also permitted the leasing of convict labor and adopted a criminal-surety system, whereby a person convicted of a MISDEMEANOR would have his fine and costs paid by a prospective employer and then be obliged to work for the surety. Though the Black Codes were soon repealed, the FREEDMEN'S BUREAU at the same time emphasized labor contracts as the nexus of the employer–employee relationship for former slaves, and this later encouraged the use of contracts as a device for forcing black labor.

In 1867, when Congress enacted the Peonage Act to abolish peonage in New Mexico Territory, it also made it applicable to "any other Territory or State of the United States." The act made it a FELONY to hold a person in a condition of peonage, or to arrest a person for that purpose.

It voided statutes and "usages" enforcing the "voluntary or involuntary service or labor of any persons as peons in liquidation of a debt or obligation, or otherwise."

United States District Judge Thomas G. Jones began the legal struggle against peonage in a vigorous GRAND JURY charge, reported as *The Peonage Cases* (1903), defining peonage broadly as "the exercise of dominion over their persons and liberties by the master, or employer, or creditors, to compel the discharge of the obligation, by service or labor, against the will of the person performing the service." In *Clyatt v. United States* (1905), the Supreme Court upheld the use of the Peonage Act for the prosecution of a peon-master. Brushing aside both STATE ACTION and DUAL SOVEREIGNTY arguments, Justice DAVID J. BREWER found authorization for direct federal power over peonage in the enforcement clause (section 2) of the THIRTEENTH AMENDMENT. But he also held that debt was the "basal fact" of peonage, thus limiting federal action to cases where an actual debt could be shown.

After publication of the "Report on Peonage" (1908) by the United States Department of Justice, prompted by discovery of occasional instances of white peonage (usually of immigrants), the Supreme Court, in BAILEY v. ALABAMA (1911), used the Peonage Act to strike down Alabama contract-enforcement statutes that permitted quitting to be *prima facie* evidence of an intent to defraud the employer. The Court held that the Peonage Act voids "all legislation which seeks to compel the service or labor by making it a crime to refuse or fail to perform it." In *United States v. Reynolds* (1914), the Court invalidated Alabama criminal-surety statutes, describing the plight of a black peon caught in them as being "chained to an everturning wheel of servitude." But peonage has proved to be a remarkably tenacious form of servitude for blacks in the rural South, highlighted by the 1921 massacre of eleven black peons by their Georgia master, and by the establishment of peonage under federal and state auspices in refugee camps after the 1927 Mississippi River flood.

While physical force or threat of prosecution plainly constitute peonage, other forms of compulsion present interpretive problems. Thus subterfuges as well as outright violations of the Peonage Act persist into the present, despite the invalidation or repeal of the state labor-contract statutes that provided the original basis of peonage. The threat of deportation has proved an effective means of keeping alien migrant workers in a condition of involuntary or underpaid labor, and lower federal courts have divided as to whether this constitutes peonage.

Bibliography
COHEN, WILLIAM   1976   Negro Involuntary Servitude in the South, 1865–1940: A Preliminary Analysis. *Journal of Southern History* 42:31–60.

DANIEL, PETE   1972   *The Shadow of Slavery: Peonage in the South, 1901–1969.*
Urbana: University of Illinois Press.
NOVAK, DANIEL A.   1978   *The Wheel of Servitude: Black Forced Labor After Slavery.*
Lexington: University Press of Kentucky.

# STRAUDER v. WEST VIRGINIA

100 U.S. 303 (1880)
## VIRGINIA v. RIVES
100 U.S. 313 (1880)
## EX PARTE VIRGINIA AND J. D. COLES
100 U.S. 339 (1880)

Leonard W. Levy

On a day in 1880 the Supreme Court handed down three opinions that fixed the constitutional law of JURY DISCRIMINATION for over half a century. The effect of the three, taken collectively, barred overt state denial of the rights of blacks to serve on juries and effectively barred blacks from jury service in the South. Anything so crude as an announced and deliberate effort to exclude persons on ground of race was unconstitutional; but if official policy did not refer to race and yet blacks were systematically excluded by covert practices, the Constitution's integrity remained unimpaired. No estimate can be made of the miscarriages of justice that occurred in the South and border states where only whites sat in judgment in civil cases involving the property of blacks or in criminal cases involving their life and liberty over a period of at least fifty-five years.

*Strauder* was a case in which official state policy was overtly discriminatory on racial grounds. West Virginia by statute declared that only whites might serve on juries. Justice WILLIAM STRONG, for the Court, holding the act to be a violation of the EQUAL PROTECTION clause of the FOURTEENTH AMENDMENT, declared that denying citizens the right to participate in the administration of justice solely for racial reasons "is practically a brand upon them, affixed by law; an assertion of their inferiority, and a stimulant to that race prejudice which is an impediment to securing to individuals of the race that equal justice which the law aims to secure to all others." The Court also sustained the constitutionality of a section of the CIVIL RIGHTS ACT OF 1866 by which Congress authorized the removal of a case from a state court to a federal court in order to prevent the denial of CIVIL RIGHTS by the state court. Justice STEPHEN J. FIELD and NATHAN CLIFFORD dissented without opinion.

In *Ex Parte Virginia and J. D. Coles,* the Court sustained the constitutionality of an act of Congress which provided that no qualified person should be disqualified because of race for service as a grand or petit juror in any court, state or federal. Coles, a county court judge of Virginia charged with selecting jurors, excluded from jury lists all black persons. He was indicted by the United States and was liable to be fined $5,000. On petition for a writ of HABEAS CORPUS, he alleged that the federal court had no JURISDICTION over him and that the act of Congress was unconstitutional. Strong declared that under the Fourteenth Amendment, Congress could reach any act of a state that violated the right of black citizens to serve on juries or their right to be tried by juries impartially selected without regard to race. The act of Judge Coles was the act of the state of Virginia, for a state acts through its officers and agents, none of whom may deny the equal protection of the laws. By so ruling, the Court prepared the ground for the doctrine of STATE ACTION. Field and Clifford, again dissenting, thought he act of Congress regulated purely local matters and destroyed state autonomy.

The effects of *Strauder* and *Ex Parte Virginia* were vitiated by the *Rives* decision. Two black men, indicted for the murder of a white man, sought to have their cases removed from a state court to a federal court on the ground that the GRAND JURY that indicted them and the PETIT JURY summoned to try them were composed entirely of whites. The prisoners claimed that the jury lists should include one third blacks, in proportion to the population, and, most important, that no blacks had ever been allowed to serve on juries in the county where they were to be tried. In this case the record did not show, as it did in the other two, overt and direct exclusion of blacks. Strong, for the Court, this time supported by Field and Clifford concurring separately, simply stated, without further ado, that the "assertions" that no blacks ever served on juries in the county "fall short" of showing the denial of a civil right or the existence of racial discrimination. The defendants might still be tried impartially. Similarly, they had no right to a jury composed in part of members of their race. A mixed jury, said the Court, is not essential to the equal protection of the laws. There was no "unfriendly legislation" in this case. In effect the Court placed upon black prisoners the burden of proving deliberate and systematic exclusion on ground of race. As a result, blacks quickly disappeared from jury service in the South.

Bibliography

SCHMIDT, BENNO C.   1983   Juries, Jurisdiction, and Race Discrimination: The Lost Promise of *Strauder v. West Virginia. Texas Law Review* 61:1401–1499.

# CIVIL RIGHTS ACT OF 1875

18 Stat. 335

Leonard W. Levy

On his deathbed Senator CHARLES SUMNER (Republican, Mass.) implored a congressional friend, "You must take care of the civil rights bill,—my bill, the civil rights bill, don't let it fail." Since 1870 Sumner had sought to persuade Congress to enact a law guaranteeing to all people, regardless of race or religion, the same accommodations and facilities in public schools, churches and cemeteries incorporated by public authority, places of public amusement, hotels licensed by law, and common carriers. Sumner had contended that racial SEGREGATION was discriminatory, that SEPARATE BUT EQUAL facilities were inherently unequal, and that compulsory equality would combat prejudice as much as compulsory segregation fostered it. Opponents claimed that the FOURTEENTH AMENDMENT protected the privileges of United States CITIZENSHIP only, not those of state citizenship to which the bulk of CIVIL RIGHTS attached. Opponents also claimed that Congress had no constitutional power to protect civil rights from violation by private persons or businesses.

School DESEGREGATION was unpopular among northern Republicans and hated by southern Democrats. After the election of 1874 resulted in a Democratic victory in the House, supporters of Sumner's bill settled for "half a loaf" by consenting to the deletion of the provisions on education, churches, and cemeteries. A black congressman from South Carolina agreed to the compromise because the school clause jeopardized the Republican party in the South and subordinated the educational needs of blacks to their right to be desegregated. Teaching the "three Rs" to the children of former slaves was more important than risking their educational opportunities by demanding their admission to "white" schools.

In February 1875 the lame-duck 43rd Congress, 2nd session, voting along party lines in both houses, passed the modified bill which President ULYSSES S. GRANT signed into law on March 1. The Civil Rights Act of 1875, the last Reconstruction measure and the last civil rights act until 1957, was the most important congressional enactment in the field of PUBLIC ACCOMMODATIONS until the CIVIL RIGHTS ACT OF 1964. The act of 1875 affirmed the equality of all persons in the enjoyment of transportation facilities, in hotels and inns, and in theaters and places of public amusement. Theoretically such businesses, though privately owned and operated, were like public utilities, exercising public functions for the benefit of the public and subject to public regulation. Anyone violating the statute was civilly liable for $500 damages and, on conviction in federal court, subject to a fine of not more than $1,000 or imprisonment for not more than one year. In 1883 the Supreme Court held the statute unconstitutional in the CIVIL RIGHTS CASES.

Bibliography

KONVITZ, MILTON R.   1961   *A Century of Civil Rights*.  New York: Columbia University Press.

# COMPROMISE OF 1877

## C. Vann Woodward

Four of the sectional compromises in nineteenth-century America were efforts to settle quarrels by mutual concessions and forestall danger of violence. Three of the four efforts were temporarily successful, and only the fourth, that of 1861, broke down in failure. For the next sixteen years, during the Civil War and Reconstruction, differences were resolved by resort to force. The Compromise of 1877 differed from the earlier ones in several ways, one of them being that its main purpose was to foreclose rather than to forestall resort to armed force. Since the Republican party was committed to force when necessary to protect freedmen's rights under the constitutional amendments and CIVIL RIGHTS acts of the Reconstruction period, any repudiation of such commitments had to be negotiated discreetly.

Under President ANDREW JOHNSON and President ULYSSES S. GRANT, the government had been backing away from enforcement of freedmen's rights almost from the start. In part the result of white resistance in the South, this retreat from Reconstruction was also a consequence of the prevalence of white-supremacy sentiment in the North. In the elections of 1874, regarded by some as a referendum on Reconstruction, the Republican House majority of 110 was replaced by a Democratic majority of sixty. And in the ensuing presidential election of 1876 the Democratic candidate, Samuel J. Tilden, won a majority of the popular votes and was conceded 184 of the 185 electoral votes required for election. He also claimed all the nineteen contested votes of South Carolina, Florida, and Louisiana, the only southern states remaining under Republican control. But so did his Republican opponent, Rutherford B. Hayes, who also claimed the election. The impasse was solved by an agreement between the two political parties (not the sections) to create a bipartisan electoral commission of fifteen to count the votes. An unanticipated last minute change of one member of the commission gave the Republicans a majority of one, and by that majority they counted all contested votes for Hayes. That eliminated Tilden, but to seat Hayes required formal action of the House. The Democratic majority, enraged over what they regarded as a "conspiracy" to rob them of their victory, talked wildly of resistance and started a filibuster.

Foreseeing the victory of Hayes, southern Democrats sought to salvage whatever they could out of defeat. Their prime objective was "home rule," which meant not only withdrawal of troops that sustained Republican rule in South Carolina and Louisiana but also a firm Republican commitment to abandon use of force in the future for defending rights of freedmen, carpetbaggers, and scalawags. This amounted to the virtual nullification of the FOURTEENTH and FIFTEENTH AMENDMENTS and the CIVIL RIGHTS ACT. In return southern conservatives promised to help confirm Hayes's election, and many Democrats of the old Whig persuasion promised to cooperate with the new administration, but not to defect to the Republican party unless it abandoned "radicalism."

With control of the army and the submission of enough northern Democrats, Republicans could have seated Hayes anyway. But the southerners exploited Republican fears of resistance and skillfully played what they later admitted was "a bluff game." An old Whig himself, Hayes fell in with the idea of reconstituting his party in the South under conservative white leaders in place of carpetbaggers. He not only pledged "home rule" but promised to appoint a conservative southern Democrat to his cabinet and sweetened his appeal to that constituency by publicly pledging generous support to bills for subsidizing "INTERNAL IMPROVEMENTS of a national character" in the South. Hayes's election was confirmed only two days before he took office.

As in earlier sectional compromises, not all the terms of that of 1877 were fulfilled, but the main ones were. Hayes appointed a southern Democrat his postmaster general, chief dispenser of patronage, and placed many other white conservatives in southern offices. Bills for federal subsidies to internal improvements met with more success than ever before. The troops sustaining Republican rule in the two states were removed and Democrats immediately took over. In the CIVIL RIGHTS CASES (1883) the Supreme Court erected the STATE ACTION barrier, severely limiting the reach of the Fourteenth Amendment. The Court's opinion was written by Justice JOSEPH P. BRADLEY, who had been a member of the 1877 electoral commission. More important than all this was the pledge against resort to force to protect black rights. That commitment held firm for eighty years, until the military intervention at Little Rock, Arkansas, in 1957. This set a record for durability among sectional compromises.

Bibliography

GILLETTE, WILLIAM  1980  *Retreat from Reconstruction, 1869–1879.* Baton Rouge: Louisiana State University Press.

POLAKOFF, KEITH J.  1973  *The Politics of Inertia: The Election of 1876 and the End of Reconstruction.* Baton Rouge: Louisiana State University Press.

WOODWARD, C. VANN  1966  *Reunion and Reaction: The Compromise of 1877 and the End of Reconstruction.* Boston: Little, Brown.

# CIVIL RIGHTS CASES

## 109 U.S. 3 (1883)

### Leonard W. Levy

In an opinion by Justice JOSEPH P. BRADLEY, with only Justice JOHN MARSHALL HARLAN dissenting, the Supreme Court ruled that Congress had no constitutional authority under either the THIRTEENTH or the FOURTEENTH AMENDMENT to pass the CIVIL RIGHTS ACT OF 1875. Holding that act unconstitutional proved to be one of the most fateful decisions in American history. It had the effect of reinforcing racist attitudes and practices, while emasculating a heroic effort by Congress and the President to prevent the growth of a Jim Crow society. The Court also emasculated the Fourteenth Amendment's enforcement clause, section five. The tragedy is that the Court made the Constitution legitimize public immorality on the basis of specious reasoning.

The *Civil Rights Cases* comprised five cases decided together, in which the act of 1875 had been enforced against innkeepers, theater owners, and a railroad company. In each of the five, a black citizen was denied the same accommodations, guaranteed by the statute, as white citizens enjoyed. The Court saw only an invasion of local law by the national government, contrary to the powers reserved to the states under the TENTH AMENDMENT. Bradley began his analysis with the Fourteenth Amendment, observing that its first section, after declaring who shall be a citizen, was prohibitory: it restrained only STATE ACTION. "Individual invasion of individual rights is not the subject-matter of the amendment." Its fifth section empowered Congress to enforce the amendment by appropriate legislation. "To enforce what? To enforce the prohibition," Bradley answered. He ignored the fact that the enforcement section applied to the entire amendment, including the CITIZENSHIP clause, which made all persons born or naturalized in the United States and subject to its jurisdiction citizens of the United States and of the states in which they reside. As Harlan pointed out, citizenship necessarily imports "equality of civil rights among citizens of every race in the same state." Congress could guard and enforce rights, including the rights of citizenship, deriving from the Constitution itself. Harlan reminded the Court of its opinion in STRAUDER v. WEST VIRGINIA (1880), where it had said that "a right or immunity created by the constitution or only guaranteed by it, even without any express delegation of power, may be protected by congress."

But Bradley took the view that the legislative power conferred upon Congress by the Fourteenth Amendment does not authorize enactments on subjects "which are within the domain of state legislation. . . . It does not authorize congress to create a code of municipal law for regulation of private rights." Congress can merely provide relief against state action that violates the amendment's prohibitions on the states. Thus, only when the states acted adversely to the rights of citizenship could Congress pass remedial legislation. But its legislation could not cover the whole domain of CIVIL RIGHTS or regulate "all private rights between man and man in society." Otherwise, Congress would "supersede" the state legislatures. In effect the Court was saying that the Reconstruction amendments had not revolutionized the federal system. In effect the Court also warned the states not to discriminate racially, lest Congress intervene, as it had in the CIVIL RIGHTS ACT OF 1866, which the Court called "corrective" legislation against state action. In the cases under consideration, however, the discrimination derived from purely private acts unsupported by state authority. "The wrongful act of an individual, unsupported by any such authority, is simply a private wrong" that Congress cannot reach. Congress can, of course, reach and regulate private conduct in the normal course of legislation, penalizing individuals; but, Bradley explained, in every such case Congress possesses under the Constitution a power to act on the subject.

Under the Thirteenth Amendment, however, Congress can enact any legislation necessary and proper to eradicate SLAVERY and "all badges and incidents of slavery," and its legislation may operate directly on individuals, whether their acts have the sanction of state authority or not. The question, then, was whether the Thirteenth Amendment vested in Congress the authority to require that all persons shall have equal accommodations in inns, public conveyances, and places of public amusement. The Court conceded that the amendment established "universal civil and political freedom throughout the United States" by abolishing slavery, but it denied that distinctions based on race or color abridged that freedom. Where, Bradley asked, does slavery, servitude, or badges of either arise from race discrimination by private parties? "The thirteenth amendment," he declared, "has respect, not to distinctions of race, or class, or color, but to slavery." The act of the owner of an inn, or theater, or transportation facility in refusing accommodation might inflict an ordinary civil injury, recognizable by state law, but not slavery or an incident of it. "It would be running the slavery argument into the ground," Bradley insisted, "to make it apply to every act of discrimination which a person may see fit to make" as to his guests, or those he will take in his coach, or those he will admit to his concert. On the theory that mere discrimination on account of race or color did not impose badges of slavery, the Court held that the Thirteenth Amendment, like the Fourteenth, did not validate the Civil Rights Act of 1875.

The case involved questions of law, history, and public policy. Harlan, dissenting, had the weight of argument as to all three, but Bradley had the weight of numbers. It was an 8–1 decision, and the eight scarcely bothered to answer the dissenter. Ignoring him might have been more discreet than trying to rebut him. He met their contentions head-on, starting with a strenuous objection to their parsimonious interpretation of national powers under the Thirteenth and Fourteenth Amendments, both of which expressly made affirmative grants of power. By contrast, Harlan demonstrated, the Court had generously construed the Constitution to support congressional enactments on behalf of slaveholders. The fugitive slave acts, which operated on private individuals, were based on a clause in the Constitution, Article 4, section 2, paragraph 3, that did not empower Congress to legislate at all. The clause merely provided that a fugitive slave be delivered up upon the claim of his owner, yet the Court sustained the acts of 1793 (PRIGG V. PENNSYLVANIA, 1842) and of 1850 (ABLEMAN V. BOOTH, 1859), implying a national power to enforce a right constitutionally recognized. The Thirteenth Amendment, as the majority admitted, established a constitutional right: civil freedom for citizens throughout the nation. And, as the majority admitted, the abolition of slavery reached the BADGES OF SERVITUDE, so that the freedmen would have the same rights as white men. Similarly, the act of 1875 reached badges of servitude, because it, like the amendments to the Constitution, aimed at erasing the assumption that blacks were racially inferior. For Harlan, RACIAL DISCRIMINATION was a badge of servitude. Bradley had distinguished the act of 1866 from the act of 1875 on the ground that the earlier statute aimed at protecting rights that only the states might deny. Harlan replied that citizens regardless of race were entitled to the same civil rights.

Harlan also demonstrated that the rights allegedly violated by purely private parties were denied by individuals and CORPORATIONS that exercised public functions and wielded power and authority under the state. Relying on a broad concept of state action, he sought to prove that the parties whom the majority regarded as private were, in contemplation of law, public or quasi-public. A railroad corporation, an innkeeper, and a theater-manager had denied accommodations to black citizens. Railroads and streetcars were common carriers, that is, they were public highways, performing state functions; they were public conveyances which, though privately owned, had been established by state authority for a public use and were subject to control by the state for the public benefit. Free citizens of any race were entitled to use such facilities. Similarly, the COMMON LAW defined innkeepers as exercising a quasi-public employment that obligated them to take in all travelers, regardless of race. Theaters were places of public amusement, licensed by the public, of which the "colored race is a part," and theaters were clothed with a public interest, in accord with MUNN V. ILLINOIS (1877). Congress had not promiscuously sought to regulate the entire body of civil rights nor had it entered the domain of the states by generally controlling public conveyances, inns, or places of public amusement. Congress had simply declared that in a nation of universal freedom, private parties exercising public authority could not discriminate on ground of race; in effect the statute reached state instrumentalities whose action was tantamount to state action.

Under the Thirteenth Amendment, Congress could reach badges of servitude; under the Fourteenth, it could reach racial discrimination by state agencies. Contrary to the Court's assertion, Congress had not outlawed racial discrimination imposed by purely private action. It had aimed at such discrimination only in public places chartered or licensed by the state, in violation of the rights of citizenship which the Fourteenth Amendment affirmed. The amendment's fifth section empowered Congress to pass legislation enforcing its affirmative as well as its prohibitory clauses. Courts, in the normal exercise of JUDICIAL REVIEW, could hold unconstitutional state acts that violated the prohibitory clauses. Accordingly, section five was not restricted to merely corrective or remedial national legislation. Congress, not the Court, said Harlan, citing McCULLOCH V. MARYLAND (1819), might choose the means best adopted to implementing the ends of the two amendments. Harlan insisted that Congress

may, without transcending the limits of the constitution, do for human liberty and the fundamentals of American citizenship, what it did, with the sanction of this court, for the protection of slavery and the rights of the masters of fugitive slaves. If fugitive slave laws, providing modes and prescribing penalties whereby the master could seize and recover his fugitive slave, were legitimate exertions of an implied power to protect and enforce a right recognized by the constitution, why shall the hands of congress be tied, so that—under an express power, by appropriate legislation, to enforce a constitutional provision granting citizenship—it may not, by means of direct legislation, bring the whole power of this nation to bear upon states and their officers, and upon such individuals and corporations exercising public functions, assumed to abridge the supreme law of the land.

Some old abolitionists, deploring a ruling that returned the freedmen to a "reign of contempt, injury, and ignominy," denounced the "new DRED SCOTT decision," but most were resigned to defeat. Racial segregation was common throughout the country. Not surprisingly *The Nation* magazine, which approved of the decision, observed that the public's general unconcern about the decision indicated "how completely the extravagant expectations as well as the fierce passions of the war have died out." The Court served "a useful purpose in thus undoing the work of Congress," said the *New York Times,* and *Harper's Weekly* agreed. Public opinion supported the Court, but justice and judicial craftsmanship were on the side of Harlan, dissenting.

Bibliography

KONVITZ, MILTON R.   1961   *A Century of Civil Rights.* New York: Columbia University Press.

WESTIN, ALAN F.   1962   The Case of the Prejudiced Doorkeeper. Pages 128–144 in Garraty, John A., *Quarrels That Have Shaped the Constitution.* New York: Harper & Row.

# *YICK WO v. HOPKINS*

## 118 U.S. 356 (1886)

### Leonard W. Levy

This is one of the basic decisions interpreting the EQUAL PROTECTION OF THE LAWS clause of the FOURTEENTH AMENDMENT. A San Francisco ordinance made criminal the conduct of a laundry business in any building not made of stone or brick, with such exceptions for wooden structures as administrative officials might make. Officials used their discretion in a grossly discriminatory manner, licensing about eighty wooden laundries run by Caucasians and denying licenses to about two hundred applicants of Chinese extraction. The Supreme Court unanimously held, in an opinion by Justice STANLEY MATTHEWS, that the ordinance, though racially neutral on its face, was applied so unequally and oppressively by public authorities as to deny equal protection. Thus the Court looked beyond the law's terms to its racially discriminatory administration and applied the benefits of the Fourteenth Amendment to Oriental ALIENS, that is, "to all persons . . . without regard to any difference of race, of color, or of nationality."

# SEGREGATION

### Kenneth L. Karst

From the beginning, RACIAL DISCRIMINATION in America has been a national phenomenon. Jim Crow was a southern name for the segregation of the races as part of a system of caste. But segregation antedated Jim Crow, and it began in the North and the West. The leading judicial decision upholding school segregation before the Civil War bears a name Northerners prefer to forget: ROBERTS V. BOSTON (1850). Blacks were either excluded entirely from PUBLIC ACCOMMODATIONS such as hotels, railroads, and theaters, or given separate accommodations. They were segregated in prisons and in churches. Several northern and western states even sought to bar the immigration of blacks; such a legal provision was adopted by Oregon voters by an eight-to-one margin.

Nor has this country's segregation been limited to blacks. As late as 1947, a federal court of appeals held that the segregation of Chicano children in a school district in California was invalid. The decision's ground was itself depressing: the state's statute authorized only the segregation of children whose ancestry was Indian, Chinese, Japanese, and Mongolian.

Still, it was the postabolition South that carried the segregation of the races to its fullest development, and blacks were the chief victims of the practice. Before slavery was abolished, of course, the dominance of whites was assured without any call for segregation. After abolition, the southern states adopted severe legal restrictions on blacks, which served to maintain white supremacy. (See BLACK CODES.) When the CIVIL RIGHTS ACT OF 1866 and the FOURTEENTH AMENDMENT not only ended these legal restrictions but also positively declared the CITIZENSHIP of the freed slaves, segregation was the southern response. By 1870, Tennessee had forbidden interracial marriages (see MISCEGENATION), and later came the "Jim Crow car" laws segregating railroad passenger seating.

Segregation was not, however, merely a creature of state legislation. It also resulted from private action: a hotel would refuse to take black guests; homeowners in a neighborhood would agree not to sell to black buyers. In such cases law played a role that was less obvious on the surface of events but was vital nonetheless. A black who sought the aid of the state courts in overcoming private discrimination would simply be turned away; state laws would deny any remedy.

Late in the nineteenth century, the Supreme Court gave its support to this system of interlocking discriminations. In the CIVIL RIGHTS CASES (1883), the Court held invalid a congressional statute forbidding racial discrimination by railroads, hotels, theaters, and restaurants. (See STATE ACTION.) And in PLESSY V. FERGUSON (1896) the Court upheld a Jim Crow car law against an EQUAL PROTECTION attack. (See SEPARATE BUT EQUAL DOCTRINE.) By the early twentieth century, the South was racially segregated to extremes that were at once tragic and ludicrous: separate telephone booths for blacks in Oklahoma; separate storage for textbooks used by black children in North Carolina and Florida schools; separate elevators for blacks in Atlanta; separate Bibles for swearing black witnesses in Georgia courts. The point of all this was nothing less than the denial to blacks of membership in a white-dominated society—the denial of citizenship itself, in defiance of the Fourteenth Amendment.

Some of the harms caused by racial segregation are harms to material interests: a black is denied accommodation at a hotel, or admission to a state university medical school (and thus to the medical profession), or the chance to live in a particular neighborhood or be a factory foreman. These material harms are serious, but the worst harms of segregation are psychic harms. The primary reason for segregating railroad passengers, of course, is to symbolize a caste system. The stigma of inferiority is a denial of a person's humanity, and the result is anguish and humiliation. The more the races are separated, the more natural it is for members of the dominant white race to see each black person not as an individual but simply as a black. Ralph Ellison, in his novel *Invisible Man* (1952), makes the point: "I am invisible, understand, simply because people refuse to see me. . . . When they approach me they see only my surroundings, themselves, or figments of their imagination—indeed, everything and anything except me. . . . You ache with the need to convince yourself that you do exist in the real world." To be a citizen, on the other hand, is to be respected as a person and recognized as a participating member in the society.

Jim Crow was a complex living system, and its dismantling would be no simple task. The field of segregation in housing exemplifies the difficulties. The NAACP's first major victory against segregation came in BUCHANAN V. WARLEY (1917), when the Supreme Court struck down a local ZONING ordinance aimed at maintaining segregated residential neighborhoods. But the decision by no means ended housing segregation, which continued as a result of private conduct. When the private discrimination was sufficiently connected with state action, as in the case of racially RESTRICTIVE COVENANTS enforced by state courts, the Fourteenth Amendment was an effective weapon against residential segregation. (See SHELLEY V. KRAEMER, 1948.) But in the absence of such state support, a landowner might simply refuse to rent or sell to blacks, and the would-be buyers would be without remedy. Two events in 1968 altered this portion of the doctrinal landscape. In JONES v. ALFRED H. MAYER CO. the Supreme Court concluded that the Civil Rights Act of 1866 forbade private discrimination in the sale of property. In the same year, Congress adopted a comprehensive fair housing law as part of the CIVIL RIGHTS ACT OF 1968. The new law forbade various forms of racial discrimination by lenders and brokers as well as private landlords and sellers. The combination of constitutional litigation and legislation aimed at ending housing segregation had achieved a radical restructuring of the law.

The restructuring of racial patterns in the neighborhoods where people live, however, has proved to be quite another matter. Middle-class blacks have largely left the core cities to live in suburbs, but the degree of racial segregation in residences has changed only slightly since 1940. The term "white flight," coined in the context of school desegregation, seems even more clearly applicable to residential patterns. It is hard to find stable interracial neighborhoods in any large city in the country, at any income level. (For discussion of related questions concerning the public schools—where continued patterns of segregation are related directly to residential segregation—see DESEGREGATION.)

In contrast, racial segregation in transportation and other public accommodations has come to an end. (See SIT-IN; CIVIL RIGHTS ACT OF 1964.) And laws forbidding interracial marriage collapsed under the double weight of equal protection and DUE PROCESS in LOVING v. VIRGINIA (1967). (See FREEDOM OF INTIMATE ASSOCIATION.) EMPLOYMENT DISCRIMINATION, too, is in retreat—including the segregation of job categories by race—as a result of enforcement of the fair employment portions of the 1964 Act.

The segregation that remains in American society, then, is chiefly residential segregation—with its concomitant, a substantial extent of separation of the races in the public schools. There is irony here: the decision in the school segregation case, BROWN v. BOARD OF EDUCATION (1954), was the critical event in the demise of Jim Crow, but our big city schools are the one set of public institutions in which the races remain largely separated. Yet Brown's impact on American life was important. The decision began more than a doctrinal movement; its implicit affirmation of the equal citizenship of all our people accelerated forces that have markedly changed not only race relations but also a wide range of other relationships formerly characterized by dominance and dependency.

It is easy now to see the social and economic changes in the country that permitted the success of the movement to end officially sponsored segregation. World War II was the great watershed. By the time the war began, there was a critical mass of educated blacks, enough to provide a national movement not only with its great chiefs but with local leadership as well—and with a trained cadre of lawyers. The war produced waves of migration of blacks out of the rural South and into the cities of the North and West, where they very soon found a political voice. In part, too, the war had been billed as a war against Nazi racism— whatever we might be doing on the home front. (See JAPANESE AMERICAN CASES, 1943–1944.) The expected postwar depression failed to appear, and the 1950s and 1960s were a time of economic expansion, conducive to a sympathetic reception for egalitarian claims. All this is familiar learning. Yet in the early 1950s there was no sense of inevitability surrounding the assault on segregation. If the sudden collapse of Jim Crow now seems inevitable, that in itself is a measure of the distance we have come. And if the end of segregation did not end a system of racial caste, that is a measure of the distance we have yet to travel.

Bibliography

BELL, DERRICK   1980   Brown v. Board of Education and the Interest-Convergence Dilemma. *Harvard Law Review*  93:518–533.

LEVY, LEONARD W. and JONES, DOUGLAS   1972   Jim Crow Education: Origins of the "Separate but Equal" Doctrine. In Levy, Leonard W., *Judgments: Essays on American Constitutional History*. Chicago: Quadrangle Books.

LITWACK, LEON F.   1961   *North of Slavery*. Chicago: University of Chicago Press.

MYRDAL, GUNNAR   1944   *An American Dilemma*. New York: Harper & Brothers.

WOODWARD, C. VANN   1966   *The Strange Career of Jim Crow*, 2nd rev. ed. New York: Oxford University Press.

# PLESSY v. FERGUSON

## 163 U.S. 537 (1896)

### Leonard W. Levy

Until BROWN V. BOARD OF EDUCATION (1954), *Plessy* was the constitutional linchpin for the entire structure of Jim Crow in America. Borrowed from LEMUEL SHAW in ROBERTS V. BOSTON (1851), the *Plessy* Court established the SEPARATE BUT EQUAL DOCTRINE: black persons were not denied the EQUAL PROTECTION OF THE LAWS safeguarded by the FOURTEENTH AMENDMENT when they were provided with facilities substantially equal to those available to white persons.

Florida enacted the first Jim Crow transportation law in 1887, and by the end of the century the other states of the old Confederacy had followed suit. Louisiana's act, which was challenged in *Plessy*, required railroad companies carrying passengers in the state to have "equal but separate accommodations" for white and colored persons by designating coaches racially or partitioning them. Black citizens, who denounced the innovation of Jim Crow in Louisiana as "unconstitutional, unamerican, unjust, dangerous and against sound public policy," complained that prejudiced whites would have a "license" to maltreat and humiliate inoffensive blacks. Plessy was a TEST CASE. Homer A. Plessy, an octoroon (one-eighth black), boarded the East Louisiana Railroad in New Orleans bound for Covington in the same state and sat in the white car; he was arrested when he refused to move to the black car. Convicted by the state he appealed on constitutional grounds, invoking the THIRTEENTH and Fourteenth AMENDMENTS. The Court had already decided in LOUISVILLE, NEW ORLEANS & TEXAS PACIFIC RY. V. MISSISSIPPI (1890) that Jim Crow cars in INTRASTATE COMMERCE did not violate the COMMERCE CLAUSE.

Justice JOHN MARSHALL HARLAN was the only dissenter from the opinion by Justice HENRY B. BROWN. That the state act did not infringe the Thirteenth Amendment, declared Brown, "is too clear for argument." The act implied "merely a legal distinction" between the two races and therefore had "no tendency to destroy the legal equality of the two races, or reestablish a state of involuntary servitude." Harlan, believing that STATE ACTION could have no regard to the race of citizens when their CIVIL RIGHTS were involved, would have ruled that compulsory racial SEGREGATION violated the Thirteenth Amendment by imposing a BADGE OF SERVITUDE.

The chief issue was whether the state act abridged the Fourteenth Amendment's equal protection clause. One reads Brown's opinion with an enormous sense of the feebleness of words as conveyors of thought, because he conceded that the object of the amendment "was undoubtedly to enforce the absolute equality of the two races before the law," yet he continued the same sentence by adding, "but in the nature of things it could not have been intended to abolish distinctions based on color. . . ." As a matter of historical fact the intention of the amendment was, generally, to abolish legal distinctions based on color. The Court pretended to rest on history without looking at the historical record; it did not claim the necessity of adapting the Constitution to changed conditions, making untenable the defense often heard in more recent years, that the decision fit the times. *Plessy* makes sense only if one understands that the Court believed that segregation was not discriminatory, indeed that it would violate the equal protection clause if it were discriminatory. Brown conceded that a statute implying a legal inferiority in civil society, lessening "the security of the right of the colored race," would be discriminatory, but he insisted that state-imposed segregation did not "necessarily imply the inferiority of either race to the other. . . ." There was abundant evidence to the contrary, none of it understandable to a Court that found fallacious the contention that "the enforced separation of the two races stamps the colored race with a badge of inferiority. If this be so, it is not by reason of anything found in the act, but solely because the colored race chooses to put that construction on it." That segregation stamped blacks with a badge of inferiority was not fallacious. The fallacy was that only they imputed inferiority to segregation. Jim Crow laws were central to white supremacist thought. That blacks were inherently inferior was a conviction being stridently trumpeted by white supremacists from the press, the pulpit, and the platform, as well as from the legislative halls, of the South. The label, "For Colored Only," was a public expression of disparagement amounting to officially sanctioned civil inequality. By the Court's own reasoning, state acts compelling racial segregation were unconstitutional if inferiority was implied or discrimination intended.

The separate but equal doctrine was fatally vulnerable for still other reasons given, ironically, by the Court in *Plessy*. It sustained the act as a valid exercise of the POLICE POWER yet stated that every exercise of that power "must be reasonable, and extend only to such laws as are enacted in good faith for the promotion of the public good, and not for the annoyance or oppression of a particular class." Jim Crow laws were not only annoying and oppressive to blacks; they were not reasonable or for the public good. The Court asserted that the question of reasonableness must be determined with reference "to the established usages, customs and traditions" of the people of the state. The proper standard of reasonableness ought to have been the equal protection clause of the Constitution, not new customs of the white supremacists of an ex-slave state. Even if the custom of segregation had been old, and it was not, the Court was making strange doctrine when implying that discrimination becomes vested with constitutionality if carried on long enough to become customary. Classifying people by race for the purpose of transportation was unreasonable because the classification was irrelevant to any legitimate purpose.

The only conceivable justification for the reasonableness of the racial classification was that it promoted the public good, which Brown alleged. The effects of segregation were inimical to the public good, because, as Harlan pointed out, it "permits the seeds of race hate to be planted under the sanction of law." It created and perpetuated interracial tensions. Oddly the Court made the public-good argument in the belief that the commingling of the races would threaten the public peace by triggering disorders. In line with that assumption Brown declared that legislation is powerless to eradicate prejudice based on hostile "racial instincts" and that equal rights cannot be gained by "enforced commingling." These contentions seem cynical when announced in an opinion sanctioning inequality by sustaining a statute compelling racial segregation. The argument that prejudice cannot be legislated away overlooked the extent to which prejudice had been legislated into existence and continued by Jim Crow statutes.

Harlan's imperishable dissent repeated the important Thirteenth Amendment argument that he had made in the CIVIL RIGHTS CASES (1883) on badges of servitude. That amendment, he declared, "decreed universal civil freedom in the country." Harlan reminded the Court that in STRAUDER v. WEST VIRGINIA (1880), it had construed the Fourteenth Amendment to mean that "the law in the States shall be the same for the black as for the white" and that the amendment contained "a necessary implication of a positive immunity, or right . . . the right to exemption from unfriendly legislation against them distinctively as colored—exemption from legal discriminations, implying inferiority in civil society, lessening the security of their enjoyment of rights which others enjoy. . . ." To Harlan, segregation was discriminatory per se. The state act was unreasonable because segregation was not germane to a legitimate legislative end. He meant that the Fourteenth Amendment rendered the state powerless to make legal distinctions based on color in respect to public transportation. A railroad, he reminded the Court, was a public highway exercising public functions available on the same basis to all citizens. "Our Constitution," said Harlan, "is color-blind, and neither knows nor tolerates classes among citizens." He thought the majority's decision would prove in time to be as pernicious as DRED SCOTT v. SANDFORD (1857). As for the separate but equal doctrine, he remarked that the "thin disguise" of equality would mislead no one "nor atone for the wrong this day done."

*Plessy* cleared the constitutional way for legislation that forced the separation of the races in all places of public accommodation. Most of that legislation came after *Plessy*. In the CIVIL RIGHTS CASES, the Court had prevented Congress from abolishing segregation, and in *Plessy* the Court supported the states in compelling it. Not history and not the Fourteenth Amendment dictated the decision; it reflected its time, and its time was racist. As Justice Brown pointed out, even Congress in governing the DISTRICT OF COLUMBIA had required separate schools for the two races. The Court did not invent Jim Crow but adapted the Constitution to it.

Bibliography

KLUGER, RICHARD   1973   *Simple Justice: The History of Brown v. Board of Education and Black America's Struggle for Equality.*  Pages 71–83. New York: Knopf.

OBERST, PAUL   1973   The Strange Career of *Plessy v. Ferguson. Arizona Law Review* 15:389–418.

OLSON, OTTO, ed.   1967   *The Thin Disguise: Turning Point in Negro History: Plessy v. Ferguson.*  New York: Humanities Press.

WOODWARD, C. VANN   1971   The National Decision Against Equality. Pages 212–233 in Woodward, *American Counterpoint: Slavery and Racism in the North–South Dialogue.*  Boston: Little, Brown.

# JOHN MARSHALL
# HARLAN
## (1833–1911)

### Henry J. Abraham

Among the Justices of the Supreme Court, few have provoked more diverse reactions from colleagues, contemporaries, and later generations than the first Justice John Marshall Harlan. Despite a distinguished tenure of over thirty-three years (1877–1911), during which he participated in many cases of constitutional significance and established himself as one of the most productive, independent, and voluble members of the Court, both jurists and historians were inclined to hold Harlan in low esteem from his death in 1911 to the middle of the twentieth century. But two signal events in 1954—the Court's implicit adoption of Harlan's famous solitary dissent in PLESSY v. FERGUSON (1896) in its decision of the public school SEGREGATION cases, BROWN v. BOARD OF EDUCATION and BOLLING v. SHARPE, and President DWIGHT D. EISENHOWER's appointment of his distinguished grandson and namesake to the highest bench—prompted historians to reevaluate the first Justice Harlan. No longer belittled and neglected, Harlan now began to be recast as a great dissenter who had foretold many of the most fundamental developments in later constitutional interpretation: the virtually complete INCORPORATION of the BILL OF RIGHTS into the FOURTEENTH AMENDMENT; the inherent inequality of racial segregation; and the plenary power of Congress under the COMMERCE CLAUSE. How can one account for the wide disparity between the traditional and revisionist interpretations of Mr. Justice Harlan?

Harlan was born in 1833 in Kentucky, the son of a two-term Whig member of the United States House of Representatives. A stern Presbyterian, young Harlan grew up during the worsening estrangement of the South and the Union. Kentucky, as a border state, was sharply divided. Harlan was graduated from Centre College, and, at twenty, completed his law courses at Transylvania University and was admitted to the Kentucky bar.

Harlan participated actively as a moderate in the political struggles that racked the country on the eve of the Civil War. In 1859 he ran for Congress, but was narrowly defeated. A traditional southern gentleman and conservative, he refused to join the Republican party or to support ABRAHAM LINCOLN's 1860 campaign. He supported the Constitutional Union party which sought the peaceful preservation of the status quo.

After the attack on Fort Sumter, Kentucky declined to furnish troops. Harlan volunteered to fight on the northern side and, in the fall of 1861, organized the Tenth Kentucky Volunteer Infantry. Harlan rose rapidly to the rank of colonel and served as acting commander of a brigade until he resigned his military commission in 1863 upon the death of his father.

Shortly after returning to civilian life, Harlan campaigned for the Constitutional Union party and was elected attorney general of Kentucky, a post he held until 1867. Harlan stumped for General George McClellan in the presidential election of 1864, bitterly criticizing the Lincoln administration. He opposed the THIRTEENTH AMENDMENT and continued to hold slaves until forced to free them.

In 1867, however, Harlan changed his party affiliation, becoming the unsuccessful Republican gubernatorial candidate. As a southern slaveholder and Whig he had long sought to support both slavery and a strong national government—a position that grew increasingly difficult in the political environment of *antebellum* Kentucky, where supporters of slavery based their political programs on opposition to the federal government. In the end Harlan resolved his dilemma in favor of the national government. Contending that he would rather be right than consistent, Harlan publicly repudiated his views favoring slavery and defended the civil war amendments as necessary to the reconstruction of the Union. A second try for the Kentucky governorship in 1871 also ended in failure.

At the national level, Harlan supported ULYSSES S. GRANT in the presidential election of 1868 and had attained sufficient prominence by 1872 to have been proposed as a vice-presidential candidate. Four years later Harlan led the Kentucky delegation to the Republican convention. When it became apparent that his friend, Benjamin Bristow, could not win, Harlan threw the Kentucky delegation's support to RUTHERFORD B. HAYES, enabling Hayes narrowly to defeat James G. Blaine and obtain the nomination.

On October 16, 1877, President Hayes nominated Harlan to the Supreme Court, an appointment that was widely regarded as a payment for political services rendered. Until five days before his death on October 15, 1911, for almost thirty-four years, Harlan served on the Court. With the exception of JOHN MARSHALL and JOSEPH STORY, none of its members up to that time had taken part in so many decisions that ultimately so crucially affected the future of American constitutionalism.

Harlan served on the Supreme Court during a period of rapid social and economic change. Although the era of Reconstruction had passed, the effect of the postwar amendments on the federal system remained a topic of bitter constitutional dispute. The Court was also increasingly obliged to rule on constitutional challenges to the validity of state and federal statutes purporting to regulate the economy in the public interest.

Harlan brought to the Court two fundamental convictions drawn from his upbringing and early experiences in Kentucky politics. He believed in a strong national government, especially in the spheres of commerce and economic development. Hence Harlan would view federal laws regulating the economy much more favorably than similar state initiatives. Second, he would ardently support the rights of blacks, although he had developed that posture only late in his political career. While Harlan never wavered in his judicial support for black rights and a strong national economy, the political implications of his Whig principles varied widely during his judicial tenure. When he came to the Court in 1877 Harlan quickly established himself as its foremost defender of private contracts against state regulation since Marshall. Indeed, throughout his long career Harlan closely scrutinized any state law that impinged on private property rights. He often voted to invalidate such statutes under the contract, JUST COMPENSATION, or EQUAL PROTECTION clauses.

After the passage of the INTERSTATE COMMERCE ACT of 1877 and the SHERMAN ANTITRUST ACT of 1890, however, Harlan came to look quite favorably upon national, as opposed to state, regulation of the economy. Harlan's Whig philosophy explains much of his apparent inconsistency in decisions concerning private property rights. Harlan generally upheld national ECONOMIC REGULATION, but often voted to strike down state economic regulations that discriminated against interstate commerce without furthering significantly an important state interest under the POLICE POWER.

During his thirty-four years on the Court, Harlan articulated a broad body of constitutional principles respecting both governmental powers and individual rights. A convinced believer in legislative authority and judgment, he abhorred and denounced what he viewed as "judicial legislation" and advocated a straightforward application of the law as set forth in the Constitution and legislative enactments. But when it came to determining the provisions of a given law, his view was unique: "It is not the words of the law but the internal sense of it that makes the law: the letter is the body; the sense and reason of the law is the soul" (CIVIL RIGHTS CASES, 1883).

Justice Harlan lifted the practice of employing LEGISLATIVE INTENT as a guide to the sound construction of the law to the level of a philosophical principle. In addition, he, above all others, had an all but religious reverence for the Constitution as the fundamental instrument of the ideals of American democracy. A fervent Marshall disciple, he viewed the Court as the ultimate guardian of the Constitution. Harlan also adhered to Marshall's views on the proper distribution of powers within the federal system.

With respect to congressional power under the INTERSTATE COMMERCE clause, Harlan was a liberal national constitutionalist, with an almost slavish devotion to Chief Justice Marshall's opinions in general, and GIBBONS v. OGDEN (1824) in particular. Harlan displayed his broad interpretation of the commerce power most forcefully in opinions construing the Interstate Commerce Act of 1887 and the Sherman Antitrust Act of 1890. He dissented in *Texas & Pacific Railroad Co. v. Interstate Commerce Commission* (1896) and INTERSTATE COMMERCE COMMISSION v. ALABAMA MIDLAND RAILWAY Co. (1897) when the Court interpreted the Interstate Commerce Act as not granting the commission the power either to void discriminatory railroad rates or to set nondiscriminatory rates itself. Harlan believed that these decisions went far "to make that commission a useless body for all practical purposes, and to defeat many of the important objectives designed to be accomplished by the various enactments of Congress relating to interstate commerce. . . ." Congress eventually agreed, amending the Interstate Commerce Act to give the commission the powers for which Harlan had contended in his dissents.

When the Court emasculated the Sherman Antitrust Act, Justice Harlan, again in dissent, registered his strong advocacy of congressional power and the spirit of the law. In UNITED STATES v. E. C. KNIGHT Co. (1895) the Court narrowly interpreted the Sherman Act as applying to monopolies in interstate commerce but not to intrastate monopolies in manufacture of goods; it also stated that Congress lacked power under the commerce clause to regulate manufacturing. In the majority's view, "Commerce succeeds to manufacture, and is not a part of it." Yet Harlan insisted that the statute applied because the goods, although manufactured in one state, entered into interstate commerce. Four decades later, in the WAGNER ACT CASES (1937), Harlan's expansive view of congressional power under the commerce clause would become the generally accepted view.

Although Harlan held to a broad interpretation of national power under the commerce clause, he nonetheless supported some positive uses of STATE POLICE POWER that affected interstate commerce. He believed that, although a state might not—under the guise of inspection laws—discriminate against meat imported from out of state (MINNESOTA v. BARBER, 1890), it might require certain passenger stops of interstate railroad trains unless Congress had superseded local laws. Indeed, Harlan thought that state power should prevail if the statute in question affected interstate commerce "only incidentally" and furthered an important state interest under the police power—as was the case with state laws prohibiting the importation or sale of intoxicating liquor (BOWMAN v. CHICAGO & NORTHWESTERN RAILWAY, 1888). Whether agreeing or dissenting, however, Harlan consistently stood for the freedom of commerce and the rights of citizens of other states. While he upheld state enactments genuinely aiming to protect the public morals, safety, health, or convenience, he strongly expressed his disapproval of those that appeared to have been enacted for the ulterior purpose of discriminating against commerce from other states.

Although fervently opposed to Justice STEPHEN J. FIELD's NATURAL RIGHTS philosophy, Harlan strongly defended the Bill of Rights and, in spite of his border state origin, became a vigorous and eloquent advocate of a nationalistic interpretation of the Thirteenth, Fourteenth, and FIFTEENTH AMENDMENTS. Harlan's most celebrated CIVIL RIGHTS dissent, *Plessy v. Ferguson* (1896), became law in the unanimous Warren Court holding in *Brown v. Board of Education* (1954). It was in *Plessy,* dissenting alone from the Court's decision upholding a Louisiana "Jim Crow" train-segregation statute under the SEPARATE BUT EQUAL doctrine, that Harlan had warned: "The thin disguise of 'equal' accommodations . . . will not mislead anyone, nor atone for the wrong this day done. . . ."

However, it was his dissent in the CIVIL RIGHTS CASES (1883) that Harlan considered as his most notable. There the majority ruled that Congress lacked power under the Fourteenth Amendment to protect blacks against private discrimination; Harlan, in contrast, argued that Congress could prohibit discrimination "by individuals or CORPORATIONS exercising public functions or authority, against any citizen because of his race or previous condition of servitude."

In these and other cases involving racial discrimination, Harlan demonstrated his belief that the Thirteenth Amendment meant more than the mere prohibition of one person's owning another as property. He urged that the framers of the Thirteenth, Fourteenth, and Fifteenth Amendments could not have expected the very states that had held blacks in bondage willingly to protect their new civil rights. Harlan thus championed congressional authority to define and regulate the entire body of civil rights of citizens.

Although Justice Harlan's dissents in racial segregation cases have received widespread attention, some of the most critical questions presented to the Court during his tenure centered on what later came to be termed the INCORPORATION DOCTRINE. Harlan joined the Court after a pattern of decisions had been set. Alone, except for Field, among Justices of his time, Harlan viewed the due process clause of the Fourteenth Amendment as encompassing at least the first eight amendments of the Bill of Rights (for example, HURTADO v. CALIFORNIA, 1884), a stand for which he was still severely castigated more than sixty years later by Justice FELIX FRANKFURTER, in ADAMSON v. CALIFORNIA (1947).

The process of "selective incorporation" of Bill of Rights guarantees, which was nearly complete by the end of the Warren Court, vindicated Justice Harlan's position in practice, if not in theory.

Interestingly, the emphasis accorded Harlan's famous dissents in civil rights cases concerning life and liberty interests resulted in a widespread neglect of his staunch defense of property rights. In CONTRACT CLAUSE cases involving states' attempts either to void or alter their obligations to bondholders, or to amend corporate charters without express reservation of the right to do so, Harlan strongly asserted the contractual rights of the individual. Under the equal protection clause Harlan voted to strike down state laws that imposed special contractual duties on corporations without imposing similar obligations on individuals.

More significant, Harlan wrote the opinion in CHICAGO, BURLINGTON & QUINCY RAILROAD CO. v. CHICAGO (1898), frequently cited as the first "incorporation" of a Bill of Rights provision, the Fifth Amendment's just compensation clause, into the Fourteenth Amendment's due process clause. The famous rate case of SMYTH V. AMES (1898) provided an indication of how far Harlan would go in striking down, under SUBSTANTIVE DUE PROCESS principles, an exercise of state police power. Speaking for the Court, he voided a Nebraska statute that pegged intrastate freight rates, on the grounds that the rates were so low as to deprive railroads of property without due process of law. A public utility, asserted Harlan, has a judicially enforceable constitutional right to a "reasonable return" upon the "fair value" of its operating assets. (See FAIR RETURN ON FAIR VALUE.)

Harlan's constitutional doctrines evoked diverse reactions from contemporaries and later generations: patronization, neglect, disdain, and praise. His colleague and friend, Justice DAVID J. BREWER, described Harlan as a simple man who "retired at eight, with one hand on the Constitution and the other on the Bible, safe and happy in perfect faith in justice and righteousness." Justice OLIVER WENDELL HOLMES patronized him in private as "old Harlan . . . the last of the tobacco-spitting judges." Contemporaneous observers of the Court viewed Harlan as a militant dissenter who was inflexible on civil rights.

How could Harlan's contemporaries and historians in the first half of the twentieth century have held him in such low esteem when the prophetic nature of his many dissents appears so obvious today? Part of the answer is that traditional and revisionist interpreters of Justice Harlan have employed widely different analytical perspectives. Viewed narrowly in comparison with his contemporaries, Harlan was simply an "eccentric exception" on the Court. Many of his most famous dissents were solos. His constitutional doctrines were often "out of tune with the times."

Harlan's eccentricity, however, was principled. In a letter of 1870

Harlan described his conception of the proper role of a Justice as that of "an independent man, with an opportunity to make a *record* that will be remembered long after he is gone." Throughout his tenure on the Court Harlan was constantly concerned with broad questions of the public interest; consequently his opinions often contained extraneous matter, referring to circumstances with no direct bearing on the case at hand.

When the Court in POLLOCK v. FARMERS' LOAN & TRUST COMPANY (1895) decided that a tax on the income from land and personal property constituted DIRECT TAXATION and thereby held unconstitutional the recently enacted Federal Income Tax Act, Harlan vehemently dissented. He correctly warned that the Court's decision would make a constitutional amendment necessary for the imposition of the income tax. Harlan's contemporaries, however, saw his denunciation of judicial legislation and his appeals to practical considerations as ignorance of the principles of legal argumentation.

Recent admirers have perhaps too strongly emphasized Harlan's opinion on civil rights and CIVIL LIBERTIES, recasting him as a Jeffersonian Democrat. Although he strongly defended the Bill of Rights against STATE ACTION and private action clothed in public functions, Harlan viewed himself as a staunch adherent to the views of John Marshall and rejected THOMAS JEFFERSON's states' rights views. Moreover, Harlan was one of the most vigorous defenders of individual property rights ever to sit on the Court, as his opinion in ADAIR v. UNITED STATES (1908) illustrated. His STRICT CONSTRUCTION of the contract and just compensation clauses and his adherence to substantive property protections under the due process clause have been soundly rejected by subsequent Courts.

The composite figure emerging from history is that of a Southern gentlemen of the nineteenth century—absolute confidence in the correctness of his own views; a firm belief that human beings could clearly discern between right and wrong; and an inability to understand, once he had made this distinction, how any reasonable man could disagree with him. An ardent disciple of Chief Justice Marshall's views of the proper judicial role and the nature of the federal system, Harlan was an egalitarian when confronted with questions of civil rights.

But today's distinction between property and liberty interests, with enhanced judicial solicitude for the latter, found no place in Harlan's constitutional philosophy. This antebellum slaveholder applied substantive due process equally to liberty and property interests.

Although Harlan's legacy thus contains elements out of tune with contemporary constitutional fashion, many of his dissents presaged what our nation would become in the second half of the twentieth century. Succeeding generations owe a great debt to this solitary dissenter. Because his philosophy contained a touch of immortality, he will be numbered among the great Justices of the Supreme Court (and he was so voted as one of but twelve "greats" in a 1970 study).

Bibliography

ABRAHAM, HENRY J.   1955   John Marshall Harlan: A Justice Neglected. *Virginia Law Review* 41:871–891.

CLARK, FLOYD B.   1915   *The Constitutional Doctrines of John Marshall Harlan.* Baltimore: Johns Hopkins University Press.

FRIEDMAN, LEON and ISRAEL, FRED L.   1969   Pages 1281–1295 in *The Justices of the United States Supreme Court, 1789–1969.* New York: Chelsea House.

WATT, RICHARD F. and ORLIKOFF, RICHARD M.   1953   The Coming Vindication of Mr. Justice Harlan. *Illinois Law Journal* 44:13–40.

WESTIN, ALAN F.   1958   The First Justice Harlan: A Self-Portrait from his Private Papers. *Kentucky Law Journal* 46:321–357.

WHITE, G. EDWARD   1975   John Marshall Harlan I: The Precursor. *American Journal of Legal History* 19:1–21.

# SEPARATE BUT EQUAL DOCTRINE

Kenneth L. Karst

The first type of racial SEGREGATION law to spread over the South was the "Jim Crow car" law, requiring blacks and whites to be seated separately in railroad passenger cars. When the Supreme Court held such a law valid in PLESSY V. FERGUSON (1896), the majority concluded that, so long as the facilities for each race were equal, the enforced separation of the races did not itself impose any inequality on black persons. In support of this separate but equal DOCTRINE, the Court drew on a pre-Civil War decision in Massachusetts, upholding racial segregation in the public schools. (See ROBERTS V. BOSTON, 1850.)

Although the doctrine originated in the context of state regulation of private conduct, it was soon extended to validate segregation in state-operated facilities. The races were separated by the law's command in courtrooms; in the public schools (see GONG LUM V. RICE, 1927); in state offices; in public parks, beaches, swimming pools, and golf courses; in prisons and jails. Some state institutions, such as universities, simply excluded blacks altogether; in most southern states there were separate state colleges for blacks. Throughout this system of segregation, the formal assumption was that facilities for blacks and whites might be separate, but they were equal.

Given the undoubted fact that segregation was imposed for the purpose of maintaining blacks in a condition of inferiority, the very term separate but equal is internally inconsistent. But the *Plessy* opinion had rejected the claim that racial separation itself imposed on blacks an inequality in the form of inferiority. (See BADGES OF SERVITUDE.) Yet *Plessy* set the terms of judicial inquiry in a way that ultimately undermined the separate but equal principle. The question of *justifications* for inequality was largely neglected; the Court focused on the question whether inequality *existed*.

In railroad cars, it was easy to achieve a rough equality of physical facilities. Similarly, a public swimming pool might be reserved for whites three days a week, reserved for blacks three days, and closed the other day. In education, however, inequalities of enormous proportion persisted up to the decision in BROWN V. BOARD OF EDUCATION (1954) and beyond. Black colleges lacked professional schools; black high schools emphasized vocational training and minimized preparation for college. In physical plants, teachers' salaries, levels of teacher training, counseling services, curricula—in every measurable aspect—the separate education offered blacks was anything but the equal of the education offered whites.

One strategy devised by the NAACP for ending school segregation was thus the filing of lawsuits aimed at forcing school boards to equalize spending for black education—at crushing expense. At the same time, a direct assault was made on segregation in higher education, and especially graduate education, where it was easiest to prove the inequality of facilities. (See MISSOURI EX REL. GAINES V. CANADA, 1938; SWEATT V. PAINTER, 1950.) These decisions, following *Plessy*'s lead, focused on the bare question of inequality. Inevitably, these cases came to touch the question whether segregation itself implied unequal education. The *Brown* opinion pursued that inquiry, found educational inequality in the fact of enforced separation, and—without discussing any purported justifications for segregation—held school segregation unconstitutional.

Separate but equal thus ended its doctrinal sway in the field of education. Within a few years the Supreme Court, in a series of PER CURIAM opinions consisting entirely of citations to *Brown,* had invalidated all state-sponsored segregation. The separate but equal doctrine was laid to rest.

Bibliography

LEVY, LEONARD W. and JONES, DOUGLAS  1972  Jim Crow Education: Origins of the "Separate but Equal" Doctrine. In Levy, Leonard W., *Judgments: Essays on American Constitutional History.*  Chicago: Quadrangle Books.

OBERST, PAUL  1973  The Strange Career of *Plessy v. Ferguson. Arizona Law Review* 15:389–418.

WOODWARD, C. VANN  1966  *The Strange Career of Jim Crow,*  2nd rev. ed. New York: Oxford University Press.

# DISCRETE AND INSULAR MINORITIES

Edward J. Erler

The idea of the "discrete and insular minority" originated in the now famous footnote four of the opinion in UNITED STATES V. CAROLENE PRODUCTS COMPANY (1938). Justice HARLAN F. STONE, writing for only a plurality of the Court, queried—without answering the question— "whether prejudice against discrete and insular minorities may be a special condition, which tends seriously to curtail those political processes ordinarily to be relied upon to protect minorities, and which may call for a correspondingly more searching judicial inquiry." In the wake of the Court's about-face in 1937, Justice Stone was serving notice that the Court might not accord the same deference to statutes directed at "discrete and insular minorities" that it would to statutes directed at ECONOMIC REGULATION.

The Court made little use of the concept until the early 1970s, when it began to delineate the class characteristics of such groups. Included were groups that had been "saddled with such disabilities, or subjected to such a history of purposeful unequal treatment, or relegated to such a position of political powerlessness as to command extraordinary protection from the majoritarian political process." Although race, nationality, and alienage seem to have been firmly established as class characteristics of the "discrete and insular minority," the Court has refused to extend such class status to illegitimates, the poor, or conscientious objectors.

REGENTS OF THE UNIVERSITY OF CALIFORNIA V. BAKKE (1978) presented the question of the "discrete and insular minority" in a new light. The question in *Bakke* was whether the same "solicitude" should be applied to test a governmental action designed to benefit rather than injure a "discrete and insular" minority. The university, citing *Carolene Products,* argued that STRICT SCRUTINY was reserved exclusively for "discrete and insular minorities." Four Justices agreed that a white male needed no special protection from the political process that authorized the actions of the university. Justice LEWIS F. POWELL rejected this argument: "the 'rights created by the . . . FOURTEENTH AMENDMENT are, by its terms, guaranteed to the individual. The rights established are personal rights. . . .' The guarantee of EQUAL PROTECTION cannot mean one thing when applied to one individual and something else when applied to a person of another color."

In FULLILOVE v. KLUTZNICK (1980) the Court, for the first time since the JAPANESE AMERICAN CASES (1943–1944), upheld a racial classification that was expressed on the face of a law. *Fullilove* involved a challenge to an act of Congress authorizing federal funds for local public works projects and setting aside ten percent of those funds for employment of businesses owned by Negroes, Hispanics, Orientals, AMERICAN INDIANS, and Aleuts. Chief Justice WARREN E. BURGER, writing for a plurality, called for judicial deference to Congress's power under section 5 of the Fourteenth Amendment, as equivalent to "the broad powers expressed in the NECESSARY AND PROPER CLAUSE. . . ." The irony was that the idea of the "discrete and insular minority" in its inception was designed to curtail such deference when racial classifications were involved.

BENIGN RACIAL CLASSIFICATIONS, it is sometimes said, are justified because they do not involve the stigma of INVIDIOUS DISCRIMINATION. The recipients of the benefits that accrue from the "benign" classification are not branded as members of an "inferior race" as they would be if the classification were an invidious one. This theory erects "stigma" as the standard for equal protection rights. Absent any such stigma the implication is that the Constitution is not offended, even if individuals must bear burdens created by a classification that otherwise would be disallowed by the equal protection clause. As Burger stated in *Fullilove*, " 'a sharing of the burden' by innocent parties is not impermissible." To use the idea of stigma as a racial class concept is, in effect, to translate equal protection rights into class rights.

But the intrusion of class into the Constitution is a dangerous proposition, one that is at odds with the principles of the constitutional regime— principles ultimately derived from the proposition that "all men are created equal." Class considerations explicitly deny this equality because they necessarily abstract from the individual and ascribe to him class characteristics that are different—and necessarily unequal—from those of individuals outside the class. A liberal jurisprudence must disallow all class considerations. When there is a conflict between two different "discrete and insular minorities," which should be accorded preference? No principle can answer this question. And the question is not merely theoretical. The Court has already faced this dilemma in cases such as UNITED JEWISH ORGANIZATIONS v. CAREY (1977) and *Castenada v. Partida* (1977), and in a pluralistic society it is inevitable that many more such cases will arise. Equal protection can be the foundation of a genuine liberal jurisprudence only if it applies to individuals. As Justice JOHN MARSHALL HARLAN remarked in his powerful dissent in PLESSY V. FERGUSON (1896), the case that established the SEPARATE-BUT-EQUAL DOCTRINE, "[o]ur Constitution is color-blind, and neither knows nor tolerates classes among citizens. In respect of CIVIL RIGHTS, all citizens are equal before the law." This is undoubtedly still the essential principle of liberal government.

JAMES MADISON argued, in THE FEDERALIST #10, that in a large, diverse republic with a multiplicity of interests it was unlikely that there would ever be permanent majorities and permanent minorities; thus there would be little probability that "a majority of the whole will have a common motive to invade the rights of other citizens." On this assumption, the majorities that do form will be composed of coalitions of minorities that come together for limited self-interested purposes. The majority will thus never have a sense of its own interest as a majority.

By and large, the solution of the Founders has worked remarkably well. There have been no permanent majorities, and certainly none based exclusively on race. Understanding American politics in terms of monolithic majorities and "discrete and insular minorities"—as the Supreme Court appears to do—precludes the creation of a common interest that transcends racial class considerations. By transforming the Fourteenth Amendment into an instrument of class politics, the Court risks either making a majority faction more likely by heightening the majority's awareness of its class status as a majority, or transforming the liberal constitutional regime into one no longer based on majority rule.

Bibliography

ELY, JOHN H.  1980  *Democracy and Distrust: A Theory of Judicial Review.*  Pages 75–77 and 135–179. Cambrige, Mass.: Harvard University Press.

ERLER, EDWARD J.  1982  Equal Protection and Personal Rights: The Regime of the "Discrete and Insular Minority." *Georgia Law Review*  16:407–444.

KARST, KENNETH L. and HOROWITZ, HAROLD W. 1974  Affirmative Action and Equal Protection. *Virginia Law Review*  60:955–974.

# JAPANESE AMERICAN CASES

*Hirabayashi v. United States*
320 U.S. 81 (1943)

*Korematsu v. United States*
323 U.S. 214 (1944)

*Ex parte Endo*
323 U.S. 283 (1944)

## Kenneth L. Karst

For more than a month after the Japanese attack on Pearl Harbor in December 1941, no one of high authority in the armed services or elsewhere in the national government suggested seriously that persons of Japanese ancestry should be moved away from the West Coast. The Army's historian wrote that in February and March of 1942 the military estimates were that "there was no real threat of a Japanese invasion" of the area. Yet by March 1942 a program was fully underway to remove about 120,000 persons from their West Coast homes and jobs and place them in internment camps in the interior of the country. About 70,000 of these people were citizens of the United States; two out of every five people sent to the camps were under the age of fifteen or over fifty. All were imprisoned for an indefinite time without any individualized determination of grounds for suspicion of disloyalty, let alone charges of unlawful conduct, to be held in custody until their loyalty might be determined. (See PREVENTIVE DETENTION.) The basis for their imprisonment was a single common trait—their Japanese ancestry.

The military services came to discover the "military necessity" of relocating the Japanese Americans in response to pressure from the West Coast congressional delegations and from other political leaders in the region—including, to his later regret, EARL WARREN, then attorney general of California. These politicians were responding, in turn, to a clamor from certain newspapers and labor unions, along with (as U.S. Attorney General FRANCIS BIDDLE later listed them) "the American Legion, the California Joint Immigration Committee, the Native Sons and Daughters of the Golden West, the Western Growers Protective Association, the California Farm Bureau Federation [and] the Chamber of Commerce of Los Angeles." The groups' campaign was aided by newspaper accounts of American military defeats and Japanese atrocities in the early days of the war, and by false reports of sabotage at Pearl Harbor. Anti-Asian racism, long a feature of California, now had a focus. In Hawaii, which *had* been attacked, no evacuation was proposed; persons of Japanese ancestry constituted almost one third of that territory's population. On the West Coast, Japanese Americans barely exceeded one percent of the population; thus, no political force resisted the mixture of fear, racism, and greed. "The Japanese race is an enemy race," said General John DeWitt in his official report to the War Department. Once the Army urged wholesale evacuation, the opposition of Biddle and the Justice Department was unavailing. President FRANKLIN D. ROOSEVELT sided with the Army, and the evacuation began.

The program, first established by EXECUTIVE ORDER 9066 and then partly ratified by Congress, called for three measures in "military areas"— that is, the entire West Coast. First, persons of Japanese descent were placed under curfew at home from 8:00 P.M. to 6:00 A.M. Second, they would be excluded from "military areas" upon military order. Third, they would be "relocated" in internment camps until their "loyalty" could be determined. The loyalty-determining process was leisurely; as late as the spring of 1945 some 70,000 persons remained in the camps.

The three parts of the program, all of which raised serious constitutional problems, were considered separately by the Supreme Court in three cases: *Hirabayashi v. United States* (1943), *Korematsu v. United States* (1944), and *Ex Parte Endo* (1944).

The *Hirabayashi* case offered the Court a chance to rule on the validity of both the curfew and the exclusion orders. A young American citizen was charged with violating the curfew and refusing to report to a control station to be evacuated from Seattle, where he lived. He was convicted on both counts, and sentenced to three months of imprisonment. In June 1943 the Supreme Court unanimously upheld the curfew violation conviction, and said that it need not consider the validity of the exclusion order, because the two sentences were to run concurrently.

Not until December 1944 did the Court reach the other parts of the evacuation program. In *Korematsu,* the Court divided 6–3 in upholding an order excluding an American citizen from his home town, San Leandro, California. On the same day, the Court in *Endo* avoided deciding on the constitutional validity of internment. Instead, it concluded that the act of Congress ratifying the evacuation program had not authorized prolonged detention of a citizen whose loyalty was conceded. The Court assumed that some brief detention was implicitly authorized as an incident of an exclusion program aimed at preventing espionage and sabotage. Any further detention would have to rest on an assumption the Court was unwilling to make: that citizens were being detained because of their ancestry, in response to community hostility. Justice OWEN

ROBERTS, concurring in the result, found congressional authority for internment in the appropriation of funds to operate the camps. Reaching the constitutional issues the majority had avoided, he concluded the Endo's detention violated "the guarantees of the BILL OF RIGHTS . . . and especially the guarantee of DUE PROCESS OF LAW."

The Japanese American cases have made two positive contributions to the development of egalitarian constitutional doctrine. The *Hirabayashi* and *Korematsu* opinions were links in a chain of precedent leading to the Supreme Court's recognition that the Fifth Amendment's due process clause contains a guarantee of equal protection as a substantive limit on the conduct of the national government. (See BOLLING V. SHARPE, 1954; EQUAL PROTECTION OF THE LAWS.) And *Korematsu* first announced the principle that legal restrictions on the civil rights of a racial group are "suspect." (See SUSPECT CLASSIFICATIONS.) Even so, these decisions deserve Eugene Rostow's epithet: "a disaster." The Supreme Court's evasion of issues, its refusal to examine the factual assumptions underlying the "military necessity" of evacuation—in short, its failures to perform as a court—are easier to forgive than to excuse. There is little comfort in the fact that the Court's *Hirabayashi* and *Korematsu* opinions were authored by Justices celebrated as civil libertarians.

Chief Justice HARLAN FISKE STONE wrote for a unanimous Court in *Hirabayashi,* approaching the validity of the curfew not so much as a question about the liberties of a citizen but as a question about congressional power. The WAR POWERS, of course, are far-reaching; they include, as Justices often repeat, "the power to wage war successfully." Thus, for Stone, the only issue before the Court was whether there was "a RATIONAL BASIS" for concluding that the curfew was necessary to protect the country against espionage and sabotage in aid of a threatened invasion. As to that necessity, the Chief Justice said: "We cannot close our eyes to the fact, demonstrated by experience, that in time of war residents having ethnic affiliations with an invading enemy may be a greater source of danger than those of a different ancestry." There was no effort to examine into the likelihood of invasion, or to specify what experience demonstrated the "fact" assumed. The one hard fact was that no sabotage or espionage had been committed by persons of Japanese ancestry at the time of the Hawaii attack or afterward. (California's Attorney General Warren had been equal to that challenge, however: ". . . that is the most ominous sign in our whole situation. It convinces me more than perhaps any other factor that the sabotage we are to get, the fifth column activities that we are to get, are timed just like Pearl Harbor was timed. . . .")

Another question remained: Why impose wholesale restrictions on persons of Japanese ancestry, when Germans and Italians were being investigated individually? Here the Court took refuge in a presumption:

"We cannot say that the war-making branches of the Government did not have ground for believing that in a critical hour [disloyal] persons could not readily be isolated and separately dealt with. . . ." This is the classical language of "rational basis" review; government officials have made a factual determination, and a court "cannot say" they are mistaken. That standard of review serves well enough to test the reasonableness of a congressional conclusion that some type of activity substantially affects INTERSTATE COMMERCE. It is utterly inappropriate to test the justification for selectively imposing restrictions on a racial minority.

Justice HUGO L. BLACK began his opinion for the majority in *Korematsu* by recognizing this difference. Racial distinctions, he said, were "immediately suspect," and must be subjected to "the most rigid scrutiny." Following that pronouncement, however, all judicial scrutiny of the racial discrimination at hand was abandoned. The opinion simply quoted the "We cannot say" passage from the *Hirabayashi* opinion; stated, uncritically, the conclusions of the military authorities; observed that "war is an aggregation of hardships"; and—unkindest cut—concluded that "Citizenship has its responsibilities as well as its privileges."

Justice Roberts, dissenting, argued that Korematsu had been subjected to conflicting orders to leave the military area and to stay put, a plain due process violation. It was left to Justice FRANK MURPHY—in his finest hour—to expose the absence of imperial clothing. He demonstrated how the "military" judgment of the necessity for evacuation had departed from subjects in which Army officers were expert and had embarked on breathtaking sociological generalization: the Japanese American community were "a large, unassimilated, tightly knit racial group, bound to an enemy nation by strong ties of race, culture, custom and religion" (quoting General DeWitt).

Decades later, Peter Irons discovered in government archives irrefutable evidence that government officers had deliberately misled the Supreme Court on questions directly related to the claim of military necessity for the evacuations. In response to this evidence, in the mid-1980s federal district courts set aside the convictions of Gordon Hirabayashi, Fred Korematsu, and Minoru Yasui (whose conviction had been affirmed along with Hirabayashi's).

Justice ROBERT H. JACKSON, dissenting in *Korematsu*, said, in effect: There is nothing courts can do to provide justice in this case, or in any case in which the military and the President are determined to take action in wartime; yet we should not lend our approval to this action, lest we create a precedent for similar extraconstitutional action in the future. Of all the oft-noted ironies of the Japanese American cases, this topsy-turvy prediction may be the most ironic of all. *Korematsu* as a judicial precedent has turned out to provide a strong doctrinal foundation for the Supreme Court's vigorous defense of racial equality in the years since mid-century. The disaster of the Japanese American cases was not doctrinal. It was instead the betrayal of justice there and then for Gordon Hirabayashi, Fred Korematsu, Minoru Yasui, and some 120,000 other individuals—and thus for us all.

Bibliography

GRODZINS, MORTON   1949   *Americans Betrayed: Politics and the Japanese Evacuation.*  Chicago: University of Chicago Press.

IRONS, PETER   1983   *Justice at War.*  New York: Oxford University Press.

ROSTOW, EUGENE V.   1949   The Japanese American Cases—A Disaster. *Yale Law Journal* 54:489–533.

# CIVIL RIGHTS DIVISION

Theodore Eisenberg

Created by Order of the Attorney General No. 3204, February 3, 1939, the Civil Rights Section (originally named the Civil Rights Unit) of the Justice Department became the federal government's principal CIVIL RIGHTS litigation unit. The order creating the Section called for a study of federal law to assess its utility in enforcing civil rights. The study, which stated the legal basis and goals of the Section's early civil rights enforcement efforts, suggested the need for TEST CASES to resolve uncertainties about the scope and constitutionality of the only statutory weapons then available to the Section, the surviving Reconstruction-era civil rights legislation. The Section's test cases include UNITED STATES V. CLASSIC (1941), an important precedent establishing authority to prosecute offenses relating to PRIMARY ELECTIONS, and SCREWS V. UNITED STATES (1945), which allowed the application of the criminal provisions of the CIVIL RIGHTS ACT OF 1866 to misconduct by state police officers.

The Civil Rights Section's growth reflects a general increase in national concern with civil rights matters. As of 1947, the Section is reported never to have had more than eight or ten lawyers and professional workers on its staff. In 1950, the section more than doubled in size. The CIVIL RIGHTS ACT OF 1957 upgraded the Section to the status of Division by providing for an additional assistant attorney general. By 1965, the Division had eighty-six attorneys and ninety-nine clerical workers. By 1978, there were 178 attorneys and 203 support personnel.

The Division's principal activity consists of litigation. It enforces the CIVIL RIGHTS ACTS OF 1957, 1960, 1964, and 1968, the VOTING RIGHTS ACT OF 1965, the Equal Credit Opportunity Act, the 1866 act's criminal provisions, laws prohibiting PEONAGE and involuntary servitude, and various other laws. It does so through direct actions or through AMICUS CURIAE appearances in private cases. An administration's civil rights priorities are reflected in the categories of cases emphasized by the Division. In the early 1960s the Division emphasized voting rights cases. From 1965 to 1967, DESEGREGATION of education was its priority issue. By 1967, employment litigation became a priority item. Creation of a Task Force on Sex Discrimination in 1977 reflected a growing concern with sex discrimination.

Bibliography

CARR, ROBERT K. 1947 *Federal Protection of Civil Rights: Quest for a Sword.* Ithaca, N.Y.: Cornell University Press.

# CIVIL RIGHTS COMMISSION

Theodore Eisenberg

THE CIVIL RIGHTS ACT OF 1957 created the Commission on Civil Rights to investigate alleged deprivations of VOTING RIGHTS, to study and collect information concerning denials of EQUAL PROTECTION, and to appraise federal laws and policies with respect to equal protection of the laws. Subsequent legislation restated and expanded the commission's concerns to include denials of rights on the basis of color, race, religion, national origin, sex, age, or handicap. Initially, the commission was to issue a series of reports and expire upon issuance of its final report, but Congress repeatedly has extended the commission's reporting duties and life. The commission lacks power to enforce any antidiscrimination or other CIVIL RIGHTS laws.

By the standards of later civil rights legislation, creation of the commission seems an innocuous event. But at the time even this mild gesture drew substantial southern opposition. The commission's "snoopers," one southern congressman argued, "would cause inestimable chaos, confusion, and unrest among [the South's] people and would greatly increase the tension and agitation between the races there."

Because of the commission's advisory nature, measuring its accomplishments is difficult. In the 1960s, the commission's early reports helped to inform Congress about the need for voting rights legislation. And it clearly has served the function, added to its mandate in 1964, of a national clearinghouse for information about denials of equal protection. But the commission also has played a somewhat larger political role. In most administrations the commission's views are more egalitarian than the President's. The commission thus serves as a gadfly that both makes official sounding pronouncements and commands media attention. Administrations hear the commission even if they do not always listen to it.

Bibliography

United States Commission on Civil Rights 1961 *Report.* Pages xv–xviii. Washington, D.C.: U.S. Government Printing Office.

# RESTRICTIVE COVENANT

Kenneth L. Karst

Until the Supreme Court ruled their judicial enforcement unconstitutional in SHELLEY V. KRAEMER (1948), restrictive covenants were widely employed to achieve the racial SEGREGATION of urban neighborhoods in America. A restrictive covenant is a contract among owners of land, mutually limiting the uses of land covered by the covenant. Many such covenants have benign purposes: all the owners on a residential block, for example, might agree that houses will be set back thirty feet from the street. Racial covenants, however, limited the occupancy of homes on the basis of the occupants' race. They rested on an ugly premise: excluding blacks or Asians would, as one Louisiana court put it, make a neighborhood "more attractive to white people."

Such covenants were commonly adopted by landowners, or written into deeds of newly developed land, beginning in the late nineteenth century. Under existing property law, they were enforceable not only against their signers, but against the signers' heirs, assignees, and purchasers—at least so long as "conditions" had not changed. The use of the covenants accelerated after the Supreme Court decided, in BUCHANAN V. WARLEY (1917), that municipal ZONING ordinances specifying where persons of one race or another might live were unconstitutional. The typical covenant ran for twenty-five years, but some ran for fifty years or even in perpetuity.

Restrictive covenants cannot be said to be the sole cause, or even the primary cause, of residential segregation before 1948. The poverty of most blacks was itself a severe restriction on the purchase of homes; and middle-class blacks who could afford to buy were steered to "colored sections" by real estate brokers and lenders. (The latter practices became violations of federal law only in 1968.) Yet the covenants surely played their part in the segregative process, a part they could play only because they were enforceable in court.

If an owner started to build a house too close to the street, in violation of a restrictive covenant, the neighbors would be entitled to an INJUNCTION ordering the owner to stop. They might also be entitled to damages, if they could demonstrate some loss. But, subject to the covenant's limitations, the owner would be entitled to occupy the property, or sell it to any purchaser. The owner of property subject to a racial covenant, however, could not—so long as the covenant was enforceable—sell it to blacks for their use as a residence. The racial covenants, then, not only restricted black would-be buyers but also restricted the owners' free alienation of property—an interest recognized in the COMMON LAW since the thirteenth century. Yet the state courts regularly enforced the covenants.

The Supreme Court lent its approval in 1926, in CORRIGAN V. BUCKLEY, holding that judicial enforcement of a racial covenant did not even raise a substantial federal question; any discrimination was private action, not STATE ACTION. (The case arose not in a state, covered by the FOURTEENTH AMENDMENT, but in the DISTRICT OF COLUMBIA. The Court correctly sensed, however, that a similar problem would arise if an EQUAL PROTECTION guarantee were found applicable to governmental action in the District.)

Over the next two decades, the NAACP searched for opportunities to bring to the Court new challenges to the judicial enforcement of racially restrictive covenants. They finally succeeded in Shelley, where the Court did find state action in a state court's injunctive relief to enforce a covenant against black buyers of a home. On the same day, in Hurd v. Hodge (1948), the Court reached a comparable result in an attack on judicial enforcement of a covenant in the District of Columbia. No constitutional issue was decided in Hurd; the Court based its decision on "the public policy of the United States."

Five years later, the Court took away the last remaining weapon of persons who would seek to use racial covenants as a way of keeping their neighborhoods white. In BARROWS V. JACKSON (1953) the Court held that a state court violated the Fourteenth Amendment by using a covenant as a basis for awarding damages against persons who sold their house to black buyers.

One of the worst features of the racial covenants was their contribution to the symbolism of black inferiority. The removal of that symbolism, wherever it may be found, is necessary if the Fourteenth Amendment's promise of equal CITIZENSHIP is to be fulfilled. But ending the judicial enforcement of racial covenants did not end residential segregation, a phenomenon that has declined only slightly since 1940.

Bibliography

HENKIN, LOUIS   1962   Shelley v. Kraemer: Notes for a Revised Opinion. University of Pennsylvania Law Review 110:473–505.
VOSE, CLEMENT E.   1959   Caucasians Only. Berkeley: University of California Press.

# Racial Equality in the Modern Era

# NAACP LEGAL DEFENSE & EDUCATIONAL FUND

Jack Greenberg

The NAACP Legal Defense & Educational Fund, Inc., was founded in 1939 by board members of the National Association for the Advancement of Colored People to conduct the legal program of the association through a corporation qualified to receive tax deductible contributions. The association was not tax exempt, because it lobbied. Board members of the association served on the board of the Fund; the Fund's director and some of its lawyers also were employees of the association.

In 1957 the Internal Revenue Service (IRS) objected to the interlocking staff and board because it enabled an organization not tax exempt to influence one entitled to tax exemption. The IRS required termination of the interlocking arrangement. Thereafter the Fund and the association were no longer formally linked, and the Fund functioned entirely independently with its own board, staff, budget, and policies. The Fund has since represented individuals and organizations with no relationship to the association at all as well as members and branches of the association.

In 1984 the Fund's staff consisted of twenty-four lawyers, with offices in New York and Washington, D.C., and several hundred cooperating lawyers across the United States. Its budget was $6.7 million. It has served as a model for the public interest law movement generally, including other legal defense funds, such as those dealing with discrimination against Hispanics, Asians, women, the handicapped, homosexuals, and the aged, as well as public interest firms representing environmental, consumer, migrant worker, and other groups.

The Fund's director-counsel was THURGOOD MARSHALL, who served until 1961 and was succeeded by Jack Greenberg, who directed the organization until 1984, when he was succeeded by Julius L. Chambers. The Fund has been involved in most of the leading cases dealing with racial discrimination in the United States, including BROWN V. BOARD OF EDUCATION (1954), which held unconstitutional racial SEGREGATION in public education, the principle of which was ultimately extended to all other governmental activities. *Brown* was the culmination of a planned litigation effort which built upon earlier Fund cases involving RACIAL DISCRIMINATION in graduate and professional schools. In the 1960s, the Fund provided representation in most of the cases generated by the

CIVIL RIGHTS movement, including representation of MARTIN LUTHER KING, JR. Thereafter, following passage of the Civil Rights Acts of the mid-1960s, the Fund brought most of the leading cases enforcing those laws. The Fund has represented civil rights claimants in more than 2,000 cases dealing with education, employment, VOTING RIGHTS, housing, PRISONERS' RIGHTS, CAPITAL PUNISHMENT, health care, and other areas of the law.

Bibliography

RABIN, ROBERT L.   1976   Lawyers for Social Change: Perspectives on Public Interest Law. *Stanford Law Journal* 28:207–261.

# THURGOOD MARSHALL

## (1908–   )

Mark V. Tushnet

Thurgood Marshall, the first black Justice of the Supreme Court, was born in Baltimore in 1908. After graduation from Lincoln University in Pennsylvania, Marshall attended Howard University Law School. Graduating first in his class in 1933, Marshall became one of CHARLES H. HOUSTON's protégés. He began practice in Baltimore, where he helped revitalize the local branch of the National Association for the Advancement of Colored People (NAACP). Houston, who had become special counsel to the NAACP in New York, was developing a program of litigation designed to attack segregated education in the South; Marshall joined the NAACP staff as Houston's assistant in 1936.

Of all the Justices who have served on the Supreme Court, Marshall has the strongest claim to having contributed as much to the development of the Constitution as a lawyer as he has done as a judge. At the start of his career, race relations law centered on the SEPARATE BUT EQUAL DOCTRINE. In his initial years at the NAACP, Marshall brought a number of lawsuits challenging unequal salaries paid to black and white teachers in the South. After Marshall succeeded Houston as special counsel in 1938, he became both a litigator and a coordinator of litigation, most of it challenging segregated education. He also successfully argued a number of cases involving RACIAL DISCRIMINATION in the administration of criminal justice before the Supreme Court. When social and political changes during World War II led to increased black militancy and support for the NAACP, Marshall was able to expand the NAACP's legal staff by hiring an extremely talented group of young, mostly black lawyers. Although he continued to conduct some litigation, Marshall gradually assumed the roles of appellate advocate and overall strategist. Relying on his staff to generate helpful legal theories, he selected the theory most likely to accomplish the NAACP's goals. This process culminated in the five lawsuits decided by the Supreme Court as BROWN v. BOARD OF EDUCATION (1954). Marshall had used his staff to develop these cases and the legal theory that segregation was unconstitutional no matter how equal were the physical facilities. After the Supreme Court held that segregation was unconstitutional and that it should be eliminated "with ALL DELIBERATE SPEED," Marshall and the NAACP staff devoted much of their attention to overcoming the impediments that southern states began to place in the way of DESEGREGATION. These impediments included school closures and investigations and harassment of the NAACP and its lawyers.

Marshall left the NAACP in 1961, having been nominated by President JOHN F. KENNEDY to a position on the UNITED STATES COURT OF APPEALS for the Second Circuit. His confirmation to that position was delayed by southern opposition for over eleven months. During Marshall's four years on the Second Circuit, he wrote an important opinion holding that the DOUBLE JEOPARDY clause applied to the states, anticipating by four years the position that the Supreme Court would adopt in BENTON v. MARYLAND (1969), a decision written by Justice Marshall. He also urged in dissent an expansive interpretation of statutes allowing persons charged with crimes in state courts to remove those cases to federal court. (See CIVIL RIGHTS REMOVAL.) Marshall was nominated as solicitor general by President LYNDON B. JOHNSON in 1965. He served as solicitor general for two years, during which he supervised the disposition of criminal cases imperiled by illegal WIRETAPPING. Johnson appointed him in 1967 to succeed Justice TOM C. CLARK on the Supreme Court.

Justice Marshall's contributions to constitutional development have been shaped by the fact that for most of his tenure his views were among the most liberal on a centrist or conservative Court. As he had at the NAACP, and as have most recent Justices, Marshall relied heavily on his staff to present his views forcefully and systematically in his opinions.

For a few years after Marshall's appointment to the Court, he was part of the liberal bloc of the WARREN COURT. Despite the tradition that newly appointed Justices are not assigned important majority opinions, Justice Marshall wrote several important free speech opinions during his first two years on the Court. In STANLEY v. GEORGIA (1969), he held that a state could not punish a person merely for possessing obscene materials in his home; the only justification for such punishment, guaranteeing a citizenry that did not think impure thoughts, was barred by the FIRST AMENDMENT. AMALGAMATED FOOD EMPLOYEES UNION v. LOGAN VALLEY PLAZA (1968) recognized the contemporary importance of privately owned SHOPPING CENTERS as places of public resort, holding that centers must be made available, over their owners' objections, to those who wish to picket or pass out leaflets on subjects of public interest. PICKERING v. BOARD OF EDUCATION (1968) established the right of public employees to complain about the way in which their superiors were discharging their responsibilities to the public.

With the appointment of four Justices by President RICHARD M. NIXON, Justice Marshall rapidly found himself in dissent on major civil liberties issues. *Stanley* was limited by *United States v. Reidel* (1971) to private possession and not extended to what might have seemed its logical corollary, acquisition of obscene material for private use. *Logan Valley Plaza* was overruled in HUDGENS V. NATIONAL LABOR RELATIONS BOARD (1976), and *Pickering* was limited by a relatively narrow definition of complaints relating to public duties in *Connick v. Myers* (1983). Marshall became part of a small liberal bloc that could prevail only by attracting more conservative members, who could be kept in the coalition by allowing them to write the majority opinions. In the series of death penalty cases, for example, Justice Marshall stated his conclusion that capital punishment was unconstitutional in all circumstances, but when a majority for a narrower position could be found to overturn the imposition of the death penalty in a particular case, he joined that majority.

Thus, after 1970, Marshall rarely wrote important opinions for the Court regarding FREEDOM OF SPEECH, CRIMINAL PROCEDURE, or EQUAL PROTECTION. Two of his opinions in cases about the PREEMPTION of state law by federal regulations, *Jones v. Rath Packing Co.* (1977) and *Douglas v. Seacoast Products* (1977), seem likely to endure as statements of general principle. More often he was assigned to write opinions in which a nearly unanimous Court adopted a "conservative" position. For example, in *Gillette v. United States* (1971), Justice Marshall's opinion for the Court rejected statutory and constitutional claims to exemption from the military draft by men whose religious beliefs led them to oppose participation in some but not all wars. Undoubtedly because of his race and because of his desire to see a majority support positions helpful to blacks, Marshall rarely wrote important opinions in cases directly implicating matters of race, although he did write two significant dissents, one defending AFFIRMATIVE ACTION in REGENTS OF THE UNIVERSITY OF CALIFORNIA V. BAKKE (1978), and another emphasizing blacks' lack of access to political power in MOBILE V. BOLDEN (1980). But Justice Marshall's major contributions have come in areas where the experience of race has historically shaped the context in which apparently nonracial issues arise.

Marshall occasionally received the assignment in important civil liberties cases. His opinion in POLICE DEPARTMENT OF CHICAGO V. MOSLEY (1972) crystallized the equality theme in the law of freedom of speech. There he emphasized the importance for free expression of the rule that governments may not regulate one type of speech because of its content, in a setting where speech with a different content would not be regulated: "[G]overnment may not grant the use of a forum to people whose views it finds acceptable, but deny use to those wishing to express less favored or more controversial views. . . . Selective exclusions . . . may not be based on content alone, and may not be justified by reference to content alone." Unless it were prohibited, discrimination based on content would allow governments, which ought to be controlled by the electorate, to determine what the electorate would hear. Although the *Mosley* principle is probably stated too broadly, because differential regulation of categories of speech such as OBSCENITY or COMMERCIAL SPEECH is allowed, still it serves as a central starting point for analysis, from which departures must be justified.

His opinion in *Memorial Hospital v. Maricopa County* (1974) synthesized a line of cases regarding the circumstances in which a state might deny benefits such as nonemergency medical care for INDIGENTS to those who had recently come to the state. If the benefit was so important that its denial could be characterized as a penalty for exercising the RIGHT TO TRAVEL, it was unconstitutional.

Because of the relatively rapid shift in the Court's composition, most of Justice Marshall's major contributions to the constitutional development have come through dissents. Several major dissenting opinions by Justice Marshall have helped shape the law of equal protection. The opinions criticize a rigid approach in which classifications based on race and a few other categories are to be given STRICT SCRUTINY while all other classifications must be "merely rational." Marshall, in dissents in DANDRIDGE V. WILLIAMS (1970) and SAN ANTONIO INDEPENDENT SCHOOL DISTRICT V. RODRIGUEZ (1973), offered a more flexible approach. He argued that the courts should examine legislation that affects different groups differently by taking into account the nature of the group—the degree to which it has been discriminated against in the past, the actual access to political power it has today—and the importance of the interests affected. Under this "sliding scale" approach, a statute differentially affecting access to WELFARE BENEFITS might be unconstitutional while one with the same effects on access to public recreational facilities might be permitted. A majority of the Court has not explicitly adopted the "sliding scale" approach, but Justice Marshall's sustained criticisms of the rigid alternative have produced a substantial, though not entirely acknowledged, acceptance of a more nuanced approach to equal protection problems.

As *Logan Valley Plaza* showed, Justice Marshall has urged, usually in dissent, an expansive definition of those actors whose decisions are subject to constitutional control. In JACKSON V. METROPOLITAN EDISON Co. (1974) the majority found that the decision of a heavily regulated utility to terminate service for nonpayment was not "state action" under any of the several strands of that DOCTRINE. Justice Marshall's dissent argued that state involvement was significant when looked at as a whole and, more important, pointed out that on the majority's analysis the utility could, without constitutional problems, terminate service to blacks. On the assumption, confirmed in later cases, that the result is incorrect, Justice Marshall's argument effectively demonstrated that the "state action" doctrine is actually a doctrine about the merits of the challenged decision: if it is a decision that the Justices believe should not be controlled by the Constitution, there is no "state action," whereas if it is a decision that the Justices believe should be controlled by the Constitution, there is state action.

Finally, after joining the seminal opinion in GOLDBERG v. KELLY (1968), which held that the Constitution defined the procedures under which public benefits, the "new property" of the welfare state, could be taken away, Justice Marshall dissented in later cases where the Court substantially narrowed the scope of *Goldberg*. His position, in cases such as BOARD OF REGENTS v. ROTH (1972), has been that everyone must be presumed to be entitled to those benefits, and that the presumption can be overcome only after constitutionality-defined procedures have been followed.

In most of the areas of law to which Justice Marshall's opinions have made significant contributions the linked strands of race and poverty appear. Discrimination by nominally private actors and suppression of speech on racial issues have played an important part in the black experience. Similarly, wealth and poverty as grounds for allocating public resources are classifications closely linked to race. Justice Marshall's desire to adopt a more flexible approach to equal protection law stems from his awareness that only such an approach would allow the courts to address difficulties that the ordinary routines of society cause for the poor. For example, his dissent in *United States v. Kras* (1973) objected to the imposition of a fifty dollar filing fee on those who sought discharges of their debts in bankruptcy. But it would be misleading to conclude that Thurgood Marshall's most important role in constitutional development was what he did as a Justice of the Supreme Court. Rather it was what he did as a lawyer for the NAACP before and after the decision in *Brown v. Board of Education*.

Bibliography

KLUGER, RICHARD   1976   *Simple Justice*. New York: Knopf.

# BROWN v. BOARD OF EDUCATION

## 347 U.S. 483 (1954)
## 349 U.S. 294 (1955)

### Kenneth L. Karst

In the dual perspectives of politics and constitutional development, *Brown v. Board of Education* was the Supreme Court's most important decision of the twentieth century. In four cases consolidated for decision, the Court held that racial SEGREGATION of public school children, commanded or authorized by state law, violated the FOURTEENTH AMENDMENT's guarantee of the EQUAL PROTECTION OF THE LAWS. A companion decision, BOLLING V. SHARPE (1954), held that school segregation in the DISTRICT OF COLUMBIA violated the Fifth Amendment's guarantee of DUE PROCESS OF LAW.

*Brown* illustrates how pivotal historical events, viewed in retrospect, can take on the look of inevitability. To the actors involved, however, the decision was anything but a foregone conclusion. The principal judicial precedent, after all, was PLESSY V. FERGUSON (1896), which had upheld the racial segregation of railroad passengers, partly on the basis of an earlier Massachusetts decision upholding school segregation. More recent Supreme Court decisions had invalidated various forms of segregation in higher education without deciding whether *Plessy* should be overruled. Just a few months before the first *Brown* decision, Robert Leflar and Wylie Davis outlined eleven different courses open to the Supreme Court in the cases before it.

The four cases we now call *Brown* were the culmination of a twenty-year litigation strategy of the NAACP, aimed at the ultimate invalidation of segregation in education. (See SEPARATE BUT EQUAL DOCTRINE.) Part of that strategy had already succeeded; the Supreme Court had ordered the admission of black applicants to state university law schools, and had invalidated a state university's segregation of a black graduate student. The opinions in those cases had emphasized intangible elements of educational quality, particularly the opportunity to associate with persons of other races. (See SWEATT V. PAINTER, 1950). The doctrinal ground was thus prepared for the Court to strike down the segregation of elementary and secondary schools—if the Court was ready to occupy that ground.

The Justices were sensitive to the political repercussions their decision might have. The cases were argued in December 1952, and in the ordinary course would have been decided by the close of the Court's term in the following June or July. Instead of deciding, however, the Court set the five cases for reargument in the following term and proposed a series of questions to be argued, centering on the history of the adoption of the Fourteenth Amendment and on potential remedies if the Court should rule against segregation. The available evidence suggests that the Court was divided on the principal issue in the cases— the constitutionality of separate but equal public schools—and that Justice FELIX FRANKFURTER played a critical role in persuading his brethren to put the case over so that the incoming administration of President DWIGHT D. EISENHOWER might present its views as AMICUS CURIAE. It is clear that the discussion at the Court's CONFERENCE on the cases had dealt not only with the merits of the black children's claims but also with the possible reaction of the white South to a decision overturning school segregation. Proposing questions for the reargument, Justice Frankfurter touched on the same concern in a memorandum to his colleagues: ". . . for me the ultimate crucial factor in the problem presented by these cases is psychological—the adjustment of men's minds and actions to the unfamiliar and the unpleasant."

When Justice Frankfurter wrote of "the adjustment of men's minds," he had whites in mind. For blacks, Jim Crow was an unpleasant reality that was all too familiar. It is not surprising that the Justices centered their political concerns on the white South; lynchings of blacks would have been a vivid memory for any Justice who had come to maturity before 1930. In any event the Court handled the *Brown* cases from beginning to end with an eye on potential disorder and violence among southern whites.

Chief Justice FRED M. VINSON, who had written the opinions invalidating segregation in higher education, appeared to some of his brethren to oppose extending the reasoning of those opinions to segregation in the public schools. Late in the summer of 1953, five weeks before the scheduled reargument of *Brown,* Vinson died suddenly from a heart attack. With *Brown* in mind, Justice Frankfurter said, in a private remark that has since become glaringly public, "This is the first indication I have ever had that there is a God."

Vinson's replacement was the governor of California, EARL WARREN. At the *Brown* reargument, which was put off until December, he did not say much. In conference, however, Warren made clear his view that the separate but equal doctrine must be abandoned and the cases decided in favor of the black children's equal protection claim. At the same time, he though the Court should avoid "precipitous action that would inflame more than necessary." The conference disclosed an apparent majority for the Chief Justice's position, but in a case of such political magnitude, a unanimous decision was devoutly to be wished. The vote was thus postponed, while the Chief Justice and Justice Frankfurter sought for ways to unite the Court. Near-unanimity seems to have been achieved by agreement on a gradual enforcement of the Court's decision. A vote of 8–1 emerged late in the winter, with Justice ROBERT H. JACKSON preparing to file a separate concurrence. When Jackson suffered a heart attack, the likelihood of his pursuing an independent doctrinal course diminished. The Chief Justice circulated a draft opinion in early May, and at last Justice STANLEY F. REED was persuaded of the importance of avoiding division in the Court. On May 17, 1954, the Court announced its decision. Justice Jackson joined his brethren at the bench, to symbolize the Court's unanimity.

The opinion of the Court, by Chief Justice Warren, was calculatedly limited in scope, unilluminating as to doctrinal implications, and bland in tone. The South was not lectured, and no broad pronouncements were made concerning the fate of Jim Crow. *Plessy* was not even over-ruled—not then. Instead, the opinion highlighted two points of distinction: the change in the status of black persons in the years since *Plessy,* and the present-day importance of public education for the individual and for American society. Borrowing from the opinion of the lower court in the Kansas case (*Brown* itself), the Chief Justice concluded that school segregation produced feelings of inferiority in black children, and thus interfered with their motivation to learn; as in the graduate education cases, such intangibles were critical in evaluating the equality of the educational opportunity offered to blacks. In *Plessy,* the Court had brushed aside the argument that segregation stamped blacks with a mark of inferiority; the *Brown* opinion, on the contrary, stated that modern psychological knowledge verified the argument, and in a supporting footnote cited a number of social science authorities. (See LEGISLATIVE FACTS.) Segregated education was inherently unequal; the separate but equal doctrine thus had no place in education.

In the ordinary equal protection case, a finding of state-imposed inequality is only part of the inquiry; the Court goes on to examine into justifications offered by the state for treating people unequally. In these cases the southern states had argued that segregation promoted the quality of education, the health of pupils, and the tranquillity of schools. The *Brown* opinion omitted entirely any reference to these asserted justifications. By looking only to the question of inequality, the Court followed the pattern set in earlier cases applying the separate but equal doctrine. However, in its opinion in the companion case from the District of Columbia, the Court added this remark: "Segregation in public education is not reasonably related to any proper governmental objective. . . ." With those conclusory words, the Court announced that further inquiry into justifications for school segregation was foreclosed.

The *Brown* opinion thus presented a near-minimum political target, one that could have been reduced only by the elimination of its social science citations. Everyone understood the importance of educational opportunity. Nothing was intimated about segregation in PUBLIC ACCOMMODATIONS or state courthouses, hospitals, or prisons. Most important of all, the Court issued no orders to the defendant school boards, but set the cases for yet another argument at the next term on questions of remedy: should segregation be ended at once, or gradually? Should the Supreme Court itself frame the decrees, or leave that task to the lower courts or a SPECIAL MASTER?

A full year passed before the Court issued its remedial opinion. *Brown II,* as that opinion is sometimes called, not only declined to order an immediate end to segregation but also failed to set deadlines. Instead, the Court told the lower courts to require the school boards to "make a prompt and reasonable start" toward "compliance at the earliest practicable date," taking into account such factors as buildings, transportation systems, personnel, and redrawing of attendance district lines. The lower courts should issue decrees to the end of admitting the plaintiff children to the schools "on a racially nondiscriminatory basis with ALL DELIBERATE SPEED. . . ."

This language looked like—and was—a political compromise; something of the sort had been contemplated from the beginning by Chief Justice Warren. Despite the Court's statement that constitutional principles could not yield to disagreement, the white South was told, in effect, that it might go on denying blacks their constitutional rights for an indefinite time, while it got used to the idea of stopping. Unquestionably, whatever the Court determined in 1954 or 1955, it would take time to build the sense of interracial community in the South and elsewhere. But in *Brown II* the Court sacrificed an important part of its one legitimate claim to political and moral authority: the defense of principle. A southern intransigent might say: after all, if *Brown* really did stand for a national principle, surely the principle would not be parceled out for separate negotiation in thousands of school districts over an indefinite time. The chief responses of the white South to the Court's gradualism were defiance and evasion. (See DESEGREGATION.) In 1956 a "Southern Manifesto," signed by nineteen Senators and 82 members of the House of Representatives, denounced *Brown* as resting on "personal political and social ideas" rather than the Constitution. One Mississippi senator, seeking to capitalize on the country's recent anticommunist fervor, called racial integration "a radical, pro-Communist political movement." President Eisenhower gave the decision no political support, promising only to carry out the law of the land.

Criticism of another sort came from Herbert Wechsler, a Columbia law professor with impressive credentials as a CIVIL RIGHTS advocate. Wechsler argued that the Supreme Court had not offered a principled explanation of the *Brown* decision—had not supported its repeated assertion that segregation harmed black school children. Charles L. Black, Jr., a Texan and a Yale professor who had worked on the NAACP briefs in *Brown,* replied that all Southerners knew that Jim Crow was designed to maintain white supremacy. School segregation, as part of that system, must fall before a constitutional principle forbidding states deliberately to disadvantage a racial group. This defense of the *Brown* decision is irrefutable. But the *Brown* opinion had not tied school segregation to the system of Jim Crow, because Chief Justice Warren's strategy had been to avoid sweeping pronouncements in the interest of obtaining a unanimous Court and minimizing southern defiance and violence.

Within a few years, however, in a series of PER CURIAM orders consisting only of citations to *Brown,* the Court had invalidated state-supported segregation in all its forms. In one case *Plessy* was implicitly overruled. Jim Crow was thus buried without ceremony. Yet the intensity of the southern resistance to *Brown* shows that no one had been deceived into thinking that the decision was limited to education. Not only did the occasion deserve a clear statement of the unconstitutionality of the system of racial segregation; political practicalities also called for such a statement. The Supreme Court's ability to command respect for its decisions depends on its candid enunciation of the principles underlying those decisions.

Both *Brown* opinions, then, were evasions. Even so, *Brown* was a great decision, a personal triumph for a great Chief Justice. For if *Brown* was a culmination, it was also a beginning. The decision was the catalyst for a political movement that permanently altered race relations in America. (See SIT-IN; CIVIL RIGHTS ACT OF 1964; VOTING RIGHTS ACT OF 1965.) The success of the civil rights movement encouraged challenges to other systems of domination and dependency: systems affecting women, ALIENS, illegitimate children, the handicapped, homosexuals. Claims to racial equality forced a reexamination of a wide range of institutional arrangements throughout American society. In constitutional/doctrinal terms, *Brown* was the critical event in the modern development of the equal protection clause as an effective guarantee of equal CITIZENSHIP, a development that led in turn to the rebirth of SUBSTANTIVE DUE PROCESS as a guarantee of fundamental personal liberties. After *Brown,* the federal judiciary saw itself in a new light, and all Americans could see themselves as members of a national community.

Bibliography

BELL, DERRICK 1980 Brown v. Board of Education and the Interest-Convergence Dilemma. *Harvard Law Review* 93:518–533.

BLACK, CHARLES L., JR.   1960   The Lawfulness of the Segregation Decisions. *Yale Law Journal* 69:421–430.

KLUGER, RICHARD   1975   *Simple Justice*. New York: Knopf.

LEFLAR, ROBERT A. and DAVIS, WYLIE H.   1954 Segregation in the Public Schools—1953. *Harvard Law Review* 67:377–435.

WECHSLER, HERBERT   1959   Toward Neutral Principles of Constitutional Law. *Harvard Law Review* 73:1–35.

WILKINSON, J. HARVIE, III   1979   *From Brown to Bakke*. New York: Oxford University Press.

# *BOLLING v. SHARPE*

## 347 U.S. 497 (1954)

### Kenneth L. Karst

In the four cases now known as BROWN V. BOARD OF EDUCATION (1954), the Supreme Court held that racial SEGREGATION of children in state public schools violated the FOURTEENTH AMENDMENT's guarantee of the EQUAL PROTECTION OF THE LAWS. *Bolling,* a companion case to *Brown,* involved a challenge to school segregation in the DISTRICT OF COLUMBIA. The equal protection clause applies only to the states. However, in previous cases (including the JAPANESE AMERICAN CASES, 1943–1944) the Court had assumed, at least for argument, that the Fifth Amendment's guarantee of DUE PROCESS OF LAW prohibited arbitrary discrimination by the federal government.

The Court in *Bolling* also drew on OBITER DICTA in the Japanese American Cases stating that racial classifications were suspect, requiring exacting judicial scrutiny. Because school segregation was "not reasonably related to any proper governmental objective," the District's practice deprived the segregated black children of liberty without due process. Chief Justice EARL WARREN wrote for a unanimous Court.

The Court concluded its Fifth Amendment discussion by remarking that because *Brown* had prohibited school segregation by the states, "it would be unthinkable that the same Constitution would impose a lesser duty on the Federal Government." Critics have suggested that what was "unthinkable" was the political implication of a contrary decision. But the notions of liberty and equality have long been understood to overlap. The idea of national CITIZENSHIP implies a measure of equal treatment by the national government, and the "liberty" protected by the Fifth Amendment's due process clause implies a measure of equal liberties. Doctrinally as well as politically, a contrary decision in *Bolling* would have been unthinkable.

# ALL DELIBERATE SPEED

Kenneth L. Karst

Chief Justice EARL WARREN achieved a unanimous decision in BROWN v. BOARD OF EDUCATION (1954) by assuring that enforcement of school DESEGREGATION would be gradual. Ordinarily, state officials found to be violating the Constitution are simply ordered to stop. *Brown II* (1955), however, instructed lower courts to insist only that offending school boards make "a prompt and reasonable start," proceeding toward full desegregation with "all deliberate speed."

This calculatedly elusive phrase was contributed by Justice FELIX FRANKFURTER, who had borrowed it from an old opinion by Justice OLIVER WENDELL HOLMES. Holmes attributed it to English EQUITY practice, but he may also have seen it in Francis Thompson's poem, "The Hound of Heaven." Whatever the phrase's origins, it was a thin cover for compromise. The objective presumably was to allow time for the white South to become accustomed to the end of SEGREGATION, in the hope of avoiding defiance of the courts and even violence. Robert Penn Warren, a southern man of letters who had not studied quantum mechanics, even tried to make gradualism in desegregation a historical necessity: "History, like nature, knows no jumps."

The South responded not with accommodation but with politically orchestrated defiance. A full decade after *Brown I,* two percent of southern black children were attending integrated schools. By 1969, the Supreme Court explicitly abandoned "all deliberate speed"; in ALEXANDER v. HOLMES COUNTY BOARD OF EDUCATION school boards were told to desegregate "at once."

No one pretends that the Supreme Court could have ended Jim Crow overnight, certainly not without support from Congress or the President. Yet the Court's decisions can command respect only when they are understood to rest on principle. *Brown II,* widely seen to be precisely the political accommodation it was intended to be, did not merely consign a generation of southern black school children to segregated schools. The decision weakened the Court's own moral authority in the very process gradualism was designed to aid.

Bibliography

WILKINSON, J. HARVIE, III  1979  *From Brown to Bakke.* New York: Oxford University Press.

# EARL WARREN

## (1891–1974)

### Anthony Lewis

The fourteenth Chief Justice of the United States, Earl Warren presided over the most sweeping judicial reinterpretation of the Constitution in generations. He served from October 1953 to June 1969. In that time the SUPREME COURT, overruling the doctrine that SEPARATE BUT EQUAL facilities for black persons satisfied the requirement of EQUAL PROTECTION, outlawed official racial SEGREGATION in every area of life. The Court ended the long-established rural bias of legislative representation by opening the question to judicial scrutiny and then ruling that citizens must be represented equally in state legislatures and the national House of Representatives. It imposed constitutional restraints for the first time on the law of LIBEL, hitherto a matter entirely of state concern. It applied to the states the standards set by the BILL OF RIGHTS for federal CRIMINAL PROCEDURE: the right of all poor defendants to free counsel, for example, and the prohibition of unreasonable SEARCHES AND SEIZURES, enforced by the EXCLUSIONARY RULE. It limited government power to punish unorthodox beliefs and enlarged the individual's freedom to express herself or himself in unconventional, even shocking ways.

The WARREN COURT, as it was generally called, had as profound an impact on American life as any Supreme Court since the time of JOHN MARSHALL. It was extraordinary not only in the scale but in the direction of its exercise of power. From Marshall's day to the Court's clash with President FRANKLIN D. ROOSEVELT in the 1930s judges had exercised a conservative influence in the American system. Shortly before his appointment to the Court in 1941 ROBERT H. JACKSON wrote that "never in its entire history can the Supreme Court be said to have for a single hour been representative of anything except the relatively conservative forces of its day." But the Warren Court in its time was perhaps *the* principal engine of American liberal reform.

Earl Warren seemed an unlikely figure to lead such a judicial revolution. He was a Republican politician, the elected attorney general of California and for three terms its phenomenally popular governor. In 1948 he was the Republican candidate for vice-president, on the ticket headed by Thomas E. Dewey. On naming him Chief Justice, President DWIGHT D. EISENHOWER emphasized his "middle-of-the-road philosophy." Yet within a few years billboards in the South demanded Warren's

216

IMPEACHMENT, and the paranoid right charged that he was doing the work of communism. Putting aside the rantings of extremists, there was no doubt that Chief Justice Warren consistently favored liberal values and unembarrassedly translated them into constitutional doctrine. Where did that commitment come from in a man whose appearance was that of a bland, hearty political figure?

There were in fact clues in his life and earlier career. He was born in Los Angeles in 1891, the son of a Norwegian immigrant who worked for the Southern Pacific Railroad. He knew poverty and personal tragedy. As a young man he was a railroad callboy, waking up the gangs, and he saw men with their legs cut off in accidents carried in on planks. His father was murdered, the murderer never found: a traumatic event that must have helped to point Warren in the direction of justice, legal and social. He put himself through college and law school at the University of California. After a brief try at private practice he spent all his life in public office, as a local prosecutor and crusading district attorney before winning statewide office.

In California politics he at first had the support of conservatives. As attorney general he blocked the nomination of Max Radin, a law professor known as a legal realist, to the state supreme court because Radin was a "radical." As attorney general and governor Warren was a leading proponent of the World War II federal order removing all persons of Japanese ancestry from the West Coast and putting them in desolate camps; opposing their return in 1943, he said, "If the Japs are released, no one will be able to tell a saboteur from any other Jap." (In a memoir published after his death, Warren wrote: "I have since deeply regretted the removal order and my own testimony advocating it, because it was not in keeping with our American concept of freedom and the rights of citizens. . . .")

But in 1945 Warren astounded political California by proposing a state program of prepaid medical insurance. Characteristically, he did so not for ideological but for human, practical reasons: he had fallen ill and realized how catastrophic serious illness would be for a person without resources. Then, in his last two terms as governor, he became an apostle of liberal Republicanism. A later Democratic governor, Edmund G. Brown, said Warren "was the best governor California ever had. . . . He felt the people of California were in his care, and he cared for them."

Many Americans and other people around the world saw that same paternal image in Earl Warren the Chief Justice, for he became an international symbol. He represented the hope of authority bringing justice to the downtrodden, an American vision of change by law rather than by rebellion. A single case gave Warren that status: BROWN V. BOARD OF EDUCATION, the 1954 school segregation decision. In recent years the Supreme Court had chipped away at PLESSY V. FERGUSON, the 1896 decision allowing what were termed "separate but equal" facilities but what were almost always in fact grossly inferior schools and other public institutions for blacks. Yet in 1953 seventeen southern and border states, with forty percent of the national enrollment, still confined black children to separate public schools; moreover, there was involved here, unlike higher education, the compulsory daily association of children. The emotional content of the legal question was high. The Court had given the most gingerly handling to the question, restoring the issue to the calendar for reargument.

Warren became Chief Justice before the second argument. The following May he delivered the opinion for a unanimous Court holding public school segregation unconstitutional. The unanimity was itself a striking feature of the result, and a surprising one. Expected southern resistance made unanimity politically essential, but the known attitudes of some members of the Court had suggested the likelihood of dissents. Richard Kluger's exhaustive study has demonstrated that the new Chief Justice played a crucial part in his management of the process inside the Court. After argument he delayed formal discussion of the cases in conference to avoid the development of rigid positions among the nine Justices. Then he stated as his view that the separate-but-equal doctrine could not be maintained unless one thought blacks inherently inferior: an approach likely to induce shame in any judge prepared to argue for that outcome. He persuaded his colleagues even then to avoid a formal vote but to continue discussing the cases, in tight secrecy, among themselves. He wrote an opinion in simple terms. Finally, he persuaded reluctant members of the Court to join for the sake of unanimity. A law clerk present at a late meeting between the Chief Justice and the most reluctant, STANLEY F. REED, remembers him saying, "Stan, you're all by yourself in this now. You've got to decide whether it's really the best thing for the country."

What is known about the process of decision in the school cases throws lights on one question asked during his lifetime: did Chief Justice Warren exercise leadership or have influence in the Court beyond his own vote in conference? He shared that bench with men of strong personality and conviction: in particular HUGO L. BLACK, who said the judicial duty was to follow the literal language of the Constitution and found in it absolutes, and FELIX FRANKFURTER, who scorned absolutes and said the Court should defer to the political branches of government in applying the uncertain commands of the Constitution. Warren came to the Court utterly inexperienced in its work; how could he have effective influence? The school cases show that he did.

No Chief Justice can command his associates' beliefs. If Warren had served with different, more conservative colleagues, many of the views that made history might have been expressed by him in dissent. Changes while he was on the Court greatly affected the trend of doctrine, in particular the retirement of Justice Frankfurter in 1962 and his replacement by ARTHUR J. GOLDBERG, who was much readier to join Warren in intervening on behalf of liberal values. But the identification of that Court with its Chief Justice, for all its logical imperfection, has substantial basis in reality.

Warren wrote the opinions of the Court not only in *Brown* but in later cases that dramatically overturned expectations. The most important of these—Warren himself thought them the weightiest decisions of his years on the Court—were the REAPPORTIONMENT cases. A divided Supreme Court in COLEGROVE V. GREEN (1946) had refused to entertain an attack on numerical inequality in political districts, an opinion by Justice Frankfurter saying that courts must stay out of the "political thicket." In 1962 the Warren Court, in an opinion by Justice WILLIAM J. BRENNAN, overthrew that doctrine of reluctance and said that federal courts could consider issues of fairness in districting. The decision in BAKER V. CARR left open the substantive questions: must the population be the test of equality, or may states weigh geography or other factors in districting? Does the same standard apply to both houses of legislatures? The answers were given by Chief Justice Warren in 1964, in terms so firm that some who listened in the courtroom felt as if they were at a second American constitutional convention. In REYNOLDS V. SIMS Warren said for a 6–3 majority that every house of every state legislature must be apportioned on the basis of population alone, with the districts as nearly equal as practicable. Few cases in any court ever had so direct and immediate an impact on a nation's politics; reapportionment was required in most of the fifty states, ancient legislative expectations were upset, new suburban power vindicated. Justice JOHN MARSHALL HARLAN predicted in dissent, as had Justice Frankfurter in *Baker v. Carr,* that the courts would not be able to manage the apportionment litigation—or to enforce their decisions against political resistance. But the gloomy prediction was wrong. Resistance from political incumbents quickly collapsed; nothing like the emotional public opposition to the school segregation cases developed in any region.

Emotions were aroused by Warren's opinion in MIRANDA V. ARIZONA (1966), holding that before questioning an arrested person the police must warn him that he has a right to remain silent and a right to see a lawyer first—one provided by the state if he cannot afford one—and that a confession obtained in violation of that rule is inadmissible at trial. The decision touched a nerve among police, prosecutors, and others convinced that judges were impeding the fight against crime. *Miranda* climaxed a series of cases holding local police to the standards of the Bill of Rights: for example, MAPP V. OHIO (1961), exclusion of illegally obtained evidence; GIDEON V. WAINWRIGHT (1963), RIGHT TO COUNSEL; GRIFFIN V. CALIFORNIA (1965), RIGHT AGAINST SELF-INCRIMINATION; each overruling an earlier decision. In *Spano v. New York* (1959) Warren commented: "The abhorrence of society to the use of involuntary confessions does not turn alone on their inherent untrustworthiness. It also turns on the deep-rooted feeling that the police must obey the law while enforcing the law; that in the end life and liberty can be as much endangered from illegal methods used to convict those thought to be criminals as from the actual criminals themselves." Impatient with reviewing the facts in case after case of claimed coercion, the Court under Warren sought a general prophylactic rule—and wrote it in *Miranda*.

Objection to the *Miranda* decision came not only from the law enforcement community. More dispassionate critics saw it as an example of overreaching by the Warren Court. The opinion seemed more legislative in character than judicial, laying out what amounted to a code of police procedure with little basis in precedent. Moreover, the Court did not confront a situation in which reform by other means was blocked, as it had with school segregation and malapportioned legislatures; various reformers were working on the confession problem.

Freedom of expression was another subject of fundamental constitutional development during the Warren years. The most important single decision was probably NEW YORK TIMES V. SULLIVAN (1964), holding that a public official may not recover libel damages unless the statement was published with knowledge of its falsity or in reckless disregard of truth or falsity. That opinion was by Justice Brennan. Justice WILLIAM O. DOUGLAS wrote for the Court in LAMONT V. POSTMASTER GENERAL (1965), holding that a statute requiring the post office to detain "Communist political propaganda" from abroad unless the addressee requested its delivery violated the FIRST AMENDMENT—the first federal statute that the Supreme Court ever held invalid under that amendment. Warren joined in these and other expansive decisions. He wrote for a 5–4 majority in UNITED STATES V. ROBEL (1967), striking down a law that forbade the employment in defense plants of any member of an organization required to register under the Subversive Activities Control Act. Warren's opinion for a unanimous Court in *Bond v. Floyd* (1966) held that the Georgia legislature could not exclude a duly elected member because he had expressed admiration for draft resisters.

The one area of expression in which Warren departed from the majority of his colleagues was OBSCENITY. He thought that local and national authorities should have a relatively free hand to combat what he evidently regarded as a social evil. Thus, while in *Miranda* imposing a national standard for fair pretrial procedures in criminal cases, he argued in dissent in JACOBELLIS V. OHIO (1964) that each local community should be allowed to fix its own standard of obscenity, a view that became the law under Chief Justice WARREN E. BURGER in MILLER V. CALIFORNIA (1973). Another example of a departure from Warren's usual approach came when gambling was involved. He generally favored broad application of the right against self-incrimination; but when the rule was applied for the benefit of a gambler in MARCHETTI V. UNITED STATES (1968), he alone dissented. Once again he saw a social evil.

Scholarly critics of Chief Justice Warren saw the obscenity and gambling cases as illustrating a fundamental shortcoming in a judge: a concern to reach particular results rather than to work out principles applicable whoever the parties in a case might be. In Warren's view, it seemed, justice consisted not in providing a philosophically satisfactory process and basis of decision but in seeing that the right side, the good side, won in each case. Many of the commentators regretted the lack of a consistent doctrinal thread in his opinions. There was nothing like Justice Black's exaltation of the constitutional text, or Justice Frankfurter's institutional concern for self-restraint.

G. Edward White, in a full-length study of Warren's work, rejected the general scholarly view that Warren had no rudder as a judge and lacked craftsmanship. He was an ethicist, White concluded, who saw his craft as "discovering ethical imperatives in a maze of confusion"— and in the Constitution. Thus the prosecutor so hard on corruption that he was called a boy scout, the Californian politician who stood aloof from party machines lest he be sullied, became a judicial enforcer of ethical imperatives. In general his sympathy lay with the little person, with victims, with people excluded from the benefits of our democracy. But he also was in the tradition of the American Progressives, who thought that government could be made to work for the people. Those two themes came together in the reapportionment cases, decisions designed to make democracy work better by making the electoral process fairer. John Hart Ely, in an analysis of judicial review as practiced in the Warren years, suggested that many of the pathbreaking decisions had a democratic structural purpose: to assure access for the powerless and thus make the system work.

There was a directness, a simplicity in Warren's opinions on the largest issues. "Legislators represent people," he wrote in the reapportionment cases, "not acres or trees. Legislators are elected by voters, not farms or cities or economic interests. . . . The weight of a citizen's vote cannot be made to depend on where he lives." When the Court held unconstitutional a statute depriving a native-born American of his citizenship for deserting the armed forces in time of war, TROP V. DULLES (1958), Warren for a plurality argued that EXPATRIATION WAS A CRUEL AND UNUSUAL PUNISHMENT in violation of the Eighth Amendment. The death penalty would not have been "cruel," he conceded, but the deprivation of citizenship was, for it caused "the total destruction of the individual's status in organized society" and cost him "the right to have rights."

Warren's whole career suggests that he was a person born not to muse but to act—and to govern. That view provides a connecting thread through all the offices he held. In each he exerted his powerful abilities in the ways open to him. As a prosecutor he fought crime. As wartime attorney general and governor he was a patriot, worrying about spies. In the postwar years, he turned to the social problems of an expanding California. As Chief Justice, too, he was committed to action, to using the opportunities available to make an impression on American life: to break the pattern of malapportionment, to attack local police abuses, to condemn racial discrimination. The instinct to govern did not leave Earl Warren when he put on a robe.

Many regarded him as a heroic figure because he put aside philosophical concerns and technical legal issues and dealt squarely with what he considered outrageous situations. And there were outrages in American life: official racism, political discrimination, abuse of police authority, suppression of free expression. Warren as Chief Justice had the conviction, the humanity, and the capacity for growth to deal effectively with those issues inside that prickly institution, the Supreme Court. But there were those who shared Justice LEARNED HAND's doubts about rule by judges, however beneficent. "For myself," Hand wrote in 1958, with the contemporary Supreme Court in mind, "it would be most irksome to be ruled by a bevy of Platonic Guardians, even if I knew how to choose them, which I assuredly do not." Earl Warren may have been the closest thing the United States has had to a constitutional Platonic Guardian, dispensing law without any sensed limit of authority except what he saw as the good of society. He was a decent, kindly law-giver. But the exercise of such power by other judges—before and after Warren—has not always had kindly or rational results. The questions about judicial power remain after its extraordinary uses in the Warren years.

Bibliography

ELY, JOHN HART    1980    Democracy and Distrust: A Theory of Judicial Review. Cambridge, Mass.: Harvard University Press.

KLUGER, RICHARD    1975    Simple Justice: The History of Brown v. Board of Education and Black America's Struggle for Equality. New York: Knopf.

SCHWARTZ, BERNARD    1983    Superchief. Garden City, N.Y.: Doubleday.

WHITE, G. EDWARD    1982    Earl Warren: A Public Life. New York: Oxford University Press.

# SOUTHERN MANIFESTO

## (March 11, 1956)

### Paul L. Murphy

Southern politicians generally opposed the Supreme Court's ruling in BROWN V. BOARD OF EDUCATION (1954). Virginia and other states resurrected the doctrine of INTERPOSITION, and Georgia threatened NULLIFICATION. The most considered statement of segregationist constitutional theory was the declaration against INTEGRATION made by ninety-six southern congressmen and senators, in March 1956, led by Senator Harry F. Byrd of Virginia. The manifesto argued: *Brown* represented a clear abuse of judicial power; the FOURTEENTH AMENDMENT, which did not mention education, was not intended to affect state educational systems; PLESSY V. FERGUSON (1896) was still good law; DESEGREGATION would cause chaos and confusion in the states affected. The manifesto called upon the people of the states to "resist forced integration by any lawful means" and concluded with a pledge "to use all lawful means to bring about a reversal of this decision which is contrary to the Constitution, and to prevent the use of force in its implementation." Federal response to such abstract defiance was notably lacking, although a group of distinguished leaders of the American bar denounced attacks on the Supreme Court as "reckless in their abuse, . . . heedless of the value of JUDICIAL REVIEW and . . . dangerous in fomenting disrespect for our highest law."

Bibliography

MUSE, BENJAMIN 1964 *Ten Years of Prelude: The Story of Integration Since the Supreme Court's 1954 Decision.* New York: Viking.

# DESEGREGATION

Derrick A. Bell

Freed finally of slavery's shackles, blacks in America began the long quest for racial equality. Desegregation, a generic term used to describe elimination of the SEGREGATION and RACIAL DISCRIMINATION that non-whites confronted at life's every turn, has been the equivalent of their Holy Grail.

While blacks have attacked barriers based on color across a spectrum that includes VOTING, employment, housing, the administration of justice, access to public facilities, and even sex and marriage, the elimination of discrimination in the public schools has been and remains the most important goal for black Americans in their continuing struggle against racism in this country.

At an early time in the nation's history, blacks hoped an already hostile society might at least share their fear, as a black minister phrased it, "for our rising offspring to see them in ignorance in a land of gospel light." That petition presented in 1787 to the Massachusetts legislature sought a separate school for Boston's black children whose parents had withdrawn them from the harassment and ridicule heaped on them by white teachers and students in some of the new nation's first public schools.

The legislature denied the petition, which reflected fears shared by succeeding generations of black parents who all during the nineteenth century filed dozens of law suits with state courts seeking relief from the racial discrimination they found in the public schools. Depending on the times and the character of the discrimination they faced, black parents have sought equal educational opportunity for their children through the advocacy of either racially separate or integrated schools.

With few exceptions, the courts were no more sympathetic to these petitions than were the school boards whose policies sometimes excluded black children from the public schools entirely and always subjected them to conditions that left little doubt as to which students were deemed members of the superior race. In ROBERTS V. CITY OF BOSTON (1850) a state court rejected a school desegregation petition almost two decades before the adoption of the FOURTEENTH AMENDMENT; three decades after its ratification, the United States Supreme Court concluded in PLESSY V. FERGUSON (1896) that the Fourteenth Amendment did not prohibit state-sanctioned segregation, citing the *Roberts* decision as support for the reasonableness of what it called SEPARATE BUT EQUAL facilities. *Plessy* provided the Constitution's blessing for laws throughout the South that required racial segregation not only in public schools, but in every possible public facility, including cemeteries and houses of prostitution.

The law and much of society enforced the "separate" phase of the *Plessy* standard to the letter, but the promise of "equal" facilities received only the grudging attention of a public whose racial attitudes ranged from apathy to outright hostility. Deep-South states spent far less for the schooling of black children than for whites. Despite a major effort to equalize segregated schools as a means of forestalling the steadily increasing number of CIVIL RIGHTS challenges in the 1950s, the South as a whole expended an average of $165 for every white child, and only $115 for each black in 1954, the year in which segregated schools were ruled unconstitutional.

More than a half century after its *Plessy* decision, the Supreme Court in BROWN v. BOARD OF EDUCATION (1954) reviewed the "separate but equal" DOCTRINE in the light of education's importance for children in a modern society, and concluded that the Fourteenth Amendment's EQUAL PROTECTION clause was violated by segregated schools "even though the physical facilities and other 'tangible" factors may be equal. . . ."

Chief Justice EARL WARREN's ringing rhetoric in the *Brown* opinion condemned racially segregated schooling as "inherently unequal." He found that the separation by the state of children in grade and high schools solely on the basis of race "generates a feeling of inferiority as to their status in the community that may affect their hearts and minds in a way unlikely ever to be undone."

This decision was the result of long years of planning and litigation by the NAACP, and the committed work of lawyers including THURGOOD MARSHALL and Robert L. Carter, social scientists like Kenneth Clark, and hundreds of courageous black parents and their children. The decision, most blacks were convinced, required the elimination of segregated school facilities. Black parents knew that state-mandated black schools were a racial insult, and most hoped that if their children attended schools with whites, they would more likely gain access to the same educational resources as white children.

But the determination of civil rights groups representing an ever-increasing number of black parents seeking to join in school desegregation suits was met by the equally determined and, at least initially, far more powerful resistance of southern whites who strongly opposed sending their children to school with blacks and greatly resented the federal coercion involved in school desegregation orders which they equated with the occupation of the region by Union forces following the Civil War.

Arguably, opposition by southern working class whites could be predicated on the basis that, by invalidating segregation laws, *Brown* betrayed post-Reconstruction promises of white superior status made to them by policymakers in return for political support given during periods when populist movements sought to challenge the monopoly of economic power held by the upper class.

Although the Supreme Court refused to turn the clock back to 1868 to determine whether the framers of the Fourteenth Amendment had intended to condone segregated schools, an examination of post-Reconstruction history shows that policies of segregation reflected a series of political compromises through which working class whites settled their demands for social reform and greater political power. C. Vann Woodward and other historians have shown that segregated schools and facilities were established by legislatures at the insistence of the white working classes who saw color barriers as official confirmation that the society's policymakers would maintain even the poorest whites in a permanent status superior to that designated for blacks.

While not willing to acknowledge that its school desegregation decision would deprive whites of long-held rights of superior status based on race, the Court in *Brown v. Board of Education II* (1955), signaled that it was aware of the major social upheaval its ruling would require. Rejecting the black petitioners' requests for immediate relief, the Court chose a procedure that would permit the individual resolution of administrative and academic problems. It mandated only a "prompt and reasonable start toward full compliance," and returned the cases to the district courts with the admonition that orders and decrees be entered to admit plaintiffs to public schools on a racially nondiscriminatory basis "with ALL DELIBERATE SPEED. . . ."

But the Court's conciliatory efforts did not avoid and may have encouraged a period of massive resistance by southern elected officials, a rise in the Ku Klux Klan and other white supremacist groups, and a general upswing in economic intimidation and threats of physical violence against blacks deemed responsible for or participants in the civil rights movement. The Court met open resistance in Little Rock, Arkansas, and elsewhere with firm resolve, as in COOPER V. AARON (1958), but for several years condoned pupil placement laws and other procedural devices clearly designed to frustrate any meaningful compliance with the *Brown* mandate.

Federal courts were far less cautious in applying the *Brown* decision as the controlling precedent in cases challenging racial segregation in other public facilities. Thus, in the first half-dozen years following *Brown*, civil rights groups succeeded in desegregating state-operated places of recreation, government buildings, and transportation facilities.

Finally, in 1964, during the height of the SIT-IN protest movement that was bringing an end to "Jim Crow" policies in many hitherto segregated privately owned facilities not covered by the Fourteenth Amendment, the Court indicated that the time for mere deliberate speed had run out, in GRIFFIN V. SCHOOL BOARD OF PRINCE EDWARD COUNTY (1964). But the success of a decade of white resistance to school desegregation was reflected in the statistics. In the eleven states of the old Confederacy, a mere 1.17 percent of black students were attending school with white students by the 1963–1964 school year. The dirgelike progress of school desegregation finally gained momentum through a series of far-reaching lower court orders combined with the federal government's enforcement of Title VI of the CIVIL RIGHTS ACT OF 1964. This provision required the cut-off of federal financial assistance to entities that followed racially discriminatory policies. The federal government's enforcement of Title VI was seldom vigorous, but even the threat of losing the federal monies made available under a host of new antipoverty and educational assistance programs in the late 1960s persuaded hundreds of southern school districts that some form of compliance was in their best interests.

In 1968, the Supreme Court in GREEN V. NEW KENT COUNTY SCHOOL BOARD virtually eliminated the offer by a school board of "freedom of choice" to all children as a sufficient compliance with desegregation requirements. The decision was hailed by civil rights lawyers who believed that the *Brown* mandate could not be implemented unless public schools were rendered nonidentifiable by race. This goal, articulated in the *Green* case by Justice WILLIAM J. BRENNAN as requiring school boards to formulate plans that promise "realistically to convert promptly to a system without a 'white' school and a 'Negro' school, but just schools," was furthered when the Court applied the *Green* standard to a large, urban school district in North Carolina in SWANN V. CHARLOTTE-MECKLENBURG BOARD OF EDUCATION (1971). A few years later, the Court held a large northern school district subject to a similar standard in KEYES V. SCHOOL DISTRICT NO. 1 OF DENVER, COLORADO (1973). (See SCHOOL BUSING.)

But while the percentage of children attending desegregated schools increased impressively, opposition to school desegregation remained. Resistance focused on plans like those approved in both *Swann* and *Keyes* requiring the transportation of children in order to achieve a measure of desegregation in each school roughly equivalent to the percentages of white and nonwhite children in the district as a whole. Opponents had gained national political strength, and their support likely played an important role in the election of RICHARD M. NIXON as President in 1968. The Nixon administration adopted policies that had the effect of slowing the federal government's participation in the school desegregation campaign, but the Supreme Court rejected Administration-sponsored delay requests in ALEXANDER V. HOLMES COUNTY BOARD OF EDUCATION (1969) and *Carter v. West Feliciana Parish School Board* (1970), although not without cracks in the solid front of unanimous opinions the Court had handed down in school desegregation cases since *Brown I.*

By 1974, in MILLIKEN V. BRADLEY, an APPEAL from lower court orders requiring the consolidation with the seventy percent black Detroit school system of fifty-three predominantly white suburban school districts, those cracks had grown into a chasm between divergent viewpoints on the appropriateness of school desegregation remedies. The insistence of civil rights lawyers that courts had unlimited discretion to impose racial-balance oriented plans to remedy proven segregation resulted in a significant change in the standards for proving school district liability for violating the Constitution.

In a 5–4 decision, the Court in *Milliken* held that federal courts could not impose multidistrict remedies to cure a single district's segregation absent findings that the other included school districts had failed to operate unitary school systems within their districts, or were responsible for the segregation in the other districts. Proof of this character could be found in few districts without histories of official, state-mandated segregation, and thus plans to desegregate large, urban school districts through metropolitanwide plans were rendered inoperable.

By the late 1970s, roughly half of all nonwhite children in the nation resided in the country's twenty to thirty largest school districts. Minority children averaged sixty percent of the school population in these districts and close to seventy percent in the ten largest districts. Politically if not physically, desegregation in these districts on the *Green-Swann* model became increasingly difficult.

Lower courts, impressed by detailed prescriptions of racial wrongdoing by urban school boards, continued at the urging of civil rights lawyers to grant relief requiring reassignments and busing to change the racial makeup of schools. But the Supreme Court, now quite divided, set increasingly difficult liability standards in cases from Dayton and Columbus, Ohio; Omaha, Nebraska; Austin, Texas; Milwaukee, Wisconsin; and Indianapolis, Indiana. Plans requiring wholesale reassignment of children in these districts were finally approved, mainly because the proof of past discrimination was so clear. There was little judicial enthusiasm for continued reliance on a remedial process about which there was so much controversy as to its effectiveness even among civil rights proponents.

By this time, a great many black communities were questioning the continued validity of the "neither black schools nor white schools" desegregation approach that had stood as an article of faith since the early post-*Brown* years. Disenchantment was prompted by the hundreds of black schools closed and the scores of black teachers and principals dismissed in the course of the school desegregation process. In addition, black parents were discovering that the sacrifice involved in busing children across town to mainly white schools did not always eliminate racial discrimination. More litigation had to be prosecuted to challenge resegregation tactics as varied as the use of standardized tests to track black students into virtually all-black classrooms, to the exclusion of blacks from extracurricular programs. In most desegregated school systems, black students were far more likely to be suspended and expelled for disciplinary violations than white students. Black parents able to enroll their children in desegregated schools all too often found themselves protesting policies of in-school discrimination quite similar to those that had led their late eighteenth-century predecessors to petition for separate schools.

The NAACP and the few other groups who sponsored most school desegregation litigation remained firm in their belief that identifiably black schools would always be inferior and must be eliminated. But local black groups in several cities including Atlanta, St. Louis, Detroit, Dallas, Boston, and Portland, Oregon, decided that mainly black schools in black neighborhoods might provide effective schooling for their children if black parents could be involved more closely in faculty hiring, curriculum selection, and other policymaking aspects of these schools.

In 1975, a court of appeals approved in CALHOUN v. COOK, over the vigorous objection of the national NAACP office, a settlement of a twenty-year-old Atlanta school case providing full faculty and employee desegregation but only limited pupil desegregation in exchange for a school board promise to hire a number of blacks in top administrative positions, including a black superintendent of schools.

A few years later, in *Milliken v. Bradley II* (1977), the Supreme Court approved without dissent a Detroit desegregation plan that gave priority to a range of "educational components" while limiting pupil desegregation in the district that was by now more than eighty percent black to a provision that no school be less than thirty percent black. The Court though was unable to decide and left standing a lower court ruling that an almost all-black subdistrict created by the Dallas school desegregation plan met school desegregation standards. The record showed both that housing patterns and geographical conditions would have made desegregation difficult and that much of the black community in the subdistrict supported its retention.

Public resistance to school desegregation continued into the 1980s even though the likelihood of new court orders was lessened by the Supreme Court's application of higher standards of proof even in litigation where metropolitan relief was not sought. For example, California voters approved an amendment to their state constitution barring state courts from ordering racial balance remedies in cases where, absent a finding that the school board was guilty of a specific intent to discriminate, the Fourteenth Amendment would not require racial balance relief. The

Supreme Court upheld this provision in *Crawford v. Los Angeles Unified School District* (1982).

Civil rights organizations mobilized to meet such challenges, but local black groups increasingly opted for programs that promised to provide equal educational opportunity in neighborhood schools. At the same time, many black parents either moved to suburban areas or sent their children out of their neighborhoods to enable them to attend predominantly white schools.

The quest for effective schooling in the 1980s mirrors those made by black parents in the 1780s and during all the periods between. They and their children have recognized that neither separate schools nor integrated schools will automatically eliminate racist policies intended to provide priority to white children for scarce educational resources. School desegregation programs mandated by the *Brown* decision, and earnestly sought in hundreds of court cases, have served to slow but have not otherwise much discouraged those policies.

Beyond the real gains made by blacks during the *Brown* years, there remain millions of black and other minority children whose schooling remains both segregated and inferior. For them, there is ample basis for parental fears as they watch their rising offspring grow "in ignorance in a land of gospel light."

Bibliography

BELL, DERRICK A.    (1973)1980    *Race, Racism and American Law.*  Boston: Little, Brown.

KALODNER, HOWARD I. and FISHMAN, JAMES J., EDS.    1978    *Limits of Justice: The Courts' Role in School Desegregation.*  Cambridge, Mass.: Ballinger.

KLUGER, RICHARD    1976    *Simple Justice: The History of Brown v. Board of Education and Black America's Struggle for Equality.*  New York: Knopf.

WOODWARD, C. VANN    (1955)1974    *The Strange Career of Jim Crow.*  New York: Oxford University Press.

# COOPER v. AARON
## 358 U.S. 1 (1958)

### Kenneth L. Karst

For several years after its decision in BROWN V. BOARD OF EDUCATION (1954–1955), the Supreme Court gave little guidance or support to the lower courts charged with supervising the DESEGREGATION of the public schools. In this case, however, the Court was confronted with direct defiance of *Brown* by a state's highest officials, and it met that challenge head-on.

Even before the *Brown* remedial opinion in 1955, the school board of Little Rock, Arkansas, had approved a plan for gradual desegregation of the local schools, and the federal district court had upheld the plan. Just before the opening of the fall 1957 term, the state governor, Orval Faubus, ordered the state's National Guard to keep black children out of Little Rock's Central High School. The attorney general of the United States obtained an injunction against the governor's action, and the children entered the school. A hostile crowd gathered, and the children were removed by the police. President DWIGHT D. EISENHOWER was thus prodded into his first significant act supporting desegregation; he sent Army troops to Central High to protect the children, and eight black students attended the school for the full academic year.

In February 1958, the school board asked the district court, in *Cooper v. Aaron,* for a delay of two and one-half years in the implementation of its plan, and in June the court agreed, commenting on the "chaos, bedlam and turmoil" at Central High. In August the federal court of appeals reversed, calling for implementation of the plan on schedule. The Supreme Court, in an unusual move, accelerated the hearing to September 11, and the next day it issued a brief order affirming the decision of the court of appeals. Later the Court published its full opinion, signed by all nine Justices to emphasize their continued unanimous support of *Brown.*

The opinion dealt quickly with the uncomplicated merits of the case, saying that law and order were not to be achieved at the expense of the constitutional rights of black children. The Court then added a response to the assertion by the Arkansas governor and legislature that the state was not required to abide by *Brown,* because *Brown* itself was an unconstitutional assumption of judicial power.

The response scored two easy points first: the Constitution, under the SUPREMACY CLAUSE, is "the supreme Law of the Land," and MARBURY v. MADISON (1803) had held that it was the province of the judiciary to "say what the law is." The Court's next step, however, was not self-evident: *Marbury* meant that the federal courts are supreme in expounding the Constitution; thus *Brown* was the supreme law of the land, binding state officers. This view, which carried the assertion of judicial power further than *Marbury* had taken it, has been repeated by the Court several times since the *Cooper* decision.

*Cooper's* importance, however, was not so much doctrinal as political. It reaffirmed principle at a crucial time. The televised pictures of black children being escorted into school through a crowd of hostile whites galvanized northern opinion. The 1960 election brought to office a president committed to a strong civil rights program—although it took his death to enact that program into law.

# MARTIN LUTHER KING, JR.

## (1929–1968)

David J. Garrow

Martin Luther King, Jr., preeminent leader of the black freedom movement of the 1950s and 1960s, repeatedly challenged America to live up to the egalitarian principles set forth in the three Reconstruction era amendments. "If we are wrong, the Constitution of the United States is wrong," King told his Alabama colleagues in an unpublished speech on December 5, 1955, the day that Montgomery's black citizens began a year-long campaign against discriminatory seating practices on city buses. Victory in that struggle catapulted King to national prominence as an exponent of nonviolent protest against racial oppression, and throughout the twelve remaining years of his life King pursued and expanded his challenge to injustice and exploitation internationally as well as domestically.

Pointing out in his 1964 book, *Why We Can't Wait,* that the United States was "a society where the supreme law of the land, the Constitution, is rendered inoperative in vast areas of the nation" because of explicit RACIAL DISCRIMINATION, King described the CIVIL RIGHTS struggle as a resumption "of that noble journey toward the goals reflected in the PREAMBLE to the Constitution, the Constitution itself, the BILL OF RIGHTS and the THIRTEENTH, FOURTEENTH, and FIFTEENTH AMENDMENTS." Protest campaigns in segregationist strongholds such as Birmingham and Selma, Alabama, stimulated national support for landmark legislative achievements such as the CIVIL RIGHTS ACT OF 1964 and the VOTING RIGHTS ACT of 1965, and produced an all-but-complete victory over de jure segregation by the middle of that decade.

Recognizing that other evils more subtle than segregation also tangibly afflicted the daily lives of millions of black people, King broadened his attack to include all forms of poverty and economic injustice, saying that the movement had to go beyond civil rights to human rights. That progression, coupled with King's outspoken condemnations of America's militaristic foreign policy, particularly its participation in the VIETNAM WAR, led King to advocate basic changes in American society reaching far beyond his previous attacks on racial discrimination.

Identified as a prominent advocate of CIVIL DISOBEDIENCE against immoral segregation statutes even before his influential 1963 "Letter from Birmingham Jail," King defended his position by reference to the long tradition of NATURAL RIGHTS thinking. In his early years of civil rights activism King said that peaceful, willing violation of such statutes forced courts to void unconstitutional provisions, but toward the end of his life King expanded his argument, contending that the weightier moral demands of social justice sometimes required that nondiscriminatory laws also be violated. If any laws blocked the oppressed from confronting the nation with moral issues of human rights and economic justice, then such laws rightfully could be breached. Although King until 1966 had believed that depicting the brutalities of racism best attracted national support for civil rights, in his final years King repeatedly suggested that protesters might have to coerce concessions from unwilling federal officials by obstructing the orderly functioning of society until the desired policy changes were made.

King's challenge to American racism helped to close the gap between constitutional principles and discriminatory practices; his broader struggle against other forms of human injustice left a legacy that will stimulate future generations for years to come.

Bibliography

GARROW, DAVID J.    1986    *Bearing the Cross: Martin Luther King, Jr., and the Southern Christian Leadership Conference, 1955–1968.*  New York: William Morrow.

KING, MARTIN LUTHER, JR.    1964    *Why We Can't Wait.*  New York: New American Library.

# CIVIL RIGHTS ACT OF 1964

78 Stat. 241

Theodore Eisenberg

The Civil Rights Act of 1964 signified many changes. For JOHN F. KEN-NEDY, prompted by southern resistance to DESEGREGATION orders and violent responses to peaceful CIVIL RIGHTS protests, proposing the measure symbolized an aggressive new attitude toward RACIAL DISCRIMINA-TION. For LYNDON JOHNSON, who supported the act after Kennedy's assassination, it marked a turn away from southern regionalism and toward national leadership on civil rights matters. For Congress, the act ended a century of nonexistent or ineffective civil rights laws and was the first civil rights measure with respect to which the Senate invoked CLOTURE. For blacks, the act was the first major legislative victory since Reconstruction and the most far-reaching civil rights measure in American history.

The act consists of eleven titles. Titles I and VIII reinforce voting rights provisions of the CIVIL RIGHTS ACTS OF 1957 and 1960 and limit the use of LITERACY TESTS to measure voter qualifications. (See also VOT-ING RIGHTS ACT OF 1970.) Titles III and IV, in provisions deleted from the bills that became the 1957 and 1960 acts, authorize court actions by the ATTORNEY GENERAL to challenge segregated public facilities and schools. Title V amends provisions governing the CIVIL RIGHTS COMMIS-SION. Title IX authorizes appeal from orders remanding to state courts civil rights cases that have been removed to federal court and authorizes the Attorney General to intervene in EQUAL PROTECTION cases. Title X establishes a Community Relations Service to assist communities in resolving discrimination disputes. Title XI deals with miscellaneous matters. The most important parts of the law are Title II, forbidding discrimination in PUBLIC ACCOMMODATIONS; Title VI, forbidding discrimination in federally assisted programs; and Title VII, forbidding EMPLOYMENT DIS-CRIMINATION. In 1972, Congress extended Title VII's coverage to most government employees. It does not cover religious institutions.

Congress shaped the 1964 act with a keen awareness of previously declared constitutional limitations on ANTIDISCRIMINATION LEGISLATION. Title II's ban on discrimination in public accommodations and Title

VII's ban on employment discrimination are limited to those entities whose operations affect INTERSTATE COMMERCE. By limiting these provisions to establishments and employers affecting commerce, Congress sought to avoid the CIVIL RIGHTS CASES' (1883) determination that Congress lacks power under the FOURTEENTH AMENDMENT to outlaw discrimination by private citizens, even in such a quasi-public area as that of public accommodations. Unlike its power to enforce the Fourteenth Amendment, Congress's COMMERCE CLAUSE power is not limited to STATE ACTION. In HEART OF ATLANTA MOTEL, INC. v. UNITED STATES (1964) and KATZENBACH v. McCLUNG (1964) the Court upheld Title II as a valid exercise of the commerce power and the power to regulate interstate travel. Under the Court's subsequent decision in JONES v. ALFRED H. MAYER CO. (1968), much of Title II and Title VII would be valid as congressional enforcement of the THIRTEENTH AMENDMENT. Title VI's ban on discrimination in federally assisted programs was tied to another constitutional provision, Congress's TAXING AND SPENDING POWER.

Judicial interpretation seems to have avoided another potential constitutional problem attending Title VII. Under a 1972 amendment to Title VII, employers must accommodate an employee's religious practices if the employer is able to do so without undue hardship. In *Trans World Airlines, Inc. v. Hardison* (1977), the Supreme Court held that the statute does not require an employer to bear more than a DE MINIMIS cost to accommodate an employee's religious preferences. If Title VII were interpreted to mandate substantial concessions to religiously based employee work preferences, it might raise serious problems under the FIRST AMENDMENT'S ESTABLISHMENT OF RELIGION clause.

With the 1964 act's constitutional vulnerability minimized shortly after enactment, the way was clear for its development. Title II, banning racial discrimination in public accommodations, was the act's symbolic heart, providing immediate and highly visible evidence that blacks, as equal citizens, were entitled to equal treatment in the public life of the community. But Title II generated little litigation, for compliance was swift throughout the South once the principle of equal access was established. Equalizing employment opportunity was a goal that would take longer to accomplish. Thus in operation, Title VII has dwarfed all other titles combined, frequently generating a huge backlog of cases in the agency charged with Title VII's administration, the Equal Employment Opportunity Commission (EEOC), and leading to thousands of judicial decisions.

The proof necessary to establish a Title VII violation repeatedly occupies the Supreme Court. Two leading cases, *McDonnell Douglas Corp. v. Green* (1973) and GRIGGS v. DUKE POWER CO. (1971), approve alternative methods of proof in Title VII cases. Under *McDonnell Douglas,* a plaintiff alleging discrimination by an employer must, after exhausting the necessary remedies with the EEOC or a state antidiscrimination agency, show that the plaintiff applied and was rejected for a job for which the plaintiff was qualified, and that the employer continued to try to fill the position. An employer must then justify its actions. Under *Griggs,* in an extension of Title VII not necessarily contemplated by the 1964 Congress, proof that an employment selection criterion has a disproportionate adverse impact on minorities requires the employer to show that the selection standard is required by business necessity. After *Griggs,* statistically based Title VII cases, and threats to bring such cases, became a widespread method for pressuring employers to hire more minority and female workers. Few employers are both able to prove the business necessity of employment tests or other hiring criteria and willing to incur the expense of doing so.

The 1964 act, particularly Title VII, is not without its ironies. First, opponents of the act amended it to include sex discrimination in the hope that such an amendment would weaken the bill's chances for passage. But the bill passed with the additional ban that revolutionized at least the formal status of female workers. And in the case of sex discrimination, Title VII reaches beyond traditional refusals to hire or obvious pay disparities. When the Court held in *General Electric Co. v. Gilbert* (1976) that excluding pregnancy from a health plan does not constitute discrimination on the basis of sex, Congress amended Title VII to overturn the result. *Los Angeles Department of Water and Power v. Manhart* (1978) marks some sort of outer limit on Title VII's protection of female workers. The Court held Title VII to proscribe a requirement that females, who live longer than males and therefore can expect to receive greater total retirement benefits from a pension plan, contribute more to a pension than males contribute. In the case of sex, religion, or national origin discrimination, Title VII provides a defense if these factors constitute a bona fide occupational qualification, a defense sometimes difficult to separate from that of business necessity. The Supreme Court found in *Dothard v. Rawlinson* (1977) that a bona fide occupational qualification justifies requiring male prison guards for at least some classes of male prisoners.

Second, although the BURGER COURT generally has been viewed as conservative in the field of civil rights, Title VII owes much of its practical importance to Chief Justice WARREN E. BURGER's opinion for the Court in *Griggs v. Duke Power Co. Griggs* removed the requirement that discriminatory intent be an element of Title VII cases. This holding, in addition to its significance for Title VII, has been incorporated in other areas, including discrimination in housing under the CIVIL RIGHTS ACT OF 1968. *New York City Transit Authority v. Beazer* (1979), in which the Court refused to invalidate an employment selection standard (exclusion of drug users) with disparate impact on minorities, may signify some retrenchment from the full force of the *Griggs* principle. And in *International Brotherhood of Teamsters v. United States* (1977), the Court refused to extend *Griggs* to invalidate seniority systems that predate Title VII. But the Court never has directly questioned *Griggs*. In UNITED STEELWORKERS OF AMERICA v. WEBER (1979), the Burger Court concluded that Title VII permitted at least some private AFFIRMATIVE ACTION employment programs.

Although Title VII deservedly receives most of the attention paid to the 1964 act, Title VI is also an important antidiscrimination law. In REGENTS OF THE UNIVERSITY OF CALIFORNIA V. BAKKE (1978) it provided the setting for the Court's first important pronouncement on affirmative action programs. Many subsequent antidiscrimination laws, such as Title IX of the EDUCATION AMENDMENT OF 1972, the AGE DISCRIMINATION ACT OF 1975, and the REHABILITATION ACT of 1973 are modeled after Title VI. Title VI is the principal antidiscrimination measure for programs receiving federal funds that are not affected by other antidiscrimination measures. In the case of public institutions, however, there is much overlap between Title VI's prohibitions and those contained in the Fourteenth Amendment. The Supreme Court has been ambiguous in describing the relationship between the two. In *Bakke,* a majority of Justices suggested that Title VI and the Constitution are coterminous, but it did not purport to overturn the Court's earlier holding in LAU v. NICHOLS (1974), widely read as extending Title VI to cases of discrimination not banned by the Constitution.

The contributions of the 1964 act to racial equality defy precise measurement, but surely they have been weighty. Beyond the tangible changes the act brought to the public life of southern communities and to the entire American workplace lie enormous changes in attitudes and everyday personal relations. Those who believe that "you can't legislate morality" would do well to ponder the lessons of the Civil Rights Act of 1964.

Bibliography

DORSEN, NORMAN; BENDER, PAUL; NEUBORNE, BURT; and LAW, SYLVIA 1979 *Emerson, Haber and Dorsen's Political and Civil Rights in the United States,* 4th ed. Vol. II:581–608, 902–1062, 1172–1220. Boston: Little, Brown.

LARSON, ARTHUR and LARSON, LEX K. 1981 *Employment Discrimination.* New York: Matthew Bender.

SCHLEI, BARBARA L. and GROSSMAN, PAUL 1976 *Employment Discrimination Law.* Washington, D.C.: Bureau of National Affairs.

SULLIVAN, CHARLES A.; ZIMMER, MICHAEL J.; and RICHARDS, RICHARD F. 1980 *Federal Statutory Law of Employment Discrimination.* Indianapolis: Bobbs-Merrill.

# EMPLOYMENT DISCRIMINATION

Reginald Alleyne

Employment discrimination on grounds of race, sex, nationality, or religion may be challenged under two acts of Congress. One of the statutes, now codified as Title 42 of the United States Code, Section 1981, is a survivor of the CIVIL RIGHTS ACT OF 1866, enacted for the protection of former slaves. As originally enacted, the statute was not seen as an employment discrimination statute. It conferred upon blacks the right to make and enforce contracts, to sue and to enjoy on a par with whites the protection of laws. The act was passed pursuant to Congress's authority under Section 2 of the THIRTEENTH AMENDMENT, and Congress proposed the FOURTEENTH AMENDMENT in order to assure the act's validity. After the Reconstruction era, however, it and other Reconstruction-era civil rights legislation fell into disuse until the 1960s. Not until *Johnson v. Railway Express Agency, Inc.* (1975) did the United States Supreme Court confirm the application of Section 1981 to RACIAL DISCRIMINATION in private-sector employment. This statute's use in employment discrimination cases has become secondary to reliance on Title VII of the CIVIL RIGHTS ACT OF 1964, which was enacted by Congress as part of a comprehensive statute prohibiting discrimination on grounds of race, sex, religion, or national origin in employment, PUBLIC ACCOMMODATIONS, and federally funded programs.

Enactment of the 1964 Act followed a long period of civil rights DEMONSTRATIONS against the kinds of discrimination the act prohibited. For twenty years preceding the enactment of Title VII, more than 200 fair employment practice bills had been proposed in the Congress, but none had passed. Allegations of a Title VII violation often are accompanied by additional allegations of a Section 1981 violation.

Another survivor of Reconstruction-era legislation now codified as 42 United States Code 1985(c), was originally designed to protect blacks from Ku Klux Klan violence. The Supreme Court, in *Great American Federal Savings and Loan Association v. Novotny* (1979), rejected the view that Section 1985(c) provides an independent remedy for the adjudication of rights protected by Title VII.

The constitutionality of Title VII of the 1964 act was never seriously questioned. The power of Congress to enact Title VII, either under

239

the COMMERCE CLAUSE or to enforce the FOURTEENTH AMENDMENT, seems to have been assumed. In 1972 Congress extended the coverage of Title VII to include employment discrimination by state and local governments. Subsequently, it was argued that back-pay awards and attorneys' fees levied by a federal court against a state under the amended Title VII violated the jurisdictional limitations of the ELEVENTH AMENDMENT. However, in FITZPATRICK v. BITZER (1976) the Supreme Court rejected that argument, holding that the 1972 amendment was a valid exercise of Congress's enforcement power under Section 5 of the FOURTEENTH AMENDMENT.

Bibliography

COMMENT 1980 Developments in the Law—Section 1981. *Harvard Civil Rights–Civil Liberties Law Review* 15:29–277.

DEAN, JOHN P. 1978 Title VII and Public Employers: Did Congress Exceed Its Powers? *Columbia Law Review* 78:372–408.

HILL, HERBERT 1977 The Equal Employment Opportunity Acts of 1964 and 1972: A Critical Analysis of the Legislative History and Administration of the Law. *Industrial Relations Law Journal* 2:1–96.

# PUBLIC ACCOMMODATIONS

Kenneth L. Karst

The refusal of hotels, restaurants, theaters, and other public accommodations to serve blacks was not exclusively a southern phenomenon. In the South, however, the practice was an essential part of a system of racial dominance and dependency, long after the THIRTEENTH AMENDMENT abolished slavery and the FOURTEENTH AMENDMENT recognized the CITIZENSHIP of the freed slaves. Aware of the role played by this form of RACIAL DISCRIMINATION in the system of white supremacy, Congress adopted the CIVIL RIGHTS ACT OF 1875, the last major CIVIL RIGHTS act of the Reconstruction era. The law prohibited public accommodations, including railroads along with the types already mentioned, from denying access to any person on account of race. The Supreme Court held this law unconstitutional, saying that when Congress enforced the Fourteenth Amendment it had no power to reach private action. (See CIVIL RIGHTS CASES, 1883; STATE ACTION.)

Later came the Jim Crow laws—state laws requiring racial SEGREGATION in all manner of public places, including public accommodations. This practice received the Court's blessing in PLESSY V. FERGUSON (1896), a case involving the segregation of seating in railroad cars. (See SEPARATE BUT EQUAL DOCTRINE.) By the end of the nineteenth century, the denial of access for blacks to public accommodations in the South was firmly rooted in both law and custom.

Soon after the Supreme Court decided BROWN V. BOARD OF EDUCATION (1954), the modern civil rights movement turned to the problem of access to public accommodations. The reason for direct action such as freedom rides and SIT-INS was not that seats in the front of the bus arrive at a destination before back seats do, or that black college students yearn to perch on lunch counter stools. Public accommodations became a target for civil rights demonstrators for exactly the same reason that they had been made the vehicles for racial discrimination in the first place: segregation and the refusal of service to blacks were powerful symbols of racial inferiority, highly visible denials of the entitlement of blacks to be treated as persons and citizens. Employment discrimination and housing discrimination might touch material interests of great importance, but no interest is more important than self-respect. The primary target of the civil rights movement was the stigma of caste.

Within a few years after the *Brown* decision, the Supreme Court had held unconstitutional nearly the whole range of Jim Crow laws. Racial segregation practiced by state institutions, or commanded or authorized by state laws, failed the test of the Fourteenth Amendment even before Congress reentered the public accommodations field. In most of the states of the North and West, civil rights laws commanded equal access not only to public accommodations—such laws merely reinforced the common law duties of innkeepers and common carriers—but also to other businesses. In the South, however, private discrimination continued in most hotels, restaurants, and barber shops. The Supreme Court was repeatedly invited to decide whether the Fourteenth Amendment established a right of access to such places, free of racial bias, but the Court repeatedly declined the invitation. (See BELL V. MARYLAND, 1964.)

As part of the CIVIL RIGHTS ACT OF 1964, Congress adopted a comprehensive public accommodations law, forbidding discrimination in the same types of places that had been covered by the 1875 act. (Railroads were forbidden to discriminate by modern interpretations of the INTERSTATE COMMERCE ACT of 1887.) Before the year was out, the Supreme Court had upheld the public accommodations portion of the 1964 act, on the basis of the power of Congress to regulate interstate commerce. (See HEART OF ATLANTA MOTEL V. UNITED STATES, 1964.)

The 1964 act is limited in its coverage, reaching an establishment only if it "affects commerce" or if its discrimination is "supported by STATE ACTION." The act exempts both private clubs and small rooming houses lived in by their proprietors. Now that the Supreme Court has interpreted the CIVIL RIGHTS ACT OF 1866 as a broad guarantee against private racial discrimination in the sale of property and other contracting, and validated the law as a congressional enforcement of the Thirteenth Amendment, at least some of the limitations of the 1964 act have been made irrelevant. For example, a barber shop is covered by the 1964 act if it is located in a covered hotel, but not if it is independent. Under recent interpretations of the 1866 act, any barber shop would violate the law by refusing service on the basis of the customer's race. (See JONES V. ALFRED H. MAYER CO., 1968; RUNYON V. McCRARY, 1976.)

The substantive core of the Fourteenth Amendment is a principle of equal citizenship. (See EQUAL PROTECTION OF THE LAWS.) Even in the absence of civil rights legislation, that principle demands that the organized community treat each of us, irrespective of race, as a respected, participating member. Racially based denial of access or segregation in places of public accommodations—even those privately owned—is a deliberate denial of the status of equal citizenship, as the sit-in demonstrators knew and helped the rest of us to understand.

Bibliography

LEWIS, THOMAS P.   1963   The Sit-in Cases: Great Expectations. *Supreme Court Review* 1963:101–151.

POLLITT, DANIEL H.   1960   Dime Store Demonstrations: Events and Legal Problems of the First Sixty Days. *Duke Law Journal* 1960:315–365.

WOODWARD, C. VANN   1966   *The Strange Career of Jim Crow,* 2d (rev.) ed. New York: Oxford University Press.

# OPEN HOUSING LAWS

Theodore Eisenberg

Many believe housing, the last major area covered by Congress's 1960s CIVIL RIGHTS program, to be the key to at least short-term progress in INTEGRATION. Despite numerous ANTIDISCRIMINATION LAWS, segregated housing patterns threaten much of the civil rights agenda, including integrated public education. Yet until the 1960s the federal government promoted segregated housing. Federal housing agencies, such as the Federal Housing Administration, required racially RESTRICTIVE COVENANTS in federally assisted projects. In Executive Order 11063 (1962), President JOHN F. KENNEDY prohibited housing discrimination in federal public housing and in housing covered by mortgages directly guaranteed by the federal government. Title VI of the CIVIL RIGHTS ACT OF 1964, which outlawed discrimination in programs receiving federal financial assistance, extended the ban to nearly all federally assisted housing.

Title VIII of the CIVIL RIGHTS ACT OF 1968 was the first comprehensive federal open housing law. Title VIII bans discrimination on the basis of race, color, religion, or national origin in the sale, lease, and financing of housing, and in the furnishing of real estate brokerage services. A 1974 amendment extends the ban to discrimination on the basis of sex. Title VIII exempts single-family houses sold or rented by owners and small, owner-occupied boarding houses. Congress's consideration of Title VIII was affected by the assassination of Martin Luther King, Jr. House opponents of the measure had tried to delay its consideration in the hope that intervening national events would sway Congress against it. But during the delay, Dr. King was assassinated and passage of the act followed swiftly.

Courts have construed Title VIII to cover activities other than the direct purchase, sale, or lease of a dwelling. For example, Title VIII prohibits discriminatory refusals to rezone for low-income housing. Most courts find that practices with greater adverse impact on minorities, even if undertaken without discriminatory purposes, impose some burden of justification. This view links Title VIII litigation to a similar line of EMPLOYMENT DISCRIMINATION cases decided under Title VII of the Civil Rights Act of 1964.

To enforce its provisions, Title VIII authorizes the secretary of housing and urban development to seek to conciliate disputes, but the Department of Housing and Urban Development (HUD) initially must defer to state or local housing agencies where state law provides relief substantially equivalent to Title VIII. In *Gladstone, Realtors v. Village of Bellwood* (1979) the Supreme Court held that Title VIII also authorized direct civil actions in federal court without prior resort to HUD or to state authorities. An ATTORNEY GENERAL finding a pattern or practice of housing discrimination is authorized to seek relief in federal court.

Two months after Title VIII's enactment the Supreme Court found Section 1982, Title 42, United States Code, a remnant of section 1 of the CIVIL RIGHTS ACT OF 1866, to be another federal open housing law. Section 1982 grants all citizens the same right "as is enjoyed by white citizens" to purchase and lease real property. In JONES V. ALFRED H. MAYER CO. (1968) the Court construed section 1982 to prohibit a racially motivated refusal to sell a home to a prospective black purchaser. In *Sullivan v. Little Hunting Park, Inc.* (1969) the Court found that violations of section 1982 may be remedied by damages awards or by injunctive relief. There are, therefore, two federal open housing laws, which, in the area of RACIAL DISCRIMINATION, overlap. But section 1982 contains none of Title VIII's exemptions, provides for none of its administrative machinery, and contains no express list of remedies.

Bibliography

BELL, DERRICK A., JR.   1980   *Race, Racism and American Law,* 2nd ed. Boston: Little, Brown.

DORSEN, NORMAN; BENDER, PAUL; NEUBORNE, BURT; and LAW, SYLVIA   Emerson, Haber and Dorsen's *Political and Civil Rights in the United States,* 4th ed. II:1063–1149. Boston: Little, Brown.

# SCHOOL BUSING

Kenneth L. Karst

Before BROWN v. BOARD OF EDUCATION (1954–1955) was decided, many a southern child rode the bus to school, passing on the way a bus headed in the other direction, loaded with children of another race. The busing of children was "one tool" used to maintain a system of school SEGREGATION. As late as 1970, before the Supreme Court had approved a single busing order, about forty percent of the nation's children rode buses to school. The school bus had permitted the replacement of rural one-room schoolhouses with consolidated schools; in the city, riding the bus had been thought safer than walking. School busing did not become the object of majoritarian anger until the 1970s, when the Supreme Court described it as "one tool" for dismantling a segregated system and affirmed its use not only in the South but also in the cities of the North and West.

In a rural southern county, the simplest form of DESEGREGATION might drastically reduce school busing; racial living patterns would permit integration of the schools through the discontinuation of racial assignments and assignment of children to the schools nearest their homes. In the cities, however, residential segregation had been so thorough that the abandonment of racial assignments and the substitution of a neighborhood school policy would not end the separation of school children by race. The question was asked: Would the Supreme Court insist on more than the end of racial assignments—on the actual mixing of black and white children in the schools—by way of dismantling segregation produced by deliberate official policy? In SWANN v. CHARLOTTE-MECKLENBURG BOARD OF EDUCATION (1971), the Court answered that question affirmatively. Then, in KEYES v. SCHOOL DISTRICT NO. 1 (1973) and COLUMBUS BOARD OF EDUCATION v. PENICK (1979), the Court extended *Swann*'s commands to the North and West, in ways that blurred the DE FACTO/DE JURE distinction. Once a constitutional violation is found, even in remote acts of deliberate segregation by a school board, then as a practical matter the district court's remedial goal becomes "the greatest possible degree of actual desegregation"—and that, in a large city, means the busing of massive numbers of children for the purpose of achieving the maximum practicable RACIAL BALANCE.

Apart from the busing ordered by courts, some busing for integration purposes has resulted from voluntary programs, mostly involving the

246

busing of minority children to schools formerly populated by non-Hispanic whites. Political resistance has been directed not to those programs but to busing ordered by a court over the opposition of the school board and of large numbers of parents and children. The most outspoken protest has come from white parents. The responses of school board majorities have varied, from political warfare in Boston and Los Angeles to the "let's-make-it-work" attitude in Columbus.

President RICHARD M. NIXON, whose first electoral campaign adopted a "Southern strategy" and whose campaign for reelection included an attack on school busing, proposed congressional legislation to restrict busing. In 1974 Congress purported to forbid a federal court to order a student's transportation to a school "other than the school closest or next closest to his place of residence." This statute's constitutionality would have been dubious but for a proviso that canceled its effect: the law was not to diminish the authority of federal courts to enforce the Constitution.

The school busing issue has forced a reevaluation of the goals of desegregation. In *Brown* the chief harm of school segregation imposed by law was said to be the stigma of inferiority, which impaired black children's motivation to learn. The fact of separation of the races in urban schools may or may not have the same stigmatic effect—even though deliberately segregative governmental actions have contributed to residential segregation in cities throughout the nation. Stigma aside, it is far from clear that racial isolation alone impairs minority children's learning. In communities with substantial Hispanic or Asian-American populations, concerns about the maintenance of cultural identity are apt to be expressed in opposition to taking children out of neighborhood schools and away from bilingual education programs. The call for "community control" of schools is heard less frequently in black communities today than it was around 1970, but some prominent black CIVIL RIGHTS leaders have placed increasing emphasis on improvement of the schools and decreasing emphasis on the busing of children.

Part of the reason for this shift in emphasis surely is a sense of despair over the prospects of busing as an effective means of achieving integration. Social scientists disagree on the amount of "white flight" that has resulted from court-ordered busing. Some demographic changes are merely extensions of a long-established pattern of middle-class migration to the suburbs. The Supreme Court in MILLIKEN v. BRADLEY (1974) made clear that metropolitan relief, combining city and suburban districts for purposes of school integration, was allowable only in rare circumstances. "White flight" can also take the form of withdrawal of children from public schools; recent estimates suggest that about one-fifth of the students in the nation's private schools have fled from desegregation orders. In this perspective, the neighborhood school is seen not only as a focus for community but also, less appetizingly, as a means for controlling children's associations and passing social advantage from one generation to the next. Either strategy of "white flight" costs money. It is no accident that the hottest opposition to court-ordered school busing has come from working-class neighborhoods, where people feel that they have been singled out to bear a burden in order to validate an ideal they have come to doubt.

School busing for integration purposes has come under strong political attack. Neither Congress nor a state can constitutionally prohibit busing designed to remedy *de jure* segregation. However, state measures limiting busing designed to remedy *de facto* segregation may or may not be upheld, depending on the legislation's purposes and effects. (See WASHINGTON V. SEATTLE SCHOOL DISTRICT NO. 1, 1982; CRAWFORD V. LOS ANGELES BOARD OF EDUCATION, 1982.)

Sadly, it is realistic to assume the continuation of urban residential segregation, which has diminished only slightly since 1940, despite nearly half a century of civil rights litigation and legislation. (Even the migration of increasing numbers of middle-class black families to the suburbs has not significantly diminished residential segregation.) Given that assumption, the nation must choose between accepting racially separate schools and using school busing to achieve integration. The first choice will seem to many citizens a betrayal of the promise of *Brown*. The second choice faces opposition strong enough to threaten not only the nation's historic commitment to public education but also its commitment to obedience to law. The resolution of this dilemma is a challenge not only to courts but also to school board members and citizens, demanding imagination, patience, and good will in quantities far beyond their recent supply.

Bibliography

BELL, DERRICK A., JR.   1976   Serving Two Masters: Integration Ideals and Client Interests in School Desegregation Litigation. *Yale Law Journal* 85:470–516.

DIMOND, PAUL R.   1985   *Beyond Busing: Inside the Challenge to Urban Segregation*. Ann Arbor: University of Michigan Press.

FISS, OWEN M.   1975   The Jurisprudence of Busing. *Law and Contemporary Problems* 39:194–216.

WILKINSON, J. HARVIE, III   1979   *From Brown to Bakke*. New York: Oxford University Press.

# VOTING RIGHTS ACT OF 1965 AND ITS AMENDMENTS

### 79 Stat. 437 (1965)

Theodore Eisenberg

Despite Congress's efforts in the CIVIL RIGHTS ACTS of 1957, 1960, and 1964 to protect the right to vote, the case-by-case approach of these laws proved ineffective in dealing with denials of VOTING RIGHTS to millions of blacks. By 1965, only seventy-one voting rights cases had been filed by the Department of Justice. And in 1964 only 19.4, 6.4, and 31.8 percent of eligible blacks were registered to vote in Alabama, Mississippi, and Louisiana, respectively. In Louisiana, comparable white registration stood at 80.2 percent.

The Voting Rights Act of 1965, amended in 1970, 1975, and 1982, provided additional protection of the right to vote. The 1965 act's most extraordinary features, its preclearance requirements, applied only to states or political subdivisions with low voter registration or participation. In such jurisdictions, most of which were in the South, the act suspended literacy, educational, and character tests of voter qualifications used to deny the right to vote in any elections. In addition, with a view to New York's Puerto Rican population, the act prohibited conditioning the right to vote on any English comprehension requirement for anyone who had completed sixth grade in a school in which the predominant classroom language was other than English. States and political subdivisions subject to the suspension of voting tests were barred from implementing other voting practices that had the effect of denying or abridging the right to vote without obtaining preclearance from a federal court or the ATTORNEY GENERAL.

The Voting Rights Act Amendments of 1970 and 1975 enhanced the preclearance provisions. The 1965 act's coverage had been triggered by low electoral participation in the 1964 election. The 1970 amendments extended the preclearance requirement through 1975 and suspended voting qualification tests or devices until 1975 in all jurisdictions, not just in jurisdictions covered by other provisions of the original 1965 act. The 1975 amendments extended the preclearance requirement through 1982 and suspended tests or devices indefinitely. The 1970 and 1975 amendments also added 1968 and 1972 to 1964 as years in which low electoral participation would trigger the act's coverage. The 1982 amendments imposed new preclearance standards to be effective until 2007.

The Supreme Court has taken an expansive view of the procedures covered by the act's preclearance requirement. In *Allen v. State Board of Elections* (1969), *Dougherty County Board of Education v. White* (1978), and other cases, the Court applied the act to voting practices that might affect minority voter effectiveness, as well as to practices directly limiting voter registration. Under these rulings, the act's preclearance requirements would govern changes in voting districts, or a county board of education's requirement that employees seeking elective office take an unpaid leave of absence.

A change in voting procedure raises the question whether the change triggers the act's preclearance requirement by having the effect of denying or abridging the right to vote. In deciding whether the requisite effect exists, the Supreme Court has held that the act covers effects even if they are not discriminatorily motivated. This standard, which is more stringent than the purposeful discrimination requirement the Court applies under the FOURTEENTH AMENDMENT and FIFTEENTH AMENDMENT, was upheld against constitutional attack in *Rome v. United States* (1980).

In addition to the preclearance requirements, the 1965 act included a nationwide prohibition upon voting qualifications or standards that deny or abridge voting rights on account of race. This prohibition applies whether the governmental unit is subject to the act's preclearance requirements or not. And, unlike the preclearance requirements, which apply only to changes in voting procedures, it applies to procedures that have long been in effect. A plurality opinion in MOBILE v. BOLDEN (1980) suggested that this provision only proscribed purposeful discrimination prohibited by the Constitution. In the 1982 amendments, however, Congress rejected a purposeful discrimination requirement and set forth standards governing findings of discriminatory effect.

In one of its remedies, the 1965 act continued and expanded a method of guaranteeing voting rights initiated in the FORCE ACT OF 1871. On a showing of widespread denials of voting rights, the act authorized a federal court to appoint federal voting examiners who themselves would examine and register voters for all elections, thereby superseding state election officials.

Addressing problems not covered by the 1965 act, the 1970 amendments lowered from twenty-one to eighteen the minimum voting age for all elections, prohibited states from imposing RESIDENCY REQUIREMENTS in presidential elections, and provided for uniform national rules for absentee voting in presidential elections. The 1975 amendments also sought to overcome linguistic barriers to political participation by requiring bilingual elections in certain political subdivisions. These language provisions brought Texas and Florida under the act's coverage. The 1982 amendments changed the expiration date of these provisions from 1985 to 1992, and added voter assistance provisions for the handicapped.

In general, the 1965 act and amendments have fared well in the Supreme Court. In SOUTH CAROLINA V. KATZENBACH (1966) and KATZEN-BACH V. MORGAN (1966) the Court upheld the constitutionality of the act. Following the Court's decision in NATIONAL LEAGUE OF CITIES V. USERY (1976) that certain integral state operations are beyond Congress's power to regulate under the COMMERCE CLAUSE, the constitutional attack was renewed. In *Rome v. United States* (1980) the Court held this argument inapplicable to cases involving Congress's power to enforce the Civil War amendments. In UNITED JEWISH ORGANIZATIONS OF WILLIAMSBURGH, INC. V. CAREY (1977) the Court held that use of racial criteria to favor minority voters in an effort to comply with the Voting Rights Act did not violate the Fourteenth or Fifteenth Amendments. In OREGON V. MITCHELL (1970) the Supreme Court sustained most of the 1970 amendments but invalidated lowering the voting age in state and local elections. The latter ruling in *Mitchell,* however, soon was overturned by the TWENTY-SIXTH AMENDMENT.

The Voting Rights Act has been the most measurably successful CIVIL RIGHTS statute. In most southern states the gap between black and white voter registration shrank dramatically, and the number of elected black officials tripled between 1970 and 1975. Overt racial appeals no longer are a routinely successful part of southern political campaigns. The 1975 amendments confirmed a shift in attitude on civil rights matters. For the first time in the twentieth century, a majority of southern congressmen voted in favor of a federal civil rights statute.

Bibliography

BELL, DERRICK A., JR.   1980   *Race, Racism and American Law,* 2nd ed. Boston: Little, Brown.

DORSEN, NORMAN; BENDER, PAUL; NEUBORNE, BURT; and LAW, SYLVIA 1979   Emerson, Haber, and Dorsen's *Political and Civil Rights in the United States,* 4th ed. Vol. 2:609–685. Boston: Little, Brown.

UNITED STATES SENATE, COMMITTEE ON THE JUDICIARY   1982   Senate Report No. 97–417, 97th Congress, 2d Session.

# ANTIDISCRIMINATION LEGISLATION

Theodore Eisenberg

From its inception, antidiscrimination legislation has shaped and been shaped by the Constitution. Antidiscrimination legislation's very existence is attributable to developments in constitutional law. Enactment of such legislation usually reflects a relatively favorable atmosphere for the promise of equality embodied in the THIRTEENTH, FOURTEENTH, and FIFTEENTH AMENDMENTS. When the values underlying these amendments are in decline, antidiscrimination legislation is not enacted, and often is not enforced.

Federal antidiscrimination laws have been enacted during two time periods. During the first period, which commenced near the end of the Civil War, Congress enacted the CIVIL RIGHTS ACT OF 1866, the Civil Rights Act of 1870, the FORCE ACT OF 1871, the Civil Rights Act of 1871, and the CIVIL RIGHTS ACT OF 1875. These early provisions, portions of which survive, exemplify two basic forms of antidiscrimination legislation. Some provisions, such as section 1 of the 1871 act (now section 1983) and section 3 of the 1866 act were purely remedial. They provided remedies for violations of federal rights but created no new substantive rights. Other provisions, such as section 1 of the 1866 act and section 16 of the 1870 act (now sections 1981 and 1982), were express efforts to change substantive law by fostering greater equality between black and white Americans.

The COMPROMISE OF 1877 marks the end of the first era during which antidiscrimination legislation flourished. Afterward, congressional and judicial developments favored neither enactment nor enforcement of antidiscrimination legislation. In the CIVIL RIGHTS REPEAL ACT of 1894 the first Democratic Congress since the Civil War repealed the few effective remnants of post-Civil War antidiscrimination legislation. A favorable climate for legislative implementation of the post-Civil War constitutional amendments did not reemerge until the late 1950s and early 1960s. There were no significant antidiscrimination statutes in the intervening years.

As the constitutional amendments were given new vigor by the WARREN COURT, however, antidiscrimination legislation experienced a renaissance. Modern statutes, including the CIVIL RIGHTS ACTS OF 1957,

1960, 1964, and 1968, protect against discrimination in voting, employ-ment, education, and housing. They represent a second era of federal antidiscrimination legislation, sometimes called part of the second recon-struction.

As in the case of earlier antidiscrimination statutes, the primary reason for enactment was to protect blacks from RACIAL DISCRIMINATION. Again, two kinds of provisions were enacted. Some provisions, such as the 1957 and 1960 Acts and Title VI of the 1964 act, are remedial in tone (though not always so interpreted) and do not purport to create new substantive rights. Others, such as Title VII of the 1964 act, which prohibits private discrimination in employment, confer new substantive rights.

Modern antidiscrimination legislation contains a recognizable sub-category that has been the fastest growing area of antidiscrimination law. Until about 1960 or 1970, antidiscrimination legislation could be equated with laws prohibiting one or more forms of racial discrimination. Subsequently, however, legislation prohibiting discrimination surfaced in many areas. For example, the AGE DISCRIMINATION ACT OF 1975, the Age Discrimination in Employment Act, the REHABILITATION ACT OF 1973, the DEVELOPMENTALLY DISABLED AND BILL OF RIGHTS ACT, the Education of Handicapped Children Acts, the Equal Pay Act, and the EDUCATION AMENDMENTS OF 1972 provide substantial protection to the aged, to the handicapped, and to women. Building on a technique first employed in Title VI of the 1964 act, most of these provisions apply only to programs or entities receiving federal financial assistance.

Although constitutional values can be viewed as the raison d'être of antidiscrimination legislation, the relationship between the Constitu-tion and antidiscrimination laws runs much deeper. Their more complex relationship may be divided into two parts. First, antidiscrimination legis-lation has been the setting for judicial and congressional decisions con-cerning the scope of congressional power. One of the few universally agreed upon facts about the history of the Fourteenth Amendment is that it was meant to place the first major antidiscrimination statute, the Civil Rights Act of 1866, on firm constitutional footing. Before ratifi-cation of the Fourteenth Amendment, doubts were expressed about Congress's power under the Thirteenth Amendment to ban racially dis-criminatory state laws. Many believe that the Fourteenth Amendment was meant primarily to constitutionalize the 1866 Act's prohibitions. With the Fourteenth Amendment in place by 1868, Congress reaffirmed the 1866 Act's bans by reenacting them as part of the Civil Rights Act of 1870. Some claim that the 1866 Act is so akin to a constitutional provision that its surviving remnants should be interpreted more like constitutional provisions than statutory ones.

Soon after this initial interplay between the Constitution and antidiscrimination laws, a foundation of constitutional interpretation grew out of litigation under antidiscrimination statutes. In a line of cases commencing with UNITED STATES V. CRUIKSHANK (1876) and culminating in UNITED STATES V. HARRIS (1883) and the CIVIL RIGHTS CASES (1883), the Court relied on what has come to be known as the STATE ACTION doctrine to invalidate antidiscrimination measures. The *Civil Rights Cases* invalidated the last piece of nineteenth-century civil rights legislation, the Civil Rights Act of 1875. In so doing the Court not only limited the Fourteenth Amendment to prohibiting state action but also rendered a narrow interpretation of the Thirteenth Amendment as a possible source of congressional power to enact antidiscrimination statutes.

The state action doctrine was not the only early limit on antidiscrimination legislation. In UNITED STATES V. REESE (1876) the Court found sections 3 and 4 of the Civil Rights Act of 1870, which prohibited certain interferences with voting, to be beyond Congress's power to enforce the Fifteenth Amendment because the sections were not limited to prohibiting racial discrimination. These limitations on antidiscrimination legislation carried over into the early twentieth century.

But some early antidiscrimination legislation survived constitutional attack and shifting political stances in Congress. For example, in Ex PARTE YARBROUGH (1884) the Court sustained use of section 6 of the 1870 act (now section 241) to impose criminal sanctions against private individuals who used force to prevent blacks from voting in federal elections. And in *Ex parte Virginia* (1880), the Court sustained the federal prosecution of a state judge for excluding blacks from juries in violation of section 4 of the 1875 act. (See STRAUDER V. WEST VIRGINIA, 1880.)

The two lines of early constitutional interpretation of antidiscrimination laws have never been fully reconciled. As a result of the early limits on congressional power to enact antidiscrimination legislation, modern civil rights statutes have been drafted to reduce potential constitutional attacks. Thus, much of the Civil Rights Act of 1964 operates only on individuals and entities engaged in some form of INTERSTATE COMMERCE. Other portions of the 1964 act, and many other modern antidiscrimination laws, are based on Congress's TAXING AND SPENDING POWERS. By tying antidiscrimination legislation to the COMMERCE CLAUSE or the spending power, Congress hoped to avoid some of the constitutional problems that plagued early legislation enacted under the Thirteenth, Fourteenth, and Fifteenth Amendments.

A potential clash between the Court and Congress over the constitutionality of modern antidiscrimination legislation has not surfaced. The modern Court sustains antidiscrimination legislation even in the face of troublesome nineteenth-century precedents. In a landmark holding barely reconcilable with portions of the *Civil Rights Cases,* the Court in

JONES V. ALFRED H. MAYER COMPANY (1968) found that Congress has power under the Thirteenth Amendment to ban private racial discrimination in housing. Later, in RUNYON V. McCRARY (1976), the Court acknowledged Congress's power to outlaw racial discrimination in private contractual relations, including those relations involved in a child's attendance at a private segregated school. In GRIFFIN V. BRECKENRIDGE (1971) the Court relied on the Thirteenth Amendment to sustain a remnant of the 1871 act allowing for causes of action against private conspiracies to violate federal rights. The case undermined *United States v. Harris* and overruled an earlier contrary decision, *Collins v. Hardyman* (1948). Another antidiscrimination statute, the VOTING RIGHTS ACT OF 1965, provided the setting for important decisions in KATZENBACH V. MORGAN (1966) and SOUTH CAROLINA V. KATZENBACH (1966), which found Congress to have broad discretion to interpret and extend Fourteenth Amendment protection to situations which the judiciary had not found violative of the Fourteenth Amendment.

There is a second respect in which constitutional provisions and antidiscrimination legislation influence each other. From the beginning, their relationship has gone beyond one of merely testing the constitutionality of a particular antidiscrimination statute. Interpretation of one set of provisions has shaped the other. This interplay began with the Civil Rights Act of 1866. Soon after ratification of the Fourteenth Amendment, the question arose as to what constituted "the PRIVILEGES AND IMMUNITIES of citizens of the United States" referred to in the Fourteenth Amendment. In the SLAUGHTERHOUSE CASES (1873) the Court's first decision construing the Fourteenth Amendment, Justice STEPHEN J. FIELD argued in dissent that section 1 of the 1866 act provided Congress's interpretation of at least some of the privileges or immunities of United States citizens. Although Field's view did not prevail—the Court limited the privileges or immunities clause to a narrow class of rights—even the majority view of the privileges or immunities clause may have had a profound effect on subsequent development of antidiscrimination legislation.

This effect stems from the strong linguistic parallel between the Fourteenth Amendment's privileges or immunities clause and the rights listed as protected by many antidiscrimination laws. Sections 1983 and 242 protect persons against deprivations of their federal "rights, privileges or immunities." Section 1985(3) refers in part to "equal privileges and immunities." Section 241 refers to any federal "right or privilege." In subsequent cases brought under antidiscrimination statutes, federal courts, relying on the *Slaughterhouse Cases'* narrow interpretation of the Fourteenth Amendment's privileges or immunities clause, plausibly could render a similar narrow interpretation of the antidiscrimination statute. Not until MONROE V. PAPE (1961) did the Court settle that the rights, privileges, and immunities protected by section 1983 include at least all rights secured by the Fourteenth Amendment.

Just as CONSTITUTIONAL INTERPRETATION influenced early antidiscrimination laws and vice versa, modern antidiscrimination legislation influences constitutional interpretation. In GRIGGS V. DUKE POWER COMPANY (1971) the Court found that an employer's selection criteria with unintentional disparate effect on a minority could lead to a violation of Title VII of the Civil Rights Act of 1964. This and earlier Supreme Court cases generated pressure to find violative of the Fourteenth Amendment government action with uneven adverse effects on minorities. Not until WASHINGTON V. DAVIS (1976) and ARLINGTON HEIGHTS V. METROPOLITAN HOUSING DEVELOPMENT CORPORATION (1977) did the Court expressly reject the *Griggs* standard as a basis for constitutional interpretation. And in REGENTS OF THE UNIVERSITY OF CALIFORNIA V. BAKKE (1978), a major theme of the opinions is the relationship between the antidiscrimination standards embodied in Title VI of the Civil Rights Act of 1964 and those of the Fourteenth Amendment.

Judicial hostility to the Reconstruction CIVIL RIGHTS program and subsequent congressional inaction left much of the civil rights field to the states. Early Massachusetts legislation covered school desegregation and PUBLIC ACCOMMODATIONS, but few other states enacted protective laws prior to 1883 and some laws that had been enacted by southern Reconstruction legislatures were repealed.

The *Civil Rights Cases'* invalidation of the Civil Rights Act of 1875 triggered the first major group of state antidiscrimination laws. Within two years of the decision, eleven states outlawed discrimination in public accommodations. Modest further legislative developments occurred before World War II, including legislation aimed at violence generated by the Ku Klux Klan, some northern prohibitions on school segregation, and some categories of employment discrimination.

The next widespread state civil rights initiative, which covered employment discrimination, drew upon experience under the wartime Committee on Fair Employment Practices. New York's 1945 Law Against Discrimination, the first modern comprehensive fair employment law, established a commission to investigate and adjudicate complaints and became a model for other states' laws. Resort to administrative agencies, now possible in the vast majority of states, remains the primary state method of dealing with many categories of discrimination.

Bibliography

BARDOLPH, RICHARD    1970    *The Civil Rights Record.*  New York: Crowell.
KONVITZ, MILTON R.    1961    *A Century of Civil Rights.*  New York: Columbia University Press.

Murray, Pauli 1961 *States' Laws on Race and Color.* New York: Woman's Division of Christian Service, The Methodist Church.

U.S. Commission on Civil Rights 1970 *Federal Civil Rights Enforcement Effort.* Washington, D.C.: U.S. Government Printing Office.

# FEDERAL PROTECTION OF CIVIL RIGHTS

Theodore Eisenberg

Although the story of federal protection of CIVIL RIGHTS is most conveniently told chronologically, two themes warrant separate mention. First, federal protection of civil rights has a paradoxical relationship with STATES' RIGHTS. All civil rights legislation has been opposed or limited in response to the argument that the federal government ought not involve itself in areas of state responsibility. The Supreme Court repeatedly has voiced this concern and, in the past, invalidated civil rights legislation partly on this ground. Deference to state law enforcement prerogatives always has been a centerpiece of Justice Department civil rights enforcement policy. And for many years Congress repeatedly rebuffed so basic a measure as antilynching legislation in the name of states' rights. Yet the original federal civil rights statutes, and their underlying constitutional amendments, were responses to outrages by states or to private outrages that states failed to ameliorate. Given the origins of the need for federal protection of civil rights, states' interests may have received undue weight in shaping federal civil rights policy.

Second, there is a seedy underside to the topic of federal protection of civil rights. For many years the federal government was more involved with denying blacks' rights than with protecting them. Well into the twentieth century federal employment policy included racial SEGREGATION and exclusion. DE JURE segregation in Washington, D.C., and the armed forces, government participation in segregated and racially isolated housing projects, racially prejudiced federal judges, and other circumstances demonstrate the depth of federal involvement in discrimination. Since the 1940s, however, there has been a trend toward increased federal protection of civil rights.

The Bureau of Refugees, Freedmen, and Abandoned Lands (the FREEDMEN'S BUREAU), created near the end of the Civil War, may be viewed as the federal government's initial civil rights enforcement effort. The Bureau's statutory charge, "the control of all subjects relating to refugees and freedmen from rebel states," enabled it to perform a variety of social welfare functions. But this first effort to assist blacks was tainted by, among other factors, the Bureau's role in establishing the oppressive system of southern labor contracts. Although Bureau agents invalidated particularly harsh terms, such as those providing for corporal punishment, much depended on the local agent's views. The Bureau and the Union Army, no less than southern legislatures, felt most comfortable when blacks were on plantations under contract and not seeking their fortune in urban areas.

With few exceptions, federal protection of blacks via the Freedmen's Bureau terminated in 1868. Congress's other Reconstruction legislation employed a variety of techniques to protect civil rights. The CIVIL RIGHTS ACT OF 1866 and the FORCE ACT of 1870 imposed penalties on those who enforced discriminatory features of the southern BLACK CODES, and the 1870 act made it a crime to conspire to hinder a citizen's exercise of federal rights. The 1870 act also provided special protection for black VOTING RIGHTS and the Force Act of 1871 went further by providing for the appointment of federal supervisors to scrutinize voter registration and election practices. The Civil Rights Act of 1871 authorized civil actions and additional criminal penalties against those who violated constitutional rights and authorized the president to use federal forces to suppress insurrections or conspiracies to deprive "any portion or class of . . . people" of federal rights. The CIVIL RIGHTS ACT OF 1875, the culmination of the Reconstruction period civil rights program, imposed civil and criminal sanctions for discrimination in PUBLIC ACCOMMODATIONS, public conveyances, and places of amusement.

Armed with the criminal provisions of the civil rights program, federal prosecutors brought thousands of cases in southern federal courts and established criminal actions as the primary vehicle through which the federal government protected civil rights. This burst of protective activity, along with the rest of Reconstruction, disintegrated with the COMPROMISE OF 1877 and the attendant withdrawal of federal troops from the South. In 1878, only twenty-five federal criminal civil rights prosecutions were brought in southern federal courts.

There are many reasons why federal criminal prosecutions were and are ineffective to protect civil rights. First, shortly after enactment of the post-Civil War ANTIDISCRIMINATION LEGISLATION, the Supreme Court limited Congress's power to protect civil rights. UNITED STATES v. REESE (1876) and JAMES v. BOWMAN (1903) invalidated portions of the 1870 act. UNITED STATES v. HARRIS (1883) and *Baldwin v. Franks* (1887) struck down the CRIMINAL CONSPIRACY section of the 1871 act and the CIVIL RIGHTS CASES (1883) found the 1875 act to be unconstitutional. These and other cases, including the SLAUGHTERHOUSE CASES (1873) and UNITED STATES v. CRUIKSHANK (1876), also narrowly construed constitutional provisions and statutory provisions that were not struck down. The entire federal statutory civil rights program therefore depended upon those provisions that, almost by happenstance, survived judicial scrutiny. And some of these were eliminated by the CIVIL RIGHTS REPEAL ACT of 1894 and a reorganization of federal law in 1909.

The principal criminal provisions that survived, now sections 241 and 242 of Title 18, United States Code, are not well suited to protecting civil rights. They always have been plagued by doubts about the particular rights they protect and the conduct they reach, and more generally by doubt about the federal government's role in law enforcement. Similar difficulties characterized federal civil remedies to protect civil rights. Finally, southern juries, until recently all white, have rarely convicted whites for violating the rights of blacks.

From the Compromise of 1877 until about 1940, reference to federal "protection" of civil rights would be misleading. Racism in America peaked in the early twentieth century, a fact reflected in the federal government's attitude toward blacks. THEODORE ROOSEVELT's lunch with Booker T. Washington summarized his administration's concern with civil rights. Roosevelt's successor, WILLIAM HOWARD TAFT, did not even lunch with Washington, and under Taft and WOODROW WILSON segregation in federal employment was adopted. Neither Warren Harding nor Calvin Coolidge showed any inclination to rise above the worst racial attitudes of their times. As secretary of commerce, HERBERT HOOVER did desegregate the Census Bureau.

Attorney General FRANK MURPHY's decision in 1939 to establish a CIVIL RIGHTS DIVISION within the Department of Justice represented a noticeable shift in federal enforcement activity. The new section studied the dormant post-Civil War statutes and adopted an enforcement program that led to such important decisions as UNITED STATES v. CLASSIC (1941) and SCREWS v. UNITED STATES (1945). Federal criminal civil rights prosecutions, however, did not grow beyond several dozen cases a year. But two decades later, in MONROE v. PAPE (1961), these cases served as precedents in establishing private enforcement of civil rights through SECTION 1983, TITLE 42, UNITED STATES CODE.

Creation of the Civil Rights Division combined with other events to generate pressure for progress in the civil rights field. In June 1941, President FRANKLIN D. ROOSEVELT issued an EXECUTIVE ORDER creating a Fair Employment Practices Committee (FEPC). A response to defense needs and black political pressure, the executive order prohibited discriminatory employment practices on account of race, color, creed, or national origin in government service, in defense industries, and by trade unions. The order, administered by the FEPC, helped many northern blacks to obtain defense jobs and encouraged many southern blacks to move north.

But the nation was not ready for an aggressive federal civil rights program. Roosevelt himself was reluctant to propose or endorse civil rights legislation. In the 1930s, he even refused to endorse an antilynching bill pending in Congress. And where Roosevelt did act, Congress balked. Until 1944, the President's Emergency Fund financed the FEPC. Congress then required congressional approval for all executive expenditures. In 1946, the FEPC expired for lack of funds and subsequent efforts to establish a statutory FEPC failed.

The end of World War II seemed to trigger or coincide with renewed violence against blacks. Following a Democratic party defeat in the 1946 congressional elections, President HARRY S. TRUMAN, in Executive Order 9008, created a presidential civil rights committee to conduct inquiries and to recommend civil rights programs. In its report, *To Secure These Rights,* the committee made far-reaching recommendations in the areas of voting, employment, and federally assisted programs, many of which would be enacted in the 1960s. Although President Truman recommended legislation based on the commission's report, his administration's civil rights accomplishments were to be on other fronts.

Truman, like other presidents, fostered civil rights most effectively in areas not requiring legislative action. Southern political power in Congress precluded significant civil rights legislation. In 1947, under black and liberal pressure, Truman authorized the Justice Department to submit an amicus curiae brief opposing judicial enforcement of racially RESTRICTIVE COVENANTS. Some believe this brief to have been influential in the Supreme Court's decision in SHELLEY V. KRAEMER (1948), which rendered racially restrictive housing covenants judicially unenforceable. From 1948 through 1951, Truman issued a series of executive orders which prohibited discrimination by defense contractors, established a committee to study compliance with government contract provisions prohibiting discrimination, provided processes for handling EMPLOYMENT DISCRIMINATION complaints in federal departments and agencies, and called for equality of treatment and opportunity in the armed services.

Civil rights enforcement received little attention early in the administration of DWIGHT D. EISENHOWER, but there were important exceptions to this pattern. Executive Order 10479 (1953) extended the antidiscrimination provisions previously required in defense contracts to all government procurement contracts. And after BROWN V. BOARD OF EDUCATION (1954), Eisenhower could not avoid civil rights issues. Southern recalcitrance in the face of *Brown* led to a federal–state confrontation in Little Rock, Arkansas, which was settled through the presence of federal troops. (See COOPER V. AARON, 1958.) But Little Rock marked no general turning point in the administration's enforcement efforts. Even when armed with increased authority to investigate denials of voting rights by the CIVIL RIGHTS ACT OF 1957, the Justice Department brought few cases.

JOHN F. KENNEDY's administration also began with little impetus toward substantial civil rights achievement. But the rising tide of civil rights activity, increased public awareness, and continued southern resistance to DESEGREGATION made new federal–state confrontations inevitable. In May 1961, federal marshals were employed to protect freedom-riders. In September 1962, in connection with efforts to integrate the University of Mississippi, heavily outnumbered federal marshals and federalized National Guard troops withstood an assault by segregationists. Only the arrival of thousands of federal troops restored order. In the Birmingham crisis of 1963, which gained notoriety for the brutal treatment of demonstrators by state and local law enforcement officers, the federal government tried to act as a mediator. The administration's inability under federal law to deal forcefully with situations like that in Birmingham led Kennedy to propose further federal civil rights legislation.

Within the executive branch, the Interstate Commerce Commission, at the administration's request, promulgated stringent rules against discrimination in terminals. Armed with the CIVIL RIGHTS ACTS OF 1957 and 1960, the Civil Rights Division established by the 1957 Act conducted massive voter registration suits but secured only token improvements in black registration. Sometimes the judges blocking progress were Kennedy appointees. In November 1962 President Kennedy issued an executive order prohibiting discrimination in public housing projects and in projects covered by direct, guaranteed federal loans. And in executive orders in 1961 and 1963 Kennedy both required AFFIRMATIVE ACTION by government contractors and extended the executive branch's antidiscrimination program in federal procurement contracts to all federally assisted construction projects.

Soon after LYNDON B. JOHNSON succeeded to the presidency, he publicly endorsed Kennedy's civil rights legislation. Due in part to his direct support, Congress enacted the CIVIL RIGHTS ACT OF 1964, the most comprehensive civil rights measure in American history. The act outlaws discrimination in public accommodations, in federally assisted programs, or by large private employers, and it extends federal power to deal with voting discrimination. Title VII of the act created a substantial new federal bureaucracy to enforce antidiscrimination provisions pertaining to employment. The 1964 act also marked the first time that the Senate voted cloture against an anti-civil rights filibuster.

Despite the efforts of the Kennedy and Johnson Justice Departments, the Civil Rights Acts of 1957, 1960, and 1964 proved inadequate to protect black VOTING RIGHTS. Marches and protests to secure voting rights led to violence, including an infamous, widely reported confrontation in Selma, Alabama, in which marchers were beaten. In March 1965, President Johnson requested new voting rights legislation. He included in his speech to the nation and a joint session of Congress the words of the song of the civil rights movement, "We shall overcome," thus emphasizing the depth of the new federal involvement in civil rights. By August, the VOTING RIGHTS ACT OF 1965 was in place. Within ten years of its passage many more than a million new black voters were registered without great fanfare, with corresponding gains in the number of black elected officials. In 1968, after the assassination of Martin Luther King, Jr., Congress enacted a fair housing law as part of the CIVIL RIGHTS ACT OF 1968.

Unlike the Reconstruction civil rights program, Congress's 1960s civil rights legislation survived judicial scrutiny. In a series of cases from 1964 to 1976, the Supreme Court both sustained the new civil rights program and revived the Reconstruction-era laws. In *Katzenbach v. McClung* (1964) and HEART OF ATLANTA MOTEL v. UNITED STATES (1964) the Court rejected constitutional attacks on the public accommodations provisions of the 1964 act. In SOUTH CAROLINA v. KATZENBACH (1966) and KATZENBACH v. MORGAN (1966) the Court rebuffed state challenges to the Voting Rights Act of 1965. And in JONES v. ALFRED H. MAYER CO. (1968) and RUNYON v. MCCRARY (1976) the Court interpreted the Civil Rights Act of 1866 to fill important gaps in the coverage of the 1964 and 1968 acts.

With the passage and sustaining of the 1964, 1965, and 1968 acts and the revival of the 1866 act, the legal battle against RACIAL DISCRIMINATION at least formally was won. The federal civil rights program encompassed nearly all public and private purposeful racial discrimination in public accommodations, housing, employment, education, and voting. Future civil rights progress would have to come through vigorous enforcement, through programs aimed at relieving poverty, through affirmative action, and through laws benefiting groups other than blacks.

Just as the civil rights movement was running out of traditional civil rights laws to support, two other issues brought federal civil rights protection near its outer limits. The comprehensive coverage of federal civil rights laws did not eliminate the inferior status of blacks in American society. Pressure mounted for assistance in the form of affirmative action programs. But these programs divided even the liberal community traditionally supportive of civil rights enforcement. Affirmative action, unlike antidiscrimination standards, meant black progress at the expense of what many believed to be legitimate opportunities of innocent individuals. In its most important aspects affirmative action survived the initial series of statutory and constitutional attacks.

In the 1970s, civil rights enforcement became engulfed in another controversy: whether to bus school children for purposes of desegregation. (See SCHOOL BUSING.) President RICHARD M. NIXON's 1968 "Southern strategy" included campaigning against busing. Within six months of Nixon's inaugural, the Justice Department for the first time opposed the NAACP LEGAL DEFENSE AND EDUCATION FUND in a desegregation case. But under the pressure of Supreme Court decisions, and given the momentum of the prior administration's civil rights efforts, the Nixon administration did help promote new levels of southern integration. The administration, however, continued to lash out at "forced busing."

School desegregation also triggered a legislative backlash. In the 1970s the Internal Revenue Service, under the pressure of court decisions, sought to foster integration by denying tax benefits to private segregated academies and their benefactors. Congress, however, intervened to limit the Service's use of funds for such purposes. Similarly, Congress restrained executive authority to seek busing as a remedy for school segregation.

In the 1960s and 1970s, federal protection of civil rights reached beyond race. In the Age Discrimination in Employment Act, the AGE DISCRIMINATION ACT OF 1975, the REHABILITATION ACT OF 1973, and other measures, Congress acted to protect the aged and the handicapped. And the Equal Pay Act of 1963, the Civil Rights Act of 1964, and the EDUCATION AMENDMENTS OF 1972 increased federal protection against sex discrimination. In each of these areas, attachment of antidiscrimination conditions to federal disbursements became a significant vehicle for civil rights enforcement.

Bibliography

BERMAN, WILLIAM C.   1970   *The Politics of Civil Rights in the Truman Administration*. Columbus: Ohio State University Press.

BRAUER, CARL M.   1977   *John F. Kennedy and the Second Reconstruction*. New York: Columbia University Press.

CARR, ROBERT K.   1947   *Federal Protection of Civil Rights: Quest for a Sword*. Ithaca, N.Y.: Cornell University Press.

GRESSMAN, EUGENE   1952   The Unhappy History of Civil Rights Legislation. *Michigan Law Review* 50:1323–1358.

HARVEY, JAMES C.   1973   *Black Civil Rights During the Johnson Administration*. Jackson: University and College Press of Missouri.

KONVITZ, MILTON R.   1961   *A Century of Civil Rights*. New York: Columbia University Press.

LITWACK, LEON F.   1979   *Been in the Storm So Long: The Aftermath of Slavery*. New York: Knopf.

# SECTION 1983, TITLE 42, UNITED STATES CODE

## (Judicial Interpretation)

### Theodore Eisenberg

Few statutes have fluctuated in importance as wildly as section 1983. From near total disuse—twenty-one reported cases from 1871 to 1920—it became one of the most litigated provisions of federal law. This drastic change is attributable both to developments in constitutional law and to developments peculiar to section 1983.

Section 1983's ascension matches the twentieth-century expansion of constitutional rights. As originally enacted in the Civil Rights Act of 1871, section 1983 at most provided a cause of action for deprivations, under color of state law, of constitutional rights. Until relatively recently, citizens had few constitutional rights enforceable against the states. In section 1983's early years, the modern expansions of the EQUAL PROTECTION and DUE PROCESS clauses had not occurred, the STATE ACTION doctrine immunized a broad range of activity from constitutional scrutiny, and the FOURTH AMENDMENT was in the infancy of its constitutional development.

An ill-considered dichotomy between classes of constitutional rights also hindered section 1983's growth. In an influential separate opinion in HAGUE V. CIO (1939), Justice HARLAN FISKE STONE argued that section 1983's jurisdictional counterpart, section 1343(3), should be interpreted to authorize federal courts to hear cases involving personal rights but not to hear cases involving mere property rights. This view influenced many courts' interpretations of section 1983 itself, again with limiting effect. In *Lynch v. Household Finance Corporation* (1972) the Court rejected the personal rights/property rights distinction. Paradoxically, a similar dichotomy between personal interests and economic interests continues to shape, indeed govern, interpretation of the equal protection clause.

Section 1983's text generated interpretive problems that might have hindered its widespread use even if the Constitution had enjoyed a broader scope. As enacted, section 1983 protected "rights, privileges or immunities" secured by the Constitution. Its scope therefore depended upon what were viewed as rights, privileges, or immunities secured by the Constitution. Until the SLAUGHTERHOUSE CASES (1873), one might have thought the rights, privileges, or immunities so secured simply to be all constitutional rights. But the *Slaughterhouse Cases* narrowly interpreted the FOURTEENTH AMENDMENT's privileges or immunities clause to protect only a small subclass of constitutional rights. Some courts adopted a similar interpretation of section 1983. In addition, section 1983 reaches only deprivations "under color of" state law. Not until well into the twentieth century was it clearly recognized that behavior not authorized by state law might constitute action under COLOR OF LAW. A narrowly construed Constitution, the shadow cast by the *Slaughterhouse Cases,* the state action doctrine, and section 1983's text combined to minimize section 1983's importance.

In the 1920s, section 1983 provided actions for some deprivations of VOTING RIGHTS. Perhaps the Court relied on the section when, in NIXON v. HERNDON (1927), it allowed a damage action to go forward against state officials. In *Lane v. Wilson* (1939), another voting rights case, the Court expressly referred to section 1983 in approving a damage action. But these cases did not erode the important limitations on section 1983.

The erosion process commenced with early twentieth-century cases that construed state action to include some actions taken in violation of state law, and with EX PARTE YOUNG (1908), which held that the ELEVENTH AMENDMENT does not bar injunctive actions against state officials. In the 1940s, criminal CIVIL RIGHTS decisions also interpreted the phrase "under color of" law to include some unauthorized action. MONROE v. PAPE (1961) capped the process by interpreting section 1983 to protect at least all constitutional rights embodied in the Fourteenth Amendment and by holding the color of law requirement in section 1983 to be satisfied by the unauthorized action of police officers. *Monroe,* together with the wide expansion of constitutional rights of the 1950s and 1960s, assured section 1983's importance.

But section 1983's growth triggered a reaction, one that began with *Monroe* itself. If every constitutional violation generated a cause of action for damages there must be limits as to when defendants actually would be held liable. In *Monroe,* the Court, giving a questionable reading to section 1983's history, held that the section was not meant to render cities liable for constitutional violations. This limitation survived until MONELL v. DEPARTMENT OF SOCIAL SERVICES (1978), when the Court held that cities may be liable under section 1983 but that, in yet another questionable reading of the section's history, Congress did not intend cities to be liable for acts of city officials unless the acts constituted "official policy," a phrase destined to be the subject of much litigation. The reaction also includes some sentiment to impose an EXHAUSTION OF REMEDIES requirement in one or more classes of section 1983 cases.

With respect to individual defendants, the Court in a series of cases read into section 1983 an array of LEGISLATIVE, JUDICIAL, prosecutorial and EXECUTIVE IMMUNITIES. And in QUERN v. JORDAN (1979) the Court held that section 1983 was not meant to abrogate the Eleventh Amendment immunity of states. In OWEN v. CITY OF INDEPENDENCE (1980), however, the Court declined to extend to municipalities the good faith defense available to executive officials. The reaction to section 1983's expansion may also encompass a series of cases, including *Parratt v. Taylor* (1981), PAUL v. DAVIS (1976), INGRAHAM v. WRIGHT (1977), and *Estelle v. Gamble* (1976), narrowly interpreting constitutional rights. If a private cause of action accompanies every constitutional right, the Court may be hesitant to "constitutionalize" many rights. Finally, the Court held in *Carey v. Piphus* (1978) that a violation of PROCEDURAL DUE PROCESS, standing alone, will not support a substantial recovery of damages; to recover more than nominal damages a plaintiff in such a case must show actual harm. The Court left open the question whether this rule would apply to other types of constitutional violation.

For many years, courts disagreed over whether section 1983 provided a cause of action for violations of federal statutes by state officials. The REVISED STATUTES of 1874, which were not supposed to make substantive changes in the law, expanded section 1983's wording to include "laws." Over a century later, in *Maine v. Thiboutot* (1980), the Court interpreted section 1983 to provide a cause of action for at least some federal statutory claims.

Bibliography

EISENBERG, THEODORE    1982    Section 1983: Doctrinal Foundations and an Empirical Study. *Cornell Law Review* 67:482–556.

———    1981    *Civil Rights Legislation.* Charlottesville, Va.: Michie Co.

FRIENDLY, HENRY J.    1973    *Federal Jurisdiction: A General View* Pp. 87–107. New York: Columbia University Press.

NAHMOD, SHELDON H.    1979    *Civil Rights & Civil Liberties Litigation.* Colorado Springs, Colo.: Shepard's.

NOTE    1977    Developments in the Law: Section 1983 and Federalism. *Harvard Law Review* 90:1133–1361.

# WASHINGTON v. DAVIS
## 426 U.S. 229 (1976)

### Theodore Eisenberg

This landmark decision concerns the relevance of a decision maker's motives in EQUAL PROTECTION cases. Black candidates for the Washington, D.C., police force alleged that the District's selection criteria had an adverse discriminatory effect upon the employment prospects of minorities and that the effect violated the FOURTEENTH AMENDMENT's equal protection clause and ANTIDISCRIMINATION LEGISLATION. In an opinion by Justice BYRON R. WHITE, the Supreme Court held that discriminatory effects, standing alone, are insufficient to establish an equal protection violation. Proof of purposeful discrimination is necessary. The Court also rejected the candidates' statutory claim. In an opinion that did not address the constitutional question, Justice WILLIAM J. BRENNAN, joined by Justice THURGOOD MARSHALL, dissented from the Court's disposition of the statutory issue. In a concurring opinion, Justice JOHN PAUL STEVENS discussed the relationship between discriminatory effects and proof of discriminatory intent and articulated his reasons for rejecting the statutory claim.

In settling a long-standing controversy over whether a decision maker's motives may constitute the basis for an equal protection claim, the Court climbed two interesting doctrinal hills. Prior to *Davis,* cases such as *Whitcomb v. Chavis* (1971) and *White v. Regester* (1973) expressly had suggested that unintentional disproportionate effects on a minority may constitute the basis for an equal protection claim. Justice White's opinion ignores these precedents but warns against the broad consequences of such a HOLDING. Such a rule "would raise serious questions about, and perhaps invalidate, a whole range of tax, welfare, public service, regulatory, and licensing statutes that may be more burdensome to the poor and to the average black than to the more affluent white."

In addition, contrary to *Davis*'s holding, a line of opinions dating back to FLETCHER v. PECK (1810) and reaffirmed in UNITED STATES v. O'BRIEN (1968) and PALMER v. THOMPSON (1971), clearly had stated that legislators' motives may not form the basis of constitutional attacks on statutes. Without alluding to all of the relevant precedents, the Court reinterpreted *Palmer* and suggested that some of its language had constituted mere OBITER DICTA.

As a practical matter, *Davis,* when combined with subsequent similar

cases such as ARLINGTON HEIGHTS v. METROPOLITAN HOUSING DEVELOP-
MENT CORP. (1977) and MOBILE V. BOLDEN (1980), curtailed litigants'
ability to bring successful equal protection claims. Proof of intentional
discrimination is difficult to obtain and judges are reluctant to deem
officials intentional wrongdoers. Indeed, it was six years after *Davis* before
the Court, in *Rogers v. Lodge* (1982), sustained a finding of intentional
discrimination in a racial equal protection case.

# AFFIRMATIVE ACTION

Henry J. Abraham

The Supreme Court's momentous decisions in BROWN V. BOARD OF EDU-
CATION and BOLLING V. SHARPE (1954), and its subsequent implementation decision in *Brown II* (1955), were followed by a long string of
rulings designed to render meaningful and effective the egalitarian promise inherent in the FOURTEENTH AMENDMENT. Compulsory racial SEGREGA-
TION was at last no longer constitutionally permissible; the Fourteenth
Amendment's guarantee of the EQUAL PROTECTION OF THE LAWS had
become the effective law of the land for all levels of the public sector.

But in the judgment of a good many Americans, equality *qua* equality, even when conscientiously enforced with an even hand, would neither
suffice to enable those previously deprived on racial grounds to realize
the promises of equality of opportunity, nor would it atone, and provide
redress, for the ravages wrought by two centuries of past discrimination.
Consequently, as strongly urged by President LYNDON B. JOHNSON, programs were established in both the public and the private realms that
were designed to go well beyond "mere" equality of opportunity and
provide not only remedial but preferential compensatory action, especially in the worlds of EDUCATION and employment. Labeled "affirmative
action"—as distinguished from "neutrality"—these programs were insti-
tuted to bring about increased minority employment opportunities, job
promotions, and admissions to colleges and universities, among others.
Understandably, affirmative action programs quickly became controversial because of their resort to RACIAL QUOTAS, also called euphemistically
"goals" or "guidelines." Their proponents' justification has been that
to provide an absolute measure of full equality of opportunity based
upon individual merit does not suffice; that, given the injustices of the
past, both preferential and compensatory treatment must be accorded
through "affirmative action" that all but guarantees numerically targeted
slots or posts based upon membership in racial groups or upon gender.
Most critics of the policy's underlying philosophy have not necessarily
objected to "affirmative action" policies such as aggressive recruiting,
remedial training (no matter what the expense), and perhaps not even
to what Justice LEWIS F. POWELL in REGENTS OF THE UNIVERSITY OF
CALIFORNIA V. BAKKE (1978) termed a justifiable "plus" consideration
of race along with other equitable factors. They do, however, object

strenuously to policies that represent, or may be regarded as sanctioning, "reverse discrimination," generally characterized by the resort to such devices as the *numerus clausus,* that is, rigid quotas set aside to benefit identifiable racial groups, as in the controversial case of UNITED STEEL-WORKERS OF AMERICA v. WEBER (1979); to double standards in grading, ranking, and similar requirements on the employment, educational, and other relevant fronts of opportunity; and to "set aside" laws that guarantee specified percentages of contracts to minority groups, as in FULLILOVE v. KLUTZNICK (1980).

The basic issue, while philosophically replete with moral and ethical considerations, was ultimately bound to be fought out on the legal and constitutional front, thus engendering judicial decisions. Several provisions of the CIVIL RIGHTS ACT OF 1964, as amended—for example, Titles IV, VI, VII, and IX—seemed quite specifically not only to forbid racial, sexual, and other discrimination per se but also to proscribe the use of racial and related quotas. The Supreme Court rapidly confronted five major opportunities to address the issue; in each instance it found itself seriously divided. Each of the five decisions involved "affirmative action" and/or "reverse discrimination."

The first and second, DeFUNIS v. ODEGAARD (1974) and *Regents v. Bakke* (1978), dealt with preferential racial admissions quotas that by design advantaged nonwhite applicants and thereby ipso facto disadvantaged whites. In *De Funis* a five-member majority rendered a nondecision on the merits by ruling the case moot, because whatever the outcome of the case, Marco De Funis would be graduated by the University of Washington Law School. Justice WILLIAM O. DOUGLAS, dissenting from the MOOTNESS determination, warned that "the equal protection clause commands the elimination of racial barriers, not their creation in order to satisfy our theory as to how society ought to be organized." In *Bakke* the Court did reach the merits of the racial quota established by the University of California (Davis) medical school, ruling 5–4 (in two diverse lineups, each headed by Justice Powell) that whereas the latter's rigid quota violated Allan Bakke's rights under the Constitution and the Civil Rights Act of 1964, the use of race as a "plus" along with other relevant considerations in admissions decisions did not. The third case, *United Steelworkers v. Weber,* concerned an employer–union craft-training plan that, on its face, directly violated Title VII of the Civil Rights Act of 1964, which clearly, indeed literally, interdicts racial quotas in employment. However, with Justices Powell and JOHN PAUL STEVENS disqualifying themselves from sitting in the cases, Justice WILLIAM J. BRENNAN, speaking for a majority of five, ruled that although the letter of the law appeared to forbid the arrangement, its purpose, as reflected in the legislative history, did not. The fourth case, *Fullilove v. Klutznick,* raised the fundamental question whether Congress, notwithstanding the Fourteenth Amendment's equal protection clause, could constitutionally legislate a ten percent set-aside plan for minority-owned construction companies desirous of obtaining government contracts. "Yes," held a 6–3 plurality—actually, the Court split 3–3–3—finding such legislation to be within the federal legislature's spending and regulatory powers under Article I of the Constitution. In his scathing DISSENTING OPINION, which he read in full from the bench on the day of the decision, Justice Stevens charged that the law represented a "perverse form of reparation," a "slapdash" law that rewards some who may not need rewarding and hurts others who may not deserve hurting. Suggesting that such a law could be used simply as a patronage tool by its authors—it had, in fact, been written on the floor of the House of Representatives without having gone to committee for hearings—he warned that it could breed more resentment and prejudice than it corrected. Echoing the first Justice JOHN MARSHALL HARLAN's memorable phrase in dissent in PLESSY v. FERGUSON (1896), namely, that "our Constitution is color-blind and neither knows nor tolerates classes among citizens," Stevens asked what percentage of "oriental blood or what degree of Spanish-speaking skill is required for membership in the preferred class?" With deep feelings, he suggested sarcastically that now the government must devise its version of the Nazi laws that defined who is a Jew, musing that "our statute books will once again have to contain laws that reflect the odious practice of delineating the qualities that make one person a Negro and make another white." The fifth case, *Memphis Fire Department v. Stotts,* seemed to draw a line (although only by the narrowest of margins, 5–4) when the Justice White-authored majority opinion held that duly established bona fide nondiscriminatory seniority systems supersede affirmative action plans.

Depending upon interpretation, one person's "affirmative action" may well constitute another's "reverse discrimination". Nonetheless, it is possible to essay distinctions. Thus, "affirmative action" may be regarded as encompassing the following five phenomena, all of which would appear to be both legal and constitutional: (1) both governmentally and privately sponsored activity designed to remedy the absence of needed educational preparation by special, even if costly, primary, and/or secondary school level preparatory programs or occupational skill development, always provided that access to these programs is not bottomed upon race or related group criteria or characteristics, but upon educational or economic need; (2) special classes or supplemental training, regardless of costs, on any level of education or training from the prenursery school bottom to the very top of the professional training ladder; (3) scrupulous enforcement of absolute standards of nondiscrimination on the basis of race, sex, religion, nationality, and age; (4) above-the-table special recruiting efforts to reach out to those members of heretofore underused, deprived, or discriminated-against segments of the citizenry; (5) provided the presence of explicit or implicit merit, of bona fide demonstrated or potential ability, the taking into account of an individual's race, gender, religion as an equitable consideration—the "plus" of which Justice Powell spoke in *Bakke* —but *only* if "all other things are equal."

"Reverse discrimination," on the other hand, which is acceptable neither legally nor constitutionally, would constitute the following quartet: (1) adoption of a *numerus clausus,* the setting aside of quotas, be they rigid or semirigid, on behalf of the admission, recruitment, employment, or promotion of individuals and groups identified and classified by racial, religious, sexual, age, or nationality characteristics; such characteristics are *non sequiturs* on the fronts of individual merit and ability and may well be regarded as an insult to the dignity and intelligence of the quota beneficiaries; (2) slanting of what should be neutral qualification examinations or requirements; double standards in grading and rating; double standards in attendance, retention, and disciplinary requirements; (3) those "goals" and "guidelines" that allegedly differ from rigid quotas, and thus presumably pass legal and constitutional muster, but that, in application, are all but synonymous with enforced quotas; (4) legislative or executive "set aside" programs, such as the one at issue in the *Fullilove* case, that mandate percentage-quotas of awards and activities based upon racial, gender, and related classifications.

"Reverse discrimination" purports to justify itself as atonement for past discrimination. It sanctions the call to children to pay for the sins of their forebears; it embraces a policy that two wrongs make one right, that "temporary" discrimination is "benign" rather than "invidious" when it is designed to remedy past wrongs. Since the "temporary" all too often becomes the "permanent," temporary suspensions of fundamental rights are fraught with permanent dangers and represent prima facie denials of the equal protection of the laws guaranteed by the Fourteenth Amendment and the DUE PROCESS OF LAW guaranteed by the Fifth.

The line between "affirmative action" and "reverse discrimination" may be thin and vexatious, but it does not lie beyond recognition and establishment in our constitutional constellation.

Bibliography

DWORKIN, RONALD 1977 *Taking Rights Seriously.* Cambridge, Mass.: Harvard University Press.

GLAZER, NATHAN 1976 *Affirmative Discrimination.* New York: Basic Books.

O'NEILL, ROBERT M. 1975 *Discriminating against Discrimination.* Bloomington: Indiana University Press.

ROCHE, GEORGE C., III    1974    *The Balancing Act: Quota Hiring in Higher Education.*  La Salle, Ill.: Open Court.

ROSSUM, RALPH A.    1980    *Reverse Discrimination: The Constitutional Debate.*  New York: Marcel Dekker.

SOWELL, THOMAS    1975    *Affirmative Action Reconsidered: Was It Necessary in Academia?*  Washington, D.C.: American Enterprise Institute.

# RACIAL QUOTAS

## Kenneth L. Karst

Programs of AFFIRMATIVE ACTION, aimed at increasing opportunities for women and members of racial and ethnic minorities in employment and higher education, have sometimes taken the form of numerical quotas. In REGENTS OF UNIVERSITY OF CALIFORNIA V. BAKKE (1978) sixteen places in a state university medical school's entering class were reserved for minority applicants; in FULLILOVE V. KLUTZNICK (1980) ten percent of funds in a federal public works program were reserved for minority-owned businesses. Such quotas have been challenged as denials of the EQUAL PROTECTION OF THE LAWS, with mixed doctrinal results.

Opponents of racial quotas maintain that it is offensive to penalize or reward people on the basis of race—in short, that the Constitution is, or ought to be, colorblind. Opponents discern in quotas a subtle but pervasive racism, in the patronizing assumption that persons of particular colors or ethnic backgrounds cannot be expected to meet the standards that apply to others. This assumption, the opponents argue, is, in its own way, a BADGE OF SERVITUDE, stigmatizing the quotas' supposed beneficiaries. Some opponents see quotas as part of a general trend toward dehumanization, robbing individuals of both personal identity and human dignity, lumping them together in a collectivity based on other people's assumptions about racially defined traits.

Unfortunately for today's America, race has never been a neutral fact in this country. Those who defend affirmative action generally admit to some uneasiness about the potential abuse of racial distinctions. They argue, however, that there is no real neutrality in a system that first imposes on a racial group harsh disadvantages, readily transmitted through the generations, and then tells today's inheritors of disadvantages that from now on the rules prohibit playing favorites. If either compensation for past RACIAL DISCRIMINATION or the integration of American institutions is a legitimate social objective, the proponents argue, a government in pursuit of those objectives can hardly avoid taking race into account.

The recent attack on racial quotas draws fuel from an emotional reservoir filled two generations ago by universities that limited admission of racial and religious minorities—most notably Jews—to specified small quotas. This ugly form of discrimination was part of a systematic stigmatization and subordination of minority groups by the dominant majority.

The recent quotas are designed to remedy the effects of past discrimination, and—when they serve the objective of compensation or integration—are not stigmatizing. They do, however, use race or ethnic status as a means of classifying persons, and thus come under fire for emphasizing group membership rather than "individual merit."

The right to equal protection is, indeed, an individual right. Yet the term "individual merit" misleads in two ways. The word "individual" misleads by obscuring the fact that every claim to equality is a claim made on behalf of the group of persons identified by some set of characteristics: race, for example, or high college grades and test scores. To argue against a racial preference is not to support individual merit as against a group claim, but to argue that some other group, defined by other attributes, is entitled to preference.

"Merit" misleads by conveying the idea of something wholly intrinsic to an individual, apart from some definition of community needs or purposes. When we reward achievement, we are not merely rewarding effort, but are also giving out prizes for native talents and environmental advantages. Mainly, we reward achievement because society wants the goods produced by the combination of talents, environment, and effort. But it is also reasonable to look to past harms and potential contributions to society in defining the characteristics that deserve reward. We admit college achievers to law schools not to reward winners but to serve society with good lawyers. If it be legitimate to seek to end a system of racial caste by integrating American society, nothing in the idea of individual merit stands in the way of treating race as one aspect of "merit."

Race-conscious remedies for past governmental discrimination were approved in decisions as early as SWANN v. CHARLOTTE-MECKLENBURG BOARD OF EDUCATION (1971). Affirmative action quotas pose another question: can government itself employ race-conscious remedies for the effects of past societal discrimination? In *Fullilove*, six Justices agreed on an affirmative answer to that question, at least when Congress prescribes the remedy. *Bakke* was complicated by a statutory claim; its result—and its practical effect in professional school admissions—was a distinction between racial or ethnic quotas, which are unlawful, and the use of racial or ethnic status as "one factor" in admission, which is lawful.

The distinction was a political success; it drew the fangs from a controversy that had turned venomous. But the distinction between a quota and a racial factor is more symbol than substance. If race is a factor, it will decide some cases. How many cases? The weight assigned to race surely will be determined by reference to the approximate number of minority admittees necessary to achieve the admitting university's goals of educational "diversity." The difference between saying "sixteen out of a hundred" and "around sixteen percent" is an exercise in constitutional cosmetics—but it seems to have saved affirmative action during a critical season.

Bibliography

KARST, KENNETH L. and HOROWITZ, HAROLD W. 1974    Affirmative Action and Equal Protection. *Virginia Law Review* 60:955–974.

VAN ALSTYNE, WILLIAM W.    1979    Rites of Passage: Race, the Supreme Court, and the Constitution. *University of Chicago Law Review* 46:775–810.

# REGENTS OF UNIVERSITY OF CALIFORNIA v. BAKKE

## 438 U.S. 265 (1978)

### Kenneth L. Karst

Perhaps the Supreme Court's majority in DeFunis v. Odegaard (1974) thought a delay in deciding on the constitutionality of racial preferences in state university admissions would give time for development of a political consensus on the issue. The result was just the opposite; by the time *Bakke* was decided, the question of RACIAL QUOTAS and preferences had become bitterly divisive. Bakke, a nonminority applicant, had been denied admission to the university's medical school at Davis. His state court suit had challenged the school's program setting aside for minority applicants sixteen places in an entering class of 100. Bakke's test scores and grades exceeded those of most minority admittees. The California Supreme Court held that the racial preference denied Bakke the EQUAL PROTECTION OF THE LAWS guaranteed by the FOURTEENTH AMENDMENT.

A fragmented United States Supreme Court agreed, 5–4, that Bakke was entitled to admission, but concluded, in a different 5–4 alignment, that race could be taken into account in a state university's admissions. Four Justices thought the Davis quota violated Title VI of the CIVIL RIGHTS ACT OF 1964, which forbids the exclusion of anyone on account of race from any program aided by federal funds. This position was rejected, 5–4. Four other Justices argued that the Davis quota was constitutionally valid as a reasonable, nonstigmatizing remedy for past societal discrimination against racial and ethnic minorities. This view was rejected by Justice LEWIS F. POWELL, who concluded that the Davis quota was a denial of equal protection. His vote, along with the votes of the four Justices who found a Title VI violation, placed Bakke in Davis's 1978 entering class.

Justice Powell's opinion on the constitutional question began by rejecting the notion of a "BENIGN" RACIAL CLASSIFICATION. He concluded that the burden of remedying past societal discrimination could not constitutionally be placed on individuals who had no part in that discrimination—absent the sort of constitutional violation that had been found in school DESEGREGATION cases such as SWANN v. CHARLOTTE-MECKLENBURG BOARD OF EDUCATION (1971), where color-conscious remedies had been approved. While rejecting quotas, Justice Powell approved the use of race as one factor in a state university's admissions policy for the purpose of promoting diversity in its student body.

Race is relevant to "diversity," of course, mainly because past societal discrimination has made race relevant to a student's attitudes and experiences. And if one's membership in a racial group may be a factor in the admissions process, it may be the decisive factor in a particular case. The Powell opinion thus anticipates a preference for minority applicants; how much of a preference will depend, as he says, on "some attention to numbers"—that is, the number of minority students already admitted. The difference between such a system and a racial quota is mostly symbolic.

The press hailed Justice Powell's opinion as a judgment of Solomon. As a contribution to principled argument about equal protection doctrine, it failed. As a political solution, however, it was a triumph. The borders of preference became blurred, so that no future applicant could blame her rejection on the preference. At the same time, a university following a "diversity" approach to admissions was made safe from constitutional attack. AFFIRMATIVE ACTION was thus saved, even as Bakke was ushered into medical school and racial quotas ringingly denounced. Almost miraculously, the issue of racial preferences in higher education virtually disappeared from the political scene, and legislative proposals to abolish affirmative action were shelved. Solomon, it will be recalled, succeeded in saving the baby.

Bibliography

BLASI, VINCENT   1979   Bakke as Precedent: Does Mr. Justice Powell Have a Theory? *California Law Review* 67:21–68.

KARST, KENNETH L. and HOROWITZ, HAROLD W.   1979   The Bakke Opinions and Equal Protection Doctrine. *Harvard Civil Rights–Civil Liberties Law Review* 14:7–29.

WILKINSON, J. HARVIE, III   1979   *From Brown to Bakke*. New York: Oxford University Press.

# FULLILOVE v. KLUTZNICK
## 448 U.S. 448 (1980)

### Kenneth L. Karst

The Supreme Court's fragmentation in REGENTS OF UNIVERSITY OF CALIFORNIA V. BAKKE (1978) left open the question of the constitutionality of government-imposed RACIAL QUOTAS or preferences. The following year, in UNITED STEELWORKERS V. WEBER, the Court held that a voluntary AFFIRMATIVE ACTION plan, calling for a racial quota in hiring by a private employer and approved by a union, did not violate Title VII of the CIVIL RIGHTS OF 1964. *Fullilove* reopened *Bakke*'s question: Can government impose a racial quota to remedy the effects of past discrimination?

Congress, in a public works statute aimed at reducing unemployment, provided that ten percent of the funds distributed to each state should be set aside for contracts with "minority business enterprises" (MBE). An MBE was defined as a business at least half owned by persons who are "Negroes, Spanish-speaking, Orientals, Indians, Eskimos and Aleuts." Nonminority contractors challenged this limitation as a denial of the Fifth Amendment's guarantee of EQUAL PROTECTION, as recognized in BOLLING V. SHARPE (1954) and later cases.

The Supreme Court held, 6–3, that the MBE limitation was valid. Three Justices, speaking through Chief Justice WARREN E. BURGER, paid great deference to Congress's judgment that the racial quota was a "limited and properly tailored remedy to cure the effects of past RACIAL DISCRIMINATION." Emphasizing the flexibility provided for the law's administration, they said that the funds could be limited to MBEs that were in fact disadvantaged because of race. The other three majority Justices, speaking through Justice THURGOOD MARSHALL, took the position they had taken in *Bakke,* concluding that the racial quota was "substantially related to . . . the important and congressionally articulated goal of remedying the present effects of past racial discrimination."

Justice POTTER STEWART, joined by Justice WILLIAM H. REHNQUIST, dissented; they would forbid any statutory racial classification, allowing race-conscious remedies only in cases of proven illegal discrimination. Justice JOHN PAUL STEVENS was not prepared to take so absolute a position but dissented here because Congress had not sufficiently articulated the reasons for its racial quota and tailored its program to those reasons.

# PALMORE v. SIDOTI
## 466 U.S. 429 (1984)

### Kenneth L. Karst

When Linda Palmore was divorced from Anthony Sidoti, a Florida court awarded custody of their daughter to Palmore. Later, Sidoti sought custody on the ground that Palmore, a white woman, had been cohabiting with a black man, whom she shortly married. The state court changed the custody on the sole ground that the mother had "chosen for herself and her child, a life-style unacceptable to her father and to society." The child would, if she remained with her mother, be "more vulnerable to peer pressures" and would suffer from "social stigmatization." The Supreme Court unanimously reversed.

For the Court, Chief Justice WARREN E. BURGER reaffirmed the need for STRICT SCRUTINY of governmental action based on race. Racial prejudice indeed existed, but the potential injury from such private biases was not a constitutionally acceptable basis for the custody change. The decision has symbolic importance, but seems unlikely to make much difference in actual awards of child custody, which can be rested on a variety of grounds in the name of the "best interests of the child" without any explicit consideration of race.

# Beyond Race: The Expansion of Civil Equality

# SUSPECT CLASSIFICATION

Kenneth L. Karst

Long before the term "suspect classification" gained currency, Justice HARLAN FISKE STONE captured the idea in his opinion for the Supreme Court in UNITED STATES V. CAROLENE PRODUCTS CO. (1938). While insisting on RATIONAL BASIS as the appropriate STANDARD OF REVIEW for cases involving ECONOMIC REGULATION, Stone suggested that "prejudice against DISCRETE AND INSULAR MINORITIES [that is, religious, or national, or racial minorities] may be a special condition, which tends seriously to curtail the operation of those political processes ordinarily to be relied upon to protect minorities, and which may call for a correspondingly more searching judicial inquiry." In modern idiom, to call a legislative classification "suspect" is to suggest the possibility that it resulted from prejudice against the group it burdens, a possibility that justifies strict judicial scrutiny to assure that it is necessary to achieve a COMPELLING STATE INTEREST. In practice, most laws subject to this exacting standard are held invalid.

Irony attends the origins of the expression. Justice HUGO L. BLACK, writing for a majority in *Korematsu v. United States* (1944), one of the JAPANESE AMERICAN CASES, found no denial of EQUAL PROTECTION in an EXECUTIVE ORDER excluding American citizens of Japanese ancestry from the West Coast. Along the way to this extraordinary conclusion, however, he said: "all legal restrictions which curtail the civil rights of a single racial group are immediately suspect. That is not to say that all such restrictions are unconstitutional. It is to say that courts must subject them to the most rigid scrutiny." In *Korematsu* itself, the Court did no such thing; it paid the greatest deference to a "military" judgment that was chiefly political and steeped in racial prejudice. Yet *Korematsu*'s main doctrinal legacy was that racial classifications were suspect.

In one view, this two-stage analysis, first identifying a classification as suspect and then subjecting it to STRICT SCRUTINY, is a roundabout way of addressing the issue of illicit legislative motives. (See LEGISLATION; WASHINGTON V. DAVIS, 1976.) Strict scrutiny is required in order to allay the suspicion that a law was designed to disadvantage a minority that lacked effective power in the legislature. That suspicion is laid to rest only by a showing that the law is well designed to achieve a legitimate purpose that has real importance. In another view, a classification based on race should be subjected to strict scrutiny because the immutable characteristic of race lends itself so well to a system thought dominated by stereotype, which automatically consigns a person to a general category, often implying inferiority. This concern for stigmatic harm is part of the substantive core of the equal protection clause, the principle of equal citizenship; the concern retains vitality even in an era when members of racial minorities have become electoral majorities in many of our major cities.

A number of egalitarian decisions in the later years of the WARREN COURT suggested a wide range of classifications that were candidates for inclusion by the Supreme Court in the "suspect" category: alienage, sex, ILLEGITIMACY, age, indigency. In the event, none of these candidates was accepted fully. Some classifications disadvantaging ALIENS were held "suspect," but many were not. The Court did significantly heighten the standard of review for most cases involving claimed denials of SEX DISCRIMINATION and gave some "bite" to the rational basis standard in cases involving illegitimacy. On the whole, however, the Court's behavior since the late 1970s suggests a determination to limit expansion of the list of suspect classifications, and thus to limit the occasions for active judicial supervision of legislation.

Some racial classifications are adopted as remedies for past societal discrimination based on race. Such an AFFIRMATIVE ACTION program presents neither of the principal dangers that have been said to require strict judicial scrutiny of racial classifications. There is less reason to suspect an illicit motive when a majoritarian body such as a legislature discriminates in favor of a historically disadvantaged minority, and the risk of stigmatic harm to a racial group is much reduced. Thus, varying majorities of the Supreme Court have consistently agreed that the appropriate standard of review for such remedial legislation, including RACIAL QUOTAS, is considerably less exacting than the strictest form of strict scrutiny.

The whole "suspect classifications" idea would seem to have outlived its usefulness. Surely the Supreme Court no longer needs the doctrine to justify its highest levels of intensity of judicial review. In race cases, for example, the Court needs no such locution in order to continue imposing on government a "heavy burden of justification" of laws imposing invidious racial discrimination. Abandonment of the rhetoric of suspect classifications would promote candor, by easing the way for open recognition of the sliding scale of standards of review now serving to cloak the Court's interest balancing. It would also remove a barrier, built into the very language of suspect "classifications," to doctrinal growth in the direction of affirmative governmental responsibility to alleviate those inequalities that prevent the realization of the principle of equal citizenship.

Bibliography

BREST, PAUL A.   1976   The Supreme Court, 1975 Term—Foreword: In Defense of the Antidiscrimination Principle. *Harvard Law Review* 90:1–54.

ELY, JOHN HART   1980   Democracy and Distrust: A Theory of Judicial Review. Cambridge, Mass.: Harvard University Press.

# BRADWELL *v.* ILLINOIS

## 16 Wallace 130 (1873)

### Leonard W. Levy

*Bradwell* is the earliest FOURTEENTH AMENDMENT case in which the Supreme Court endorsed sex discrimination. Mrs. Myra Bradwell, the editor of the *Chicago Legal News,* was certified by a board of legal examiners as qualified to be a member of the state bar. An Illinois statute permitted the state supreme court to make rules for admission to the bar. That court denied Mrs. Bradwell's application for admission solely on the ground of sex, although the fact that the applicant was married also counted against her: a married woman at that time was incapable of making binding contracts without her husband's consent, thus disabling her from performing all the duties of an attorney. She argued that the PRIVILEGES AND IMMUNITIES clause of the Fourteenth Amendment protected her CIVIL RIGHT as a citizen of the United States to be admitted to the bar, if she qualified.

Justice SAMUEL F. MILLER, speaking for the Court, declared that the right to be admitted to the practice of law in a state court was not a privilege of national CITIZENSHIP protected by the Fourteenth Amendment. Justice JOSEPH P. BRADLEY, joined by Justices NOAH SWAYNE and STEPHEN J. FIELD, concurred in the JUDGMENT affirming the state court, but offered additional reasons. History, nature, COMMON LAW, and the civil law supported the majority's reading of the privileges and immunities clause, according to Bradley. The "spheres and destinies" of the sexes were widely different, man being woman's protector; her "timidity and delicacy" unfit her for many occupations, including the law. Unlike Myra Bradwell, an unmarried woman might make contracts, but such a woman was an exception to the rule. "The paramount destiny and mission of woman are to fulfill the noble and benign offices of wife and mother. This is the law of the Creator." Society's rules, Bradley added, ought not be based on exceptions. Chief Justice SALMON P. CHASE dissented alone, without opinion, missing a chance to advocate the cause of SEX EQUALITY, at least in the legal profession.

288

# NINETEENTH AMENDMENT

Deborah L. Rhode

Ratification of the women's suffrage amendment in 1920 marked the culmination of a struggle spanning three quarters of a century. Under the leadership of organizations including the National Woman's Suffrage Association and the National Women's Party, over 2 million women participated in some 900 campaigns before state and federal legislators, party officials, and referendum voters. By the time the amendment was adopted, a majority of the states had already given some recognition to women's VOTING RIGHTS.

Political agitation for enfranchisement began in 1848, at the first women's rights convention in Seneca Falls, New York. In its Declaration of Sentiments, the convention included suffrage as one of the "inalienable rights" to which women were entitled. As the century progressed, the vote assumed increasing importance, both as a symbolic affirmation of women's equality and as a means to address a vast array of sex-based discrimination in employment, education, domestic law, and related areas. Once the Supreme Court ruled in MINOR v. HAPPERSETT (1875) that suffrage was not one of the PRIVILEGES AND IMMUNITIES guaranteed by the FOURTEENTH AMENDMENT to women as citizens, the necessity for a state or federal constitutional amendment became apparent.

The struggle for women's rights was a response to various forces. Urbanization, industrialization, declining birth rates, and expanding educational and employment opportunities tended to diminish women's role in the private domestic sphere while encouraging their participation in the public sphere. So too, women's involvement, first with abolitionism and later with other progressive causes, generated political commitments and experiences that fueled demands for equal rights.

Those demands provoked opposition from various quarters. The liquor industry feared that enfranchisement would pave the way for PROHIBITION, while conservative political and religious leaders, as well as women homemakers, painted suffrage as an invitation to socialism, anarchism, free love, and domestic discord. Partly in response to those claims, many leading suffragists became increasingly conservative in their arguments and increasingly unwilling to address other causes and consequences of women's inequality. That strategy met with partial success.

As they narrowed their social agenda, women's rights organizations expanded their political appeal. The growing strength of the suffrage movement, together with women's efforts in World War I, finally helped prompt the United States to join the slowly increasing number of Western nations that had granted enfranchisement.

Yet to many leading women's rights activists, the American victory proved scarcely less demoralizing than defeat. The focus on enfranchisement had to some extent deflected attention from other issues of critical importance for women, such as poverty, working conditions, birth control, health care, and domestic relations. Without a unifying social agenda beyond the ballot, the postsuffrage feminist movement foundered, splintered, and for the next half century, largely dissolved. During that period, women did not vote as a block on women's issues, support women candidates, or, with few exceptions, agitate for women's rights. Despite their numerical strength and access to the ballot, women remained subject to a vast range of discrimination in employment, education, WELFARE BENEFITS, credit standards, family law, and related areas. Although the Nineteenth Amendment itself was urged as a ground for qualifying women to serve on juries, most courts rejected this argument except where jury service was tied to voter status.

Yet however limited its immediate affects, the Nineteenth Amendment marked a significant advance toward equal rights. Enfranchisement was a necessary if not sufficient condition for women to exercise significant political leverage. Moreover, the skills, experience, and self-esteem that women gained during the suffrage campaign helped lay the foundation for a more egalitarian social order.

Bibliography

CATT, CARRIE CHAPMAN and SHULER, NETTIE ROGERS 1970  *Woman Suffrage and Politics.* New York: Americana Library Edition.

STANTON, ELIZABETH CADY; ANTHONY, SUSAN B., GAGE, MATILDA JOSLYN; and HARPER, IDA H., eds.  1881–1922  *History of Woman Suffrage.* New York: Fowler & Wells.

# SEX DISCRIMINATION

## Ruth Bader Ginsburg

The application of constitutional principle to government action that distinguishes on the basis of sex is a late-twentieth-century development. From the 1860s until 1971, the record remained unbroken: the Supreme Court rejected every effort to overturn sex lines in the law. Equalizing the rights, responsibilities, and opportunities of men and women was not considered a judicial task; without offense to the Constitution, women could be kept off juries and barred from occupations ranging from law to bartending. Women could also be "protected" from long hours, night work, and hazardous jobs, as in MULLER V. OREGON (1908), but protection of this order limited women's opportunities and relied upon the notion that a woman "looks to her brother and depends upon him."

The Court explained its position in *Fay v. New York* (1947). The NINETEENTH AMENDMENT's ratification in 1920 gave women the vote, but only that; in other respects, the Constitution remained an empty cupboard for sex equality claims. Nearly a decade and a half later, in *Hoyt v. Florida* (1961), a unanimous bench reaffirmed the traditional view. The Court held that a volunteers-only system for females serving on juries encountered no constitutional shoal; it was rational to spare women from the obligation to serve in recognition of their place at the "center of home and family life."

Pervasive social changes following World War II undermined the *Hoyt* assumptions. That period saw unprecedented growth in women's employment outside the home, a revived feminist movement, changing marriage patterns, and a decline in necessary home-centered activity. Expansion of the economy's service sector opened places for women in traditional as well as new occupations. Curtailed population goals, facilitated by more effective means of controlling reproduction, and extended lifespans counted as well among important ingredients in this social dynamic. These last two developments created a setting in which the typical woman, for the first time, was experiencing most of her adult years in a household not dominated by child care requirements. Columbia economics professor Eli Ginzberg appraised the sum of these changes as "the single most outstanding phenomenon of our century." The BURGER COURT, not noted for its activism in other areas, responded.

Through the 1960s, the Supreme Court had explained its EQUAL PROTECTION rulings in terms of a two-tier model. Generally, challenged legislation was ranked at the lower tier and survived judicial inspection if rationally related to a permissible government objective. Exceptional cases, ranged on the upper tier, involved FUNDAMENTAL RIGHTS (voting is a prime example) or SUSPECT CLASSIFICATIONS (race is a paradigm). Review in these exceptional cases was rigorous. To survive inspection, the legislative objective had to be compelling, and the classification, necessary to its accomplishment. (See STRICT SCRUTINY; COMPELLING STATE INTEREST.)

Equal protection adjudication in gender discrimination cases prompted "in between" standards. As the 1970s wore on, the STANDARD OF REVIEW for sex-based classification inched up toward the higher tier. The process commenced with *Reed v. Reed* (1971). A unanimous Court held that an Idaho estate administration statute, giving men preference over similarly situated women, denied would-be administrator Sally Reed the equal protection of the laws. *Reed* attracted headlines; it marked the first solid break from the Supreme Court's consistent affirmation of government authority to classify by sex. The terse *Reed* opinion acknowledged no departure from precedent, but Court-watchers recognized something new was in the wind.

Less than a year and a half after the laconic *Reed* decision, the Court came within one vote of declaring sex a "suspect" category. In FRONTIERO V. RICHARDSON (1973) the Justices held 8–1 that married women in the uniformed services were entitled to the same fringe benefits as married men. Under the laws declared unconstitutional, men received a housing allowance and health care for their civilian wives automatically; women received these family benefits only if they supplied over three-fourths of the couple's support.

Four of the Justices ranked sex a suspect classification. Justice LEWIS F. POWELL, concurring, articulated a prime reservation of the remaining five Justices: our eighteenth- and nineteenth-century Constitution-makers had evidenced no concern at all about the equality of men and women before the law. The Court must tread lightly, Justice Powell cautioned, when it enters the gray zone between CONSTITUTIONAL INTERPRETATION, a proper judicial task, and constitutional amendment, a job for the people's elected representatives.

No fifth vote has emerged for explicit placement of sex at the top tier of equal protection analysis, although the Court has repeatedly acknowledged that it applies a standard considerably more exacting than the lower tier RATIONAL BASIS test. If a classification based upon gender is to withstand constitutional challenge, the defender of the sex criterion must establish what the Court in *Kirchberg v. Feenstra* (1981) called "exceedingly persuasive justification"; the sex-based distinction will be condemned unless it "substantially furthers an important government interest." In MISSISSIPPI UNIVERSITY FOR WOMEN V. HOGAN (1982) the Court noted that it was unnecessary to "decide whether classifications based upon gender are inherently suspect," for the classification challenged there could not survive even intermediate tier scrutiny. If the Court continues to review categorization by gender with the rigor displayed in many of its 1973–1982 decisions, however, the "suspect" seal may eventually be placed on accumulated precedent.

Despite the absence of a majority opinion, the 8–1 *Frontiero* JUDG-MENT was a notable way-paver for challenges to statutes that openly disadvantage or denigrate women. First, the Court did not invalidate the flawed legislation; it repaired it. Congress provided benefits for the military man's family; the Court, in effect, extended the same benefits to families in which the service member was female. Second, in contrast to the statute that figured in *Reed* —a nineteenth-century hangover repealed prospectively months before the Court heard Sally Reed's appeal—post–World War II legislation was at issue in *Frontiero*. Most significantly, *Frontiero* invalidated the type of gender line found most frequently in federal and state legislation. Wives were deemed dependent regardless of their own economic circumstances. Husbands were ranked independent unless they contributed less than one-fourth of the couple's support. In disallowing resort to this particular stereotype the Court set the stage for its subsequent disallowance of similar stereotypes in other settings.

Since *Frontiero,* with few exceptions, the Court has regularly overturned legislation explicitly invoking a male/female criterion and perceived by the Justices as denigrating women. A Utah statute that required a parent to support a son until age twenty-one but a daughter only until eighteen was struck down in *Stanton v. Stanton* (1975). Using DUE PROCESS analysis, the Court invalidated laws excluding all women from jury duty save those who volunteered (TAYLOR V. LOUISIANA, 1975) or chose not to opt out (*Duren v. Missouri,* 1979). In *Kirchberg v. Feenstra* (1981) a unanimous bench condemned Louisiana's "head and master" law, which gave the husband alone a unilateral right to dispose of property jointly owned with his wife.

Even a noncontributory welfare program—the type of governmental largess generally left untouched by the judiciary—has been revised by Court decree to eliminate the law's discrimination against women. Congress had provided for public assistance benefits to families where dependent children had been deprived of parental support because of the father's unemployment; no benefits were allowed when mother, rather than father, qualified as the unemployed parent. "Congress may not legislate 'one step at a time' when that step is drawn along the line of gender, and the consequence is to exclude one group of families [those in which the female spouse is a wage earner] altogether from badly needed subsistence benefits," Justice HARRY BLACKMUN concluded for a Court unanimous on the constitutional issue in CALIFANO V. WESTCOTT

(1979). Although the Justices divided 5–4 on the appropriate remedy (the majority extending the benefit to families of unemployed mothers, the dissenters preferring to invalidate the entire program), all subscribed solidly to the equal protection ruling.

In 1837 Sarah Grimke made this plea: "I ask no favors for my sex, I surrender not our claim to equality. All I ask of our brethren, is that they . . . take their feet . . . off our necks. . . ." Does the equal protection principle operate with the same bite when men rather than women are the victims of explicit gender-based discrimination? Constitutional doctrine after *Reed* has evolved, with some insecurity, through three stages. In the first, statutes ostensibly favoring women were upheld if they were seen as "compensatory," even if that rationalization was entirely post hoc. Then the Court recognized more consistently that gender-based classifications rooted in "romantic paternalism" reinforce stereotypes and perpetuate anachronistic social assumptions that confine women's opportunities. In the third stage, the Court attempted a reconciliation of these two strands of doctrine: a classification that favors women can survive an equal protection attack, but only if it reflects a conscious legislative choice to compensate for past, gender-based inequities.

In two first-stage decisions the Court upheld laws that appeared to favor women. *Kahn v. Shevin* (1974) involved a $15-per-year state property tax saving for widows (along with the blind and the totally disabled) but not widowers. The classification, as the Court appraised it, was genuinely "benign"—it helped some women and harmed none. Following on the heels of *Kahn,* the Court ruled, in *Schlesinger v. Ballard* (1975), that it was not a denial of equal protection to hold a male naval officer to a strict "up or out" (promotion or discharge) system, while guaranteeing a female officer thirteen years of duty before mandatory discharge for lack of promotion.

*Kahn* and *Ballard* were greeted by some in a Panglossian manner. The decisions could be viewed as offering women the best of both worlds—a High Court ready to strike down classifications that discriminate against females, yet vigilant to preserve laws that prefer or favor them. But this analysis was uncritically optimistic. The classification attacked in *Kahn* was barely distinguishable from other products of paternalistic legislators who had regarded the husband more as his wife's guardian than as her peer. And in *Ballard,* neither contender challenged the anterior discrimination that accounted, in large measure, for the navy's promoting men more rapidly than women—the drastically curtailed opportunities and assignments available to navy women.

Sex as a proxy for need, or as an indicator of past discrimination in the marital unit, is a criterion too gross to survive vigorous equal protection scrutiny. The Court eventually demonstrated its appreciation that discrimination by gender generally cuts with two edges, and is seldom, if ever, a pure favor to women. A young widower whose wage-earning wife had died giving birth to the couple's son brought suit in *Weinberger v. Wiesenfeld* (1975). The unanimous Court declared unconstitutional the SOCIAL SECURITY ACT's provision of a mother's benefit for the caretaker of a deceased wage-earner's child. As in *Frontiero,* the remedy was extension of the benefit in question to the entire class of similarly situated individuals, males as well as females. In effect, the *Wiesenfeld* judgment substitutes functional description (sole surviving parent) for the gender classification (widowed mother) employed in the statute.

The government had urged that the sex differential in *Wiesenfeld* operated "to offset the adverse economic situation of women." But the Court read the legislative history closely and rejected "the mere recitation of a benign, compensatory purpose" as a hindsight apology for laws in fact based on twin assumptions: that man's primary place is at work, woman's at home; and that a gainfully employed woman is a secondary breadwinner whose employment is less crucial to her family than her husband's.

*Wiesenfeld's* focus on actual legislative purpose set a penetrating standard for sex classifications defended as "benign" or "compensatory." Gender classifications superficially favoring women and affecting interests ranging from the purchase of beer to attendance at a nursing school have accordingly been struck down.

CRAIG V. BOREN (1976) held unconstitutional an Oklahoma law allowing young women to purchase 3.2 percent beer at age eighteen, but requiring young men to wait until age twenty-one. *Orr v. Orr* (1979) declared violative of equal protection a statute that required husbands, but never wives, to pay alimony. CALIFANO V. GOLDFARB (1977) rejected social security classifications qualifying a widow for survivor's benefits automatically, a widower only upon proof that his wife supplied three-fourths of the couple's support.

The 4–1–4 judgment in *Goldfarb,* in contrast to the *Wiesenfeld* decision on which *Goldfarb* built, was a cliffhanger. The PLURALITY OPINION concentrated on discrimination against women as breadwinners. Justice JOHN PAUL STEVENS, who cast the swing vote in favor of widower Goldfarb, focused on the discrimination against the surviving male spouse. Why this discrimination against a class of men? Like the plurality, Justice Stevens refused to accept the government's hindsight compensatory justification for the scheme. Congress, the record suggested, had ordered different treatment for widows and widowers out of longstanding "habit"; the discrimination encountered by widower Goldfarb was "merely the accidental by-product of [the legislators'] traditional way of thinking about females." Four members of the Court, in dissent, repeated a long rehearsed argument: the sex-based classification accurately reflects the station in life of most women, it operates benignly in women's favor, and it is administratively convenient. In 1980, however, the Court adhered to *Goldfarb* with a clearer (8–1) majority, in WENGLER V. DRUGGISTS MUTUAL INSURANCE CO.

The most emphatic reaffirmation of *Wiesenfeld*'s skeptical view of benign gender-based classification came in 1982, one day after expiration of the extended deadline for ratification of the proposed EQUAL RIGHTS AMENDMENT. The Court decided, 5–4, in *Mississippi University for Women v. Hogan*, that Mississippi's single-sex admissions policy for a nursing school failed to meet the heightened standard of review. Justice SANDRA DAY O'CONNOR, who, a century earlier under BRADWELL V. ILLINOIS (1873), could have been barred from practicing law without offense to the Constitution, wrote the majority opinion.

Challengers in most of the cases just surveyed contended against gross assumptions that females are (and should be) concerned primarily with "the home and the rearing of the family," males with "the marketplace and the world of ideas" (*Stanton v. Stanton*, 1975). The complainants did not assail the accuracy of these assumptions as generalizations. Rather, they questioned each law's erroneous treatment of men and women who did not fit the stereotype, and the fairness of gender pigeonholing in lieu of neutral, functional description. The traditional legislative slotting, they argued, amounted to self-fulfilling prophecy. A Court that in 1948, in GOESAERT V. CLEARY, had declared "beyond question" the constitutionality of legislation "drawing a sharp line between the sexes," was receptive in the 1970s to argument to which it would not "give ear" a generation earlier.

The Court has left a narrow passage open, however, for compensatory legislation that does not rest on traditional role-typing. In *Califano v. Webster* (1977) the Court distinguished from habitual categorization by sex a law designed, at least in part, to ameliorate disadvantages women experienced. A social security benefit calculation, effective from 1956 to 1972, established a more favorable formula for retired female workers than for retired male workers. The legislative history indicated that this scheme, unlike those in *Wiesenfeld* and *Goldfarb*, had been conceived in light of the discrimination commonly encountered by gainfully employed women, specifically, depressed wages for "women's work" and the early retirement that employers routinely forced on women but not on men. While tilting toward a general rule of equal treatment, the *Webster* PER CURIAM opinion approves genuinely compensatory classifications that are adopted for remedial reasons rather than out of prejudice about "the way women are," and are trimly tailored in scope and time to match the remedial end.

Neutrally phrased laws that disproportionately affect one sex have not attracted the heightened scrutiny generally accorded explicit gender-based classifications that serve as a proxy for a characteristic or condition susceptible of individual testing. Citing RACIAL DISCRIMINATION precedent, the Court has held that facially neutral classifications that disproportionately affect members of one sex are not necessarily sex-based. The Court has not yet considered in a constitutional setting whether official lines may be drawn based on actuarial differences, but statutory precedent indicates the answer will be "no."

"[G]ood intent or absence of discriminatory intent" does not immunize an employment practice from the equal opportunity requirement of Title VII of the CIVIL RIGHTS ACT OF 1964, which now covers both public and private employment. GRIGGS V. DUKE POWER CO., a notable 1971 Title VII race discrimination decision, so held. But in WASHINGTON V. DAVIS (1976) the Court held the *Griggs* principle inapplicable to race discrimination claims invoking the Constitution rather than Title VII. PERSONNEL ADMINISTRATOR OF MASSACHUSETTS V. FEENEY (1979) expanded the *Washington v. Davis* reasoning. *Feeney* involved an assault on exorbitant veterans' preferences in civil service as impermissibly gender-biased. Helen Feeney challenged the nation's most extreme veterans' preference—an absolute lifetime preference Massachusetts accorded veterans in a range of civil service positions. The preference had "a devastating impact upon the employment opportunities of women"; it operated to reserve top jobs for a class almost exclusively male. The purpose? Purely to aid veterans, surely not to harm women, Massachusetts (and the United States, AMICUS CURIAE) maintained. Of course, to become a veteran one must be allowed to serve her country, and the military had maintained highly restrictive quotas and more exacting qualification standards for females. When litigation in *Feeney* commenced, over ninety-eight percent of Massachusetts veterans were male.

Feeney sought accommodation of the conflicting interests—aiding veterans and opening to women civil service employment beyond the "pink-collar" ghetto. The typical "points-added" preference, she said, was not at issue, only the extreme arrangement Massachusetts had legislated, which placed a veteran with a minimum passing grade ahead of a woman with a perfect score, and did so for each promotion as well as for initial hiring. A preference so large, she argued, took too much from Pauline to pay Paul.

The Court rejected the proffered distinction between moderate and exorbitant preferences. The "discriminatory purpose" hurdle could not be surmounted absent proof that the Massachusetts preference "was originally devised or subsequently re-enacted because it would accomplish the collateral goal of keeping women in a stereotypic and predefined place in the Massachusetts Civil Service." The lawmaker must *want,* not merely anticipate, the consequences. Alone, disparate impact on one sex, however "devastating" and "inevitable," does not violate equal protection.

The discriminatory purpose requirement, as elaborated in *Feeney*, leaves a slack rein for legislative choices with foreseeable but undesigned adverse effects on one of the sexes. Suppose, for example, that the social security payments at issue in *Wiesenfeld* or *Goldfarb* had turned not on sex but on the deceased wage-earner's status as the family's principal breadwinner. In most families, husbands would fit that neutrally phrased description, wives would not. May Congress, without violating equal protection, resort to a "principal breadwinner" standard in social welfare legislation in the interest of fiscal economy? Would use of a "principal breadwinner" criterion survive constitutional review as a measure enacted "in spite of," rather than "because of" its practical effect— its reduction of the value to the family of the wife's earnings? The only, uncertain, guide is an obiter dictum from *Feeney*, in which the Court accepted that "covert" sex classifications, ostensibly neutral but in fact a pretext for sex-based discrimination, are vulnerable to equal protection attack.

Can actuarial differences, for example, in life expectancies, health records, or accident experiences, provide constitutionally valid grounds in any context for gender-based categorizations? Sex averaging has not fared well in post-1970 constitutional litigation. Thus, *Reed v. Reed* and *Frontiero v. Richardson* rejected as a basis for government action the generalization that "men [are] as a rule more conversant with business affairs than women"; *Craig v. Boren,* the fact that more 18–20-year-old males than females drink and drive; *Orr v. Orr* (1979), the reality that wives far more often than husbands "need" alimony. Legislation resting on characteristics, attributes, habits, or proclivities of the "typical man" or "typical woman" have been rejected for two reasons: they reinforce traditional restrictive conceptions of the social roles of men and women; and they burden members of one sex by employing gender as a proxy for a characteristic susceptible to individual testing or at least capable of sex-neutral description. But actuarial tables, their defenders point out, are used in situations in which individual testing is not feasible. The Court has not yet explicitly confronted actuarial tables in a constitutional context, but a Title VII decision may indicate the position the Court will take in an equal protection challenge to government action.

*Los Angeles Department of Water and Power v. Manhart* (1978) raised the question whether women could be required to pay more currently in order to receive monthly benefits on retirement equal to those received by men. The majority held the two-tier charges inconsistent with Title VII's prohibition of sex-based classification. All recognized in *Manhart* that the statement, "on the average, women live longer than men," is accurate, and that an individual's lifespan generally cannot be forecast with precision. But the majority refused to countenance a break from the general Title VII rule against sex averaging. Unquestionably, for pension purposes, women destined to die young are burdened by placement in an all-female class, and men destined to live long are benefited by placement in an all-male class. Moreover, Justice Stevens suggested for the majority, the group insurance context may not be an ideal setting for urging a distinction other than age: "To insure the flabby and the fit as though they were equivalent risks may be more common than treating men and women alike; but nothing more than habit makes one 'subsidy' seem less fair than the other." The Court adhered to *Manhart,* when invited to reconsider, or contain the holding, in *Arizona Governing Committee v. Norris* (1983).

Are women to have the opportunity to participate in full partnership with men in the nation's social, political, and economic life? Kenneth L. Karst has identified this overarching question, in its constitutional dimension, as one ripe for synthesis in the final quarter of the twentieth century. The synthesis envisioned would place within an encompassing sex equality framework cases involving explicit male/female classification as well as cases on REPRODUCTIVE AUTONOMY and pregnancy-linked regulation. That synthesis, however, may well depend on the clarity of directions from the political arena. The Court has treated reproductive choice cases under a "personal autonomy," not a "sex equality" rubric, and it has resisted argument that separate classification of pregnant women is sex-based.

In a bold 1973 ruling, ROE V. WADE, the Court struck down an anti-abortion law as unwarranted state intrusion into the decision of a woman and her doctor to terminate a pregnancy. *Roe v. Wade* has been typed aberrational—an extraordinarily activist decision issued from a bench reputedly deferential to legislative judgments. It bears emphasis, however, that the Court bypassed an equal protection argument presented for the female plaintiffs. Rather, the Court anchored stringent review to a concept of personal autonomy derived from the due process guarantee. Two decisions, particularly, had paved the way: GRISWOLD V. CONNECTICUT (1965), which held inconsistent with due process Connecticut's ban on use of contraceptives even by married couples, and EISENSTADT V. BAIRD (1972), which extended *Griswold* to strike down Massachusetts' prohibition on sales of contraceptives except to married persons by prescription.

Some speculated that *Roe v. Wade* and a companion 1973 decision, *Doe v. Bolton,* were motivated, at least in part, by concerns about unwanted children born into impoverished families. But in MAHER V. ROE (1977) the Court indicated that such speculations had been mistaken. The Court declined to extend the 1973 rulings to require state support for an indigent woman's elective abortion.

The impoverished women, on whose behalf constitutional claims to public assistance for abortion were pursued, relied primarily on the equal protection principle. They maintained that, so long as government subsidized childbirth, it could not withhold subsidy for abortion, a far less expensive, and, at least in the first trimester, less risky procedure. If government pays for childbirth but not abortion, then, the *Maher* plaintiffs argued, government intrudes upon a choice *Roe v. Wade* said the state must leave to doctor and patient. The Court, however, distinguished government prohibition from government support. Though the state could not bar access to a woman able to pay for an abortion, it was not required to buy an admission ticket for the poor woman. Rather, government could pursue a policy of encouraging childbirth (even if that policy would affect only the poor) by refusing Medicaid reimbursement for nontherapeutic abortions and by banning such abortions in public hospitals. Though widely criticized in the reproductive-choice context, the distinction between government stick and government carrot had been made in other settings to which the Court referred in its 1977 ruling.

The *Maher* logic was carried further in HARRIS v. McRAE (1980). The federal law at issue excluded even medically needed abortions from a medical benefits program. In holding, 5–4, that this exclusion violated neither the due process nor the equal protection clause, the Court reiterated the distinction drawn in *Maher:* though the government may not proscribe abortion, it need not act affirmatively to assure a poor woman's access to the procedure.

Following after the intrepid 1973 abortion decisions, the later public-funding-of-abortion rulings appear incongruous. The *Roe v. Wade* decision was not easy to reach or explain. Social and economic conditions that seem irreversible, however, suggest that the ruling made by the Court in 1973 will remain with us in the long run, while the later dispositions may eventually succumb to a different legislative view of state and national policy, and of the centrality of choice with respect to childbearing to a woman's control of her life's course.

When does disadvantageous treatment of pregnant workers operate to discriminate on the basis of sex? High Court decisions on that question display less than perfect logic and consistency.

School teachers may not be dismissed or placed on forced leave arbitrarily at a fixed stage in pregnancy well in advance of term. Such a rule conflicts with due process, the Court ruled in CLEVELAND BOARD OF EDUCATION v. LAFLEUR (1974). Similarly invoking due process, the Court held in *Turner v. Department of Employment Security* (1975) that pregnant women willing and able to work may not be denied unemployment compensation when jobs are closed to them. It is unlawful under Title VII, as interpreted by the Court in *Nashville Gas Co. v. Satty* (1977), for an employer to deprive women disabled by pregnancy of accumulated job-bidding seniority when they return to work.

But *Geduldig v. Aiello* (1974) held that a state-operated disability income protection plan could exclude pregnancy without offense to the equal protection principle. And in an analogous Title VII case, *General Electric Company v. Gilbert* (1976), the Court held that a private employer's exclusion of pregnant women from disability coverage did not discriminate on the basis of sex because all "nonpregnant persons," women along with men, were treated alike.

Lawyers may attempt to square the apparently contradictory constitutional decisions by referring to the different principles employed in the Court's analyses—equal protection in *Aiello,* due process in both *LaFleur* and *Turner.* But the particular due process theory of IRREBUTTABLE PRESUMPTIONS the Court pressed into service in *LaFleur* has lost favor with the Justices in other contexts. A factor not fully acknowledged in the written opinions, and based more on the Justices' experience than on legal analysis, may account for the divergent responses. Perhaps the able pregnant woman seeking only to do a day's work for a day's pay, or the woman seeking to return to her job relatively soon after childbirth, is a credible figure to the Court, while the woman who asserts she is disabled by pregnancy is viewed with suspicion. Is she really incapacitated physically or is she malingering so that she may stay "where she belongs"—at home tending baby?

With respect to Title VII, Congress in 1978 simplified the judicial task by prospectively overruling *General Electric.* It amended the statute to say explicitly that classification on the basis of sex includes classification on the basis of pregnancy. The Court gave the amended statute a cordial reception in *Newport News Shipbuilding of Drydock Co. v. EEOC* (1983). The congressional definition placed in Title VII is not controlling in constitutional adjudication, but the Court may be stimulated by the legislature's action to revise its view, expressed in *Aiello* and *General Electric,* that singling out "pregnant persons" is not a sex-based action. Coming full circle, there will be pressure on the Court not simply to check regulation disadvantageous to pregnant women but to uphold new-style protective legislation—for example, laws requiring employers to grant to pregnant women a voluntary leave period not accorded others with temporarily disabling physical conditions.

In what areas does the Constitution allow explicit male/female classification? A few idiosyncratic problems survive.

According to current doctrine, the Constitution affords some leeway for discrimination with respect to parental rights and relationships, at least when children are born out of wedlock. A unanimous Court held in *Quilloin v. Walcott* (1978) that an unwed father who "has never exercised actual or legal custody over his child" has no constitutional right to block adoption approved by the mother. (In contrast, the Court held in *Caban v. Mohammed* [1979] that a state statute discriminated on the basis of sex in violation of equal protection when it permitted adoption of a child born out of wedlock solely on the mother's consent, even when the father's parental relationship with the child was substantial.) And according to *Parham v. Hughes* (1979) a state may condition an unwed father's (but not an unwed mother's) right to recover for wrongful death upon his legitimation of his child by court order. The main theme of the *Parham* opinion had been sounded earlier: women and men were not similarly situated for the purpose at hand—maternity is rarely in doubt, but proof of paternity is often difficult. Hence, as the Court held in LALLI v. LALLI (1978), the state may erect safeguards against spurious filiation claims. Those safeguards may be applied even when, as in *Parham,* father and child had a close and constant relationship.

MICHAEL M. v. SUPERIOR COURT (1981) upheld, 5–4, California's "statutory rape" law, under which a male who engages in sexual intercourse with an underage female commits a crime; a female who engages in sexual intercourse with an underage male does not. Both participants in the act that precipitated the prosecution in *Michael M.* were underage.

There was no majority opinion in *Michael M.* Justice WILLIAM H. REHNQUIST wrote for the Court's plurality. He postulated as the statute's purpose, as California had argued, the prevention of teenage pregnancy, and reasoned that males and females were not similarly situated in this setting. Nature inhibited the female, for she would suffer the consequences. The law could legitimately take into account this fact of life by punishing the male, who lacked a biological deterrent. Moreover, the plurality found persuasive California's further contention that sparing the female from criminal liability might encourage her to report the unlawful activity.

Given the ancient roots of the California law, Justice WILLIAM J. BRENNAN pointed out in dissent, it was plain that the sex classification "was initially designed to further . . . outmoded sexual stereotypes" (young women are not capable of consenting to an act of sexual intercourse, young men can make such decisions for themselves). For Justice Stevens, who dissented separately, the critical question in *Michael M.* was whether "the sovereign . . . govern[s] impartially" under a statute that authorizes punishment of the male, but not the female, even "when they are equally responsible" for the disfavored conduct, indeed even "when the female is the more responsible of the two." The answer, it seemed to Justice Stevens, was clearly "no."

Although by 1980 many states had amended all of their sex crime laws to render them equally applicable to males and females, *Michael M.* touched a sensitive nerve. In view of the 4–1–4 division, the decision may well remain an isolated instance.

ROSTKER v. GOLDBERG (1981) presented the politically loaded question whether Congress could confine draft registration to males. Congress had thought about the matter and decided it in 1980. It considered, on the administration's recommendation, authorizing the President to require registration by both sexes. But it decided on registration for males only. The Court's 6–3 decision upheld the sex classification. The opinion, written by Justice Rehnquist, underlined the special deference due congressional judgments in the areas of national defense and military affairs.

The *Rostker* opinion asserted that men and women were not similarly situated for the purpose at hand because women were excluded from combat service, an exclusion "Congress specifically recognized and endorsed . . . in exempting women from registration." Reminiscent of *Schlesinger v. Ballard,* where no party challenged the dissimilar promotion opportunities for male and female naval officers, no party challenged the combat exclusion in *Rostker.* Even so, the executive branch had estimated that in the event of a major mobilization there would be a substantial number of noncombat positions in the armed services that conscripted women could fill. Against this backdrop *Rostker* may be explained as a WAR POWERS case, unlikely to have a significant influence in future sex discrimination cases.

Constitutional doctrine relating to gender discrimination, although still evolving, and variously interpreted, is nonetheless a remarkable judicial development. In contrast to race discrimination, an area in which constitutional interpretation is tied to amendments drawn with a view to the eradication of the legacy of black slavery, gender discrimination was not a concern to which the Reconstruction Congress (or the Founding Fathers) adverted. Nonetheless, the Court, since 1970, has creatively interpreted clauses of the Constitution (equal protection and, less securely, due process) to accommodate a modern vision of sexual equality in employment, in access to social benefits, in most civic duties, in reproductive autonomy. Such interpretation has limits, but sensibly approached, it is consistent with the grand design of the Constitution-makers to write a charter that would endure as the nation's fundamental instrument of government.

Bibliography

BABCOCK, BARBARA A.; FREEDMAN, ANN E.; NORTON, ELEANOR H.; and ROSS, SUSAN C.  1974  *Sex Discrimination: Causes and Remedies* (Wendy Williams, Supplement 1978). Boston: Little, Brown.

GINSBURG, RUTH BADER    1978    Sex Equality and the Constitution. *Tulane Law Review* 52:451–475.

_____ 1979    Sexual Equality under the Fourteenth and the Equal Rights Amendments. *Washington University Law Quarterly* 1979:161–178.

_____ 1983    The Burger Court's Grapplings with Sex Discrimination. In V. Blasi, ed. *The Burger Court: The Counter-Revolution That Wasn't.* Pages 132–156. New Haven, Conn.: Yale University Press.

GUNTHER, GERALD    1972    Foreword: In Search of Evolving Doctrine on a Changing Court: A Model for a Newer Equal Protection. *Harvard Law Review* 86:1–48.

KANOWITZ, LEO    1981    *Equal Rights: The Male Stake.* Albuquerque: University of New Mexico Press.

_____ 1969    *Women and the Law.* Albuquerque: University of New Mexico Press.

KARST, KENNETH L.    1976    Book Review. *Harvard Law Review* 89:1028–1036.

_____ 1977    Foreword, Equal Citizenship under the Fourteenth Amendment. *Harvard Law Review* 91:1–68.

_____ 1984    Woman's Constitution. *Duke Law Journal* 1984:447–508.

KAY, HERMA H.    (1974)1981    *Sex-Based Discrimination,* 2nd ed. St. Paul: West Publishing Co.

_____ 1985    Models of Equality. *University of Illinois Law Review* 1985:39–88.

LAW, SYLVIA    1984    Rethinking Sex and the Constitution. *University of Pennsylvania Law Review* 132:955–1040.

TRIBE, LAURENCE H.    1978    *American Constitutional Law.* Pages 1060–1077. Mineola, N.Y.: Foundation Press.

WASSERSTROM, RICHARD A.    1977    Racism, Sexism, and Preferential Treatment: An Approach to the Topics. *UCLA Law Review* 24:581–622.

# CRAIG v. BOREN

## 429 U.S. 190 (1976)

### Kenneth L. Karst

It is ironic that the leading modern decision setting the STANDARD OF REVIEW for claims of SEX DISCRIMINATION involved discrimination against men, concerning an interest of supreme triviality. Oklahoma allowed women to buy 3.2 percent beer upon reaching the age of eighteen; men, however, had to be twenty-one. A young male would-be buyer and a female beer seller challenged the law's validity. The young man became twenty-one before the Supreme Court's decision; his challenge was thus rejected for MOOTNESS. The Court held that the seller had STANDING to raise the young man's constitutional claims, and further held, 8–1, that the law denied EQUAL PROTECTION OF THE LAWS. Justice WILLIAM H. REHNQUIST dissented.

Speaking through Justice WILLIAM J. BRENNAN, the Court held that classifications based on gender were invalid unless they served "important governmental objectives" and were "substantially related to achievement of those objectives." This intermediate standard was a compromise between the two views of the majority in FRONTIERO V. RICHARDSON (1973) as to the level of judicial scrutiny of both legislative objectives and legislative means. Under the RATIONAL BASIS standard of review, the objective need be only legitimate, and the means (in equal protection language, the classification) only rationally related to its achievement. At the opposite end of the continuum of standards of review, STRICT SCRUTINY demands a legislative objective that is a COMPELLING STATE INTEREST, and means that are necessary to achieving that objective. The *Craig* standard appears to have been deliberately designed to fall between these two levels of judicial scrutiny of legislation.

In the years since *Craig,* the Supreme Court has often invalidated classifications based on sex but typically has not challenged the importance of legislative objectives. Instead, the Court generally holds that a sex classification is not "substantially related" to a legislative goal. In *Craig* itself, the Court admitted that traffic safety, the state's objective, was important, but said maleness was an inappropriate "proxy for drinking and driving."

Justice JOHN PAUL STEVENS, concurring, doubted the utility of multitiered levels of judicial scrutiny in equal protection cases, and commented that men, as a class, have not suffered "pervasive discrimination." The classification was objectionable, however, because it was "based on the accident of birth," and perpetuated "a stereotyped attitude" of young men and women. Because the state's traffic safety justification failed, the law was invalid.

# MICHAEL M. v. SUPERIOR COURT

## 450 U.S. 464 (1981)

### Kenneth L. Karst

A boy of 17½ was convicted of rape under a California statute making it a crime for a male to have intercourse with a female under 18; the girl's age was 16½. A fragmented Supreme Court voted 5–4 to uphold the conviction against the contention that the statute's SEX DISCRIMINATION—the same act was criminal for a male but not for a female—denied the EQUAL PROTECTION OF THE LAWS.

There was no opinion for the Court. The majority Justices, however, agreed in accepting the California Supreme Court's justification for the law: prevention of illegitimate teen-age pregnancies. The risk of pregnancy itself, said Justice WILLIAM H. REHNQUIST, served to deter young females from sexual encounters; criminal sanctions on young males only would roughly "equalize" deterrents.

The dissenters argued that California had not demonstrated its law to be a deterrent; thirty-seven states had adopted gender-neutral statutory rape laws, no doubt on the theory that such laws would provide even more deterrent, by doubling the number of persons subject to arrest. When both parties to an act are equally guilty, argued Justice JOHN PAUL STEVENS, to make the male guilty of a FELONY while allowing the female to go free is supported by little more than "traditional attitudes toward male–female relations."

# ROSTKER v. GOLDBERG

## 453 U.S. 57 (1981)

### Kenneth L. Karst

Men subject to registration for possible military CONSCRIPTION challenged the exclusion of women from the registration requirement as a denial of EQUAL PROTECTION. The Supreme Court, 6–3, rejected this claim. Justice WILLIAM H. REHNQUIST, for the majority, paid great deference to Congress's authority over military affairs; with the most minimal judicial second-guessing of the congressional judgment, he concluded that men and women were "not similarly situated," because any draft would be designed to produce combat troops, and women were ineligible for combat. SEX DISCRIMINATION, in other words, was its own justification.

As the dissenters demonstrated, the exclusion of women from draft registration had resulted from no military judgment at all; the President and the Joint Chiefs of Staff had urged that women be registered. Rather, Congress had heard the voice of public opinion. It is not impossible that the Court itself heard that voice. Thus do sex-role stereotypes perpetuate themselves.

# MISSISSIPPI UNIVERSITY FOR WOMEN v. HOGAN

## 458 U.S. 718 (1982)

### Kenneth L. Karst

Joe Hogan, a male registered nurse, was rejected by a state university's all-female school of nursing. A 5–4 Supreme Court held that Hogan's exclusion violated his right to EQUAL PROTECTION OF THE LAWS. For the majority, Justice SANDRA DAY O'CONNOR rejected the argument that, by excluding males, the university was compensating for discrimination against women. Rather, the all-female policy "tends to perpetuate the stereotyped view of nursing as an exclusively woman's job." The university thus failed the test set by CRAIG v. BOREN (1976) for SEX DISCRIMINATION cases. The dissenters, making a case for diversity of types of higher education, emphasized that Hogan could attend a coeducational state nursing school elsewhere in Mississippi.

# REPRODUCTIVE AUTONOMY

Ruth Bader Ginsburg

Commencing in 1942 in SKINNER V. OKLAHOMA, and most intrepidly in 1973 in ROE V. WADE, the Supreme Court has secured against unwarranted governmental intrusion a decision fundamental to the course of an individual's life—the decision whether to beget or bear a child. Government action in this area bears significantly on the ability of women, particularly, to plan and control their lives. Official policy on reproductive choice may effectively facilitate or retard women's opportunities to participate in full partnership with men in the nation's social, political, and economic life. Supreme Court decisions concerning BIRTH CONTROL, however, have not yet adverted to evolving sex equality-equal protection doctrine. Instead, high court opinions rest dominantly on SUBSTANTIVE DUE PROCESS analysis; they invoke basic liberty-autonomy values difficult to tie directly to the Constitution's text, history, or structure.

*Skinner* marked the first occasion on which the Court referred to an individual's procreative choice as "a basic liberty." The Court invalidated a state statute providing for compulsory STERILIZATION of habitual offenders. The statute applied after a third conviction for a FELONY "involving moral turpitude," defined to include grand larceny but exclude embezzlement. The decision ultimately rested on an EQUAL PROTECTION ground: "Sterilization of those who have thrice committed grand larceny, with immunity for those who are embezzlers, is a clear, pointed, unmistakable discrimination." Justice WILLIAM O. DOUGLAS's opinion for the Court, however, is infused with substantive due process tones: "We are dealing here with legislation which involves one of the basic CIVIL RIGHTS of man. Marriage and procreation are fundamental to the very existence and survival of the race." Gerald Gunther has noted that, in a period marked by a judicial hands-off approach to economic and social legislation, *Skinner* stood virtually alone in applying a stringent review standard favoring a "basic liberty" unconnected to a particular constitutional guarantee.

Over two decades later, in GRISWOLD V. CONNECTICUT (1965), the Court grappled with a state law banning the use of contraceptives. The Court condemned the statute's application to married persons. Justice Douglas's opinion for the Court located protected "zones of privacy" in the penumbras of several specific BILL OF RIGHTS guarantees. The law in question impermissibly intruded on the marriage relationship, a privacy zone "older than the Bill of Rights" and "intimate to the degree of being sacred."

In EISENSTADT V. BAIRD (1972) the Court confronted a Massachusetts law prohibiting the distribution of contraceptives, except by a registered pharmacist on a doctor's prescription to a married person. The Court avoided explicitly extending the right announced in *Griswold* beyond use to distribution. Writing for the majority, Justice WILLIAM J. BRENNAN rested the decision on an equal protection ground: "whatever the rights of the individual to access to contraceptives may be," the Court said, "the right must be the same for the unmarried and the married alike." *Eisenstadt* thus carried constitutional doctrine a considerable distance from "the sacred precincts of marital bedrooms" featured in *Griswold*.

The Court's reasoning in *Eisenstadt* did not imply that laws prohibiting fornication, because they treat married and unmarried persons dissimilarly, were in immediate jeopardy. Rather, Justice Brennan declined to attribute to Massachusetts the base purpose of "prescrib[ing] pregnancy and the birth of an unwanted child as punishment for fornication."

In 1977, in CAREY V. POPULATION SERVICES INTERNATIONAL, the Court invalidated a New York law prohibiting the sale of contraceptives to minors under age sixteen and forbidding commercial distribution of even nonprescription contraceptives by anyone other than a licensed pharmacist. Justice Brennan reinterpreted the pathmarking precedent. *Griswold,* he noted, addressed a "particularly 'repulsive' " intrusion, but "subsequent decisions have made clear that the constitutional protection of individual autonomy in matters of childbearing is not dependent on [the marital privacy] element." Accordingly, "*Griswold* may no longer be read as holding only that a State may not prohibit a married couple's use of contraceptives. Read in light of [*Eisenstadt* and *Roe v. Wade*], the teaching of *Griswold* is that the Constitution protects individual decisions in matters of childbearing from unjustified intrusion by the State."

*Roe v. Wade* declared that a woman, guided by the medical judgment of her physician, has a FUNDAMENTAL RIGHT to abort her pregnancy, a right subject to state interference only upon demonstration of a COMPELLING STATE INTEREST. The right so recognized, Justice HARRY L. BLACKMUN wrote for the Court, falls within the sphere of personal privacy recognized or suggested in prior decisions relating to marriage, procreation, contraception, family relationships, child-rearing and education. The "privacy" or individual autonomy right advanced in *Roe v. Wade* is not explicit in our fundamental instrument of government, Justice Blackmun acknowledged; however, the Court viewed it as "founded in the FOURTEENTH AMENDMENT's [and presumably the FIFTH AMENDMENT's] concept of personal liberty and restrictions upon state action." Justice

Blackmun mentioned, too, the district court's view, derived from Justice ARTHUR J. GOLDBERG's concurring opinion in *Griswold,* that the liberty at stake could be located in the NINTH AMENDMENT's reservation of rights to the people.

The Texas criminal abortion law at issue in ROE V. WADE was severely restrictive; it excepted from criminality "only a *lifesaving* procedure on behalf of the mother, without regard to pregnancy stage and without recognition of the other interests involved." In the several years immediately preceding the *Roe v. Wade* decision, the Court noted, the trend in the states had been "toward liberalization of abortion statutes." Nonetheless, the Court's rulings in *Roe v. Wade* and in a companion case decided the same day, *Doe v. Bolton* (1973), called into question the validity of the criminal abortion statutes of every state, even those with the least restrictive provisions.

The sweeping impact of the 1973 rulings on state laws resulted from the precision with which Justice Blackmun defined the state interests that the Court would recognize as compelling. In the first two trimesters of a pregnancy, the state's interest was confined to protecting the woman's health: during the first trimester, "the abortion decision and its effectuation must be left to the medical judgment of the pregnant woman's attending physician"; in the next three-month stage, the state may, if it chooses, require other measures protective of the woman's health. During "the stage subsequent to viability" (roughly, the third trimester), the state may protect the "potentiality of human life"; at that stage, the state "may, if it chooses, regulate, and even proscribe, abortion except where it is necessary, in appropriate medical judgment, for the preservation of the life or health of the mother."

Sylvia Law has commented that no Supreme Court decision has meant more to women. Wendy Williams has noted that a society intent on holding women in their traditional role would attempt to deny them reproductive autonomy. Justice Blackmun's opinion indicates sensitivity to the severe burdens, mental and physical, immediately carried by a woman unable to terminate an unwanted pregnancy, and the distressful life she and others in her household may suffer when she lacks the physical or psychological ability or financial resources necessary for child-rearing. But *Roe v. Wade* bypassed the equal protection argument presented for the female plaintiffs. Instead, the Court anchored stringent review to the personal autonomy concept found in *Griswold.* Moreover, *Roe v. Wade* did not declare an individual right; in the Court's words, the decision stated a joint right of "the woman and her responsible physician . . . in consultation."

The 1973 abortion rulings have been called aberrational, extraordinarily activist interventions by a Court reputedly deferential to STATES' RIGHTS and legislative judgments. John Hart Ely criticized *Roe v. Wade* as a decision the Court had no business making because freedom to have an abortion "lacks connection with any value the Constitution marks as special."

Archibald Cox described his own view of *Roe v. Wade* as "less rigid" then Ely's. He said in a 1975 lecture: "The Court's persistent resort to notions of substantive due process for almost a century attests the strength of our natural law inheritance in constitutional adjudication." Cox considered it "unwise as well as hopeless to resist" that strong tradition. *Roe v. Wade* nevertheless foundered, in his judgment, because the Court did not (and, he believed, could not) articulate an acceptable "precept of sufficient abstractness." The critical parts of the opinion, he commented, "read like a set of hospital rules and regulations."

Paul Freund expressed a similar concern in 1982. He thought *Roe v. Wade* epitomized a tendency of the modern Supreme Court (under Chief Justice WARREN E. BURGER as well as Chief Justice EARL WARREN) "to specify by a kind of legislative code the one alternative pattern which will satisfy the Constitution, foreclosing further experimentation by Congress or the states." In his view, "a law which absolutely made criminal all kinds and forms of abortion could not stand up; it is not a reasonable accommodation of interests." But the Court "adopted what could be called the medical point of view—making distinctions that turn on trimesters." The Court might have drawn other lines, Freund suggested; it might have adopted an ethical rather than a medical approach, for example, by immunizing abortions, in a manner resembling the American Law Institute proposal, "where the pregnancy was the result of rape or incest, where the fetus was severely abnormal, or where the mother's health, physical or mental, would be seriously impaired by bringing the fetus to term." (The Georgia statutes struck down in *Doe v. Bolton,* companion case to *Roe v. Wade,* were patterned on the American Law Institute's model.) If the Court had proceeded that way, Freund commented, perhaps "some of the bitter debate on the issue might . . . have been averted; at any rate the animus against the Court might have been diverted to the legislative halls."

Animus there has been, in the form of anti-abortion constitutional amendments introduced in Congress in 1973 and each session thereafter; proposals for "human life" legislation, in which Congress, upon the vote of a simple majority, would declare that the Fourteenth Amendment protects the life of "persons" from the moment of conception; and bills to strip the Supreme Court of JURISDICTION to decide abortion cases. State legislatures reacted as well, adopting measures aimed at minimizing the impact of the 1973 ruling, including notice and consent requirements, prescriptions for the protection of fetal life, and bans on public expenditures or access to public facilities for abortion.

Some speculated that the 7–2 judgments in the 1973 cases (Justices

BYRON R. WHITE and WILLIAM H. REHNQUIST dissented) were motivated in part by population concerns and the specter of unwanted children born to women living in grinding poverty. But in 1977, the Court voted 6–3 against pleas to extend the 1973 rulings to require public assistance for an indigent woman's elective (not medically necessary) abortion. First, in *Beal v. Doe,* the Court held that the federally established Medicaid program did not require Pennsylvania, as a condition of participation, to fund elective abortions. Second, in MAHER V. ROE the Court ruled that the equal protection clause did not command Connecticut, which furnished Medicaid funds for childbirth, to pay as well for elective abortions. Finally, *Poelker v. Doe* held that the city of St. Louis did not violate the equal protection clause by providing publicly financed hospital services for childbirth but not for elective abortions.

The impoverished Connecticut women who sought Medicaid assistance in *Maher* maintained that, so long as their state subsidized childbirth, it could not withhold subsidy for abortion, a far less expensive and, at least in the first trimester, less risky procedure. Stringent equal protection review was required, they urged, because the state had intruded on the "fundamental right" declared in *Roe v. Wade.* Justice LEWIS F. POWELL, writing for the Court, responded that the right recognized in *Roe* did not require government neutrality as to the abortion decision; it was not a right to make a choice unchecked by substantive government control. Rather, it was a right restraining government from obstructing a woman's access to private sources to effectuate her decision. Because the right *Roe v. Wade* secured, as explained in *Maher,* was not impinged upon (and because disadvantageous treatment of needy persons does not alone identify SUSPECT CLASSIFICATION requiring close scrutiny), Connecticut's funding refusal could be sustained if it related "rationally" to a "constitutionally permissible" purpose. The policies to encourage childbirth in preference to abortion and to protect potential life supported the *Maher* regulation. There was, in the Court's view, no issue here, as there had been in *Roe v. Wade,* of an attempt "to impose [the state's] will by force of law."

Although criticized as irrational in the reproductive choice context, the distinction Justice Powell drew between government carrot and government stick had been made previously in other settings. But in *Maher,* unlike other cases in which the carrot/stick distinction had figured, the state could not justify its funding bar as an attempt to conserve public funds. In comparison to the medical costs of childbirth and the subsequent costs of child-rearing borne by public welfare programs, the costs of elective abortions are insubstantial.

The *Maher* logic was carried further in HARRIS V. McRAE (1980). The federal law at issue, known as the HYDE AMENDMENT, excluded even therapeutic (medically needed) abortions from the Medicaid program. In holding, 5–4, that the Hyde Amendment survived constitutional review, the Court reiterated the distinction drawn in *Maher*. Justice JOHN PAUL STEVENS, who had joined the majority in *Maher*, switched sides in *McRae* because he discerned a critical difference between elective and therapeutic abortions in the context of the Medicaid program. Congress had established two neutral criteria for Medicaid benefits—financial need and medical need. The pregnant women who challenged the Hyde Amendment met both criteria. By creating an exception to the medical need criterion for the sole purpose of deterring exercise of the right declared "fundamental" in *Roe v. Wade*, Justice Stevens reasoned, the sovereign had violated its "duty to govern impartially."

Following the bold step in the 1973 abortion rulings, the public funding rulings appear incongruous. The direct, practical effect of the funding rulings will not endure, however, if the legislative trend again turns in the direction discernible at the time of the *Roe v. Wade* decision. National and state legislators may come to question the wisdom of a childbirth-encouragement policy trained on Medicaid-eligible women, and to comprehend more completely the centrality of reproductive autonomy to a woman's control of her life's course.

May the state require spousal consent to the abortion decision of a woman and her physician when the state itself may not override that decision? In PLANNED PARENTHOOD V. DANFORTH (1976) the Court held unconstitutional Missouri's requirement of spousal consent to a first-trimester abortion. Justice Blackmun, for the six-member majority, declared that the state may not delegate authority to any person, even a spouse, to veto abortions which the state may not proscribe or regulate. A husband, of course, has a vital interest in his wife's pregnancy, Justice Blackmun acknowledged. But the woman's stake is more compelling; therefore the final decision must rest with her.

Although government may not remove the abortion decision from the woman and her physician unless its action demonstrably serves a compelling interest in the woman's health or in potential life, a state may act to ensure the quality of the decision. In *Danforth* the Court unanimously upheld Missouri's requirement that, prior to a first-trimester abortion, a woman certify that she has given her informed, uncoerced consent. The abortion decision is stressful, the Court observed; it should be made with "full knowledge of its nature and consequences." A state's authority in this regard, however, is limited. Regulations must be genuinely necessary to secure enlightened consent; they must be designed to inform rather than persuade; and they must not interfere with the physician's counseling discretion.

In *Akron v. Akron Center for Reproductive Health* (1983) the Court, 6–3, speaking through Justice Powell, struck down a series of regulations that exceeded these limits. One regulation required the physician to tell any woman contemplating an abortion that the unborn child is a human life from conception; to tell her the details of the anatomical characteristics of the fetus; and to enumerate the physical and psychological risks of abortion. The Court held this regulation invalid because it was designed to persuade women to forgo abortions, and because it encroached upon the physician's discretion to decide how best to advise the patient. The Court also invalidated as unnecessary to secure informed, uncoerced consent a twenty-four-hour waiting period between consent and abortion and a requirement that the physician personally convey information to the woman.

The Court has not yet had occasion to pass upon a regulation designed to render the birth-control-through-contraception decision an informed one. In *Bolger v. Youngs Drug Product Corporation* (1983), however, a majority held that government may not block dissemination of information relevant to that decision. At issue was a federal statute (the Comstock Act) prohibiting the mailing of contraceptive advertisements. All eight participating Justices held the statute unconstitutional as applied to the promotional and informational literature in question because the legislation impermissibly regulated COMMERCIAL SPEECH. (Earlier, in *Carey*, the Court had invalidated an analogous state regulation on the same ground.) Five Justices joined in a further ruling that the federal statute violated the right to reproductive autonomy because it denied adults truthful information relevant to informed contraception decisions.

The trimester scheme established in *Roe v. Wade* has guided the Court's ruling on state regulation of abortion procedures. Under that scheme, the state may not interfere with a physician's medical judgment concerning the place and manner of first-trimester abortions because abortions performed at that stage are less risky than childbirth. Thus in *Doe v. Bolton* (1973), the companion case to *Roe v. Wade*, the Court invalidated a Georgia requirement that even first-trimester abortions be performed in a full-service hospital. In *Connecticut v. Menillo* (1975), however, the Court, per curiam, explicitly relied upon one of the underpinnings of *Roe v. Wade*, the need for a physician's medical judgment, to uphold a state's conviction of a nonphysician for performing an abortion.

The ban on state regulation of a physician's performance of first-trimester abortions is not absolute; it does not exclude regulation serving an important state health interest without significantly affecting the abortion decision. A unanimous bench in *Danforth* so indicated in upholding a Missouri regulation requiring maintenance of records of all abortions, for disclosure only to public health officials, for seven years.

*Roe v. Wade* declared that after the first trimester, because an abortion entails greater risks, the state's interest in women's health could justify "place and manner" regulations even if the abortion decision itself might be affected. However, the Court has attentively scrutinized procedural regulations applicable after the first trimester to determine whether, in fact, they are reasonably related to the protection of the patient's health in light of current medical knowledge. Several regulations have failed to survive the court's scrutiny. In *Doe v. Bolton,* for example, the Court struck down Georgia's requirement that a hospital committee and two doctors, in addition to the woman's physician, concur in the abortion decision. And in *Danforth,* the Court struck down a Missouri ban on use, after the first trimester, of saline amniocentesis, then the most widely used second-trimester abortion procedure. Justice Blackmun, for the majority, observed that although safer procedures existed, they were not generally available. Consequently, the regulation in practice would either require the use of more dangerous techniques or compel women to forgo abortions.

The Court had three 1983 encounters with regulations alleged to connect sufficiently with a women's health: *Akron, Planned Parenthood Association v. Ashcroft,* and *Simopoulos v. Virginia.* In *Akron* and *Ashcroft,* the Court invalidated regulations requiring that abortions, after the first trimester, be performed in licensed acute-care hospitals. Justice Powell, for the majority, said that although current medical knowledge justified this requirement during much of the relevant period, it was unnecessary during the first four weeks of the second trimester; medical advances had rendered abortions safe at that stage even when performed in less elaborate facilities. The hospital requirement significantly burdened a woman's access to an abortion by raising costs substantially; therefore it must be tied more precisely to the period in which it was necessary. In *Simopoulos,* on the other hand, the Court upheld the limitation of second-trimester abortions to licensed facilities (including nonacute care facilities licensed to perform abortions during the first four to six weeks of the second trimester).

These three decisions indicate the Court's readiness to test specific second-trimester regulations that increase the cost of abortions against advances in medical technology. However, the majority in *Akron,* although aware that medical advances had rendered early second-trimester abortions safer than childbirth, explicitly refused to extend beyond the first trimester an across-the-board proscription of burdensome "place and manner" regulations.

Only in the last stage of pregnancy, after viability, does the state's interest in potential life become sufficiently compelling to allow the state to forbid all abortions except those necessary to preserve the woman's health. The point at which viability occurs is a medical judgment, the Court said in *Roe v. Wade, Danforth,* and *Colautti v. Franklin* (1979); the state may not establish a fixed measure of that point after which nontherapeutic abortions are illegal.

When postviability abortions occur, may the state impose manner requirements in the interest of preserving a viable fetus? The answer appears to be yes, if the regulations are not overbroad. In *Danforth* the Court invalidated a regulation requiring the physician to exercise due care to preserve the fetus; the regulation was not limited to postviability abortions. In *Ashcroft,* however, a 5–4 majority sustained a law requiring a second physician to attend a postviability abortion and attempt to preserve the life of the fetus. Even the dissenters agreed that such a regulation could stand if trimmed; they objected to Missouri's regulation because it required a second physician even at abortions using techniques that eliminated any possibility of fetal survival.

Dissenting in *Akron,* Justice SANDRA DAY O'CONNOR, joined by Justices White and Rehnquist, strongly criticized the Court's trimester approach to the regulation of abortion procedures. *Roe v. Wade's* medical model, she maintained, had been revealed as unworkable in subsequent cases. Advances in medical technology would continue to move forward the point during pregnancy when regulation could be justified as protective of a woman's health, and to move backward the point of viability, when the state could forbid abortions unless they were necessary to preserve the patient's life or health. The *Roe v. Wade* framework thus impelled legislatures to adjust their laws to changing medical practices, and called upon courts to examine legislative judgments, not as jurists applying "neutral principles" but as "science review boards."

More fundamentally, Justice O'Connor disapproved the interest balancing exhibited by the Court in the 1973 decisions. Throughout pregnancy, she said, the state has "compelling interests in the protection of potential human life and in maternal health." (In *Beal* the Court had said that the state does have an interest in potential life throughout a pregnancy, but that the interest becomes *compelling* only in the postviability stage.) Justice O'Connor's analysis, it appears, would permit from the beginning of pregnancy the regulation *Roe v. Wade* permits only in the final trimester: state proscription of abortion except to preserve a woman's health.

Vagueness doctrine has occasionally figured in the Court's review of state regulation of abortion procedures. In *Colautti,* the Court invalidated as too vague to supply adequate notice a statute attaching a criminal sanction to a physician's failure to exercise due care to preserve a fetus when there is "sufficient reason to believe that the fetus may be viable." And in *Akron,* a vagueness handle was employed to strike down a provision mandating the sanitary and "humane" disposal of aborted fetuses.

Minors have constitutional rights, but state authority over CHILDREN'S RIGHTS is greater than over adults'; the state may protect minors because of their immaturity and "peculiar vulnerability," and in recognition of "the importance of the parental role in child rearing." Justice Powell so observed in his plurality opinion in *Bellotti v. Baird* (1979), and no Justice has disagreed with these general statements. In concrete cases concerning the reproductive autonomy of minors, however, the Court has been splintered.

In *Danforth,* the Court invalidated, 5–4, a law requiring a parent's consent for most abortions performed on unmarried women under the age of eighteen. The majority did not foreclose a parental consent requirement for minors unable to make the abortion decision in an informed, mature manner.

The Court "continue[d] the inquiry" in *Bellotti.* Massachusetts required unmarried minors to obtain the consent of both parents or, failing that, the authorization of a state judge "for good cause shown." The Court voted 8–1 to invalidate the law, but split 4–4 on the rationale. Justice Stevens, writing for four Justices, thought the case governed by *Danforth.* Justice Powell, writing for four other Justices, attempted to provide guidance for state legislators. The abortion decision is unique among decisions facing a minor, he observed; it cannot be postponed until attainment of majority, and if the fetus is carried to term, the new mother will immediately face adult responsibilities. A blanket requirement of parental consent, using age as a proxy for maturity, was too sweeping. Yet the state's interest in ensuring the quality of a minor's abortion decision and in encouraging family participation in that decision would justify a law requiring either parental consent or the determination of an independent decision maker that abortion is in the minor's best interest, or that she is mature enough to decide for herself.

Justice Powell's *Bellotti* framework, although by 1983 only a two-member view, became, in *Akron* and *Ashcroft,* the de facto standard governing consent statutes. In *Ashcroft,* the Court upheld, 5–4, a statute conditioning a minor's abortion on either parental consent or a juvenile court order. Justice Powell and Chief Justice Burger voted to uphold the provision because, as indicated in *Bellotti,* the juvenile court must authorize an abortion upon finding that the abortion is in the minor's best interest or that the minor is mature enough to make her own decision. Three other Justices viewed the consent requirement as imposing "no undue burden on any right that a minor [arguably] may have to undergo an abortion." Four Justices dissented because the statute permitted an absolute veto, by parent or judge, "over the decision of the physician and his patient."

In *Akron,* however, the Court struck down, 6–3, an ordinance requiring all minors under age fifteen to have either parental or judicial consent. Because *Akron* failed to provide explicitly for a judicial determination of the minor's maturity, Justice Powell and the Chief Justice joined the four *Ashcroft* dissenters in condemning the consent provision.

With respect to contraception, no clear statement has emerged from the Court on the extent of state and parental authority over minors. In *Carey* the Court, 7–2, struck down a ban on the distribution of contraceptives to persons under age sixteen. The state sought to justify the measure as a means of deterring sexual activity by minors. There was no majority decision, but six Justices recognized that banning birth control would not in fact deter sexual activity.

May the state require parental consent to the minor's use of contraceptives? At least five Justices, it appears from the *Carey* decision, would state unequivocally that minors have no right to engage in sexual activity in face of disapproval of the state and of their parents. But it is hardly apparent that any minor-protective interest supports stopping the young from effectuating a decision to use nonhazardous contraceptives when, despite the views or commands of the state and their parents, they do engage in sexual activity.

Arguably, such a provision would serve to preserve parental authority over a decision many people consider a moral one. *Danforth* indicated that this end is insufficient to justify requiring parental consent for an abortion. Yet, as Justice Powell's *Bellotti* opinion illustrates, at least some Justices consider the abortion decision unique. Perhaps the issue will remain undecided. For practical reasons, lawmakers may be deterred from conditioning a minor's access to contraceptives on parental consent or notification. Many minors whose parents would wish them to use birth control if they engaged in sexual activity would nevertheless fail to seek parental consent for fear of disclosing their sexual activities. As five Justices indicated in *Carey*, deliberate state policy exposing minors to the risk of unwanted pregnancies is of questionable rationality.

In *Akron*, which came to the Court a decade after *Roe v. Wade*, Justice Powell acknowledged the continuing argument that the Court "erred in interpreting the Constitution." Nevertheless, *Akron* commenced with a reaffirmation of the 1973 precedent. As *Akron* itself illustrates, the Court typically has applied *Roe v. Wade* to restrict state efforts to impede privately financed access to contraceptives and abortions.

It appears safe to predict continued "adher[ence] to STARE DECISIS in applying the principles of *Roe v. Wade*." But other issues remain beyond the zone of secure prediction. Current opinions do not indicate whether the Court eventually will relate its reproductive autonomy decisions to evolving law on the equal status of men and women. Nor can one forecast reliably how science and population will influence the next decades' legislative and judicial decisions in this area.

The development of a safe, efficient, inexpensive morning-after pill, for example, may alter the reproductive autonomy debate by further blurring distinctions between contraceptives and abortifacients, and by sharply reducing occasions for resort to clinical procedures. A development of this order may diminish in incidence and detail both legislative

activity and constitutional review of the kind sparked in the decade
following *Roe v. Wade.* Moreover, it is at least possible that a different
question will confront the Court by the turn of the century: If population
size becomes a larger governmental concern, legislators may change
course, and measures designed to limit childbirth may become the focus
of constitutional controversy.

Bibliography

BREST, PAUL   1981   The Fundamental Rights Controversy: The Essential Con-
tradictions of Normative Constitutional Scholarship. *Yale Law Journal*
90:1063–1112.

BYRN, ROBERT   1973   An American Tragedy: The Supreme Court on Abortion.
*Fordham Law Review*  41:807–862.

COX, ARCHIBALD   1976   *The Role of the Supreme Court in American Government.*
New York: Oxford University Press.

DEMBITZ, NANETTE   1980   The Supreme Court and a Minor's Abortion Decision. *Columbia Law Review*  80:1251–1263.

DESTRO, ROBERT   1975   Abortion and the Constitution: The Need for a Life
Protective Amendment. *California Law Review*  63:1250–1351.

ELY, JOHN HART   1973   The Wages of Crying Wolf: A Comment on *Roe v.
Wade. Yale Law Journal*  82:920–949.

ESTREICHER, SAMUEL   1982   Congressional Power and Constitutional Rights:
Reflections on Proposed "Human Life" Legislation. *Virginia Law Review*
68:333–458.

FREUND, PAUL   1983   Storms over the Supreme Court. *American Bar Association
Journal*  69:1474–1480.

HEYMANN, PHILIP and BARZELAY, DOUGLAS   1973   The Forest and the Trees:
*Roe v. Wade* and its Critics. *Boston University Law Review*  53:765–784.

LAW, SYLVIA   1984   Rethinking Sex and the Constitution. *University of Pennsylvania Law Review*  132:955–1040.

PERRY, MICHAEL   1976   Abortion, the Public Morals, and the Police Power:
The Ethical Function of Substantive Due Process. *UCLA Law Review*  23:689–
736.

————   1978   The Abortion Funding Cases: A Comment on the Supreme
Court's Role in American Government. *Georgetown Law Journal*  66:1191–
1245.

REGAN, DONALD   1979   Rewriting *Roe v. Wade. Michigan Law Review*  77:1569–
1646.

TRIBE, LAURENCE H.   1978   *American Constitutional Law*   Pages 921–934.
Mineola, N.Y.: Foundation Press.

# *ROE v. WADE*

410 U.S. 113 (1973)
*DOE v. BOLTON*
410 U.S. 179 (1973)

Kenneth L. Karst

In these cases the Supreme Court confronted the emotionally charged issue of abortion. The decisions invalidated two states' abortion laws—and, by inference, similar laws in a majority of states. As a result, the Court was plunged into prolonged and intense controversy, ranging from questions about the bearing of morality on constitutional law to questions about the proper role of the judiciary in the American system of government. The Court held unconstitutional a Texas law forbidding abortion except to save the pregnant woman's life and also invalidated several features of a Georgia law regulating abortion procedures and limiting abortion to Georgia residents.

The two women whose fictitious names grace the cases' titles were pregnant when they filed their actions in 1970, but not at the time of the Supreme Court's decision. The Court nonetheless held that their cases were not moot; rigid application of the MOOTNESS doctrine would prevent appellate review of an important issue that was capable of repetition. Nine doctors were also held to have STANDING to challenge the Georgia law; the intervention of a doctor under prosecution in Texas was held improper under the equitable ABSTENTION principle of YOUNGER v. HARRIS (1971); and a Texas married couple was denied standing because the woman had not been pregnant. The Court thus proceeded to the constitutional merits.

The *Roe* opinion, by Justice HARRY A. BLACKMUN, reviewed the history of abortion laws and the recent positions on abortion taken by medical groups and the American Bar Association, but the Court grounded its decision on neither history nor current professional opinion. Instead, the Court relied on a constitutional right of PRIVACY previously recognized in GRISWOLD V. CONNECTICUT (1965) and now relocated in the "liberty" protected by the DUE PROCESS clause of the FOURTEENTH AMENDMENT. This right included "a woman's decision whether or not to terminate her pregnancy," which decision was a FUNDAMENTAL INTEREST that could be restricted only on a showing of a COMPELLING STATE INTEREST.

The Court identified two state interests that would qualify as "compelling" at different stages in pregnancy: protection of maternal health and protection of potential life. Before discussing these interests, however, the Court dealt with a preliminary question: whether a fetus was a PERSON within the meaning of the Fourteenth Amendment. In an abortion, of course, it is not the state that denies life to a fetus; presumably the point of the Court's question was that if a fetus were a "person," the amendment should not be read to bar a state from protecting it against being aborted. The Court concluded, however, that a fetus was not a "person" in the amendment's contemplation. In reaching this conclusion, Justice Blackmun said: "We need not resolve the difficult question of when life begins." Absent a consensus among doctors, philosophers, or theologians on the issue, "the judiciary, at this point in the development of man's knowledge, is not in a position to speculate as to the answer." In any event, the law had never recognized the unborn "as persons in the whole sense." That conclusion alone, however, could not dispose of the question of the state's power. A state can constitutionally protect beings (or even things) that are not persons—including fetuses, which surely can be protected by law against certain kinds of experimentation or disposal, even though the law may be motivated by a feeling that fetuses share our common humanity.

The Court did recognize the state's interests in protecting maternal health and potential life; each would become "compelling" at successive stages of pregnancy. During the first trimester of pregnancy, neither interest is compelling; the abortion decision and its implementation must be left to the woman and her doctor. During the second trimester, the interest in maternal health becomes sufficiently compelling to justify some state regulations of the abortion procedure. When the fetus becomes "viable"—capable of life outside the womb, around the beginning of the third trimester of pregnancy—the state's interest in potential life becomes sufficiently compelling to justify prohibiting abortion except to preserve the "life or health" of the mother.

This scheme of constitutional rights has the look of a statute and evidently was influenced by New York's liberal law and the American Bar Association's model abortion law. Investigative reporters tell us that the three-part scheme resulted from negotiation among the Justices, and it is hard to see it as anything but a compromise between banning abortion altogether and turning over the entire abortion decision to the pregnant woman.

Justice BYRON R. WHITE, dissenting, complained that the Court had permitted abortion to satisfy "the convenience, whim or caprice of the putative mother." Chief Justice WARREN E. BURGER, concurring, responded that the Court had rejected "any claim that the Constitution requires abortion on demand" in favor of a scheme relying on doctors' "medical judgments relating to life and health." The Court's opinion deals ambiguously with the doctor's decisional role. At one point it states that the abortion decision "must be left to the medical judgment of the pregnant woman's attending physician." Yet the Court's decision rests on the constitutional right to privacy, which includes "a woman's decision whether or not to terminate her pregnancy." Very likely Justice Blackmun, a former general counsel of the Mayo Clinic, was influenced by the medical authorities he cited. Indeed, the Blackmun and Burger opinions both convey an inclination to convert abortion issues into medical questions. Linking the state's power to forbid abortions with "viability" is one example—although it is unclear how the Court will respond when medical technology permits the preservation of very young fetuses outside the womb. Similarly, a supposed lack of medical consensus made the Court reluctant to decide when life begins.

The issues in *Roe,* however, were not medical issues. First, there is no medically correct decision concerning an abortion when the pregnant woman's health is not endangered. Second, there is no lack of medical consensus about what happens in the normal process of reproduction from insemination to birth. In some sense "life" begins at conception; to say otherwise is not to make a medical judgment but to decide a question of law or morality. The problem before the Court in *Roe* was to determine whether (or when) a state could constitutionally protect a fetus. The state's interest in potential life surely begins at the time of conception, and arguably before. Yet if *Griswold* and EISENSTADT v. BAIRD (1972) remained good law, the state could not constitutionally protect that interest by forbidding contraception. Most people do not equate the use of "morning after" pills or intrauterine devices with murder, although these forms of "contraception" are really ways of effecting abortion after conception. In 1973 no state was enforcing its abortion laws against such practices. Yet the argument that "life" begins at conception, for purposes of defining legal or moral rights, embraced the claims of both the newest embryo and the eight-month fetus. There was evident artificiality in the Court's selection of "viability" as the time when the state's concerns for potential life became "compelling," but there would have been artificiality in any resolution of the issue of state power other than an all-or-nothing decision.

In *Roe*'s companion case, *Doe v. Bolton,* the Court held invalid four provisions of Georgia law, requiring that abortions be: (1) performed in hospitals accredited by the Joint Commission on Accreditation of Hospitals; (2) approved by hospital staff committees; (3) approved in each case by two physicians other than the pregnant woman's doctor; and (4) limited to Georgia residents. The latter requirement was an obvious violation of Article IV's PRIVILEGES AND IMMUNITIES clause, and the other three were held to impose unreasonable restrictions on the constitutional right recognized in *Roe*.

The *Roe* opinion has found few defenders; even the decision's supporters are inclined to offer substitute justifications. *Roe*'s critics divide roughly into two groups: those who regard abortion as murder, and those who think the Supreme Court exceeded its proper institutional bounds, failing to ground its decision in the Constitution and merely substituting its own policy judgment for that of the people's elected representatives.

The latter criticism touched off an impressive succession of essays on JUDICIAL REVIEW. It was the former group of critics, however, who dominated the politics of abortion. The "right to life" movement was, for a time, one of the nation's most effective "single issue" groups, achieving enough respect from legislators to permit the adoption of laws withdrawing governmental financial aid to poor women who seek abortions. (See MAHER v. ROE, 1977; HARRIS v. McRAE, 1980.) Various constitutional amendments to overturn *Roe* were proposed in Congress, but none was submitted to the states for ratification. In the early 1980s Congress considered, but did not adopt, a bill declaring that "human life begins from the moment of conception." Congress also heard proposals to withdraw federal court jurisdiction over abortion cases. (See JUDICIAL SYSTEM.) Yet the *Roe* decision has weathered all these political storms.

*Roe*'s stability as a precedent is founded on the same social and political base that initially supported the decision. It was no accident that *Roe* was decided in the 1970s, when the movement against SEX DISCRIMINATION was winning its most important constitutional and political victories. The abortion question was not merely an issue between pregnant women and their unwanted fetuses; it was also a feminist issue, going to women's position in society in relation to men. Even today American society imposes a greater stigma on unmarried women who become pregnant than on the men who father their children, and society still expects women to take the major responsibility for contraception and child care. The implications of an unwanted pregnancy or parenthood for a woman's opportunities in education, employment, and personal association—indeed, for the woman's definition of self—are enormous. Justice White's dissenting remark, that abortion regulation is an issue about which "reasonable men may easily and heatedly differ," perhaps said more than he intended to say.

Bibliography

ELY, JOHN HART 1973 The Wages of Crying Wolf: A Comment on *Roe v. Wade*. *Yale Law Journal* 82:920–949.

HENKIN, LOUIS   1974   Privacy and Autonomy. *Columbia Law Review* 74:1410–1433.

Symposium on the Law and Politics of Abortion. 1979 *Michigan Law Review* 77:1569–1646.

TRIBE, LAURENCE H.  1978  *American Constitutional Law.*  Pages 923–934. Mineola, N.Y.: Foundation Press.

WOODWARD, BOB and ARMSTRONG, SCOTT   1979   *The Brethren: Inside the Supreme Court.*  Pages 165–189, 229–240. New York: Simon & Schuster.

# EQUAL RIGHTS AMENDMENT

Deborah L. Rhode

In March 1972, Congress proposed an Equal Rights Amendment (ERA) to the United States Constitution. The amendment provided:

Section 1. Equality of rights under the law shall not be denied or abridged by the United States or by any State on account of sex.

Section 2. The Congress shall have the power to enforce, by appropriate legislation, the provisions of this article.

Section 3. The Amendment shall take effect two years after the date of ratification.

In May 1982, the extended deadline for ratification expired without the necessary approval from three-fourths of the states; fifteen had never ratified and five had voted to rescind their ratification. Challenges to the legality of those rescissions and to Congress's extension of the ratification deadline became moot.

Proponents subsequently reintroduced the amendment in Congress, thus continuing a campaign that began a half-century earlier. Some version of an equal rights amendment had surfaced in every congressional term between 1923 and 1972. In the view of most proponents, the text adopted in 1972 was designed to prohibit gender classifications except those concerning personal privacy, physical characteristics, or past discrimination. The rationale was that a constitutional prohibition would avoid piecemeal remedies for various forms of discrimination. Such a mandate would also subject sex-based classifications to a more rigorous standard of review than that prevailing under FOURTEENTH AMENDMENT doctrine, which allows discrimination substantially related to an important state purpose.

Although conceived as a measure to unite women, the amendment has often divided them. Throughout its history, the ERA campaign has triggered fundamental controversies about the meaning of equality and the means to attain it in a society marked by significant disparities in sexual roles. Much debate has centered not on legal entitlements but on cultural aspirations. Dispute has focused on the amendment's effect concerning laws purportedly advantaging women, such as protective labor legislation, marital support requirements, and military service exemptions. Particularly during the earlier part of the century, opponents contended that equality in formal mandates could never secure equality in fact. So long as female wage earners and homemakers were more economically vulnerable than men, a demand for equal rights appeared out of touch with social realities. By contrast, ERA proponents contended that protective legislation had often "protected" women from opportunities for higher paid vocations, and had legitimated stereotypes on which invidious discrimination rested. Supporters also noted that by the time Congress proposed the amendment in 1972, much sex-based regulation had been either invalidated or extended to men, and that which remained could be cast in sex-neutral terms.

So too, much of the discrimination that the amendment was originally designed to redress was, by the 1970s, illegal under various judicial, executive, and legislative mandates. Accordingly, the ERA ratification campaign frequently focused on symbolic rather than legal implications. To proponents, a constitutional mandate would serve as an important affirmation of women's equal status and as a catalyst for change in social practices beyond the scope of legal regulation. For opponents, however, the amendment's symbolic subtext represented an assault less on gender discrimination than on gender differences, and an invitation for further encroachments on states' rights.

In the ratification struggle of the 1970s, ERA supporters lacked the leverage to make their interests felt. But if the equal rights campaign helps inspire and empower women to expand their political influence, then the struggle itself may prove more important than its constitutional consequences.

Bibliography

BOLES, JANET 1979 *The Politics of the Equal Rights Amendment: Conflict and the Decision Process.* New York: Longmans.

BROWN, BARBARA A.; EMERSON, THOMAS I.; FALK, GAIL; and FREEDMAN, ANN E. 1971 The Equal Rights Amendment: A Constitutional Basis for Equal Rights for Women. *Yale Law Journal* 80:872–985.

RHODE, DEBORAH L. 1983 Equal Rights in Retrospect. *Journal of Law and Inequality* 1:1–72.

# PORNOGRAPHY

## Catherine Hancock

The Supreme Court's OBSCENITY decisions define the forms of pornography that are protected from censorship by the FIRST AMENDMENT. As a practical matter, this protection is quite broad. Most pornography is also a unique kind of speech: about women, for men. In an era when sexual equality is a social ideal, the constitutional protection of pornography is a vexing political issue. Should pornographic imagery of male dominance and female subordination be repudiated through censorship, or will censorship inevitably destroy our commitment to free speech?

In ROTH v. UNITED STATES (1957) the Court found obscene speech to be unworthy of First Amendment protection because it forms "no essential part of any exposition of ideas." Yet precisely because of pornography's ideational content, some of it was deemed harmful and made criminal. The Court could avoid examining the specific nature of this harm, once it had located obscenity conveniently outside the constitutional pale. But it could not avoid defining obscenity, and thereby identifying the justification for its censorship.

The essential characteristic of "obscene" pornography is its appeal to one's "prurient interest," which is a genteel reference to its capacity to stimulate physical arousal and carnal desire. But such pornography must also be "offensive," and so, to be censored, sex-stimulant speech must be both arousing and disgusting. The meaning of offensiveness depends upon the subjective judgment of the observer, and is best captured by Justice POTTER STEWART's famous aphorism in JACOBELLIS V. OHIO (1964): "I know it when I see it."

Given the limitations of the criminal process, obscenity laws did not make offensive pornography unavailable in the marketplace. As HARRY KALVEN, JR. pointed out, few judges took the evils of obscenity very seriously, although constitutional rhetoric made the law appear to be "solemnly concerned with the sexual fantasies of the adult population." The Court's chief goal was the protection of admired works of art and literature, not the elimination of pornographic magazines at the corner drug store. Sporadic obscenity prosecutions may occur in jurisdictions where the "contemporary community standard" of offensiveness allows convictions under MILLER v. CALIFORNIA (1973). But the constitutional validity of a legal taboo on "hard-core" pornography became largely irrelevant to its suppliers and consumers, even as that material became sexually explicit and more violent in its imagery during the 1970s.

That same decade saw a legal revolution in equality between the sexes, embodied in judicial decisions based on the guarantees of EQUAL PROTECTION and DUE PROCESS. Women won legal rights to control and define their own sexuality, through litigation establishing rights to contraception and abortion, and through legislative reforms easing restrictions on prosecutions for sexual assault. Pornography also became a women's issue, as feminists such as Catharine MacKinnon attacked it as "a form of forced sex, a practice of sexual politics, an institution of gender inequality." Women marched and demonstrated against films and magazines portraying them as beaten, chained, or mutilated objects of sexual pleasure for men. In 1984, their protests took a legal form when MacKinnon and Andrea Dworkin drafted an ordinance adopted by the Indianapolis City Council, outlawing some types of pornography as acts of SEX DISCRIMINATION.

By using the concept of equal protection as a basis to attack pornographic speech, the council set up a dramatic assault upon First Amendment doctrine, making embarrassed enemies out of old constitutional friends. As a strategic matter, however, the council needed a COMPELLING STATE INTEREST to justify censorship of speech that did not fall into the obscenity category. The ordinance defined offensive pornography more broadly than *Miller*'s standards allow, because it went beyond a ban on displays of specific human body parts or sexual acts. Instead, it prohibited the "graphic sexually explicit subordination of women" through their portrayals as, for example, "sexual objects who enjoy pain or humiliation," or "sexual objects for domination, conquest, violation, exploitation, possession or use."

As a philosophical matter, sex discrimination is a good constitutional metaphor for the harms attributed to pornography, namely, the loss of equal CITIZENSHIP status for women through the "bigotry and contempt" promoted by the imagery of subordination. But as a matter of DOCTRINE, the causal link between the social presence of pornography and the harms of discrimination is fatally remote. Free speech gospel dictates that "offensive speech" may be censored only upon proof of imminent, tangible harm to individuals, such as violent insurrection (BRANDENBURG V. OHIO, 1969), a physical assault (COHEN V. CALIFORNIA, 1971), or reckless tortious injury to reputation (NEW YORK TIMES V. SULLIVAN, 1964). The closest historical analogue to the creation of a cause of action for classwide harm from speech is the criminal GROUP LIBEL statute upheld by a 5–4 Supreme Court in BEAUHARNAIS V. ILLINOIS (1952). But this remedy has been implicitly discredited by *New York Times* and *Brandenburg*, given its CHILLING EFFECT upon uninhibited criticism of political policies and officials.

It came as no surprise when early court decisions struck down Indianapolis-type ordinances as void for vagueness, as an unlawful PRIOR

RESTRAINT on speech, and as an unjustified restriction of protected speech as defined by the earlier obscenity decisions. The courts could accept neither the equal protection rationale nor the breadth of the ordinances' scope, as both would permit too great an encroachment upon the freedoms of expression and consumption of art, literature, and political messages. Ironically, it is the potentially endemic quality of the imagery of women's subordination that defeats any attempt to place a broad taboo upon it.

Eva Feder Kittay has posed the question, "How is it that within our society, men can derive a sexual charge out of seeing a woman brutalized?" Her answer to that loaded question is that our conceptions of sexuality are permeated with conceptions of domination, because we have eroticized the relations of power: men eroticize sexual conquering, and women eroticize being possessed. Pornography becomes more than a harmless outlet for erotic fantasies when it makes violence appear to be intrinsically erotic, rather than something that is eroticized. The social harm of such pornography is that it brutalizes our moral imagination, "the source of that imaginative possibility by which we can identify with others and hence form maxims having a universal validity."

The constitutional source for an analysis of brutalizing pornography lies in the richly generative symbols of First Amendment law itself. That law already contains the tolerance for insistence "on observance of the civic culture's norms of social equality," in the words of Kenneth L. Karst. Any acceptable future taboo would be likely to take the form of a ban on public display of a narrowly defined class of pictorial imagery, simply because that would be a traditional, readily enforceable compromise between free speech and equality. Any taboo would be mostly symbolic, but it would matter. Only by limiting the taboo can we avoid descending into the Orwellian hell where censorship is billed as freedom.

Bibliography

BRYDEN, DAVID   1985   Between Two Constitutions: Feminism and Pornography. *Constitutional Commentary* 2:147–189.

KALVEN, HARRY, JR.   1960   The Metaphysics of Obscenity. *Supreme Court Review* 1960:1–45.

KITTAY, EVA FEDER   1983   Pornography and the Erotics of Domination. Pages 145–174 in Carol C. Gould, ed., *Beyond Domination: New Perspectives on Women and Philosophy.* Totowa, N.J.: Rowman & Allanheld.

MACKINNON, CATHARINE A.   1984   Not a Moral Issue. *Yale Law & Policy Review* 2:321–345.

NOTE   1984   Anti-Pornography Laws and First Amendment Values. *Harvard Law Review* 98:460–481.

# ILLEGITIMACY

Kenneth L. Karst

The Anglo-American law of illegitimacy derives from two interrelated purposes of our institutional progenitors. First, imposing the legal disabilities of illegitimacy on a child was seen as a punishment of the parents for their sin. More importantly, the law of legitimacy supported a system of male control over economic resources. The chief effect of the principle of bastardy-as-punishment was to disable illegitimate children from making claims against their deceased fathers' estates. Similarly, formal marriage was the only basis for a woman's claim to inherit from the man who fathered her children. Thus the punishment was reserved for unmarried women and their children. Unmarried fathers, far from being punished, were strengthened in their power to control the transmission of wealth and status. As the Supreme Court began to recognize in two 1968 decisions, these themes are modern as well as medieval.

The cases were LEVY V. LOUISIANA and *Glona v. American Guarantee & Liability Insurance Co.* On EQUAL PROTECTION grounds, the Court invalidated provisions of Louisiana's wrongful death statute that allowed damages to a surviving child for the death of a parent, and vice versa, only in cases of legitimate parentage. From that time forward, most of the Court's decisions on illegitimacy have dealt with laws regulating inheritance by illegitimate children (especially from their fathers), and laws restricting the right to death damages or benefits in cases of illegitimacy. Both in their results and in their doctrinal explanations, these decisions have pursued a crooked path.

Much of the early doctrinal uncertainty surrounded the question of the appropriate STANDARD OF REVIEW. *Levy* and *Glona* purported to apply the RATIONAL BASIS standard, but in fact they represented a more demanding judicial scrutiny. There were good reasons for categorizing illegitimacy as a SUSPECT CLASSIFICATION that would demand STRICT SCRUTINY of the state's asserted justifications. As the Court has said more than once, it is "illogical and unjust" to burden innocent children because their parents have not married. The status of illegitimacy is out of the child's control. Illegitimates have suffered historic disadvantage. The status has been the centuries-old source of stigma; such legislative classifications are apt to be the result of habit, prejudice, and stereotype rather than serious attention to public needs. After a series of cases characterized by doctrinal instability, in *Mathews v. Lucas* (1976) the Court rejected the assimilation of illegitimacy to the suspect classifications category. The Court did remark, however, that its standard of review in such cases was "not a toothless one."

Part of the reason for the tortuous doctrinal path from *Levy* and *Glona* to *Mathews v. Lucas* was that the Justices were closely divided on the general issue of the Court's approach to illegitimacy as a legislative classification; in these circumstances, trifling factual distinctions tended to affect the decisions of cases. Even after *Mathews v. Lucas* this pattern continued, as TRIMBLE v. GORDON (1977) and LALLI v. LALLI (1978) illustrate—although the Court has identified a verbal formula for its standard of review: An illegitimacy classification must be "substantially related to a permissible state interest." As Justice LEWIS F. POWELL said for a plurality in *Lalli,* the Court's concern for the plight of illegitimates must be measured against a state's interest in "the just and orderly disposition of property at death." A seventeenth century probate lawyer would not be surprised to learn that the justice and order emerging from *Lalli* offered protection for a father's estate against the claims of illegitimate children, even though paternity had been established beyond question.

The Supreme Court has invoked its intermediate standard of review to invalidate state laws imposing severe time restrictions on suits to establish paternity and compel fathers to support children born outside marriage. But if *Lalli* validated an ancient tradition of domination through control over the transmission of wealth and status, *Parham v. Hughes* (1978), just four months later, validated the tradition of the illegitimacy relation as punishment for sin. An illegitimate child and his mother were killed in an automobile accident. State law would have allowed only the mother to sue for wrongful death damages, if she had survived. Given the mother's death, the father would have been entitled to bring the suit if he had formally legitimated the child. Although he had not undertaken formal legitimation proceedings, the father had signed the child's birth certificate, and had supported the child and visited him regularly; the child had taken the father's name. The Court upheld the state's denial of a right to sue, 6–3.

The state court in *Parham* had said the law was a means of "promoting a legitimate family unit" and "setting a standard of morality." The *Parham* dissenters, focusing on SEX DISCRIMINATION, faulted the state for doing its promoting and standard-setting selectively, along lines defined by gender. The decision also intruded seriously on the FREEDOM OF INTIMATE ASSOCIATION. The father–son relationship was complete in every sense but the formal one. Four members of the majority said it was all right, nevertheless, for the state to "express its 'condemnation of irresponsible liaisons beyond the bounds of marriage' " by denying the father the right to damages for the death of his son. In other words, the father should be ashamed of himself.

In *Glona,* the Court had rejected precisely this sort of reasoning. The fact that the legislature was "dealing with sin," the Court said, could not justify so arbitrary a discrimination as the denial of wrongful death damages. *Glona* had involved the claim of a mother, and mothers of illegitimate children have been the historic victims of a system of illegitimacy in a way that fathers have not. But *Parham* involved a man who not only sired a child but was a father to him. What had been protected in *Glona* was not merely the damages claim of a mother, but the status of the intimate relationship between a mother and her son. The *Parham* law's arbitrariness lay in its assumption that significant incidents of the parent-child relationship should be denied because of the absence of a formal marriage. Seen in this light, the law's discrimination demands some substantial justification for its invasion of the freedom of intimate association. *Glona* teaches that the required justification is not to be found in the state's wish to punish "sin." The Supreme Court plainly is not yet prepared to hold that the status of illegitimacy is itself constitutionally defective. When that day arrives, however, *Glona* will serve as a precedent.

Bibliography

PERRY, MICHAEL J.   1979   Modern Equal Protection: A Conceptualization and Reappraisal. *Columbia Law Review*  79:1023–1084.

WALLACH, ALETA and TENOSO, PATRICIA   1974   A Vindication of the Rights of Unmarried Mothers and Their Children: An Analysis of the Institution of Illegitimacy, Equal Protection, and the Uniform Parentage Act. *University of Kansas Law Review*  23:23–90.

# FREEDOM OF INTIMATE ASSOCIATION

Kenneth L. Karst

Since the 1960s the Supreme Court has decided scores of cases dealing with marriage and divorce, family relationships, the choice whether to procreate, and various forms of intimate association outside the traditional family structure. Although the factual settings of these cases and their opinions' doctrinal explanations have been diverse, in the aggregate they represent the emergence of a constitutional freedom of intimate association.

The Court had asserted as early as MEYER V. NEBRASKA (1923) and PIERCE V. SOCIETY OF SISTERS (1925) that the Constitution protected the freedom to marry and raise one's children, and SKINNER V. OKLAHOMA (1942) had subjected a compulsory STERILIZATION law to STRICT SCRUTINY. But the modern beginning for the freedom of intimate association was Justice WILLIAM O. DOUGLAS's opinion for the Court in GRISWOLD V. CONNECTICUT (1965). Although that case involved a prosecution of the operators of a BIRTH CONTROL clinic for dispensing advice on contraception and the means to achieve it, the focus of the opinion was a married couple's right to use contraceptive devices. Justice Douglas located that right in a "zone of privacy," created by "penumbras" of various specific guarantees in the BILL OF RIGHTS. He did not specify the scope of the new RIGHT OF PRIVACY, and one product of *Griswold* has been a distinguished body of literature rich with suggested approaches to that issue. In *Griswold* itself, however, the chief object of constitutional protection was the marital relationship.

*Griswold* has become a major precedent for several lines of doctrinal development. The right to marry has been recognized as a SUBSTANTIVE DUE PROCESS right in LOVING V. VIRGINIA (1967) and ZABLOCKI V. REDHAIL (1978). The right to use contraceptives has been extended to unmarried persons in EISENSTADT V. BAIRD (1972) on an EQUAL PROTECTION theory, and even the right to advertise and sell them has been defended in CAREY V. POPULATION SERVICES INTERNATIONAL (1977) on the basis of the FIRST AMENDMENT and the privacy right of potential buyers, married or not. These protections of intimate relationships outside marriage have been complemented by heightened scrutiny of legislative classifications visiting disadvantage on the status of ILLEGITIMACY. *Griswold* 's most famous doctrinal outgrowth was ROE v. WADE (1973), which squarely placed the new constitutional right of privacy within the liberty protected by substantive due process, and held that the right included a woman's freedom to choose to have an ABORTION.

Here as elsewhere, constitutional doctrine has followed in the wake of social change. After World War II the movement for racial equality accelerated, bringing new awareness and new acceptance of a cultural diversity extending well beyond differences based on race. By the 1970s the feminist movement had succeeded in engaging the nation's attention and changing attitudes of both men and women toward questions of "woman's role," and in particular toward marriage and the family. The white, middle-class "housewife marriage," with the father working and the mother and children at home in a one-family suburban house, may still be the image most often called to mind by general references to "the family." The image, however, represents less than half of America's population. The "wife economy" is now obsolete; increased longevity will place further strains on lifetime marriage; women now know they can choose marriage without motherhood, or motherhood without marriage; racial and ethnic minorities will not again accept the idea that the diversity of their forms of intimate association is merely pathological. Indeed, large numbers of middle-class white couples are openly living together without marrying. What has changed is not so much the fact of diversity as the range of the acceptable in intimate association.

A strong egalitarian theme runs through our society's collective recognition of these changes; it is natural that both due process and equal protection have provided doctrinal underpinnings for the freedom of intimate association. As abstractions, "liberty" and "equality" may sometimes be in tension, but here they have nourished each other. As the civil rights movement sought to advance equality under the banner of "freedom," so the abortion rights movement has sought a new status for women under the banner of "choice."

Taking account of doctrinal development in this area, the Supreme Court, in its opinion in *Roberts v. United States Jaycees* (1984), referred for the first time to a "freedom of intimate association." "[C]ertain kinds of highly personal relationships," said the Court, had been afforded substantial constitutional protection: "marriage; childbirth; the raising and education of children; and cohabitation with one's relatives." The Court noted that these relationships tended to involve relatively small numbers of persons; a high degree of selectivity in beginning and maintaining the affiliations; and "seclusion from others in critical aspects of the relationship." Their constitutional protection reflected "the realization that individuals draw much of their emotional enrichment from close ties with others. Protecting these relationships from unwarranted state interference therefore safeguards the ability independently to define one's identity that is central to any concept of liberty."

For half a century the Court has performed much of its judicial interest-balancing by adjusting the STANDARDS OF REVIEW of the constitutionality of legislation. As the *Jaycees* opinion noted, heightened judicial scrutiny results when the Court perceives the importance of the values or interests impaired when government restricts freedom or imposes inequality. The Court has spoken of procreation as a "basic" right, and has labeled "fundamental" both the right to marry and the freedom of choice "whether to bear or beget a child." To understand what these characterizations may imply for the constitutional status of other forms of intimate association, it is necessary to ask why REPRODUCTIVE AUTONOMY and the freedom to marry are so important. To answer that question requires analysis of the substantive values that may be at stake in intimate associations.

The term "intimate association" is used here to mean a close and familiar personal relationship with another that is in some significant way comparable to a marriage or family relationship. Its connecting links may take the form of living together in the same quarters, or sexual intimacy, or blood ties, or a formal relationship, or some mixtures of these, but in principle the idea of intimate association also includes close friendship, with or without any such links. The values of intimate association are undeniably elusive; they are not readily reducible to items on a list. Yet such an exercise is implicit in any attempt to illuminate the principle underlying the decisions on marriage and reproductive choice. The potential values in intimate associations can be grouped in four clusters: society, caring and commitment, intimacy, and self-identification.

Intimate association implies some expectation of access of one person to another's physical presence, some opportunity for face-to-face encounter. A couple's claim of the right to live together, with or without a sexual relationship, directly implicates this interest in another's society; so does a divorced parent's claim of a right of access to a child in a former spouse's custody, or a prison rule wholly denying visitation rights. Other impairments of the interest in an intimate's society are indirect, as when welfare aid to a mother's family is terminated because she is living with a man. The latter case offers opportunity for manipulation; it might be characterized as a denial of no more than a money payment, or as a denial of the society of an intimate. To allow a claim of constitutional right to turn on such question-begging seems intolerable; yet that is just what the Supreme Court typically does in cases of indirect interference with the values of intimate association. Concededly, not every impairment of the freedom to enjoy an intimate's society requires the same degree of justification, but there is little to be said for distracting attention from substantive interest-balancing by engaging in definitional legerdemain.

For most people, mutual caring and commitment are the chief values of intimate association. Caring implies commitment, for it requires an effort to know another, trust another, hope for another, and help another develop. The commitment in question is not a legal commitment enforceable by law, but a personal commitment, the sense that one is pledged to care for another and intends to keep the pledge. It is possible to be committed to an association one has not chosen; a young child exercises no choice in forming an association with her family and yet may feel wholly committed to them. Still, the value of commitment is usually heightened for the partners to an intimate association when they know there is real and continuing choice to maintain the association. The caring partner continually reaffirms her autonomy and responsibility by choosing the commitment, and the cared-for partner gains in self-respect by seeing himself through his partner's eyes as one who is worth being cared for. Furthermore, although commitment means an expectation of constancy over time, it is not paradoxical to say that effective legal shelter for this value must offer protection to casual intimate associations as well as lasting ones. Such a casual association may ripen into a durable one, and the value of commitment is fully realizable only in an atmosphere of freedom to choose whether a particular association will be fleeting or enduring. Finally, to limit the law's protection to lasting intimate associations would require intolerable inquiries into private behavior and private intentions.

Intimacy, in the context of intimate associations, is more than privacy in its ordinary sense of nondisclosure. When we speak of intimate friends, or of persons who share an intimate relationship, we refer to the intimacy of a close and enduring association, that is, intimacy in the context of caring and commitment. This sort of intimacy is something that a person can share with only a limited number of others, for it requires time and effort to know another and deal with her as a whole person.

Intimate associations are powerful influences over the development of most people's personalities. Not only do these associations give an individual his best chance to be seen (and thus to see himself) as a whole person rather than an aggregate of social roles; they also serve as statements to others. As the legal consequences of cohabitation come to approximate those of marriage, and as divorce becomes more readily available, marriage itself takes on a special significance for its expressive content as a statement that the couple wish to identify with each other. The decision whether to have a child is also a major occasion for self-identification. To become a parent is to assume a new status in the eyes of oneself and others. Plainly the freedom to choose one's intimate associations is at the heart of this notion of association-as-statement. And, just as the freedom of political nonassociation is properly recognized as a FIRST AMENDMENT right, the freedom not to form an intimate association is similarly linked to the freedom of expression.

These four sets of intimate associational values—society, caring and commitment, intimacy, and self-identification—coalesce in an area of the human psyche that is awkward to discuss in lawyers' language. Yet even before the *Jaycees* opinion the Supreme Court had occasionally suggested its awareness of the reasons why such values are important. In *Eisenstadt,* for example, Justice WILLIAM J. BRENNAN spoke of "unwarranted governmental intrusion into matters so fundamentally affecting a PERSON as the decision whether to bear or beget a child." Although the word "person" usually is no more than a prosaic reference to an individual, its use in this passage resonates in the registers of matters personal and the human personality. If freedoms relating to marriage and family and reproductive choice are "fundamental," the reason is that these concerns lie close to the center of one's sense of self.

Not all governmental restrictions on associational freedom are intrusive in the same degree on the values of intimate association. The constitutional freedom of intimate association is not a rule for decision but an organizing principle, demanding justification for governmental intrusions on close personal relationships in proportion to the magnitude of invasion of intimate associational values. One complicating feature of this interest-balancing is that the law's interference with the freedom of intimate association usually is not direct. Instead, government typically conditions some material benefit (employment, inheritance, welfare payments, Social Security) on the candidate's associations in fact or formal associational status.

In DANDRIDGE V. WILLIAMS (1970), for example, a state proportioned welfare benefits to family size but set an absolute limit on aid to any one family. The Supreme Court, treating the law as a restriction on money payments and ignoring its potential effects on family size, subjected it only to RATIONAL BASIS scrutiny. In CLEVELAND BOARD OF EDUCATION V. LAFLEUR (1974), however, pregnant school teachers were required to take a long maternity leave. The Court, emphasizing the right to procreate, rigorously scrutinized the law under the IRREBUTTABLE PRESUMPTIONS doctrine. This sort of question-begging without explanation, far from being aberrational, has been the norm for the Court's treatment of indirect restrictions on intimate association. It is not unusual for the Court to conceal its interest-balancing behind definitional assumptions.

When a state conditions a benefit on a formal associational status such as marriage or legitimacy of parentage, a further analytical complication arises. The state controls entry into the status as well as its legal consequences. Judicial evaluation of such a restriction on benefits must take into account the ease of entry. Alternatively, a law restricting entry into a formal associational status must be evaluated partly on the basis of the consequences of the status, including eligibility for benefits. The opportunities for circular reasoning are evident; only close attention to the associational values at stake will permit noncircular resolutions. The formal status of marriage, for example, must be seen not merely as a bureaucratic hurdle on the road to material benefits but also as a statement of the partners' commitment and self-identification.

In protecting the freedom of intimate association the Supreme Court has followed several different doctrinal paths. The *Griswold* opinion drew on the First Amendment's freedom of political association partly by way of analogy and partly in support of the Court's "zone of privacy" theory. Later decisions have both extended *Griswold*'s results in the name of equal protection and recharacterized its right of privacy as a substantive due process right. For a brief time in the 1970s the Court even used the rhetoric of PROCEDURAL DUE PROCESS and irrebuttable presumptions to defend the freedom of intimate association—a development which some Justices called a disguised form of equal protection or substantive due process. Today the freedom's most secure doctrinal base is substantive due process; yet both the First Amendment and the equal protection clause counsel judicial sensitivity to the need to protect intimate associations that are unconventional or that may offend majoritarian morality. In a society that expresses its cultural diversity in a rich variety of family forms and other personal relationships, these constitutional claims of freedom and equality will overlap.

Whatever its doctrinal context, a claim to freedom of intimate association depends on the nature and magnitude of the intrusion into the substantive values of intimate association, weighed against the governmental interests asserted to justify the intrusion. To give life to this abstraction it is necessary to examine the freedom of intimate association in operation as an organizing principle in particular subject areas. The Supreme Court's decisions can be grouped in seven overlapping categories: marriage and husband–wife relations; divorce; nonmarital relationships; procreation; illegitimacy; family autonomy; and homosexual relationships.

The Supreme Court's clear recognition of a constitutional right to marry by no means forecloses a state from regulating entry into marriage. Some restrictions, in fact, promote the principle of associational choice: minimum age requirements, for example, or requirements demanding minimum competency to understand the nature of marriage. Other restrictions aimed at promoting public health, such as mandatory blood tests, also seem likely to pass the test of strict judicial scrutiny. It is less clear that the balance of state interests against the freedom of associational choice should uphold a prohibition against POLYGAMY, or a refusal to allow homosexuals a status comparable to marriage, or a prohibition on marriage between first cousins. Yet it is safe to predict that homosexual marriage will not gain judicial blessing in the immediate future, and that the constitutionality of incest and polygamy laws will not be questioned seriously in any future now foreseeable. The Supreme Court, after all, is an instrument of government in a human society. Still, in theory, any direct state prohibition of marriage must pass the test of strict scrutiny, and indirect restriction on the right to marry requires justification proportioned to the restriction's likely practical effects as a prohibition.

The freedom of intimate association speaks not only to state interference with the right to marry but also to state intrusion into the relations between husband and wife. A marriage is more than a list of contractual duties; the partners deal with each other on many levels, both practical and emotional, and their relations are necessarily diffuse rather than particularized, exploratory rather than fixed. Spouses who are committed to stay together in an intimacy characterized by caring need to heal their relationship for the future, not settle old scores. Long before *Griswold* recognized a married couple's constitutional right to autonomy over the intimacies of their relationship, our nonconstitutional law largely maintained a "hands-off" attitude toward interspousal disputes. This tradition once supported a system of patriarchy now discredited; today the values of intimate association counsel the state to leave the partners to an ongoing marriage alone and let them work out their own differences—or, if they cannot, to terminate the marriage with a minimum of state interference.

Although the Supreme Court has not formally recognized a constitutional "right to divorce" comparable to the right to marry, both in principle and in practical effect such a right can be derived from the Court's decisions. The freedom of intimate association demands significant justification for state restrictions on exit from a marriage. The relevance to divorce of the associational value of self-identification is evident. Even the value of commitment bears on such a case, and not merely because divorce is the legal key to remarriage. For those who choose to stay married, their commitment is heightened by the knowledge that it is freely chosen. The Constitution apart, state laws setting conditions for divorce have virtually eliminated the requirement of a showing of one partner's fault. The restrictions that remain concern ACCESS TO THE COURTS, and involve limitations such as filing fees, as in BODDIE V. CONNECTICUT (1971), or RESIDENCE REQUIREMENTS, as in SOSNA V. IOWA (1975).

When a marriage terminates, nothing in the principle of associational choice militates against judicial enforcement of interspousal contracts governing the division of property. Once the union is dissolved, application of the usual rules of contract law to postdissolution obligations threatens none of the values of intimate association and demands no special justification. (Issues of child custody, which do require careful balancing of associational values, are discussed along with other parent–child questions.)

When a couple live together in a sexual relationship without marrying, the associational values of society, caring, and intimacy are all present in important degrees. Although the couple's association may not be so definitive a statement of self-identification as marriage would be, such a statement it surely is. Even the commitment implicit in such a union, although it may be tentative, usually is not trivial. If the couple see the union as a trial marriage, it takes on the instrumental quality that the *Griswold* court saw in sexual privacy. The Supreme Court's decisions on contraception and abortion have extended that right of privacy to unmarried persons. In 1968 the Court construed federal welfare legislation to prevent a state from terminating a mother's benefits merely because she had a man, not her husband, living in the house; Justice Douglas, concurring, would have held the state's attempted regulation of the mother's morals a denial of equal protection, by analogy to the Court's then recent decisions on illegitimacy. Some classifications based on marital status plainly are unconstitutional.

It seems no more than a matter of time before the Court, recognizing the expansion of the boundaries of the acceptable in intimate association, follows the logic of the contraception cases and holds invalid state laws forbidding fornication and unmarried cohabitation. Many lower courts have reached similar results, typically without addressing constitutional issues. Most of the cases have involved the claims of unmarried women denied employment, or child custody, or admission to the bar because they were living with men. The freedom of intimate association is, in important part, a product of the movement for equality between the sexes.

So are the Supreme Court's decisions on reproductive choice. "Birth control is woman's problem," said Margaret Sanger in 1920; it still is. The right to procreate, which another generation's Court called "one of the basic civil rights to man," is now matched with the constitutional right of man and woman alike to practice contraception and with a woman's right to have an abortion, even over her husband's objection. Although the right to choose "whether to bear or beget a child" is not reducible to an aspect of the freedom of intimate association, it is in part an associational choice. Given today's facility of contraception and abortion, generally one can choose whether to be a parent. The *Skinner* opinion properly connected marriage and procreation. An unmarried couple living together recognize this linkage when they decide to marry because they "want to have a family." Children are valued not only for themselves and the associations they bring but also as living expressions of their parents' caring for—and commitment to—each other. The decision whether to have a child is, in part, a choice of social identification and self-concept; it ranks in importance with any other a person may make in a lifetime.

Not only the right to be a parent, protected in *Skinner,* but also the right to choose to defer parenthood or to avoid it altogether implicates the core values of intimate association. *Griswold* and its successor decisions, defending these values in the context of nonassociation, protect men and women—but particularly women—against the enforced intimate society of unwanted children, against an unchosen commitment and a caring stained by reluctance, against a compelled identification with the social role of parent. Coerced intimate association in the shape of forced child-bearing or parenthood is no less serious an invasion of the sense of self than is forced marriage.

*Griswold* and its successors also protect the autonomy of a couple's association, whether it be a marriage or an association of unmarried intimates. The point was explicitly made in the *Griswold* opinion concerning marital autonomy, and *Eisenstadt v. Baird* (1972) effectively gave unmarried couples the same power to govern the intimacies of their association. What emerges from these decisions, along with *Skinner* and *LaFleur,* is not an absolute rule but a requirement of appropriate justification when the state burdens the decision whether to procreate.

The Supreme Court has focused on equal protection in dealing with the constitutionality of laws defining the incidents of illegitimacy. There is obvious unfairness in visiting unequal treatment on an illegitimate child in order to express the state's disapproval of her parents. Yet the freedom of intimate association suggests an additional perspective: the unfairness of state-imposed inequality between persons in traditional marriage/family relationships and those in other comparable forms of intimate association. In particular, the illegitimacy laws discriminate against unmarried women and their children—as, indeed, such laws have done from their medieval beginnings. The principle of legitimacy of parentage assumes not only that a child needs a male link to the rest of the community but also that the claim of the child's mother to social position depends on her being granted the status of formal marriage. In historical origin and in modern application, the chief function of the law of illegitimacy is to assure male control over the transmission of wealth and status. Deviance from the principle of legitimacy is most likely in subgroups whose fathers lack wealth and status; it is no accident that the incidence of illegitimacy in our society is highest among the nonwhite poor.

As increased numbers of middle-class couples live together without marrying, surely there will be changes in the legal status of unmarried mothers and their children. In the perspective of the freedom of intimate association, the constitutional basis for the whole system of illegitimacy appears shaky. If the informal union of an unmarried couple is constitutionally protected, the relationship between that union's children and their parents is also protected. Significant impairment of the substantive values of such an intimate association must find justification, in proportion to the impairment, in state interests that cannot be achieved by other less intrusive means.

Ever since *Meyer v. Nebraska* (1923) and *Pierce v. Society of Sisters* (1925) judges and commentators have assumed that the Constitution protects the autonomy of the traditional family against excessive state interference. Those two decisions rested on substantive due process grounds, and they have been cited often by the Supreme Court during the modern revival of substantive due process as a guarantee of personal liberty. When a family is united concerning such matters as the children's education, only a COMPELLING STATE INTEREST will justify state interference with the family's choice.

When a family is not united, however, the constitutional principle of family autonomy is an imperfect guide. Generally, the law assumes that children prosper under their parents' control. For very young children, this assumption is little more than a corollary of the family autonomy principle. As children mature, however, it becomes sensible to speak of the continuing family relationship as a matter of choice. Within the family that stays together, parent–child relations are, from some point in a child's teenage years forward, a matter of intrafamily agreement. Even when parental discipline is the rule, it rests on the child's consent, once the child is capable of making an independent life. Not surprisingly, the Supreme Court held invalid a state law giving an unmarried minor female's parents the right to veto her decision to have an abortion. (See PLANNED PARENTHOOD OF MISSOURI v. DANFORTH, 1976.)

The freedom of intimate association thus counsels severe restrictions on the state's power to intervene either to enforce parental authority or to oppose it—just as considerations of intramarital associational choice and harmony dictate that state intervention into the husband–wife relationship be limited to cases of urgent necessity, such as wife abuse. Conceding that most children want and need parental discipline, it remains true that invoking the state's police officers and juvenile halls to enforce that discipline is destructive of the values of intimate association. For mature children, those values depend on their willingness to identify with their parents and to be committed to maintaining a caring intimacy with them. In cases of a parent's incapacity or serious neglect, state intervention into the zone of family autonomy may be constitutionally justified. Yet removals of children from parental custody and terminations of parental rights are extreme measures, intruding deeply into the values of intimate association—not only for parents but also for children. The most compelling justification is therefore required for so drastic a state intervention, justification found in the child's needs, not any interest the state may have in punishing parental misbehavior. The Supreme Court's refusal in LASSITER v. DEPARTMENT OF SOCIAL SERVICES (1981) to extend the full reach of the RIGHT TO COUNSEL to indigent parents in termination proceedings seems an unstable precedent.

While a marriage lasts, the law is no more likely to interfere in interspousal disputes over child-rearing than it is in other controversies between husband and wife. When a marriage ends, an agreement between the separating parents over child custody usually will prevail, absent some overriding factor such as the associational choice of a mature child. A custody contest upon divorce, involving competing claims of rights of association, demands discretionary, whole-person evaluations rather than application of specific rules of law. The Constitution comes to bear on such decisions only marginally, as appellate courts seek to assure that trial judges do, in fact, consider the whole persons before them and do not disqualify parents from custody by informally substituting unconstitutional "rules" for the discretion that is appropriate. Such a "rule," for example, might disqualify on the basis of a parent's race— or, as in PALMORE v. SIDOTI (1984), the race of the parent's spouse—or religion, or unmarried cohabitation, or sexual preference. *Stanley v. Illinois* (1972) is an instructive analogy; there the Supreme Court held that a law disqualifying a natural father from custody of his illegitimate child upon the mother's death was an unconstitutional irrebuttable presumption of unfitness.

It is now established beyond question that the "liberty" protected by the two due process clauses protects "freedom of personal choice in matters of marriage and family life"—Justice POTTER STEWART's words, concurring in *Zablocki v. Redhail* (1978). If the logic of that freedom extends beyond formal marriage and beyond the nuclear family, the reason is that the human family is a social artifact, not an entity defined in nature. In MOORE v. CITY OF EAST CLEVELAND (1977) a plurality of four Justices admitted the traditional "extended family" into the circle of due process protection, and that opinion is now regularly cited as if it were an OPINION OF THE COURT. The freedom Justice Stewart described is comprehensible only in the light of intimate associational values that are also found in families that depart significantly from traditional models. One result of the movement for women's liberation has been the increased adoption of alternative living arrangements: couples living together outside marriage; single mothers with children, sometimes combining with other similar families. Other groupings such as communes for the young and the old are responses to what their members see as the failings of traditional arrangements. These people do not risk prosecution under cohabitation laws or other "morals" statutes; they may, however, risk the loss of material benefits.

Any governmental intrusion on personal choice of living arrangements requires substantial justification, in proportion to its likely influence in coercing people out of one form of intimate association and into another. In DEPARTMENT OF AGRICULTURE v. MORENO (1973) the Supreme Court demanded such justification for a law denying food stamps to households composed of "unrelated" persons, and found it lacking. Yet in *Village of Belle Terre v. Boraas* (1974) the Court made no search for justification beyond minimum rationality, and upheld a ZONING ordinance designed to screen out nontraditional families and applied to exclude occupancy of a home by six unrelated students. In design, the *Belle Terre* ordinance was a direct assault on the freedom of intimate association, an attempt to stamp out forms of personal association departing from a vision of family life that no longer fit a large proportion of the population. *Belle Terre*'s standing as a precedent surely will weaken as the Court comes to take seriously its own rhetoric about "family" values in nontraditional families. One occasion for such rhetoric was the opinion in *Smith v. Organization of Foster Families* (1977), recognizing the values of intimate association in a foster family.

Laws prohibiting homosexual conduct are only rarely enforced against private consensual behavior. The middle-class homosexual couple thus have each other's society, including whatever sort of intimacy they want; they care for each other and are committed to each other in the degree they choose. What government chiefly denies them is the dignity of self-identification as equal citizens, along with certain forms of employment and other material benefits that may be reserved for partners to a formal marriage.

Whatever may have been the original purpose of laws forbidding homosexual sex, today one of their chief supports is a wish to regulate the content of messages about sexual preference. One fear is that the state, by repealing its restrictions, will be seen as approving homosexual conduct. The selective enforcement of these laws is itself evidence that one of the main policies being pursued is the suppression of expression; the laws are enforced mainly against those who openly advertise their sexual preferences. The immediate practical effect of this enforcement pattern is to penalize public self-identification and expression, some of which is political expression in support of "gay liberation." Even thoroughgoing enforcement would severely impair expression, along with the values of caring and intimacy. For a homosexual, a violation of these laws is the principal form that a sexual expression of love can take.

The denial of the status of marriage, or some comparable status, does not merely limit homosexuals' opportunities for expressive self-identification; material benefits also are frequently conditioned on marriage. Some commentators argue that a state's refusal to recognize homosexual marriage raises a problem of sex discrimination, and others contend that homosexuality should be regarded as a SUSPECT CLASSIFICATION for equal protection purposes. In any case, the heart of the constitutional problem lies in the freedom of intimate association. Although the denial of formal recognition of a homosexual couple's union may not demand the same compelling justification that would be required by a total prohibition of homosexual relations, it nonetheless seems unlikely that government could meet any requirement of justification that was not wholly permissive.

The burden of justification is of critical importance in the area of regulation of homosexual conduct, precisely because most such regulations are the product of folklore and fantasy rather than evidence of real risk of harm. If, for example, the state had to prove that a lesbian mother, by virtue of that status alone, was unfit to have custody of her child, the effort surely would demonstrate that the operative factor in the disqualification was not risk of harm, but stigma. The results of serious constitutional inquiry into harms and justifications in such cases are easy to predict. First, however, that serious inquiry must be made, and the Supreme Court showed in *Doe v. Commonwealth's District Attorney* (1976) that it was not eager to embark on that course.

The freedom of intimate association serves as an organizing principle mainly by focusing attention on substantive associational values. In a given case, the impairment of those values is matched against the asserted justifications for governmental regulation. Those justifications are hard to discuss systematically, for they can be asserted on the basis of a range of interests as broad as the public welfare. One cluster of justifications, however, deserves attention: the promotion of a political majority's view of morality. The state may claim a role in socializing its citizens, and especially the young, to traditional values. When a legislature prohibits unmarried cohabitation or homosexual relations or other disapproved forms of intimate association, it does so primarily to promote a moral view and to protect the sensibilities of those who share that view. The freedom of intimate association does not wholly disable government from seeking these ends; however, as *Griswold* and its successor decisions show, neither can the state defeat every claim to the freedom of intimate association simply by invoking conventional morality.

The judicial interest-balancing appropriate to the evolution of many claims of freedom of intimate association thus must consider not only degrees of impairment of associational values but also questions of the kind raised by GOVERNMENT SPEECH cases involving official promotion of particular points of view. There is a difference, for example, between a "baby bonus" designed to assist parents with child-rearing and a state's offer of cash to any woman entering an abortion clinic, conditioned on her agreement to forgo an abortion. To say that the difference is one of degree is to remind ourselves that the judicial function in constitutional cases is one of judgment. The freedom of intimate association is not a machine that, once set in motion, must run to all conceivable logical conclusions. It is instead a constitutional principle, requiring significant justification when the state seeks to lay hands on life-defining intimate associational choices.

Bibliography

BURT, ROBERT A.    1979    The Constitution of the Family. *Supreme Court Review* 1979:329–395.

Developments in the Law—The Constitution and the Family    1980    *Harvard Law Review* 93:1156–1383.

GERETY, TOM    1977    Redefining Privacy. *Harvard Civil Rights-Civil Liberties Law Review* 12:233–296.

GLENDON, MARY ANN    1977    *State, Law and Family.* New York: North-Holland Publishing Company.

KARST, KENNETH L.    1980    The Freedom of Intimate Association. *Yale Law Journal* 89:624–692.

SYMPOSIUM    1975    Children and the Law. *Law and Contemporary Problems* 39, no. 3:1–293.

SYMPOSIUM    1979    Children and the Law. *University of California, Davis Law Review* 12:207–898.

SYMPOSIUM    1985    The Legal System and Homosexuality—Approbation, Accommodation, or Reprobation? *University of Dayton Law Review* 10:445–813.

TRIBE, LAURENCE H.    1978    *American Constitutional Law.* Chap. 15. Mineola, N.Y.: Foundation Press.

WILKINSON, J. HARVIE, III and WHITE, G. EDWARD 1977    Constitutional Protection for Personal Lifestyles. *Cornell Law Review* 62:563–625.

# ALIENS

## Kenneth L. Karst

The status of aliens—persons who are not citizens of the United States—presented perplexing constitutional problems in this country only after the great waves of IMMIGRATION began in the nineteenth century. The question seems not to have troubled the Framers of the Constitution. JAMES MADISON, in THE FEDERALIST #42, defended the power of Congress to set a uniform rule of NATURALIZATION as a means for easing interstate friction. Absent such a congressional law, he argued, State A might grant CITIZENSHIP to an alien who, on moving to State B, would become entitled to most of the PRIVILEGES AND IMMUNITIES granted by State B to its citizens. Evidently it was assumed from the beginning that aliens were not protected by Article IV's privileges and immunities clause, and it is still the conventional wisdom—although not unchallenged—that aliens cannot claim "the privileges and immunities of citizens of the United States" guaranteed by the FOURTEENTH AMENDMENT.

Alienage has sometimes been treated as synonymous with dissent, or even disloyalty. The ALIEN AND SEDITION ACTS (1798), for example, were aimed not only at American citizens who opposed President JOHN ADAMS but also at their supporters among French and Irish immigrants. The PALMER RAIDS of 1919–1920 culminated in the DEPORTATION of hundreds of alien anarchists and others suspected of SUBVERSIVE ACTIVITIES. At the outbreak of World War II, Attorney General FRANCIS BIDDLE was determined to avoid the mass internment of aliens; in the event, however, Biddle deferred to War Department pressure, and more than 100,000 persons of Japanese ancestry, alien and citizen alike, were removed from their West Coast homes and taken to camps in the interior. (See JAPANESE AMERICAN CASES, 1943–1944.)

When the KENTUCKY RESOLUTIONS (1798) protested against the Alien and Sedition Acts, they defended not so much the rights of aliens as STATES' RIGHTS. Indeed, the *rights* of aliens were not a major concern in the nation's early years. Even the federal courts' DIVERSITY JURISDICTION could be invoked in a case involving aliens only when citizens of a state were on the other side, as HODGSON v. BOWERBANK (1809) held. For this jurisdictional purpose, a "citizen" of a state still means a United States citizen who is also a state citizen. (An alien can sue another alien in a state court.) Thus, while a state can grant "state citizenship"—can allow aliens to vote, hold public office, or receive state benefits—that state citizenship does not qualify a person as a "citizen" within the meaning of the Constitution. Some states have previously allowed aliens to vote; even today, some states allow aliens to hold public office.

Most individual rights protected by the Constitution are not limited to "citizens" but extend to "people" or "persons," including aliens. An exception is the right to vote, protected by the FIFTEENTH, NINETEENTH, and TWENTY-SIXTH AMENDMENTS, which is limited to citizens. Aliens do not, of course, have the constitutional freedom of entry into the country that citizens have; aliens' stay here can be conditioned on conduct—for example, the retention of student status—that could not constitutionally be required of citizens. An alien, but not a citizen, can be deported for certain violations of law. In wartime, the property of enemy aliens can be confiscated. Yet aliens are subject to many of the obligations fastened on citizens: they pay taxes along with the rest of us, and, if Congress so disposes, they are as susceptible as citizens to CONSCRIPTION into the armed forces.

Congress, by authorizing the admission of some aliens for permanent residence, accepts those admittees as at least limited members of the national community. The CIVIL RIGHTS ACT OF 1866, for example, protects a resident alien against state legislation that interferes with the alien's earning a livelihood. The vitality of the PREEMPTION DOCTRINE in such cases no doubt rests on two assumptions: that the national government, not the states, has the primary responsibility for the nation's dealings with foreign countries, and that the regulation of another country's nationals is likely to affect those dealings.

Throughout our history, state laws have discriminated against aliens by disqualifying them from various forms of public and private employment, and from receiving public assistance benefits. Early decisions of the Supreme Court mostly upheld these laws, ignoring their evident tensions with congressional policy and rejecting claims based on the Fourteenth Amendment's EQUAL PROTECTION clause. Two decisions in 1948, OYAMA V. CALIFORNIA and TAKAHASHI V. FISH & GAME COMMISSION, undermined the earlier precedents, and in the 1970s the Court made a frontal assault on state discriminations against aliens.

A legislative classification based on the status of alienage, the Court announced in GRAHAM V. RICHARDSON (1971), was a SUSPECT CLASSIFICATION, analogous to a racial classification. Thus, justifications offered to support the classification must pass the test of STRICT SCRUTINY. State restrictions of WELFARE BENEFITS, on the basis of alienage, were accordingly invalidated. Two years later, this reasoning was extended to invalidate a law disqualifying aliens from a state's civil service, SUGARMAN V. DOUGALL (1973), and a law barring aliens from the practice of law, IN RE GRIFFITHS (1973). The string of invalidations of state laws continued with *Examining Board v. Flores de Otero* (1976) (disqualification to be a civil engineer) and *Nyquist v. Mauclet* (1977) (limiting eligibility for state scholarship aid).

In the *Sugarman* opinion, the Court had remarked that some state discriminations against aliens would not have to pass strict judicial scrutiny. The right to vote in state elections, or to hold high public office, might be limited to United States citizens on the theory that such rights are closely connected with the idea of membership in a political community. By the end of the decade, these words had become the foundation for a large exception to the principle of strict scrutiny of alienage classifications. The "political community" notion was extended to a broad category of public employees performing "government functions" requiring the exercise of discretion and responsibility. Disqualification of aliens from such jobs would be upheld if it was supported by a RATIONAL BASIS. FOLEY V. CONNELIE (1978) thus upheld a law disqualifying aliens to serve as state troopers, and AMBACH v. NORWICK (1979) upheld a law barring aliens from teaching in public schools unless they had shown an intent to become U.S. citizens. *Cabell v. Chavez-Salido* (1982) extended the same reasoning to state probation officers.

At the same time, the Court made clear that when Congress discriminated against aliens, nothing like strict judicial scrutiny was appropriate. *Mathews v. Diaz* (1976) announced an extremely deferential standard of review for such congressional laws, saying that the strong federal interest in regulating foreign affairs provided a close analogy to the doctrine of POLITICAL QUESTIONS—which suggests, of course, essentially no judicial scrutiny at all.

It was argued for a time that the preemption doctrine provides the most complete explanation of the Court's results in alienage cases. The early 1970s decisions, grounded on equal protection theory, instead might have been rested on congressional laws such as the 1866 act. The decisions on "governmental functions," seen in this light, would amount to a recognition that Congress has not admitted resident aliens to the "political community." On this theory, because Congress has not admitted "undocumented" aliens for any purpose at all, state laws regulating them would be viewed favorably. In PLYLER V. DOE (1982), the Supreme Court rejected this line of reasoning and held, 5–4, that Texas had denied equal protection by refusing free public education to children not lawfully admitted to the country while providing it for all other children. The majority, conceding that Congress might authorize some forms of state discrimination, discerned no such authorization in Congress's silence.

The preemption analysis, no less than an equal protection analysis, leaves the key term ("political community") for manipulation; on either theory, for example, the school teacher case seems wrongly decided. And the equal protection approach has one advantage that is undeniable:

it focuses the judiciary on questions that bear some relation to life—substantive questions about degrees of discrimination and proffered justifications—rather than on the metaphysics of preemption.

Bibliography

NOTE    1975    Aliens' Right to Teach: Political Socialization and the Public Schools. *Yale Law Journal* 85:90–111.

NOTE    1979    A Dual Standard for State Discrimination Against Aliens. *Harvard Law Review* 92:1516–1537.

NOTE    1979    The Equal Treatment of Aliens: Preemption or Equal Protection? *Stanford Law Review* 31:1069–1091.

NOTE    1980    State Burdens on Resident Aliens: A New Preemption Analysis. *Yale Law Journal* 89:940–961.

PRESTON, WILLIAM, JR.    1963    *Aliens and Dissenters: Federal Suppression of Radicals, 1903–1933.* Cambridge, Mass.: Harvard University Press.

ROSBERG, GERALD M.    1977    The Protection of Aliens from Discriminatory Treatment by the National Government. *Supreme Court Review* 1977:275–339.

# *PLYLER v. DOE*

457 U.S. 202 (1982)

Kenneth L. Karst

Experimenting with ignorance, the Texas legislature authorized local school boards to exclude the children of undocumented ALIENS from the public schools, and cut off state funds to subsidize those children's schooling. The Supreme Court, 5–4, held that this scheme denied the alien children the EQUAL PROTECTION OF THE LAWS. The OPINION OF THE COURT, by Justice WILLIAM J. BRENNAN, contains the potential for important future influence on equal protection DOCTRINE.

The Court was unanimous on one point: the FOURTEENTH AMENDMENT's guarantee of equal protection for all PERSONS extends not only to aliens lawfully admitted for residence but also to undocumented aliens. The question that divided the Court was what that guarantee demanded—an issue that the Court's recent opinions had typically discussed in language about the appropriate STANDARD OF REVIEW. In SAN ANTONIO INDEPENDENT SCHOOL DISTRICT v. RODRIGUEZ (1973) the Court had rejected the claim that EDUCATION was a FUNDAMENTAL INTEREST, and had subjected a state system for financing schools to a deferential RATIONAL BASIS standard. A significant OBITER DICTUM, however, had suggested that a total denial of education to a certain group of children would have to pass the test of STRICT SCRUTINY. (See GRIFFIN v. COUNTY SCHOOL BOARD OF PRINCE EDWARD COUNTY, 1964.) Furthermore, although alienage was, for some purposes, a SUSPECT CLASSIFICATION, the Court had not extended that characterization to laws discriminating against aliens who were not lawfully admitted to the country.

Justice Brennan's analysis blurred the already indistinct lines dividing levels of judicial scrutiny in equal protection cases. He suggested that some form of "intermediate scrutiny" was appropriate, and even hinted at a preference for strict scrutiny. Eventually, though, he came to rest on rhetorical ground that could hold together a five-Justice majority. Because the Texas law imposed a severe penalty on children for their parents' misconduct, it was irrational unless the state could show that it furthered "some substantial goal of the State," and no such showing had been made. In a concurring opinion, Justice LEWIS F. POWELL remarked that heightened scrutiny was proper, on analogy to the Court's decisions about classifications based on ILLEGITIMACY. Justice THURGOOD

Marshall, also concurring, repeated his argument for recognition of a "sliding scale" of standards of review, and accurately noted that this very decision illustrated that the Court was already employing such a system. No one should be surprised when the Court holds invalid a supremely stupid law that imposes great hardship on a group of innocent people.

Chief Justice WARREN E. BURGER, writing for the four dissenters, agreed that the Texas policy was "senseless." He argued nonetheless that the Court, by undertaking a "policymaking role," was "trespass[ing] on the assigned function of the political branches." In allocating scarce state resources, Texas could rationally choose to prefer citizens and lawfully admitted aliens over aliens who had entered the country without permission; for the dissenters, that was enough to validate the law.

The *Plyler* opinion was narrow, leaving open the question whether a similar burden of substantial justification would be imposed on a discrimination against undocumented aliens who were adults, or even against innocent children when the discrimination was something less than a total denial of education. Justice Brennan did suggest that judicial scrutiny might properly be heightened in cases of discrimination against aliens—even undocumented aliens—who had established "a permanent attachment to the nation." Although it is unlikely that this view could command a majority of the Court today, the remark may bear fruit in the future.

# INDIGENT

### Kenneth L. Karst

An indigent is a person too poor to provide for certain basic needs. It would be unconstitutional for a state or the national government deliberately to deny benefits or impose burdens on the basis of a person's indigency. To this extent, today's law fulfills Justice ROBERT H. JACKSON's prescription, concurring in EDWARDS v. CALIFORNIA (1941): "The mere state of being without funds is a neutral fact—constitutionally an irrelevance, like race, creed, or color." In a market economy, however, indigency is anything but an irrelevance; unrelieved, it bars access to virtually everything money can buy. Unsurprisingly, therefore, the Supreme Court has found in the Constitution affirmative obligations on government to supply to indigents certain benefits that they cannot afford to buy for themselves. These obligations are few in number; the very idea of a market economy implies de facto WEALTH DISCRIMINATION in the sense of differential access to goods and services, and in no sense has the Court declared capitalism unconstitutional. (See FREEDOM OF CONTRACT.)

The first focus for the Court's egalitarian concerns for relieving the poor from consequences of their poverty was the criminal process. In cases such as GRIFFIN v. ILLINOIS (1956) and DOUGLAS v. CALIFORNIA (1963), one doctrinal vehicle was the EQUAL PROTECTION clause. But the goal of "equal justice for poor and rich, weak and powerful alike" contained no easily discernible place to stop, and it was always clear that the Court would not require the states to make unlimited funds available so that all accused persons could match the spending of the very rich on their criminal defense. The alternative to the equality principle was insistence on minimum standards of criminal justice for everyone, and the Court's post-1950 decisions tightening those standards—not merely in areas such as the RIGHT TO COUNSEL or the setting of BAIL but throughout the criminal process—can be seen in this egalitarian light, reflecting a recognition that the criminal justice system generally bears most heavily on the poor.

A similar approach, setting minimum standards of justice, had characterized the Court's treatment of claims by the poor to access to civil courts and administrative hearings. PROCEDURAL DUE PROCESS, not equal protection, provides the doctrinal foundation for this development. A concern for hardship to the poor surely played an important role in decisions such as BODDIE V. CONNECTICUT (1971) (access to divorce courts for persons unable to afford filing fees), *Sniadach v. Family Finance Corp.* (1969) (prior hearings prerequisite for prejudgment garnishment), and GOLDBERG V. KELLY (1970) (prior hearings prerequisite for termination of WELFARE BENEFITS). But just as the Court has stopped far short of a general principle of equal access to criminal justice, so it has refused to make equality the guiding principle for its decisions on access to civil justice; in LASSITER V. DEPARTMENT OF SOCIAL SERVICES (1981) the Court denied the existence of a right to state-appointed counsel in proceedings to terminate parental rights.

The one area where the equality principle has guided the Supreme Court's treatment of poverty is the electoral process. The development began with HARPER V. VIRGINIA STATE BOARD OF ELECTIONS (1966), which invalidated a POLL TAX as a condition on voting in a state election. Property qualifications to vote, too, were invalidated, except in the elections of special-purpose districts. Not only VOTING RIGHTS but also rights of access to the ballot were secured against financial barriers that would disqualify the poor.

The early 1970s marked a turning point in the constitutional protection of indigents against the consequences of their poverty. Since that time, the Court has drawn one line after another constricting the expansion of either equal protection or due process doctrines to impose on government further affirmative obligations to relieve the burdens of poverty—even when those burdens affect the quality of an indigent's relations with government itself.

Bibliography

BRUDNO, BARBARA    1976    *Poverty, Inequality, and the Law.*  St. Paul, Minn.: West Publishing Co.

# WEALTH DISCRIMINATION

Barbara Brudno

Wealth discrimination—the state's allocation of resources on the basis of ability to pay—has received the attention of the courts only recently. Sensitivity to the plight of the poor was an outgrowth of the CIVIL RIGHTS movement of the 1960s. Thus, the first constitutional issue raised by EQUAL PROTECTION claims of the poor was whether poverty-based discrimination is analogous to RACIAL DISCRIMINATION for purposes of the applicable STANDARD OF REVIEW.

Advocates of this analogy stress the poor's lack of political power and the public's antipathy to the poor and to programs, such as welfare, enacted to ameliorate poverty. They argue that the Supreme Court should give less deference to legislative judgments when reviewing poverty discrimination claims than it does when reviewing ECONOMIC REGULATIONS challenged by those able to pursue nonjudicial means of redress. However, at no time during the more than quarter of a century since the Court's first decision in this area, GRIFFIN V. ILLINOIS (1956), has a majority of the Court ever embraced the analogy to race for purposes of equal protection review.

The *Griffin* decision held unconstitutional a state's refusal to provide an INDIGENT convicted criminal defendant with a free transcript necessary to obtain meaningful appellate review. In so holding, *Griffin* enunciated a potentially expansive principle of "equal justice": "[A] state can no more discriminate on account of poverty than on account of religion, race, or color. . . . There can be no equal justice when the kind of trial [or APPEAL] a man gets depends on the amount of money he has."

Since *Griffin*, the Supreme Court has struck down poverty-based discrimination in only a few other cases, most notably DOUGLAS V. CALIFORNIA (1963) and BODDIE V. CONNECTICUT (1971). *Douglas* held unconstitutional a state's refusal to appoint counsel for an indigent seeking appellate review of a criminal conviction; and *Boddie* held unconstitutional a state's refusal to waive court access fees which deprived an indigent plaintiff of access to the only available forum for obtaining a divorce.

In the vast majority of poverty-based discrimination cases, however, the Supreme Court has treated the poor's claims, whether they involve access to the judicial process itself, equal educational opportunity, or the very means of survival, the same as any other challenged "social and economic" regulation. Thus, the Court has applied the RATIONAL BASIS standard of review to uphold a $50 bankruptcy filing fee against a debtor too poor to pay it; a state financing system that allocated educational resources according to the tax bases of school districts; and an allocation of WELFARE BENEFITS that discriminated on the basis of family size. (See *United States v. Kras,* 1973; SAN ANTONIO INDEPENDENT SCHOOL DISTRICT v. RODRIGUEZ, 1973; DANDRIDGE v. WILLIAMS, 1971.)

Several reasons may underlie the Court's refusal actively to scrutinize legislation adversely affecting the poor. If the Court holds a payment requirement unconstitutional as applied to the poor, someone must decide who is poor enough to qualify for this affirmative relief. Moreover, such a holding may require the legislative branch to reallocate its budget to provide the funds necessary to pay for what the poor cannot afford, something which the courts are always reluctant to do, especially in times of economic recession.

Another reason for judicial restraint lies in the need for line-drawing. If not all poverty-based inequalities or deprivations are unconstitutional—as surely they are not in a market economy—then the Court must delineate those interests that are sufficiently "vital" or "fundamental" to justify stricter judicial scrutiny when the state allocates such interests through a pricing system that deprives poor people from access to them. Obvious candidates include basic necessities such as food, housing, and other means of subsistence. Beginning with its 1971 decision in *Dandridge,* however, the Supreme Court consistently has refused to treat any such interests as entitled to a heightened equal protection standard of review. Moreover, in MAHER v. ROE (1977) the Court carried this refusal to apply a meaningful equal protection standard to any discriminatory "social and economic" legislation to the extreme of validating a provision prohibiting Medicaid funding of abortion although other, including pregnancy-related medical care costs, were funded and the choice to seek an abortion rather than bear a child had been held to be constitutionally protected. Moreover, *Maher* upheld this discrimination even though, unlike the discrimination upheld in all similar prior cases, it cost rather than saved taxpayer dollars. (See HARRIS v. McRAE, 1980.)

The Court's refusal since 1971 to treat "vital interests" of the poor as comparable to constitutionally guaranteed rights is one matter. In *Maher,* however, the Court validated discrimination only among the poor and solely on the basis of the poor's attempt to exercise a constitutionally guaranteed right of choice otherwise available to everyone. The recent jurisprudence of wealth discrimination legitimates and reinforces a dual system of constitutional rights, leaving the poor—who disproportionately are composed of women, children, the aged, and racial minorities—with paper rights beyond their financial reach.

Bibliography

BINION, GAYLE   1982   The Disadvantaged Before the Burger Court: The Newest Unequal Protection. *Law & Policy Quarterly* 4:37–69.

BRUDNO, BARBARA   1976   *Poverty, Inequality, and the Law.* St. Paul, Minn.: West Publishing Co.

_____   1980   Wealth Discrimination in the Supreme Court: Equal Protection for the Poor from *Griffin* to *Maher*. Pages 229–246 in Ron Collins, ed., *Constitutional Government in America*. Durham, N.C.: Carolina Academic Press.

# AGE DISCRIMINATION

Theodore Eisenberg

The racial CIVIL RIGHTS revolution of the 1950s and 1960s generated interest in constitutional protection for groups other than racial and religious minorities. Enhanced constitutional scrutiny of SEX DISCRIMINATION may be a consequence of the civil rights struggle.

Discrimination on the basis of age, however, has not become constitutionally suspect. In MASSACHUSETTS BOARD OF RETIREMENT v. MURGIA (1976) the Supreme Court held that some forms of age classification are not suspect and sustained against EQUAL PROTECTION attack a state statute requiring uniformed state police officers to retire at age fifty. In a PER CURIAM opinion, the Court concluded that the retirement did not affect a FUNDAMENTAL RIGHT, and characterized the affected class as uniformed police officers over age fifty. Perhaps intending to leave open heightened scrutiny of some age classifications, the Court stated that the requirement in *Murgia* did not discriminate against the elderly. In light of its findings with respect to the nature of the right and the relevant class, the Court held that mere rationality, rather than STRICT SCRUTINY, was the proper STANDARD OF REVIEW in determining whether the statute violated the equal protection clause. It found that the age classification was rationally related to furthering the state's interest of protecting the public by assuring physical preparedness of its uniformed state police.

In *Vance v. Bradley* (1979) the Court, in an opinion by Justice BYRON R. WHITE, again applied the RATIONAL BASIS test and held that Congress may require retirement at age sixty of federal employees covered by the Foreign Service retirement and disability system, even though it imposes no such limit on employees covered by the Civil Service retirement and disability system. In sustaining the mandatory retirement age, the Court emphasized Congress's special consideration of the needs of the Foreign Service. "Congress has legislated separately for the Foreign Service and has gone to great lengths to assure that those conducting our foreign relations will be sufficiently competent and reliable in all respects. If Congress attached special importance to high performance in these positions . . . it was quite rational to avoid the risks connected with having older employees in the Foreign Service but to tolerate those risks in the Civil Service."

But in the legislative arena, age discrimination did feel the effects of the constitutional egalitarian revolution. Section 715 of the CIVIL RIGHTS ACT OF 1964 required the secretary of labor to report to Congress on age discrimination in employment. In 1965 the secretary reported persistent arbitrary discrimination against older Americans. In 1967, upon the recommendation of President LYNDON B. JOHNSON, and relying on its powers under the COMMERCE CLAUSE, Congress passed the Age Discrimination in Employment Act (ADEA). The act, which has been amended several times, prohibits employment discrimination against persons between the ages of forty and seventy.

In EQUAL EMPLOYMENT OPPORTUNITY COMMISSION v. WYOMING (1983), prior to its OVERRULING of NATIONAL LEAGUE OF CITIES v. USERY (1976) in GARCIA v. SAN ANTONIO METROPOLITAN TRANSIT AUTHORITY (1985), the Court sustained against a TENTH AMENDMENT attack the constitutionality of Congress's 1974 extension of the ADEA to state and local governments. In a 5–4 decision, the Court found that applying the act's prohibition to a Wyoming mandatory retirement age for game wardens would not interfere with integral state functions because the state remained free to apply reasonable standards of fitness to game wardens.

Building on a provision in Title VII of the Civil Rights Act of 1964, the ADEA allows employers to take otherwise prohibited age-based action when age is a "bona fide occupational qualification reasonably necessary to the normal operation of the particular business." In its early interpretations of this provision, the Court has not given the defense an expansive reading. In *Western Air Lines, Inc. v. Criswell* (1985), in an opinion by Justice JOHN PAUL STEVENS, the Court held that Congress's "reasonably necessary" standard requires something more than a showing that an age-based requirement is rationally connected to the employer's business. Relying on the heightened standard, the Court therefore rejected an airline's defense of its requirement that flight engineers retire at age sixty. In *Johnson v. Mayor & City Council of Baltimore* (1985) the Court held that a federal statute generally requiring federal fire fighters to retire at age fifty-five does not establish that being under fifty-five is a bona fide occupational qualification under the ADEA for nonfederal fire fighters.

In the Age Discrimination Act of 1975 (ADA), following the racial antidiscrimination model of Title VI of the Civil Rights Act of 1964, Congress prohibited discrimination on the basis of age in programs or activities receiving federal financial assistance. The ADA thus joins Title IX of the EDUCATION AMENDMENTS OF 1972 and section 504 of the REHABILITATION ACT OF 1973, which prohibit, respectively, sex discrimination and discrimination against the handicapped in federally assisted programs. The ADA vests broad authority in the secretary of health and human services to promulgate regulations to effectuate the statute's antidiscrimination mandate. Like the ADEA, the ADA contains exceptions allowing discrimination on the basis of age when age is reasonably related to the program or activity. Other specific federal spending programs contain their own statutory prohibitions on age discrimination.

Bibliography

SCHUCK, PETER H.   1979   The Graying of Civil Rights Law: The Age Discrimination Act of 1975. *Yale Law Journal* 89:27–93.

UNITED STATES DEPARTMENT OF LABOR   1965   *Report to the Congress on Age Discrimination in Employment under Section 715 of the Civil Rights Act of 1964.* Washington D.C.: Government Printing Office.

# STATE ACTION—
# BEYOND RACE

Kenneth L. Karst

For most of its century-long existence, the STATE ACTION limitation of the reach of the FOURTEENTH AMENDMENT and FIFTEENTH AMENDMENT has had its chief importance in cases involving RACIAL DISCRIMINATION. From the CIVIL RIGHTS CASES (1883) until the 1940s, the state action barrier impeded both judicial and congressional protection of CIVIL RIGHTS. As the civil rights movement gathered force in the years following World War II, relaxation of the state action limitation was essential to the vindication of the rights of blacks and others who were making claims to constitutional equality. The WARREN COURT accelerated the erosion of the state action barrier, bringing more and more private conduct within the reach of the Fourteenth Amendment. ALEXANDER M. BICKEL accurately described the effects of the Court's decisions as "egalitarian, legalitarian, and centralizing." By the late 1960s some commentators were predicting the state action doctrine's early demise.

Those predictions missed the mark; today the state action limitation remains very much alive. Yet the doctrine's revival has not signaled a return to a restricted role for the national government in protecting rights of racial equality. By the time the BURGER COURT set about rebuilding the state action barrier, the Court had provided Congress with a firm basis for federal civil rights legislation in the THIRTEENTH AMENDMENT, which has never been interpreted to contain a state action limitation. Furthermore, the Court had generously interpreted various federal civil rights laws to forbid most types of private racial discrimination that had flourished behind the state action barrier in the prewar years.

Although the revival of the state action doctrine has offered little new support for private racial discrimination, that revival has diminished the "legalitarian" and "centralizing" effects of the Warren Court's decisions. Indeed, recent Supreme Court majorities have explicitly extolled the Court's use of the state action doctrine to promote the values of individual autonomy and FEDERALISM. The Warren Court had blurred the distinction between state and society, between what is "public" and what is "private." In so doing, the Court assumed that the force of law underlay all private dealings. It is only a short step from this assumption to the judicial creation of a great many constitutional rights of private individuals against other private individuals. Justice JOHN MARSHALL HARLAN, deploring the trend, argued in UNITED STATES v. GUEST (1966) that "[the] CONSTITUTIONAL CONVENTION was called to establish a nation, not to reform the COMMON LAW."

The Burger Court has viewed its revival of the state action barrier in precisely these terms, as a contraction of the reach of the Constitution— and especially the reach of the federal judiciary—with a corresponding expansion of both individual autonomy and state SOVEREIGNTY. The Court's recent majorities have drawn a sharp distinction between society's "public" and "private" spheres, and two implications have followed. First, the Constitution limits governmental, but not private, conduct. Second, if private conduct is to be regulated by government, the preferred regulator is the state government, and not Congress or the federal courts. The result has been a marked reduction in the Fourteenth Amendment's potential applications to private conduct, even when that conduct is carried on with what the Warren Court used to call "significant state involvement."

Indeed, the very search for "significant state involvement" has been replaced by a new analytical approach. Where the Warren Court determined the existence of state action by considering the totality of interconnections between government and private conduct, today's majority separately examines various arguments for finding state action underpinning private conduct—and typically, as in JACKSON v. METROPOLITAN EDISON COMPANY (1974) and BLUM v. YARETSKY (1982), rejects those arguments one by one.

In doctrinal terms, the current majority of the Supreme Court has narrowed both of the principal avenues for finding state action in private conduct. First, the "public function" theory that informed the "white primary" cases from NIXON v. HERNDON (1927) to TERRY v. ADAMS (1953) and the "company town" decision in MARSH v. ALABAMA (1946) has been confined to cases in which the state has delegated to a private party a function traditionally performed exclusively by the state. In FLAGG BROTHERS, INC. v. BROOKS (1978) the Court even tightened its rhetoric for such cases, referring to "the sovereign function doctrine."

Second, the various types of state support that previously contributed to findings of "significant state involvement" in private conduct, having been disaggregated in the Court's analysis, have been strictly limited in their separate meanings. Thus: heavy state financial aid to a private school was insufficient to establish state action in RENDELL-BAKER v. KOHN (1982); the theory of REITMAN v. MULKEY (1967) that the state had "encouraged" private racial discrimination has yet to be employed to find state action in another case; the state's licensing and comprehensive regulation of a public utility was insufficient to establish state action in *Jackson v. Metropolitan Edison Company;* the precedent of BURTON V. WILMINGTON PARKING AUTHORITY (1961) has been restricted to cases in which government and private actors are so intimately interconnected that their relationship can be called one of "symbiosis"—or, as in LUGAR V. EDMONDSON OIL COMPANY (1982), "joint participation"; and the RESTRICTIVE COVENANT precedent of SHELLEY V. KRAEMER (1948) has become a one-case category. Even a public defender, employed by the state to represent indigent defendants in criminal cases, was held in *Polk County v. Dodson* (1981) not to be acting under COLOR OF LAW as required by SECTION 1983, TITLE 42, OF THE U.S. CODE, statutory words that are interpreted to track the state action limitation.

The insight that law—and thus the coercive power of the state—provides the foundation for claims of right in human society is not new. Indeed, the proposition teeters on the edge of tautology. To say that a person owns land, for example, is mainly a shorthand statement about the readiness of state officials to employ force to protect that person's exercise of certain rights to control the use of that land. To speak of law itself is to speak of a power relationship. In a large and complex society the point may sometimes become diffused, but the potential application of coercive power, wielded by governmental officials, is one of the chief features differentiating interactions in nearly all human societies from those in a jungle. The public/private distinction may have its uses, but candid description is not one of them.

Nonetheless, Justice WILLIAM H. REHNQUIST, writing for the Supreme Court in the *Flagg Brothers* case, reaffirmed "the 'essential dichotomy' between public and private acts" as a feature of American constitutional law. State action, for purposes of interpreting the Fourteenth Amendment, could not be found on the potential enforcement of law by state officials, but only on its actual enforcement. To rule otherwise, Rehnquist said, would "intolerably broaden" the notion of state action. Unquestionably, the public/private distinction is secure in American constitutional law.

The appeal of the public/private distinction for the judges and commentators who create constitutional DOCTRINE is readily identified. If any one value lies at the core of American CONSTITUTIONALISM, it is the protection of individual freedom against arbitrary exercises of governmental power. A central assumption in this value scheme is that a "neutral" body of law is no more than the playing field on which individuals autonomously pursue their own goals. The same assumption is also reassuring about autonomy itself—not just that autonomy is valuable, but that autonomy exists. It is hard to see how American constitutionalism could get along without some form of the public/private distinction, absent a fundamental transformation of the idea of constitutionalism.

Plainly, the public/private distinction would be compatible with a definition of state action much broader than the current one. The present restrictive interpretation of the state action limitation, in other words, serves purposes beyond the maintenance of a zone of individual freedom against arbitrary governmental interference. Those purposes are not far below the surface of the Supreme Court's recent state action opinions. The Supreme Court's current restrictive readings of the state action limitation are congenial to Justices who want to preserve state power against the intrusion of the federal government, and who want to restrict the role of the judiciary in second-guessing the political process. One's attitude toward the state action issue, as toward a great many constitutional issues in the last generation, will reflect one's general views about JUDICIAL ACTIVISM AND RESTRAINT. The consequences of these choices are not merely institutional; they affect substantive rights of liberty and equality. Every decision reinforcing the Fourteenth Amendment's state action barrier is a decision not to vindicate a claim of Fourteenth Amendment rights.

Bibliography

NOTE    1974    State Action: Theories for Applying Constitutional Restrictions to Private Activity. *Columbia Law Review*  74:656–705.

SYMPOSIUM    1982    The Public/Private Distinction. *University of Pennsylvania Law Review*  130:1289–1608.

TRIBE, LAURENCE H.    1985    *Constitutional Choices*.  Pages 246–268. Cambridge, Mass.: Harvard University Press.

# *BLUM v. YARETSKY*

457 U.S. 991 (1982)
*RENDELL-BAKER v. KOHN*
457 U.S. 830 (1982)

## Kenneth L. Karst

Following the Supreme Court's decision in BURTON v. WILMINGTON PARKING AUTHORITY (1961), commentators and lower courts began to ask whether a significant state subsidy to a private institution might make that institution's conduct into STATE ACTION, subject to the limitations of the Fourteenth Amendment. *Blum* and *Rendell-Baker* ended two decades of speculation; by 7–2 votes, the Court answered "No."

In *Blum* patients in private nursing homes complained that they had been transferred to facilities offering lesser care without notice or hearing, in violation of their rights to PROCEDURAL DUE PROCESS. Through the Medicaid program, the state paid the medical expenses of ninety percent of the patients; the state also subsidized the costs of the homes and extensively regulated their operation through a licensing scheme. The Court rejected each of these connections, one by one, as an argument for finding state action. The Constitution governed private conduct only when the state was "responsible" for that conduct; normally, such responsibility was to be found in state coercion or significant encouragement; these features were missing here.

In *Rendell-Baker* employees of a private school complained that they had been discharged for exercising their rights of FREEDOM OF SPEECH, and fired without adequate procedural protections. The Court reached neither issue, because it concluded that the action of the school did not amount to state action. Although the school depended on public funding, no state policy—no coercion or encouragement—influenced the employees' discharge.

Dissents in the two cases were written by Justices WILLIAM J. BRENNAN and THURGOOD MARSHALL, respectively. They argued that a consideration of all the interconnections between the institutions and the states, including the heavy subsidies, amounted to the kind of "significant state involvement" found in *Burton*. But considering the totality of circumstances in order to find state action is precisely what a majority of the BURGER COURT has been unwilling to do.

367